The Journey
Wisdom and S

1649–1654
STOCKHOLM

1792–1911
LONDON

BRUSSELS
1654–1669, 1791

PARIS
1721–1791, 1792

1576–1649
PRAGUE

1576
VENICE

1669–1721
ROME

WISDOM AND STRENGTH

WISDOM AND STRENGTH

The Biography of a Renaissance Masterpiece

PETER WATSON

DOUBLEDAY

NEW YORK LONDON TORONTO SYDNEY AUCKLAND

PUBLISHED BY DOUBLEDAY
a division of Bantam Doubleday Dell Publishing Group, Inc.,
666 Fifth Avenue, New York, New York 10103

DOUBLEDAY and the portrayal of an anchor with a dolphin
are trademarks of Doubleday, a division of Bantam Doubleday
Dell Publishing Group, Inc.

PHOTO CREDITS

The publisher gratefully acknowledges permission from the following sources to reprint the photographs that appear in this volume: *Wisdom and Strength*, photo of *Wisdom and Strength* in the Frick, and Henry Clay Frick; Copyright the Frick Collection, New York. Bust of Rudolf II courtesy of the Board of Trustees of the Victoria and Albert Museum. Photograph of Veronese's house in San Samuele by Osvaldo Bohm, Venice. Detail of *The Marriage at Cana* Musée du Louvre, Paris. Photo: Alinari/Art Resource. Portrait of Christina by Elbfas and portrait of Christina by Heimbach courtesy of Gripsholm Slott, Sweden. The National Art Collections. *Christina's Abdication* and Cardinal Decio Azzolino courtesy of Nationalmuseum, Stockholm. Portrait of Lebrun reproduced from Gilbert Émile-Mâle in *Paris et Ile-de-France: Memoires* (1956). New York Public Library, General Research Division, Astor Lenox & Tilden Foundations. Portrait of the Duke of Bridgewater courtesy of the Ashmolean Museum, Oxford. Bust of second Marquess of Stafford courtesy of the Virginia Museum of Fine Arts, Richmond. Portrait of the fifth Earl of Carlisle courtesy of Castle Howard Collection, Castle Howard, York. *The Siege of Prague* courtesy of Kungliga Biblioteket, Stockholm. Hope's Duchess Street gallery reproduced from Charles M. Westmacott, *British Galleries of Painting and Sculpture* (1824). The New York Public Library, Art, Prints & Photographs Division, Astor Lenox & Tilden Foundations. Painting of Deepdene courtesy of the London Borough of Lambeth Archives Department. Portrait of Lily, Duchess of Marlborough, by A. Esme Collings. Reproduced from *Country Life*, Vol. V, no. 124 (1899). Courtesy of IPC Magazines Ltd., London. Portrait of Roger Fry courtesy of the Provost and Fellows, King's College, Cambridge. Portrait of Thomas Hope courtesy of the National Portrait Gallery, London.

Library of Congress Cataloging in Publication Data
Watson, Peter.
    Wisdom and strength : the biography of a
    Renaissance Masterpiece / Peter Watson. — 1st ed.
       p. cm.
Includes index.
1. Veronese, 1528–1588. Wisdom and strength.
2. Painting—Private collections—History. I. Title.
ND623.V5A76 1989   88-30766
759.5—dc19   CIP

ISBN 0-385-18449-2
Copyright © 1989 by Peter Watson
ALL RIGHTS RESERVED
PRINTED IN THE UNITED STATES OF AMERICA
APRIL 1989
FIRST EDITION

BG

For
Kathrine

Acknowledgments

I would like to thank all the people who helped me while I was writing this book. None of them is responsible for any errors or omissions which remain. Several scholars have read all, or parts, of the manuscript and have offered suggestions for improvement or corrected errors: Dr. Richard Cocke, University of East Anglia; Dr. R. J. W. Evans, Brasenose College, Oxford; Mr. Cecil Gould, former deputy director, National Gallery, London; Dr. J. H. Shennan, University of Lancaster; Edgar Munhall, curator, The Frick Collection, New York; Mr. David Watkin, Peterhouse, Cambridge, Mr. Denys Sutton, Editor of *Apollo*, 1962–1988.

For help with research and information, I would also like to thank Bernice Davidson, research curator, The Frick Collection; Helen Glanville, picture restorer, the Dulwich Gallery, London; Rodney Merrington and Christopher Kingzett, respectively director and archivist, Agnew, London; Beverly Louise Brown, curator, National Gallery of Art, Washington, D.C.; Nancy Little, former librarian and archivist of Knoedler, New York; His Grace the late Duke of Newcastle; His Grace the Marquess of Bute; M. Jeremy Rex-Parkes, archivist of Christie's, and Francis Russell, of the Drawings Department, for making available some unpublished letters of Philippe John Tassaert; Burton Frederickson, director, the Provenance Index, The Getty Museum, Malibu, California; Per Burstrom, Director, Nationalmuseum, Stockholm; Linda Shaw, assistant keeper of the manuscripts, Nottingham University; Dr. Wolfgang Prohaska, Kunsthistorisches Museum, Vienna. Marie-Louise Sciò, for help with the Odescalchi material in Rome. For help with translation, my deepest debt is to Elisabeth Kondal, who cheerfully translated many Swedish and German documents; but I am also grateful to B. Velinsky for help with the Czech material.

The book could not have been written without the generous help of the staffs of several libraries. My first debt is to the London Library, surely the most civilized, and civilizing, library anywhere, but also to the National Fine Art Library, at the Victoria and Albert Museum; the library of the Courtauld Institute, London; the Frick Art Reference Library, New York; the Bibliothèque Nationale, Paris; the Witt (Picture) Library, London; the staff of the Bank of England Press Office for help with monetary conversions. Finally, I would like to thank Sam Vaughn, my commissioning editor, whose enthusiasm in the early stages of the book was a real boon; and Patrick Filley, whose editing skills and recommendations in the final stages were tactful and finely judged.

Contents

Chronological History and Journeys of *Wisdom and Strength*

1576	Venice	(Creation)
1576	Prague	Holy Roman Emperor Rudolf
1612	Prague	Holy Roman Emperor Matthias
1621	Prague	Holy Roman Emperor Ferdinand
1649	Sweden	(Looted by Queen Christina's army)
1654	Brussels	(En route to Rome)
1669	Rome	Queen Christina
1689	Rome	Cardinal Decio Azzolino
1692	Rome	Don Livio Odescalchi
1713	Rome	Baldassare d'Erba Odescalchi and Benedetto Cardinal Odescalchi
1721	Paris	Phillippe, Duke of Orléans (via Pierre Crozat)
1723	Paris	Louis, Duke of Orléans
1752	Paris	Louis Philippe, Duke of Orléans
1780	Paris	Philippe Égalité
1791	Brussels	Viscount Edward de Walckiers
1792	Paris	Comte Laborde Mereville

1792	London	Comte Laborde Mereville
1798	London	Duke of Bridgewater/Earl of Carlisle/ Earl of Gower (via Michael Bryan)
1799	London	Thomas Hope
1831	London	Henry Thomas Hope
1849	outside London	Henry Thomas Hope
1862	outside London	Henrietta Hope
1872	London	Lord Francis Pelham Clinton Hope
1902	London	Agnew and Colnaghi
1911	New York	Knoedler
1912	New York	Henry Clay Frick (via Roger Fry)

Introduction:
The Search for
Wisdom and Strength

This book is a biography. It describes a single life, a life that has seen many adventures, many sharp changes of fortune. It has seen war, revolution, abdication, execution, madness, sexual scandal, religious conversion, and attempted assassination. It has been a distinguished and fantastic life, unique not least for the fact that its history already stretches over four hundred years and continues to this day.

This is not the biography of a person but of a painting, a Renaissance old master. The story begins in Venice in 1576; it roams over Europe, crisscrossing the lives of a score of Emperors and Queens, Popes and cardinals, field marshals and generals, politicians and poets, French, Italian, and English nobles, and a multitude of lesser, though no less interesting, personalities. It is a story that is still unfolding in America. This one life links individuals, and objects, who are never thought of in the same breath: the mad Habsburg Emperor Rudolf II of Prague and Henry Clay Frick, coal millionaire and industrial baron of Pittsburgh and New York; Christina, the spinster Queen of Sweden, and Philippe II d'Orléans, the licentious regent of France; Choderlos de Laclos and the bulldog English dukes of Newcastle; Johannes Kepler and Lord Byron; the sinister Hope diamond and Winston Churchill.

This story may be read in two ways. It may be read first for the unusual and unexpected links which it throws up between these historical figures. All of them had a passion for art and for collecting. Whatever faults they had, and they had a few, they were, at least in this, consistent and laudable. But the story is more than that. All paintings, all works of art, are unique and contain the secrets of their own history. Some, however are more interesting and more instructive than others. They have more secrets. Most wall paintings, such as the Sistine Chapel ceiling by Michelangelo, remain where they were painted; others, though portable, have remained in the same collection for hundreds of years, like those painted by Titian for the Spanish King, Charles V, in the Prado in Madrid. But however beautiful and important these works are, there would be little to say about their history.

The idea for this book was to write a history of an art work which would not simply be interesting but would encompass within its narrative as many aspects of art history as possible. It would read like a biography but at the same time it would touch upon subjects usually met with only in more academic works. A biography of a single work, provided it is the right work, offers an unusual way to explore art history and one that, with luck, will appeal to the general reader. In tracing this single thread, all kinds of backwaters are glimpsed, which the nonspecialist may care to follow up at a later date. The narrative is thus an introduction, but only an introduction to the sheer *richness* of art history. As much as anything, it shows the general reader why the provenance, the life of a work of art is very important to the *pleasure* of many collectors, would-be collectors, and connoisseurs. It introduces the nonspecialist to the rhythms of the past, as they affect art.

It took several months simply to identify the right work, the right story to follow. This was because, in order to be a serious introduction that covered at least most of the main developments, the narrative had to meet certain criteria. Isolating those criteria and then finding a work of art which fitted the bill was itself a puzzle. In the course of it, many objects were considered; all except one were rejected. There were, in all, ten steps in the solution to this puzzle. These steps, the hidden backbone of the book, explain how a sixteenth-century Venetian oil painting now on display in New York City came to be the subject of this biography. These steps are set out now to show how the initial puzzle was solved. It was a tantalizing intellectual adventure in itself.

1. The work should be a European painting or sculpture. Buildings or stained-glass windows were obviously unsuitable, being for the most part immovable. Furniture, clocks, tapestries, silver, porcelain, manuscripts, scientific or medical instruments, and other objets d'art do not, rightly or wrongly, evoke the same sense of identification that people feel for figurative art. Nor has there been the same level of intellectual involvement with such objects as there has been with painting or sculpture. The situation is changing rapidly, but it remains true that painting and sculpture are the senior members of the fine arts.

Art from other geographical areas is no less accomplished, no less beautiful, than European art. But unlike European art, the arts of China, Japan, India, Southeast Asia, Africa, Persia, the Pacific, or South America do not have as many intimate links with the great political, religious, and cultural events which are part of the heritage of the West.

2. The work should have *moved around* a lot. If it had hung on one wall

or stood in one courtyard for hundreds of years, the likelihood was that its story would not be very enlightening.

3. The work should be by an acknowledged master rather than by an anonymous artist. There was bound to be more interest in a great artist than in an unknown one. And more to say about such an artist as well. By the same token, there would be more to learn from a quality work than a second-rate one.

4. The narrative should touch upon as many as possible of the great developments in art. This was perhaps the most important criterion of all. For me, that meant it had to be a work of the Italian Renaissance, still the greatest flowering of artistic talent the world has seen. Which also meant the story had to start in Florence, Rome, or Venice, the most interesting and most important cities of the Italian Renaissance. After that, the other great stylistic manifestations—Mannerism, Baroque, Rococo, Neoclassicism, Impressionism, abstract art—should all feature in the narrative.

Leaving Italy, the work should also have been caught up in the great historical events of Europe which exerted an effect on art and, especially, on collecting. These events included the Thirty Years' War, in historian Hugh Trevor-Roper's characterization, a time of widespread "plunder" of the arts across the Continent. The story should also take in the golden age of Dutch painting in the seventeenth century, as well as the wonderful collaboration between Popes and artists in Rome which created the Baroque; it should encompass France in the tumultuous eighteenth century and the great flux that took place as a result of the French Revolution and the Napoleonic Wars, when literally thousands of works changed hands and hundreds of collections were broken up and shipped from one country to another to create fresh collections. The narrative should be in England in the nineteenth century, the time of empire and of industrial revolution and the great British country houses. Finally, it should have left Europe, either late in the nineteenth century or early in the present one, and traveled to America. This is clearly the latest great wholesale movement of art, and the book would not be complete without it.

5. The work should have undergone physical change; that is, it should have aged. This would introduce a natural point for a discussion of the *materials* of art, an important topic that is sometimes overlooked in many art histories. More than any other, this criterion meant that the work eventually chosen would be a painting rather than a sculpture.

Furthermore, there should also be a drawing associated with the work, showing how it had been prepared and what ideas had helped to form it. Drawings, their relationship to finished oils, the fashions in collecting them, are not as much like painting as one might think.

In the same vein, the work should have been copied. In earlier times copies—true copies, not fakes—were an important subdivision of paint-ing. Indeed copies are themselves indicators of taste. The fact that a picture has been copied shows that later artists believed there was some-thing to be learned from the exercise.

6. The painting should have been owned by a succession of people who were not only intellectually interesting and politically powerful but typical collectors of their time—or at least atypical in a way that threw their contemporaries into clear relief. Art historians are becoming more and more interested in patronage, and a succession of significant patrons would throw light on the fluctuations in taste.

The painting should have belonged to one or more of the very great collections—those of the Gonzagas of Mantua, Charles I of England, one or more of the Habsburg Emperors, Catherine the Great of Russia, Queen Christina of Sweden, Popes and cardinals, the French royal fam-ily, the English lords of the Grand Tour, the great American industrialists and bankers.

7. At the same time, it should not always have been popular. This may seem odd at first, but only if a painting has been *in* and *out* of fashion would the book be able to explore how taste changes (or tastes change). Likewise, the picture should have changed in value. The price of art is rarely mentioned in conventional art histories but it is clearly of great fascination for many people.

A subsidiary part of this criterion was that the painting should be "diffi-cult." This too may seem odd at first but only because we live at a time when "pretty" or "decorative" pictures, as opposed to "serious" or "dif-ficult" ones, are much in favor. Many experts deplore the trend, pointing out that a serious or difficult picture can be much more rewarding pre-cisely because there is more to say about it, more to understand, and, once that understanding has been achieved, more satisfaction to be gained.

8. The picture should have come into contact with the art *market:* dealers and auction houses especially. Again, these are areas usually left out of most art history books. Yet they are just as much a part of art history as pure aesthetics. When art was not being plundered in earlier centuries, it was being bought and sold, just as now. The interest in prices and their relation to artistic merit is not new.

9. The narrative should also touch upon a number of other miscellane-ous elements of the art world such as the salon, the art exhibition, the art gallery or museum, art historians themselves. These would show how the appreciation and display of art has changed over the years.

10. Finally, and perhaps this was a bonus, the picture should contain within its story a mystery. Some element in the narrative should be either

controversial or unknown. After all, part of the fun, even the romance, of art history comes from the discoveries which are made from time to time in dusty archives or forgotten attics. A mystery in the story was not essential but, like a small imperfection in an otherwise perfect character, it made it more intriguing.

It was a demanding set of criteria and it took several months to find anything that fitted the bill. The chief problem was that most paintings by well-known Renaissance artists—Raphael, Titian, Leonardo da Vinci, for example—have always been popular and have moved very little, usually spending years, quite often hundreds of years, in one place. As a consequence, they throw little light on changing tastes.

In New York City, on Seventieth Street between Madison Avenue and Fifth Avenue, there is a white stone mansion of quiet grandeur. It has a large garden and terrace in the front and another garden in back. Merely two stories high, overlooking Central Park, and surrounded on three sides by huge skyscrapers, the mansion nonetheless asserts itself, gently, by virtue of its proportions, its grace, the sheer fact that there is nothing else quite like it.

The Frick Collection, named after its founder, the coke and steel millionaire Henry Clay Frick, contains what many people consider to be the most perfect collection of Western art in the world. To enter the Frick— with its perfectly proportioned and perfectly decorated rooms, its water garden of many greens, its wide staircase, its deep blue enamels and sumptuous bronzes—is to catch a privileged glimpse of the rich achievement of the European artistic impulse. All the paintings in this collection were chosen with great care and skill and with the best advice, so that although the Frick is far from being the largest collection in the world, for many devoted admirers it is the best.

In one room, near Giovanni Bellini's *St. Francis in Ecstasy,* hangs Titian's *Portrait of a Man in a Red Cap.* There are rooms full of Bouchers and Fragonards, and in halls and galleries Corots, Gainsboroughs and Van Dycks and Renoirs, sparkle like jewels.

But it is the West Gallery, the biggest room in the house, which contains the greatest number of masterpieces: two great Turners, *The Harbor of Dieppe* and *Cologne,* Vermeer's *Mistress and Maid,* in yellow, black, and peach, Goya's sinuous *The Forge,* Van Dyck's two portraits, of Frans Snyders and his wife, three Rembrandts, including *The Polish Rider,* Velázquez's crisp *King Philip IV of Spain,* Gerard David's *The Deposition,* El Greco's *Vincenzo Anastagi,* Constable's *The White Horse,* de la Tour's *The Education of the Virgin,* austere and clean, and Frans Hals's *Portrait of a*

Painter. With each artist at the very top of his form, there is perhaps no other room in the world that offers such varied visual perfection.

At the far end of this room, on either side of a double door, are two large canvases by the Venetian master Paolo Veronese. The one on the left shows a young man dressed in fine white silk which is torn at the leg. He is turning away from one woman, buxom and blond, with talons on her fingers, toward another, more restrained, rather distant woman who wears a crown of laurel leaves. The other picture, on the right, shows an older man with a full, dark beard who is dressed in a lion's skin. He is slumped against a wall in the attitude of defeat while a partially naked but otherwise sumptuously dressed woman stands over him, looking upward to a shining sun. A collection of crowns and jewels lie scattered at the foot of the picture, a cherub plays here, and on a stone pedestal are inscribed the Latin words *Omnia Vanitas*—All Is Vanity. The picture is predominantly made up of different reds, crimsons, and yellows, with rich browns mixed into the shadows.

The feel of these two canvases is quite different from anything else in the room. For the most part, those others depict actual people or places, but in the Veroneses the figures are idealized, the poses staged and unnatural. The titles are unusual, too; some would say old-fashioned. Instead of simply *Portrait of This* or *Landscape of That,* the Veronese on the left is called *An Allegory of Vice and Virtue,* while the other is called *An Allegory of Wisdom and Strength.*

The Frick allegories are also unusual in their histories, *Wisdom and Strength* most of all. The vicissitudes it has undergone in the more than four hundred years since it was painted make it perhaps the most distinguished old master. Its story encompasses almost the entire development of Western painting since the Renaissance, for the painting has moved around a great deal and has had a series of amazing adventures.

Wisdom and Strength's biography started in Venice in the late sixteenth century, when the picture was commissioned by Rudolf II, the extraordinary Habsburg Emperor who ruled the Holy Roman Empire from Prague for a quarter of a century before going mad and being replaced by his brother. The picture was commissioned when Venice was at her best: Mannerism was already developing, and the Counter-Reformation and the Inquisition, each of which affected the appearance of Veronese's work, were strong influences in artistic and daily life. A drawing of the picture exists, showing how Veronese began to conceive his composition.

In Prague, Mannerism was the dominant style, all the rage, which suited Emperor Rudolf's eclectic and mystical tastes. His collections, so different from now, are the perfect time capsule to throw into relief our assumptions about art.

When Prague was sacked in the Thirty Years' War, the pictures were hauled off as booty to Sweden, which was then a grand power governed by another extraordinary monarch, Queen Christina. One of the greatest collectors of her age (or of any other), this would-be intellectual attracted the likes of René Descartes to her court, where he gave her philosophical instruction at five o'clock in the morning. Then, when the Queen underwent a dramatic religious crisis, converted secretly to Catholicism in 1654, and abdicated, she took with her to Rome several of her favorite works of art. *Wisdom and Strength* was included.

Christina's time in the Holy City brought her into contact with several Popes, two of them great collectors like herself, several cardinals, and numerous wily politicians, such as Louis XIV and Cardinal Mazarin. Her time in Rome, when her collections were put on display, coincided with the great age of Baroque: the great sculptor Bernini was a friend and Nicolas Poussin, the French painter who spent much of his life in Rome, was a neighbor.

On Christina's death, her collections passed to one of Rome's great collectors, Don Livio Odescalchi, a nephew of the Pope. The wealthy Odescalchi was also a formidable soldier and the builder of one of the great palaces of Rome. He formed a superb collection, particularly rich in drawings. After he died, the rising fortunes of France ensured that the pictures went north again, this time to Paris. The negotiations between the Italian papal family, who was selling, and the regent of France, Philippe II, Duke of Orléans, took many years and entailed the interference of two Popes. Chief among the negotiators for the French was Pierre Crozat, a legendary figure in art history though not widely known outside it. Crozat was not a dealer as such but one of the early "amateurs" in art, whose collection (of drawings) and patronage (of Watteau, among others) lent him a distinction as a leader of taste.

The regent of France, from the cadet branch of the royal family, was every bit as extraordinary as Rudolf and Christina. The regent's lust for sexual adventure gave the world the concept of the debauched roué, as orgies of the most fantastic kind took place at his home, the Palais Royal. Yet he had exquisite taste, made the Palais Royal the most distinguished house in Europe, and gave his name to the Régence style, a direct precursor of the Rococo.

He left his collection to his heirs. They did not govern as he did but, as the second family of France, the Dukes of Orléans were closely connected with the arts and artists of the turbulent eighteenth century: Boucher, who copied *Wisdom and Strength*, Greuze, Diderot, Vigée-

Lebrun, and the development of the Salon. Tragically, all this culminated with the regent's great-grandson, Philippe-Égalité, who chose to sell the entire collection of old master paintings in order to finance his political ambitions during the French Revolution. This did him no good, however, and he was guillotined in 1793.

The collections, including *Wisdom and Strength,* then underwent a series of adventures typical of that chaotic time when Napoleon's troops and the French aristocracy in particular were transporting art, legally or otherwise, in all directions. At one stage James Christie, founder of the auction house which bears his name, considered buying Égalité's collection, as did George III (then Duke of York), but the pictures eventually entered England via several other men, who included the governor of the Bank of England. The collection was dispersed at the famous Orléans sale, the greatest art sale anywhere and at any time, in terms of the effect it had on taste.

The sale was orchestrated by a triumvirate of English nobles led by the Duke of Bridgewater (the Canal Duke) and, as a result, *Wisdom and Strength* was acquired by yet another extraordinary character, Thomas Hope, a banker of Dutch background who had made a good marriage in England. His houses, at Duchess Street in London and Deepdene in Surrey, were shrines to the Neoclassical ideal then sweeping Europe. Hope's extraordinary character extended to the entertainments given in his home, where guests had to dress to match the classical antiquities on show. Hope tried to buy a peerage for himself but failed. More successful with his pen, he published a novel, anonymously at first, that was mistaken for a work of Byron's. *Wisdom and Strength* fitted very neatly into Hope's views of art: he was always trying to marry classical ideals to more recent techniques and insights.

Hope was alive and forming his collection at a time when art was flourishing in Britain as never before. Reynolds had recently died but Turner, Blake, Raeburn, and many other great names were very much alive. The British Institution was just starting up, the National Gallery was soon to be formed in 1824 and art appreciation and art collecting were growing by leaps and bounds. Hope left his collections to his descendants, and his eldest son, Henry, moved the paintings and statues to the family's country home at Deepdene, near Guildford in Surrey. Henry also became a Tory member of Parliament and a good friend of Disraeli. Deepdene therefore became for a while a classic English country house where politicians, men of letters, artists, and scholars met for interesting weekends. Indeed, Disraeli himself, temporarily out of office, wrote his first political novel, *Coningsby,* at Deepdene and dedicated it to Henry Hope, with a comment about the pictures and glades of the house which had helped to inspire him. At this time, *Wisdom and Strength* and the other pictures kept company in Deepdene with the notorious Hope diamond, which Henry had inherited from his uncle.

The next generation of Hopes fulfilled Thomas's social ambitions, for his granddaughter married the Duke of Newcastle and became an aristocrat. Deepdene then became the second home of the family and was for a time rented out to the Churchills. The dowager Duchess of Marlborough, Lillian, married Lord William Beresford and entertained lavishly while her husband, a successful soldier in his younger days who had won the Victoria Cross, set about trying to win the Derby. Late in the nineteenth century Winston Churchill himself spent time at Deepdene and, like Disraeli before him, commented on the paintings in one of his books. As the new century was ushered in, however, Lord Francis Pelham Clinton Hope, the younger brother of the then Duke of Newcastle, who had been left the house, was forced to sell the contents bit by bit. Agnew, the firm of prominent art dealers, bought *Wisdom and Strength* and then, in partnership with two other dealers, Colnaghi in London and Knoedler in New York, sent it to America. Art dealers as we know them today thus entered the picture.

During this part of its travels, the picture and its companion piece, *Vice and Virtue,* were spotted by Roger Fry, who had recently been an assistant curator at the Metropolitan Museum of Art in New York. Along with Bernard Berenson, Wilhelm von Bode, and others, Fry was typical of the art experts coming into prominence at that time and bringing a degree of scholarship with them. Fry, besides being an influential advocate of modern art in England, was an adviser to Frick, traveled in Europe on his behalf, and acquired several pictures for him, including Rembrandt's *The Polish Rider.* Frick, one of the dozen or so industrial barons who created the great collections in North America, acquired *Wisdom and Strength* and *Vice and Virtue* from Knoedler on Fry's recommendation. It can be said that Frick's acquisitions were typical of the powerful men without whom America today would be much poorer in old masters.

Until this point, the history of *Wisdom and Strength* was no different from that of its companion piece, *Vice and Virtue,* which hangs on the other side of the doorway in the West Gallery of the Frick Collection. However, *Wisdom and Strength* alone has developed a *pentimento.* That is, a layer of paint in part of the picture—which Veronese had intended to keep hidden—has begun to assert itself and to show through. This provides a natural opportunity to examine the physical aspects of paintings, how they age and continue to change.

The provenance of *Wisdom and Strength* does not, of course, involve the history of Western art in its entirety. Most notably, neither Catherine the Great, nor the great Spanish collections, nor German art, nor the great abstract movements of modern art are more than touched upon. But even so it is a fantastic story, with many twists in the plot and a succession of very different, very extraordinary people who have owned the picture. After such an exciting life, a life which acts as an unusual introduction to the history of European painting since the Renaissance and which demonstrates the *interrelationship* of many different strands— aesthetics, market forces, religious beliefs—it is perhaps only fitting that *Wisdom and Strength* should come to rest at the Frick Collection. For, as described by the New York *Times,* the Frick is "Paradise."

When one stands in front of *Wisdom and Strength* in the West Gallery, it looks so placid, so clean, so *fresh,* that it is hard to imagine that the painting is now more than four hundred years old and has led such a turbulent life, been present at so many significant historical events, shared the company of so many powerful and extraordinary personalities. But it has, and this is its story.

I

VENICE

1.

The Figures:
Fashion and Beauty
in Renaissance Venice

Venice, 1576. A worse year for the creation of great art could not be imagined. Throughout the summer a hot sun beat down remorselessly on the new paving stones in the piazza by St. Mark's. From the middle of May right through the end of September it was uncomfortably sticky, unusually so for Venice. Moreover, the city was empty. The meat market, with its sides of lamb and legs of mutton, which was then located on the *piazzetta,* was eerily quiet; the new bakery at the Ponte della Pescheria was also empty. At the other end of town, the Rialto was abandoned, its fish market and fruit stalls at a standstill. Venice was not at her best.

Almost the only purposeful activity was a regular ferry of spindly gondolas dipping and weaving out to the island of San Erasmo. This was the golden age of gondolas in Venice: in normal times there were ten thousand of them hidden in the secret backwaters of the city, with gilded prows and little *felzi,* or cabins, lushly decorated with satin cushions in green or purple.

However, the gondolas that zigzagged across the lagoon to San Erasmo in 1576 were painted black all over. Their destination was the lazaretto, a newly founded isolation hospital on the island. The gondolas were filled with patients and for many of them it would be a one-way journey: the city was in the grip of the plague. This was before the age of medicine proper and wild, ignorant ideas about the plague's origins meant that during the epidemic life was disrupted in ways that actually made things worse. The Venetians, for instance, believed that one of the causes of plague was salt water being mixed with fresh water, so they cut back on personal hygiene. Other unfounded beliefs may not have made things materially worse but they would have added to the general confusion.

Not that Venice was a stranger to the plague. She had been afflicted no fewer than forty times since the tenth century—or, as a rough average, once every sixteen years. Every generation had to face an epidemic at least once. But the plague of 1576 in Venice, made worse by that hot, sticky summer, was among the worst, raising comparisons with the Black Death, which had devastated the city two centuries before.

Faced with the plague, the Venetians immediately ordered a blockade of the city in the belief that the disease was spread by human movement. However, this only abetted overcrowding and made the plague worse. Although blockades were imposed for health reasons, their chief effect was economic. The woolen, silk, and printing industries, heavily dependent on the movement of goods, came to a standstill. There was also a curb on association so that anyone whose livelihood depended on that, strolling players, teachers, and the like, was put out of work too. In the 1570s there were about two hundred painters in the artists' guild in Venice. That group would have been affected by the plague no less than anyone else, since its members needed pigments and canvas from the East, walnut oil from the Italian mainland outside the Veneto, and miniver hair for brushes.

The disruption caused by the blockades was made worse because the nobility and the employing classes abandoned the city at the first suspicion of the disease. Although the plague was imperfectly understood, it was obvious that it was more devastating in the towns than in the countryside. In such circumstances it is hardly surprising that plague came to be looked upon as a disease of the poor, and Venice was no exception to this rule.

Throughout 1576 the city emptied as the poor died and many rich families left for safer areas on the mainland. This in turn limited employment opportunities. Artists felt the pinch as much as anyone else as their patrons made a mass exodus from the city. The number of nobles leaving the city rose so dramatically that attendance at the governing assemblies plummeted in the summer, from thirteen hundred to three hundred. And so administrative confusion was added to medical ignorance and economic turbulence.

Bad as all that was, it paled alongside the sheer number of deaths in Venice during those months. According to official statistics, the plague claimed thirty-seven hundred victims between early August 1575 and late February 1576. Then came the deadliest phase, the hot, dry summer of that year. By the end of February 1577 another forty-three thousand had died, including Titian, who, at his death on August 28, 1576, was the most famous man of his day. Between February and July 1577, when the epidemic finally lifted, another three or four thousand had died, making a total of about fifty thousand, or 30 percent of the population of the entire city. It is no exaggeration to say that the population of Venice never recovered. Many families had been wiped out entirely and there was scarcely anyone who had not lost a close relative.

It was in these terrible circumstances that Paolo Veronese, who was then forty-eight and had been living in Venice since 1555, began his masterpiece *Wisdom and Strength*. Yet his picture conveys no hint of the dark and diseased world in which it was conceived; indeed it is essentially a clean, calm, colorful painting with an uplifting moral theme. Veronese kept his work carefully separate from the awful problems that surrounded him, a trait that was typical of the man.

With little work being commissioned that year, the order for this painting must have been flattering to Veronese, and a relief, although he was by then very well known in Venice. It arose, indirectly, from the death of the Holy Roman Emperor, Maximilian II, who died at Regensburg on October 12 from causes that had little to do with the plague. Maximilian was succeeded by his son Rudolf II, then aged twenty-four, a bizarre man, the first of several extraordinary characters to own *Wisdom and Strength*. He had a passionate interest in the occult sciences and attracted to his court all manner of curious characters, quite apart from genuine masters such as Johannes Kepler, Tycho Brahe, and one of the Bruegels. Rudolf eventually became so reclusive that, later in life, he was required to present himself at a window of his castle to prove to his subjects, who had not seen him for two years, that he was still alive.

In spite of this side to his nature, Rudolf was the greatest collector of his time. Although today he is not as well remembered as Catherine the Great or Charles I of England, his collections were easily on a par with theirs.

Rudolf was established as a collector by his father, who not only left him a number of masterpieces but also employed certain important people, such as the painter Giuseppe Arcimboldo, the musician Philippe de Monte, and the famous antiquary and art dealer Jacopo Strada. They all stayed on at the court. By the time Rudolf acceded to the throne, he had developed his own tastes and one of his first moves was to commission a number of works to celebrate his coronation. For these he turned to Paolo Veronese in Venice, whom he had admired since finishing his education with the other branch of the Habsburg family in Spain. At that time he had traveled home through northern Italy, familiarizing himself with the works of Italian artists, some of whose paintings he had been introduced to in Madrid. In addition, Veronese had recently appeared before the Inquisition in Venice, charged with putting "immoral" figures into his paintings: such notoriety would undoubtedly have appealed to the young Emperor, who was interested in anything out of the ordinary. His coronation provided the perfect opportunity to approach Veronese.

Veronese must have been immediately struck by the cruel irony of his own position. All around him was devastation and economic ruin, with discolored, festering bodies literally piling up in the streets, and the lazaretto, the isolation hospital at San Erasmo, little more than a funeral home. Against this grisly background, however, he had received a daz-zling commission from the most illustrious patron he had ever had—indeed, from the most illustrious patron anyone *could* have had.

In those days, Veronese's studio was in the Calle de Ca' Mocenigo, on the northern side of the Grand Canal. The streets were narrow and the houses close together. It was amazing he had not caught the plague and little short of a miracle that no one in his immediate family had suc-cumbed. As he ordered the large pieces of canvas and the pigments, and as he made one or two preliminary sketches to show his ideas to his brother Benedetto, who worked for him, he must have wondered whether the great commission would ever see the light of day. Every morning he would surely have examined his skin for the telltale boils and red or purple *petecchie,* or spots, which would spell the end.

He could not possibly have known that it was the beginning of an extraordinary adventure that was to last more than four hundred years.

By 1576 Veronese had developed a rather bony face, with prominent cheekbones and a high, curved nose. He wore a dark beard and was beginning to go bald. At first glance, therefore, his appearance was rather forbidding: he looked more like a stern clerk than an artist. Yet Veronese loved fine clothes and good food and, by all accounts, his nature was very gentle.

He was by that time one of the most famous men in the city. As long ago as 1556 he had been awarded a gold chain as a reward for being the best of seven painters who had decorated the great Libreria. By now his paintings occupied pride of place in many of the great public buildings, in the private palaces lining the Grand Canal, and in the churches and great monasteries of the city. His frescoes adorned the country villas on the *terraferma,* the mainland beyond the lagoon where the nobles spent their weekends. Moreover, he had made a certain style of picture all his own, and it was this distinctive mix which Rudolf wanted.

That mix had three important elements, and *Wisdom and Strength* shows each of them. In the first place, the people in the painting, though they are supposed to represent exalted gods from classical times, are real Venetians. The woman has the kind of blond beauty that was much ad-mired in sixteenth-century Venice and is dressed in the very height of fashion. The man has the classical dark good looks, the bushy hair, the hooked nose, and a soft expression in a strong head that can be found in many paintings by the great Venetians, Titian and Tintoretto as well as Veronese.

Second, the painting shows these Venetians in a classical allegory. Ve-ronese made his name by this juxtaposition, which no one thought odd at the time. Whether he painted themes from classical mythology or the familiar Christian subjects, the setting was always sixteenth-century Venice. His patrons loved to see themselves portrayed in the fabulous silks, damasks, and brocades for which the city was famous. They were adorned with jewels, lace and painted leather. *The Marriage at Cana, The Last Supper, The Finding of Moses, Venus Mourning the Death of Adonis*—no matter how dramatic or tragic the subject, Veronese's compositions are all opulent, with fine clothes or rich food or musicians highlighting and celebrating the Venetian way of life.

Third, the picture is large and even today, more than four hundred years after it was painted, still glows with a special Venetian lighting. In *Wisdom and Strength* it is always morning.

Veronese began with a drawing or, rather, several drawings. Five are known which contain elements used in *Wisdom and Strength*. Almost invariably, Veronese worked out his compositions beforehand in drawings —in all, 150 survive, in marked contrast to Titian, of whose drawings fewer than fifty are known, despite his age and vast output of paintings. Even before Veronese put pen or chalk to paper, however, there were influences at work in his mind: the composition did not arise from nowhere. Without an understanding of these influences, it is impossible now to grasp what Veronese was driving at in *Wisdom and Strength*.

The first of these influences was Venice itself, the city and its people.

The Venice That Veronese Painted

Daily life in sixteenth-century Venice was crowded and noisy. The extensive amount of building going on would have generated much of that noise. The great dynasties—the Grimani, the Corner, the Mocenigo—had all built new palazzi commissioned from the city's famous architects, Sanmicheli and Sansovino.

Political power in Venice lay solely in the hands of these nobles, persons who were entitled to sit in the *Maggior Consiglio,* the Great Council. Nobility was a legal concept, since its number was confined to the descendants of those who had been in the Great Council at the time of the "great closure" of 1296–97 or else had been brought in during the block ennoblements of 1381. In other words, at the time Veronese arrived in Venice all the nobles could trace their ancestry for well over one hundred fifty years. These genealogies were officially recognized and no one who was not inscribed in a special "Golden Book" could sit in the Great Council.

There were about two thousand nobles in the city, but the number was falling, from twenty-five hundred at the beginning of the sixteenth century to sixteen hundred in 1630. Someone like Veronese, however, who was not himself of their number, would have been much more aware of the *case,* or houses, of the nobility. The law conferred the status of noble on all the male members of a family, so it followed that any legitimate descendant, provided he did not disgrace himself, was automatically noble. By Veronese's time this meant that the two thousand male nobles could be divided into roughly seventy *case.*

Family then did not mean quite what it has come to mean for us. The family firm, or *fraterna,* was the predominant form of business organization. As a result of this, brothers, with their respective families and unmarried sisters, would often share a single palazzo and manage the family affairs in common, an arrangement that did not by any means guarantee harmony. Another factor of some importance was that primogeniture did not exist in the Venetian family; instead money would be left in trust for the family as a whole. So there was no problem of the penniless younger son bringing the family, and nobility in general, into disrepute. In fact, it tended to be the older sons who remained unmarried. This was so because they tended to have the better education, an advantage which equipped them for the Church, then seen as a major source of advancement. A good bishopric could lead to a cardinal's hat, which carried with it opportunities for lucrative nepotism.

Below the nobility were three groups of ordinary citizens. *Cittadini originarii* had to be legitimate descendants of two generations of Venetian citizens and to possess honorable status; that is, neither they nor their fathers could have practiced a mechanical occupation. Second came the body of scribes and notaries who worked mainly as clerks in the state bureaucracy. Finally there was citizenship by grace, which was bestowed on non-Venetians who met certain qualifications, either of residence or marriage. Such individuals were granted the right to trade either inside or outside the city. The citizens had no voting rights in the committees and councils of state but they did have their part to play: only a *cittadini originarii* could become the head of chancellery, who had charge of all government documents, including treaties. The holder of this important office had entry to all the great councils of state, though he was without a vote. Furthermore the official posts of all the lay religious confraternities, the *scuole grandi,* were confined to citizens. These officers were powerful in a financial, if not in a political, sense since they disbursed large sums for charitable purposes.

Life for the citizens was not as easy as life for the nobles but, given enterprise and a little luck, citizens could become wealthy and powerful. And in fact marriages between nobles and women of the citizen class were quite common, more so than the other way around because of the value of the dowry that might accompany a citizen bride.

As in many societies the great families became linked by marriage and in sixteenth-century Venice this produced two "sets" or dynasties. One was the Grimani-Barbaro set; the other was the Corner-Pisani dynasty. This was good news for Veronese because he was patronized by members of both. The Grimani, the Corner, and the Pisani were wealthy trading families and the Pisani were also bankers. All four families achieved high ecclesiastical distinction, too, and this sealed their social preeminence.

Veronese's closest links were with the Barbaro family. There were two Barbaro brothers, Daniele and Marcantonio, who were both very appreciative of his talents. Daniele especially was an example of the learned, civilized Venetian noble. Toward the end of the 1550s the Barbaro brothers commissioned Andrea Palladio to build a villa on the terra firma at Maser. Alessandro Vittoria, who, with Sansovino, was among the great Venetian sculptors, was commissioned to execute the statues, and Veronese was asked to decorate the interiors with fresco.* This combination of enlightened, intelligent patronage and the work of three great artists makes the Villa Maser probably the best of all surviving Renaissance villas. In his frescoes there, Veronese introduced a number of new devices, mainly illusionistic effects which complement Palladio's architecture and give the interior of the building a feeling of being *outside*. Veronese is at his lightest: he has a sense of humor, shows wonderful draftsmanship, and is the perfect accompanist for Palladio.

Apart from Daniele Barbaro, the noble whom Veronese was closest to was Giacomo Contarini. He was barely twenty when Veronese arrived in Venice, five years younger than the artist, but he was destined for a distinguished government career and he had encyclopedic interests, in particular in mathematics and engineering. He was close to Barbaro and a friend of Palladio's, who bequeathed his drawings to Contarini. Giacomo became the protector of Francesco Bassano and, later, of Galileo, for whom he obtained state patronage.

The intellectuals of the day used to meet at Contarini's house, which was known for its full library, especially rich in ambassadorial reports. Contarini collected paintings, sculpture, vases, and medical and cosmological instruments. Among the intellectuals who were frequent visitors were the painters Tintoretto and Palma Giovane. Like Barbaro, Giacomo Contarini appears to have been fond of Veronese and to have appreciated his gifts. It was Giacomo who commissioned the master's *Rape of Europa*

* However, this is now questioned, as some scholars allege that Vittoria's brother, Marcantonio, worked at the Villa Maser.

in 1573. And following the fire in the Doges' Palace in 1577, he and others presented a memorandum on the new decorations needed: Veronese was featured prominently in the plan.

The hope of every politically ambitious noble in Venice was to be elected doge. Such an election took place shortly after Veronese settled there. The new doge, Lorenzo Priuli, was an upright but rather dull man, but his wife, Zilia Dandolo, was a much more colorful and exciting personality and a great favorite among the people—so much so that she was bestowed with the rare honor of a "coronation" in her own right. The ceremony in which "La Priula" processed from the family palace on the Grand Canal to the Basilica of St. Mark was so complex and brilliant that all subsequent processions of dogaressas were modeled on it. The brilliance would have a marked effect on Veronese: he had seen nothing like it before, and the great formal occasion, with everyone dressed in the most sumptuous ceremonial garb, was rarely absent from his canvases after that.

As a painter, Veronese was one of the select few nonpatricians who saw the insides of the nobility's great palazzi. Since the sumptuary laws forbade ostentation, the interiors of these buildings were significantly more flamboyant than their facades. It was common, for example, for the beamed ceilings to be picked out with gilded designs and for the walls to be lined with leather, at least to a height of about five feet. The leather was gilded, too, and stamped with patterns. Above the leather the walls were covered with portraits and other paintings. The floors of the best houses were usually made of crushed marble in a variety of colors, often with heraldic devices worked into them. In Venice's damp winters, heating was achieved by enormous fireplaces which had large hoods jutting out into the rooms; the hoods were supported by caryatids carved by the best sculptors. Furniture, which was made of oak or walnut, tended to be massive and that, too, was ornately carved.

Though individuals like Barbaro and Contarini had their serious sides, the Venetian nobility were equally well known for their flamboyant lifestyle. The Venetians of Veronese's time can lay claim to being among the most fashion-conscious people of any age. A good idea of the seriousness with which the nobility took their appearance can be had from the fact that dressmakers ranked, in guild terms, as full-scale artists.

Veronese would have been familiar with Bartolomeo Bontempelli's shop "at the sign of the Calice at San Salvatore" near the Calle degli Stagneri. "Calice" means chalice or goblet, so this may have been either a tavern or a shop selling Venetian glass. And he would have known or known of Master Giovanni, who was to be found at San Lio. Bartolomeo

stocked all the most sumptuous materials, watered silk, taffeta, and flowered brocade being especially popular. Master Giovanni would cut the
materials for the women of the day, who would linger in these shops so
long that they became favorite meeting places, rather like coffee shops in
later ages. Velvets, satins, and damasks were also very popular, especially
with the motifs of birds, roses, and violets woven into them. Venetian
cloth and lace were well known and well regarded as far afield as England.

It would have been hard for Veronese to miss the dyers' shops in
Venice. The silk and wool industries in the city provided a great boon to
the dyers' art. Their establishments were scattered across the city and the
larger spaces began to take on the name *chiovere,* since there could be
found the *chiovi,* or the pins used to hang up the webs so the cloth could
dry. The hollow stones which were used to carry the poles and from
which the webs were hung may still be seen on Venetian facades today.
The trade was strictly controlled and only Venetian workmen were allowed to practice as dyers. In order to preserve their trade secrets the
dyers circulated scare stories to instill fear into the superstitious and keep
them from poking their noses into the shops. One popular story told how
a giant with a huge hat roamed the shops with a lantern. Among the dyes,
Venetian scarlet and crimson were especially famous and particularly
popular with the English and French.

Such was the concern of Venetian women with their appearance that
there was even a special trade guild created for belt and buckle makers.
These items were constantly changing shape, as was the very outline of
women, as various metal corsets came into vogue, tightened by screws or
springs, only to be replaced by stays stiffened with whalebone. To add to
their luster, handkerchiefs had gold threads running through them, as
did silk stockings. Gloves were made of painted leather and petticoats
were commonly striped in silk floss. Possibly the most extraordinary item
of clothing was the shoes worn by the women of Venice. Called pattens
or chopines and made of sturdy wood, they may be looked upon as a
forerunner of high heels. But they became exaggerated until eventually
they developed into short stilts, by means of which patrician women
could avoid the considerable filth in the streets. According to Pompeo
Molmenti, in his history of Venice, there were at one time specimens of
such shoes in the Civic Museum which were, respectively, 43 and 51
centimeters high (17 and 20 inches). The pattens were often richly decorated with brocade or jewels, but that didn't stop women falling off them
and, sometimes, suffering injury.

Jewelry was displayed, according to one observer, in a "senseless"
fashion. On one occasion Pietro Casola noted twenty-five young women

in one reception room, each wearing jewels worth at least $2,116,100 (at 1988 values).† Earrings had come into use as recently as 1525 but fans— much older—had by now extended to all classes of citizen. It was the vogue then to have not just scenes of chivalry depicted on the fans but also scenes taken from current events, often in caricature.

With clothes so popular, it is no surprise to find that the opportunities for wearing them were many and varied. A ball or banquet, a feast or wedding were all opportunities for new clothes, music, and fine food. The banquet, in which all dress in their best finery, is one of Veronese's most typical scenes.

It was nothing for Venetians to spend 400 to 500 ducats ($25,000–$35,000) on a single banquet. Often the walls of the palazzo where the ball was to be held were draped with gold cloth, and tapestries adorned the courtyards. There was dancing throughout the night with trumpets, pipes, fifes, and flutes among the orchestra. It was the fashion to dance first, and afterward clowns dressed in strange costumes would announce dinner. During dinner gymnasts might entertain, either balancing on their chins three swords, one on top of the other, or tightrope-walking. Besides the invited guests, hundreds of gawkers would gather in their gondolas outside the palazzo to watch the show going on inside. After dinner the whole ball might move out into the streets or continue on the canals in barges. The manners of the age dictated a lavish show and it was considered very bad form to skimp on anything. On the few recorded occasions when hosts did try to economize (usually by not inviting any women), the guests responded by wrecking the house and walking off with the valuables.

There was little formal dancing as we would recognize it: women sometimes danced with other women, and men with men. But grace and lightness of foot were admired and dances such as the *gagliarda,* the *cappello,* and the *torcia* were in great vogue. The dances sound strange to us now: in the *torcia* a woman holding a torch moved through the rooms of the banquet until she came across her favorite man, whom she invited to dance. The torch was then given to a third party who had the unlucky task of following the first couple to light their way as they danced. Dancing often led to more uninhibited behavior, but that did not keep away men of the cloth, who would attend in some sort of disguise.

The food at these festivities received as much attention as everything else. Vinegar soup was common and popular, as were Milanese sausages made of pigs' brains, Ferrarese sturgeon, thrushes from Perugia, and geese from the Romagna. Dishes were dressed differently, too. The

† All conversions of value are approximate. See Appendix A for a note on money.

Venetians often added scented water to their food and even gold dust, which they believed helped to strengthen the heart. The food at the banquets was often accompanied by sugar sculptures, forming statuettes of the Popes or wild animals, and even knives and forks were molded out of confectionery.

Such heavily spiced food was accompanied by a wide variety of wines: *salubri, stomacali, matricali.* In general, wines with a strong bouquet and plenty of body were preferred, like *greco,* which came from a grape originally grown in Crete, and *vernaccia,* by contrast a highly alcoholic local Venetian wine made from raisins. The wines were frequently spiked with drugs and flavored with perfumes.

Most of the grand families employed a steward whose job it was to prepare the table for the banquets. He ensured that the dining room and the table itself were adorned with fragrant flowers and other decorations, such as fish in glass tanks, baskets of fruit, which hung everywhere, and little cuddly animals, such as rabbits, which were tied with luxurious silk threads. The copper wine coolers were chased and damascened and in Venice even the toothpicks of the nobles were made of gold. Perfume was sprinkled everywhere, on the tablecloths and napkins (usually folded in the form of miters or boats), and at the beginning and end of each meal, rose water was poured over the hands of the diners from ewers of gold or silver. One final touch: the carvers were much more esteemed then than they are now and would cut the meat from a sideboard with great public show.

Veronese adopted as his own this sumptuous world of the Venetian nobles. The huge canvases which he filled with vivid velvets, damascened pitchers, and watered silks have come to represent the Venice of the sixteenth century, the Republic's golden age. Whether it is Veronese's *Portrait of a Lady* (Bella Nani), now in the Louvre, *The Supper in the House of Simon,* in Turin, or *The Family of Darius Before Alexander,* in London's National Gallery, one of the things which stands out in Veronese's work is his treatment of brocade, fur, the folds in cloth, the gold filigree which lines the pitchers of wine in the foreground, the sheen of pink or green on a velvet gown. His treatment of surfaces and of different materials is faultless. Even Bernard Berenson, perhaps the greatest of connoisseurs, asserted that Veronese has scarcely been equaled for his "painterly qualities"—and never bettered.

Wisdom and Strength is no less typical than these other masterpieces. Take first the female figure. In any Veronese the female forms, whether clothed or not, whether they appear in religious compositions or in secular allegories, all share a number of distinctive features. Pompeo Molmenti, in his *History of Venice*,‡ puts it this way: "The hair is yellow like ripe corn, the eyes blue, the cheeks round and rosy, the lips full and moist, the breast snow-white. We may take it for certain that most of the models who sat to Venetian artists were women of the people, usually full-bodied and large-limbed; the Venetian temperament admired as the ideal of female beauty the slow movement, the abundant flanks, the full breasts of the noble matrons; and the taste of the upper classes was towards the blonde type; the painters chose their models from the blonde women of the people who in most respects could hardly be distinguished from the patrician dames. It is rare to meet with a brunette in Venetian painting . . ."

Molmenti also has something to say about the dress and attitudes of these beauties. They are, he says, either "gorgeously dressed or in seductive *dishabille*." "We see them in Olympus between Jove and Apollo, or on the rocks of Naxos, or at the court of Phoenician sovereigns, or in the groves of mythological story; or else they smile from the altarpieces where the Madonna appears hardly as the mother of God, but only as the mother of men, stirred by passions that belong to the present world. . . . In these pictures we get the young and radiant noble maiden or the courtesan in all the pride of her seductive beauty. But be it the sweetness of the high-born lady or the smiling invitation of her frailer sister, both are depicted in an atmosphere of glowing and limpid light, but without passion and guileless of profound emotion. Flesh, muscle, blood, are all instinct with life, but their eyes follow no spiritual vision, nor do they reveal a struggle of the soul; they never wear that passionate expression of the modern [nineteenth-century] woman. Their physical form, so intensely attractive in itself, has no counterpart in a vivifying soul."

There could be no better description of the women in Veronese's art or of *Wisdom and Strength*. Molmenti is correct in every detail, down to the eyes which follow no spiritual vision. Examine any of Veronese's pictures: at times it seems that he has used the same woman, with the same hair, the same thick eyelids, and the same staring, expressionless eyes, over and over again. Both *Wisdom and Strength* and *Vice and Virtue* are good examples.

Of the men in Veronese's Venice there is less to say, save that they are all muscular creatures, dark-haired, usually bearded, and noticeably taller than the women. In *Wisdom and Strength* a muscular man is slumped to the right; as in many Venetian paintings he is nonetheless a noble creature, with a full head of dark hair and a marked widow's peak. He has a

‡ Molmenti published his three-volume Italian work in 1880. The English translation appeared in 1907.

strong, hooked nose, another Venetian characteristic. But although he may be a warrior, there is a softness in his expression and his face has character. The men in Veronese's work, in fact, always have more character, in the modern sense, than the women because they are less idealized and in many cases identifiable as real people. Strength could be a likeness of either the Emperor himself or even of Veronese, although that is unlikely.

Vice and Virtue, the second Frick painting, shows other aspects of Venetian manhood. The figure here is younger than in *Wisdom and Strength,* though he too is dark with a slight, wispy beard. He is dressed as a noble. Men's clothes in Venice were in general more somber than women's and they were less subject to the fads of fashion. However, one exception was made in the case of young nobles who, until they settled down to their public careers, usually at age twenty-five (the age necessary for admission to the Great Council), were not obliged to wear the toga. The color of the toga reflected a man's status and role in the Republic, but until he assumed the senior position, a young noble was free if he so wished (and he invariably did) to follow foreign fashions, the French and the Spanish styles being especially in vogue. The trade of tailor was so popular and so specialized in sixteenth-century Venice that its guild was divided into three classes: *da veste,* (for jackets), *da zipponi,* and *da calze* (hose and trousers).

Male fashion was set by a group of young men known as the Company of the Hose, who held a number of celebrations every year at which the new fashions were introduced. The basic dress of this club was a long cloak of silk brocade, velvet, or satin, with an elaborate doublet and with hose embroidered in gold and silver, sewn with pearls and gems, especially the right leg, which was "all garnished with diamonds, rubies, emeralds, sapphyres, the largest pearls and other varieties of precious jewels."

Vice and Virtue now betrays more of its secrets. The central figure is clearly a member of the Company of the Hose. He wears a silver-white doublet of silk or satin, too bright and cheerful for him to be more than twenty-five and to have been accepted yet into the Great Council. His cloak, also of fine silk, has either fallen from his shoulders or been pulled off by Vice. More important still, we can see that the hose on this young man's left leg, which is sewn with gold thread, is badly torn. In other words, this Hercules is very much a contemporary Venetian figure. The man, in shunning Vice and approaching Virtue, is also turning away from the pleasures of Venice.

Veronese's figures were not only types. In many of his compositions he included real people, though they were often idealized or younger than they actually were. He put himself in the frescoes at the Villa Maser and he put his wife Elena in his *Supper at Emmaus,* where she appears in fine clothes as the young mistress of the house; his brother Benedetto also appeared in that picture. And he sometimes put his friends in his paintings as well.

Apart from the faint possibility that "Strength" bears a slight resemblance to the Emperor, there are no recognizable faces in *Wisdom and Strength.* Probably, then, Veronese used ordinary models and his imagination. Molmenti records the use of models in his *History of Venice.* Several artists, he says, used wooden mannequins which could be pulled into any shape. But live models were also used and, according to the notebook of Lorenzo Lotto, the Venetian master who lived in the first half of the sixteenth century, the following charges were typical:

Beggarman (for saints)	8 soldi
Drawing nude women	3 lire, 10 soldi
Undressing women, only to see	12 soldi

Which would mean the beggarmen received about $3.00 (at 1988 rates) for their trouble while the women who posed nude received about $4.50.

No less than in his other works, then, the figures in *Wisdom and Strength* are typical Veronese Venetians, with the build, the looks, the coloring—even, in the case of the woman, the fashionable clothes, sumptuous, ornate, shining with splendor. Yet amid all this beauty and excess, there was another side to Venice. This underside hardly merited the title *la Serenissima.* It tells us something about Veronese and the world of the Renaissance painter to know what this Venice was, the Venice he did not paint.

The Venice Veronese Did Not Paint

To take the most unglamorous aspects first, there was in the city an ever-present and crude sexuality. There was, for instance, a thriving trade in pornographic poetry. The habit of swearing was so bad that the government set up an executive to control it (*esecutori contra la bestemmia*). This body also controlled gambling, which was equally widespread. Cards were so popular that the Republic was obliged at one time to ban their sale, and the sale of dice, too. Entire families were ruined by the gam-

bling associated with cards. And servants were pressured to denounce
their masters who held gaming tables in their homes: those whose masters were found out in some other way were punished. Servants were
usually pilloried for a first offense (by their masters) and liable to the loss
of their nose and/or ears for a second. Everyone was affected by the
gambling craze and the names of many noble families occur in the trials
of the period. It became so bad that at one point the executive even went
so far as to have its printed warning replaced by warnings carved in
stone.

Despite the Catholic Church, bigamy was by no means unknown in
sixteenth-century Venice. This was so because until the seventeenth century, it was possible to celebrate marriage in the Republic without *any*
religious rite: the only requirement was that witnesses be present. There
was usually no check on previous liaisons, and therefore whoever so
desired could take any number of spouses. Homosexuality was so common that special laws were passed in 1527, 1586, and 1598 to stamp it
out. Men even took to dressing in women's clothes and prostitutes sometimes did the reverse. According to some contemporary accounts, the
government was so worried about sodomy that it encouraged prostitutes
to sit in deliberately alluring poses in their windows to coax men back to
heterosexual desires.

Prostitution flourished despite the laws that sought to contain it. One
law restricted where courtesans could live but nonetheless they spread all
over the city. There were more than eleven thousand prostitutes in Venice, making the ratio of prostitutes to males 1 to 15, indicating a thriving
demand for their services (indeed, the government took taxes from
them). As time went by there came to be several classes of prostitute:
women who lived with their employers were called *mammole,* ordinary
harlots were known as *cortigiana,* and, at the top of the scale, there was
the *cortigiana onorata.* This last group often owned their own houses and
the author Pietro Aretino wrote about them in great detail: they were
known collectively as *Aretine.* The names of several notorious courtesans
have survived. Among the better known were Vienna Rizzi, Lucrezia
Squarcia, who wrote bad poetry, Lucia dagli Alberi, who was "beautiful
and well-born," and Stellina, only fifteen, who had "eyes that stab."
There was even published a *Catalogo di tutte le principal e più onorate cortigi-
ane,* which included the names of married prostitutes and gave their
prices. They ranged from half a crown to thirty crowns.

If a prostitute became pregnant she would take the baby to one of the
Venetian foundling hospitals. These hospitals had one particularly curi-
ous feature: each had a small hole covered by a grating set into a wall.
The hole was designed to be just large enough to fit a newborn child so

only if the mother acted promptly, before the infant grew too big, could she leave the baby anonymously. Otherwise she had to raise the child herself.

The poor in Venice were, in general, neglected by Veronese in his paintings. He had a narrower range of subject matter, and of patrons, than Tintoretto, for example. In some of the latter's paintings the apostles can be seen handing wine and bread to the deserving poor. For all her splendors, la Serenissima had its ugly side which Veronese did not record, even in his commissions for some of the great religious organizations.

In his paintings, Veronese also ignored the intellectual life of Venice, although this was an important and distinctive element.

Music, which in Veronese's paintings is usually performed by secular groups playing at huge banquets, also developed great sophistication in the churches and cathedrals. The organ was becoming very popular then, so much so that instruments were constructed out of any materials at hand, even cardboard. One of the best was at San Sebastiano, a small church south of the Grand Canal, where Veronese did so much work, and where he designed and painted the organ shutters. The perfected violin was introduced into Venice during his lifetime, in 1580, but the most famous feature on the Venetian musical front was the choir of St. Mark's, which was accompanied by instrumental groups. The Venetians were inordinately proud of this choir, in which discipline was so strict that choristers were forbidden from singing anywhere else. Popular forms of music included counterpoint in three voices and the madrigal.

Venice was also a center of the printing trade. In the last decade of the fifteenth century she had had two hundred printers, and throughout the sixteenth century books produced in Venice became progressively cheaper and more popular in style. The great Aldus Manutius invented cursive or italic type, and Venice was one of the first places to use wood-block printing for illustrations and decorations in the borders.

Books imply learning and in Venice there were three kinds of learned institution: the coterie, the academy, and the university. They formed an important side to life in the city.

There were three coteries of repute. These were private affairs at which intellectuals of all sorts were invited to discuss matters of the day. The most well known, that run by Domenico Veniero, included among its regular members the musicians Girolamo Parabosco and Adrian Willaert, the philosopher Lorenzo Contarini, Daniele Barbaro, Bernardo Tasso, Giambattista Susio, a doctor, Fortunio Spiro, an Orientalist, and Cristoforo Mielichs, an agent for the Fuggers, the famous German banking family. The poets would recite, the musicians would play, and everyone would argue.

The academies, however, were more formal. There had been academies in the city since 1484, when the Aldine Academy had been founded by Aldus Manutius. That had been dissolved, but by Veronese's time their presence was familiar: several others had come and gone, among them the Fama, the Gelosi, and the Confusi. The Vicenza Academy, of which the architect Palladio was a member, was unusually well documented and from that one can gain some idea of the subjects treated: mathematics, the origin of the winds, and good government.

Schools and universities thrived in Venice. There was a boarding school in Venice itself and another nearby in Padua. Teachers had to pass a qualifying examination and survive an inquiry about their morals. In the primary school, children learned to read from prayer books or from a series of texts put together by one Gianantonio Tagliente who made a living by writing primers on arithmetic, grammar, handwriting, and Greek. According to *Lo Scolare,* a book published in 1588, the school curriculum was as follows: ages 7–10, grammar; 10–14, logic, rhetoric, and poetry; 14–18, music, arithmetic, geometry, and astronomy; 18–22, ethics and law; 22–30, the remaining sciences. Physical education was included throughout. By 1551 each of the *sestiere,* the six regions of Venice had established a public school to teach grammar and Latin.

After school many Venetians would complete their education at the University of Padua. The university had a clinical school, an anatomical theater, a botanical garden, and a department of science and invention. In 1565 it boasted 720 students. The academic year began in November and the students came from all walks of life. The rich lived in palaces with servants while some of the poorer undergraduates lived with the professors (Galileo took in lodgers). The poorest of all were lodged in colleges that were funded by charities. The degree offered was highly respected and the degree ceremony an occasion of great pomp and majesty.

The People in Venice

With a population in the region of 170,000–175,000 (until the plague, that is) Venice was one of the largest cities in the world. As such, it contained no shortage of individuals who, although not noble, still had an impact on Veronese.

Of all the personalities whom Veronese would have heard of on his arrival in Venice, no name would have rung with more resonance than that of Pietro Aretino. He died in the year Veronese reached the city but by then his gossipy, barbed tongue had ensured that the reputation he had earned in Rome was equaled in Venice. Aretino was a shoemaker's son from Arezzo and the stories about his sharp wit started early. It was said that he was forced to leave Arezzo when he was only thirteen because he had composed a scandalous sonnet about church indulgences. In Rome, Aretino blossomed in the company of other equally colorful men. He was in and out of trouble there, much as he had been in Arezzo, but, to his credit, he did see the end coming in Rome. Before the imperial forces of Holy Roman Emperor Charles V could rout the Holy City, Aretino had left it for Venice. He settled quickly in a house overlooking the Grand Canal and was very soon a member of one of the most exclusive groups in the city, known as the triumvirate; its other members were Sansovino and the great Titian himself.

Jacopo Sansovino was born in Florence in 1486. He liked sculpture but proved more successful as an architect. He was so successful that in Rome his design for the Church of St. John the Baptist was picked in competition in preference to one by Raphael. His fame spread and he numbered three Popes among his patrons. Unlike Aretino, he did not anticipate the Sack, but as soon as the attack began he fled, intending to go to France to seek the King's favor. On the way he stopped off in Venice for provisions and the doge, hearing that he had arrived and knowing of his reputation, invited him to stay. Sansovino was asked to rescue the Basilica of St. Mark, which was rotting, its foundations undermined by water. He did such a good job that, in gratitude, the Venetian Senate made him the equivalent of chief architect of the Republic. He received a house and a handsome salary and decided to stay.

By the time the other two members of the triumvirate arrived in Venice, Titian was already well known though not as famous as he was to become. Born in the late 1480s, he was a pupil of Gentile Bellini and Giorgione. Well before Veronese arrived in the city, Titian had begun to paint in a much freer, more impressionistic way. He even used his fingertips to apply the paint, considered a notorious practice at the time. We now recognize that this was the master in the throes of inventing modern painting, but that is not how it was seen then. Veronese paid little attention to the old man's technique, though it is clear he did know about it, with several of his earlier pictures showing debts to Titian.

But Veronese could scarcely have failed to be affected by the triumvirate which was so much a part of the social scenery. The three men took to entertaining one another at graceful dinners, with good conversation, beautiful women, and excellent food. The food was often donated by other personalities and Aretino would pen pretty replies: "For the fine and excellent turkey which the affable kindness of your true courtesy sent me from Padua, I give you as many thanks as he had feathers." Titian was a man of the world who traveled to Rome, Spain, and Augsburg. He painted Aretino several times. And Sansovino included the faces of Titian and Aretino on the bronze doors he designed for the sacristy of St. Mark's.

If Aretino was the most scurrilous of the three, Sansovino was the ladies' man. Giorgio Vasari, the painter and biographer of the greatest Renaissance artists, describes the architect as "handsome and graceful, so that many ladies of rank fell in love with him." He also says that Sansovino was an intermittent victim of "some disorder caused by the escapades of his youth." Through the goings-on of the triumvirate we can get some idea of the Venice which Veronese encountered when he first arrived. Aretino, who died so soon afterward, even did that in typical style: he fell off his chair while laughing at a joke.

To someone like Veronese the triumvirate would have appeared as *the* "in" set socially. But he was a painter and so would have paid more attention to the competition in that particular field. And though Titian was preeminent, it was a time that was particularly rich in artistic talent.

Tintoretto was quite different from Titian. Far from being in the social swim, he lived in a rather out-of-the-way part of Venice, in a graceful Gothic palace on the Fondamenta dei Mori. He was ten years' Veronese's senior, with a rather rugged build and a strong but ugly head. He was the retiring sort, fond of family life and especially proud of his son Domenico, also a painter, and his daughter Marietta, who was a clever musician as well as a painter. Tintoretto often held concerts at his house and would himself accompany Marietta.

Tintoretto, who did not become really famous until the end of his career, kept a large workshop, using his son and daughter to make alterations, variations, and enlargements. His style, well worked out and very effective, employed huge canvases with lots of action, vivid color, and striking perspective, with the main incident set deep within the picture. It was also very serious and this was probably a reflection of his nature. Unlike Veronese's, Tintoretto's paintings hardly ever reflect the joyous side to Venice and in his personal life he was rather gruff. He spoke little but when he did was often quite rude, even to the powerful. On one occasion, Tintoretto met Aretino in the street shortly after the writer had made some sharp quip about him which had filtered back. Tintoretto was perfectly civil and asked Aretino to come home with him, saying he wanted to paint his portrait. Aretino, who was flattered, accepted. But no sooner was the writer properly posed in the workshop than Tintoretto whipped a dagger from his doublet. He probably never intended to harm Aretino but he had made his point: the writer never spoke ill of him again. Tintoretto also suffered a misfortune that almost certainly had an

effect on his disposition: his beloved Marietta died tragically at the age of
thirty and he mourned her for the rest of his life.

After Titian, Tintoretto, and Veronese came Andrea Schiavone, Paris
Bordone, and Jacopo Bassano. Apart from a short stay, Bassano did not
live in Venice itself, but he was well known and widely respected,
enough for him to have mattered to Veronese. Indeed, the master sent
his own son to train with Bassano, since he felt that his skills were better,
at least in some things.

Equally important to Veronese were two nonpainters: the sculptor
Alessandro Vittoria and the architect Andrea Palladio, for Veronese col-
laborated fruitfully with both men.

Andrea Palladio, "the most imitated architect in history," was born in
Padua in 1508. Christened Andrea della Gondola, he was given the
name Palladio by Count Giangiorgio Trissino, a noble from Vicenza,
who picked him out from a number of masons working on a new loggia
being added to Trissino's villa. Trissino was one of the leading intellectuals of Vicenza, a fact that was to be of some importance to Palladio, since
the Trissino household was far more than a grand house. It was, in effect,
a kind of school for young noblemen where they were given tuition in
the humanities. In this way Palladio acquired an education he otherwise
would not have had, and it was to stand him in good stead. Whether
Palladio met Daniele Barbaro through Trissino is not known; but the
count had undoubtedly helped him obtain the commission to build the
dramatic Olympian Theater for an academy in Vicenza to which Trissino
belonged. This building, with its classical auditorium and the strong
foreshortenings on its stage area, attracted a lot of attention and it may
have been this publicity that drew Barbaro to Palladio. By the time Veronese and Palladio came into contact with each other, the architect, who
was twenty years the painter's senior, already had an impressive number
of commissions under his belt and some influential friends and patrons.

Life was not all art and aristocracy, however. Venice was a bustling,
thriving, cosmopolitan port and there were all manner of people to be
found in the restaurants and bazaars near the Rialto, the main bridge, or
along the Merceria, where many of the shops were located. These people
included Veronica Franco, the most celebrated courtesan of the time,
who numbered many of the most distinguished men of the day among
her visitors. There was Tomaso Rangone, now into his sixties and a definite "character." He was both a doctor and a philologist, who professed
to teach people how to live to be a hundred and twenty. There was
Scipione Bargagli, a Sienese inventor of games that were very popular. In
one of his games, *Ortolani,* men and women dressed up as gardeners and
discussed the qualities of the mind in terms of horticulture. There was

Paolo Rizzo, a celebrated goldsmith who was known for his skill in damascening ironware—inlaying fine, ornate lines of gold and silver into the surface of swords or plates or jugs. There was the poet Bernardo Tasso, whose books were printed in Venice and whose son Torquato became even more famous as a poet. There were Giorgio Ghisi, the helmet and shield maker, and Vincenza Armani, the actress. In music there were the Gabrielis, Andrea and Giovanni, and Claudio Merulo, organist at St. Mark's, whose madrigals were all the rage.

That Veronese in his painting ignored so many aspects of Venetian life had a lot to do with the system of patronage, for it was the nobles, either as individuals or as leaders of the state or the church, who commissioned many of his works. It also had something to do with the status of painters in the sixteenth century. To a much greater extent than now, artists were used to doing what they were told. But Veronese's personality, and his own experiences in Venice, cannot be ignored. They, too, affected the form and appearance of the pictures he produced.

Veronese in Venice

Veronese was born in Verona in 1528 and was originally called Paolo Spezapreda, which meant "stonecutter," his father being a stonemason. The family lived on the left bank of the Adige as it curved through Verona, in the district known as San Paolo di Campo Marzo. Whether Veronese, the fifth child, was actually delivered in Verona is disputed. It may have been at Legnano, where his father had a commission at the time; or it may have been at Vangadizza, where there was a family called Caliari, the name he was later to adopt.

Verona was as good a place as any in which to grow up. It had been a city-state in its own right but by that time had been part of the Venetian republic for a hundred years and was by now the second city of *la Serenissima,* "the serene republic," as Venice was known by those envious of her achievements. Many travelers passed through, as the Adige was a flourishing commercial route, and there was no shortage of influences for a young painter. It may not have been as exciting as Venice or Florence or Rome but it was by no means a backwater. It was also close to Mantua where the court of the Gonzagas had for some time been a focus for painters and other artists. Veronese, who painted a *Temptation of St. Anthony* for Ercole Gonzaga, therefore grew up to be familiar with the works of such masters as Moretto, Savoldo, Giulio Romano, Parmigianino, Pisanello, and even Raphael himself, not to mention all the great Venetian masters—Bellini, Giorgione, Sebastiano del Piombo, and, above all, Titian.

Frescoes were to play an important part in Veronese's career throughout his life and, indeed, it was his ability in that sphere of painting which set him on the road to fame. The well-known architect Michele Sanmicheli saw Veronese's work and was impressed enough to have him decorate a villa he was building for a Venetian nobleman by the name of Soranzo. "La Soranza," as the villa was called, was characteristic of the period, for the nobility in *la Serenissima* had recently discovered the pleasures of the second home, for weekends and holidays, and they alternated between their palazzi on the lagoon and the countryside of the *terraferma*.

Veronese was very precocious and had found work in Venice by 1553, when he was twenty-five. His reputation had certainly preceded him because he was immediately set to work on part of the ceiling of the chamber of Venice's ruling Council of Ten. He was a success: he showed Jupiter striking the vices with his bolts, but what attracted particular attention to this new young artist were his dramatic *sottinsù*, illusionistic foreshortenings, which he must have absorbed from the works of Giulio Romano in Mantua. To them he added his own mix of silvery colors.

He settled permanently in Venice in 1555 and then, the next year, he won a gold chain for his contribution to the decoration of the great Libreria of St. Mark's, designed by Sansovino senior. It was an auspicious start for a newcomer.

If Veronese had an instant impact on Venice, what of the city's effect on him? It must have been equally stunning, for Venice in those days was little short of electrifying. In the 1550s the city was, in many ways, at the peak of her power and glory. Capital of a vast commercial and political empire which embraced the eastern basin of the Mediterranean and the countries of the Levant, Venice was a bustling, cosmopolitan metropolis. The dominions included a large part of the north Italian plain—Padua, Vicenza, and Verona, as well as Bergamo, Brescia, and Crema. It included Istria and stretches of the Dalmatian coast (now Yugoslavia). Overseas territories included Crete, producer of corn, wine, and sugar.

In the city itself, on the bridges and along the canals and little streets, or *calli,* Armenians mingled with Turks, Greeks with Albanians, slaves with barbarians, Germans with Spaniards, their varied costumes contrasting noticeably with the more solemn robes of the magistrates and senators of the Republic. The spectacle of the city itself was irresistible to a painter, and in the public buildings and private palaces there were almost unlimited opportunities for an accomplished artist to work on many commissions. Venice was made for Veronese and Veronese was made for Venice.

In the wider political and historical sweep, Venice's fortunes had begun to wane; her long, slow decline was about to begin. To the man in the street, however, that was not yet apparent: the city was thriving. Its trade with the Levant was not unchallenged but it was still very strong; and despite the discovery of the Cape routes, and America, Venice was still an important staging post between many parts of the East and western Europe, especially Germany. Veronese would have noticed the particularly heavy presence of Germans in the city, who owned the companies which shipped onward the goods coming in from the East and unloaded at Venice.

As well as being buoyant economically, Venice was also full of herself, halfway through what promised to be her best century yet. It began in a blaze of glory and went from strength to strength. In the beginning there had been the glories of Bellini, Giorgione, Sebastiano, Carpaccio, and the young Titian. Leonardo had visited the city in 1500, and Dürer came shortly thereafter. German bankers, the Fuggers and the Wechslers, were well established in the Fondaco (the commercial heart of Venice, where the warehouses were located), as were the links with their cities, Augsburg and Nuremberg. By that time Venice also had a reputation for learning and was a center of printing. In the last years of the fifteenth century one half of all the books printed in Italy were produced in Venice. One of the reasons why Venice was popular with artists was that the republican system of government meant that when a doge died commissions were not affected. An artist's contract was with the government, not an individual.

Not everything was rosy. The city lost an important trade route when Alexandria fell to the Turks, the first in a series of defeats Venice was to suffer at their hands as the century wore on. But Venice's wars were not fought on her soil, and in the first part of the century, when upheavals were taking place in Rome and Florence, she was able to remain relatively stable. Prosperity followed.

The Sack of Rome, which took place in 1527, was almost as important to the world of art as it was to the world of politics. If Florence had led the Renaissance toward the end of the fifteenth century, that leadership had passed to Rome as the *quattrocento*—the 1400s—gave way to the *cinquecento*—the 1500s. Michelangelo, Leonardo, and Raphael were all active there in the early part of the century. Now, with the Sack, the center moved again and eventually settled in Venice.

This was partly due to Titian, who had achieved such great fame that in 1530 he met the Holy Roman Emperor, Charles V, at Bologna. Titian painted the Emperor's portrait and the two men became good friends. The artist was knighted, an unheard-of honor in those days, which, as we shall see in a later chapter, throws light on the changing status of artists in the sixteenth century.

Intellectually and religiously speaking, Venice was also a liberal place by the standards of the day. The Inquisition had imposed censorship of books there, as everywhere else, but the traditional distrust of the popes and the presence of followers of so many different religions—Jews and Arabs, as well as orthodox Greeks, Protestants, and Catholics—ensured a wider range of ideas than before. Only three years after Martin Luther nailed his ninety-five theses to the door of All Saints Church in Wittenberg, a disciple of his was a guest at Venice's principal Augustinian monastery and preached in one of the churches.

On the surface, life in Venice continued much as before throughout the 1540s. The trade in spices and luxury goods was maintained; and although the number of printing presses fell, it was still greater than anywhere else. Politically, Venice was as stable as ever; the arts continued to blossom in all directions. In painting, Tintoretto could be added to Titian; in architecture, Palladio could be added to Sansovino; and in letters, Angelo Beolco Ruzante could be added to Pietro Bembo and Aretino.

With hindsight, we can see that certain events of this time foreshadowed the decline which was to be Venice's fate in the later years of the century. Pirates appeared in the Adriatic as early as 1533, and in 1540 the republic was forced to conclude a treaty with the Turkish ruler, Suleiman I, as a result of which she lost more of her territories in the East. She also felt obliged to build a fortress at the entrance to the lagoon. However, as the half century was reached, Venice was still a proud, successful city whose accomplishments were the envy of the civilized world. Veronese, therefore, could not have arrived in the city on the lagoon at a better time. The city was as ready to receive his gifts as he was anxious to offer them.

Veronese eventually settled in a fairly large house in the parish of San Samuele, now a quiet and out-of-the-way district. To get to it, one leaves St. Mark's and walks toward the Accademia, into a mainly residential area enclosed by a loop of the Grand Canal. On the left is a street which is wider than most with a number of craft and antique shops, as well as picture framers. Called Salizzada San Samuele, Veronese lived here at number 3337, on the corner of the Calle di Mocenigo. It is a large house for the area, four stories high and now painted red.

The comings and goings of famous and colorful people, the building and decoration of this or that grand palazzo, the intellectual fads and fashions were all part of the general backdrop to Veronese's life in Venice. But, from time to time, specific events stood out and involved him particularly closely. One such incident was the publication, in 1557, of Lodovico Dolce's book *Dialogo della pittura* (Dialogue on Painting). Dolce's book was in part a reply to Giorgio Vasari's *Lives of the Most Eminent Painters, Sculptors, and Architects,* in which Vasari had argued that Michelangelo was so divine that no other artist was worth anything in comparison. The Italians of the period were not alone in being especially interested in three aspects of painting which they looked upon as quite distinct: *disegno, invenzione,* and *colore.* To Vasari, Michelangelo's mastery of these three arts enabled him to produce art even more beautiful than that created in antiquity.

In reply, Dolce concentrated on color and argued for the superiority of Raphael over Michelangelo, saying that the former was more subtle and had a greater range. Furthermore, he went on to extol Titian as the best combination of artistic talents. Dolce was thus the champion of Venetian art, whereas Vasari was the most eloquent supporter of its Florentine counterpart.

Veronese was highly conscious of this debate and would occupy his own position in the divide, a divide which has recurred throughout the history of art. Indeed, Veronese's position accounts for why his paintings have been in and out of fashion while those of other artists have been either universally popular or universally unpopular. For Veronese was a magnificent draftsman, with an individual sense of color: in this he was influenced by Titian. But the *form* of his figures owes as much, if not more, to Michelangelo. His paintings show that, though Venetian, he was drawn as much to Vasari's arguments as to Dolce's. At some points in history this has been seen as a strength, at others a weakness.

Like Dolce's book, the Council of Trent provided an important political and social backdrop. The council had been meeting on and off since 1544, having been called in response to the enormous religious, and therefore political, changes that were overtaking Europe, notably the Reformation. The council would continue until 1563, when it would issue a series of proclamations that would affect art in general and Veronese in particular. Underlying the work of the council was an uncomfortable peace, between the Spanish and German Habsburgs and the French Valois, between northern Europe and southern, between Protestant and Catholic. This brittle peace would last for Veronese's lifetime but already in his day were felt the roots of unease, the feeling, perhaps unconscious, that the good times were ending.

Another event that influenced Veronese was his visit to Rome. This probably took place in the spring of 1560. He went there at the invitation of Girolamo Grimani, a member of the grand Grimani clan and procurator for St. Mark's. He went "not so much to see the pomp of the court, as was the common custom, but as a painter to see the magnificent buildings, Raphael's paintings, Michelangelo's sculpture." It is not clear if he saw Michelangelo himself while he was in Rome, but Veronese was much influenced by the great master, so it is certainly possible.

The commission for the Villa Maser came in 1560 and his next major work following that turned out to be one of the truly great and truly typical Veroneses. In June of 1562 he contracted with the Benedictine monks of the Abbey of San Giorgio Maggiore for a canvas, *The Marriage at Cana,* which is now in the Louvre. The subject is Christ's first miracle, when he turned water into wine. Oddly enough, though, what it shows is an extremely worldly banquet. All are in their best clothes, wearing silks, brocades, and gilded leather; there are fine plates loaded with rich food, damascened pitchers brimming with wine. A feeling of sumptuousness, an atmosphere of luxury, is everywhere. Furthermore, the wedding guests are being entertained with music and near the center of the canvas, in the foreground, is the ensemble. These are no ordinary musicians, however: on the bass there is the tall, rangy figure of Titian; there is Bassano on some kind of flute; Palladio and Sansovino are part of the group; and Tintoretto and Veronese himself, in white silk and pale yellow hose, are playing cellos. There are indeed religious elements: the servants have found that the water has been turned into wine; there is a timepiece signifying that, as Jesus said, "mine hour is not yet come." But the religious feeling is muted. Nevertheless, by all accounts the Benedictines loved their picture.

The next year, 1563, was marked by the ending of the Council of Trent. In Venice the council's first impact was felt in the realm of literature: censorship, though less strong in Venice than in some other cities, reduced book production, at least for a while.

In the middle 1560s, when Veronese's pictures were seen by Vasari, his art became increasingly vigorous and he began to explore more adventurous compositions. One example is the ceiling paintings originally done for the Church of the Umiltà but now in the Cappella del Rosario in Santi Giovanni e Paolo.

In this composition the perspective, which is not a new device for Veronese, is nevertheless much more effective than before: as the spectator cranes his or her neck to look at it, the movement in the painting is so strong and so perfectly tailored to its overhead position that, for a moment, giddiness sets in. Another picture from the period is *The Family of Darius Before Alexander,* now in the National Gallery in London. In earlier, busy compositions, many of Veronese's figures had, as it were, moved against one another so that although there was a lot of individual activity in a picture the figures canceled out one another and the overall effect was static (*The Marriage at Cana* is a case in point). In *Darius,* however, it is as if all the figures are caught up together in an invisible but irresistible wave sweeping across the canvas. The movement in the painting is *one* movement and the emotional impact is all the more forceful for that.

Veronese, by now well into his thirties, decided to get married. On April 17, 1566, he married Elena Badile, the daughter of his former teacher in Verona, Antonio Badile. There is no documentation about their romance, but it had then been some thirteen years since Veronese had left Verona. If he had been carrying a torch for Elena since then, he comes across as a rather diffident, retiring sort; or maybe he was exceptionally prudent and wanted to be well established financially before entering into marriage. As the 1570s were ushered in, the political situation of Venice suddenly worsened. This would have become very evident to everyone when, in 1570, Alvise Mocenigo was chosen as doge after an unusual election. There was no pomp associated with his elevation, no great procession. All the pageant was dispensed with and he ascended the throne only four days after his predecessor, Pietro Loredan, had died. The fact is that war with the Turks threatened.

The Sultan had attacked Cyprus, and Mocenigo appealed to Venice's allies for help. He approached France, the Czar, the Pope, and Philip of Spain. Only two of the four—the Pope and Philip—promised help, but even they were slow in sending it, and it took Venice more than a year to respond to the Turkish threat. The Battle of Lepanto, when it did take place, was extremely bloody. The Christian fleet discovered the Turkish armada in the Gulf of Lepanto and the line of fighting soon stretched for four miles. So hard was it that the flagships of both fleets came to grips and the Turkish commander was killed. The slaughter was horrible. Eight thousand Venetians lost their lives. Among the Spanish, Miguel de Cervantes was wounded and permanently maimed, but lived to write *Don Quixote.* Seventeen of the Turkish ships fell into enemy hands and many, many others went to the bottom. Scores of slaves were freed and five thousand prisoners taken.

One of Veronese's few purely "political" pictures was painted in response to this victory. His *Allegory of the Battle of Lepanto* is enormous in conception but very small in format. The picture is very busy and very bloody. Divided into two levels, it shows the battle at the bottom, while a celestial scene with the Virgin fills the upper half of the canvas. Thus the victory at Lepanto is attributed to divine intervention, represented in the picture by a dramatic burst of light under the Virgin and by angels throwing flaming arrows down through the storm clouds. But still there are familiar touches: although it is a far from serene picture, portraying as it does a bloody battle scene, yet the feeling of the painting is one of sumptuousness. Veronese's mastery of color is magnificent.

Veronese was now in full flood. He was still painting his huge banquet scenes, among them at this time a *Feast of St. Gregory* for the refectory of the Monte Berico Cloister in Vicenza, and his studio was full to the extent that both his brother Benedetto and his nephew, Alvise dal Friso, were employed there. With all these paintings under his belt, it must therefore have come as something of a shock for him when, in 1573, with his reputation at its height, he came into conflict with the Inquisition.

It all started because he painted another vast sumptuous feast canvas, a *Last Supper* for the Learned Dominican fathers of Santi Giovanni e Paolo, who needed to replace a painting of the same subject by Titian which had been lost in a fire. Many believe this painting to be Veronese's finest work. The picture is, in effect, a triptych, three Palladian arches with Christ in the central one and staircases leading off the canvas. Someone very like Veronese himself is at the top of the right-hand steps, arms outstretched, welcoming newcomers to the feast. The picture is lively, full of movement and light, and contains many of the usual Veronese hallmarks: fine clothes, jugs of wine, rich food, exotically garbed blacks, dogs and monkeys and it is painted in striking perspective.

In Venice, hardly anyone thought this painting unusual or out of keeping with the biblical story. And the Dominican friars were probably pleased to have such a large canvas; it was busy and they would never tire of looking at it. Nonetheless, ten months after the picture was finished and signed, Veronese was summoned before the Inquisition and asked about "certain improprieties." This has become a famous encounter in the annals of art history because in it Veronese defended himself against the Holy Office with what is, in the twentieth century, a very familiar argument but which was, at the time, something of a novelty. The essentials of the encounter are as follows:

Q: What is your profession?
A: I paint and make figures.
Q: The one clothed as a buffoon with a parrot on his wrist; for what reason have you painted him on the canvas?
A: For ornament, as is usual.
Q: How many people were at the Last Supper?
A: I believe that Christ and His Apostles were there; but when there is additional space I adorn it with figures according to fancy.

Veronese was also questioned as to whether he had been specifically requested to paint in Germans (i.e., non-Catholics), buffoons, and the like. He replied: "No, my lords. But the commission was to ornament the picture as seemed good to me. It was big and with capacity for many figures in my judgment." He was then asked directly if he thought it was fitting to introduce bizarre and alien figures in a Last Supper. "No," he replied, adding, "we painters are all a little mad. . . ." Asked if such devices and license did not aid the Protestants in slandering the Roman Church, he answered: "Unhappily, yes. But I feel obliged to follow my predecessors," and he cited Michelangelo's *Last Judgment*. Nonetheless, the Inquisitors exacted an apology from Veronese and made him promise to amend the painting within three months. He did so, but not in the way the Inquisition anticipated. The picture's title was changed to *The Feast in the House of Levi*. That was much safer, since, in the Bible, that event was attended by "publicans and sinners."

There are two threads to draw out of this encounter. First, Veronese is hardly forceful in the presentation of his views; rather, he gives his opinion but politely and apologizes when asked to. Second, he also sets out an artistic defense for what he has done that, although perfectly reasonable nowadays, was much less so at the time, given that artists did not enjoy the same freedom and universally high status they now have and were used to doing what they were told. Possibly, the whole episode says as much about the Inquisition in Venice as it does about Veronese's character. He was known, respected, and liked in Venice; he had painted enough pictures like this one before and probably no one could see what the fuss was about. As it took the Holy Office ten months to get round to prosecuting him, perhaps they did it just for form's sake.

It certainly did no harm to Veronese's reputation. The next year, when Henry III, the new Valois King of France, visited the city, Veronese was one of the artists commissioned to help prepare the fantastic welcome. It was an occasion made for him.

The doge and his senators met the King at the Lido and he formally entered Venice by passing through a ceremonial arch designed by Palladio and decorated by Veronese. By all accounts, Venice made an indelible impression on the French King. Among the many entertainments laid on in his honor was a lavish banquet where all the plates, glasses, and elaborate centerpieces were sculpted in sugar. One morning he was taken to the arsenal, where he was shown an immense keel. That evening he returned to see the same keel, now finished in every detail as a fully rigged ship, properly sailed and manned. He learned how to dance the quadrille, then all the rage in Venice, and there was also a visit to Veronica Franco, the city's most famous courtesan . . .

As Henry left Venice all must have seemed well with the city. His visit had crowned the early seventies when, following the Lepanto victory, Venice's glory had returned to her. The Doges' Palace was redecorated, after fires, and Veronese took his part in painting compositions which, as much as at any other time, celebrated and glorified Venice's triumphs and her virtues.

Yet within months the wheel had turned again. Those sinister blemishes had appeared on the skins of the people and the glory and the pomp, the feasting, and the fine clothes disappeared, to be replaced by disease and decay, starvation and death.

It was, therefore, a singular situation which faced Veronese in 1576. He had led a successful and enjoyable life in one of the most cosmopolitan and sophisticated cities of the day: indeed, he was chiefly known for being the main celebrant of that sophistication. He was acquainted with almost everyone who mattered and as an artist he had a foot in both the patrician and the intellectual camps which together made Venice essentially what it was. No one would have been more conscious than he of the straitened circumstances of the city.

That his pictures lack *any* reference to the enormous drama going on around him is surely extraordinary to modern thinking. On the other hand, would the Emperor have thanked him for intruding such grisly ideas into the pictures he had commissioned? Almost certainly not. Venice's idea of herself was shared by the world at large and even amid the most appalling difficulties Veronese never challenged that. *Wisdom and Strength* was created by a man who was a first-rate painter but did not see himself as a social critic.

2.
The Commission: Why the Emperor Chose Veronese

Rudolf II of Prague, the Habsburg Emperor who ruled the Holy Roman Empire from 1576 to 1612, was the first of twenty-three very different people to possess *Wisdom and Strength*. He was also the most mentally unbalanced. Many of the others, indeed most, were extraordinary characters, but Rudolf was the only one who was frankly mad.

The commission for the painting is the one area in the history of *Wisdom and Strength* which is in dispute. Every other detail in its provenance is known for certain. The mystery lies in whether the picture went straight from Veronese's studio to Rudolf's collection in Bohemia, or whether it went first to Albrecht, Duke of Bavaria. The fact that there *are* two rival theories about *Wisdom and Strength* introduces the very flavor of art history. One can see scholarship at work.

The Albrecht Version

Those who believe the painting went first to Albrecht base their view on an article published in a Viennese journal in 1874. According to this account, the antiquarian Jacopo Strada, who was in the service of the Holy Roman Emperor, Maximilian II (Rudolf's father), was lent for a while to Albrecht, Duke of Bavaria, to find works of art for him.

Albrecht was an enthusiastic collector who had traveled to Italy and had many distinguished Italian friends. He was keen on architecture and employed two full-time goldsmiths who, no sooner had they completed an object, would be ordered to melt it down and start again on something different. His collections included six hundred paintings, but they were works which were chosen, rather like photographs, less for their artistic merit than for the educational content and the information they contained. There were pictures of foreign costumes, of strange animals, dwarves, murderers, and other notorious criminals and no fewer than twenty-four portraits of bearded women. Yet while these curiosities appealed to him, Albrecht possessed no Dürers and almost no Italian master of note.

Strada first came into contact with Albrecht through the Fuggers, the Augsburg banking family, and made several trips to Italy on the duke's behalf, mainly to Rome and Venice. On at least three occasions, Strada made large purchases in Italy, in April 1567 and January 1568, and again in 1575, when he bought the entire collection of Doge Pietro Loredan, who, it will be recalled, had died shortly before the Battle of Lepanto. It is, however, the 1567 trip of Strada's that is most relevant.

On that trip, Strada went from Munich to Mantua to Venice, stopping also at Vicenza and Padua. In an inventory of things he bought on his travels, Strada includes:

1 gross stück Gemälde vom weitberühmten Paolo Veronese, dabei geschrieben: Omnia Vanitas (One large piece, a painting by the widely renowned Paolo Veronese, on which is written: Omnia Vanitas)

1 gross stück Gemälde vom genannten; dabei geschrieben: Honor et Virtus Post Mortem Floret (One large piece, a painting by the same artist; on which is written: Honor et Virtus Post Mortem Floret)

These details are recorded in a letter of Strada's, apparently dated June 14, 1567, in which he also recounts his visit to Mantua. His expense account lists twenty-eight pictures purchased there. Then on August 31 of that year, Strada ordered twenty-two chests sent from Venice to Vienna. The next month, on September 14, he visited Albrecht in Munich and went on to Vienna where the chests from Venice had already arrived. He sent them on to Albrecht.

According to some scholars, these documents indicate that Strada acquired *Wisdom and Strength* and its companion piece, *Vice and Virtue,* not from Veronese himself in Venice, but in Mantua. What is not clear from this chronology is whether the paintings which Strada bought already existed or were specially commissioned. If so, the commission might relate to the marriage, in 1568, of Albrecht's son, Wilhelm V, to Renata of Lorraine. This union was carried out with ostentatious expense in that year and if the two paintings *do* relate to the wedding, they would have a very specific meaning: *Vice and Virtue* was to be seen as a blessing on the young couple by Albrecht, then forty, that their honor and virtue should flourish after his death. Following this interpretation, the figure of Vice in the Frick painting is not Vice but Death, symbolized by the knife. And Virtue is not simply Virtue but, since the woman embraces the man, Marriage. "Omnia Vanitas" in *Wisdom and Strength* refers to the vanity of love, of the world; it warns the young couple not to be too obsessed with worldly goods, as Albrecht was himself, and Hercules is shown as melancholy and downward-looking to represent the triumph of wisdom over strength, since the former is more important in marriage. Albrecht was a stalwart defender of Catholicism in Reformation times in Germany, so this picture may also be seen as a warning to the young couple not to value too highly the wedding gifts they received, since many would be from Protestants.

If Albrecht did acquire the pictures, they would have passed from him to his wife Anna when he died in 1579 and then, on her death in 1587, to Rudolf. Jacopo Strada's son, Ottavio, was in Rudolf's employ at the time, so it is easy to imagine that the Emperor would have known about the paintings.

This theory appears straightforward, even if there is nothing other than the inventory entries to support it. The entries themselves are clear.

Or are they? The fact is that other scholars have come to the conclusion that the inventory entries are far from clear and the consensus of scholarly opinion now holds that both *Wisdom and Strength* and *Vice and Virtue* went straight to Rudolf's court in Prague. One reason for this view is that the Strada inventory bears no date: 1567 is quoted because everything else in the volume which contains this list refers to the years 1560–68. Another reason is that the inventory is not in Strada's handwriting. This has led some scholars to conclude that the inventory was merely a list of works offered to *a* Duke of Bavaria, meaning that the paintings listed were just copies.

The "Albrecht question" can never be resolved fully unless and until someone finds either a contract for the commission for these paintings or Veronese's own account book. Veronese himself does not help: few of his works are dated and his artistic development was not typical, in that he seems to have arrived in Venice fully formed stylistically. Technically he was so good so early on that there was not really much room for improvement or development. He seems to have had two periods during which he produced a number of allegories, one around 1567 and the other beginning in the early 1570s. So that too is not much help. Still there is the inventory. That added to the fact that Jacopo Strada's son was in Rudolf's employ while his granddaughter became the Emperor's mistress makes it perfectly easy to see the Stradas playing a hand in the transfer of the Veroneses from Munich to Prague.

Equally strong, however, is the circumstantial evidence for Rudolf himself being the commissioner of the two Frick pictures. And in fact, the official catalog of the Frick Collection has changed over the years on this issue. The original catalog, which appeared in 1949, gave many of the details of the Albrecht version. The 1968 edition, on the other hand, mentions Albrecht but leans much more to Rudolf.

The Rudolf Version

In 1563, when he was eleven, Rudolf was sent to Spain to be educated. By all accounts his education at the court of Philip II made him haughty and suspicious. But it also gave him a taste for great art. Rudolf's father, Maximilian II, had been an avid collector but it was in the comprehensive collections of Spain that Rudolf first encountered, and then passionately enjoyed, the works of Bruegel, Bosch, Raphael, Correggio, Dürer, and, above all, the great Venetian Titian.

On his way back from Spain in 1571, Rudolf stopped off in Genoa and Milan and spent time at the ducal courts in Mantua and Ferrara. He saw many great works of art and sampled the civilized atmosphere of the sophisticated Italian courts. The Gonzagas in Mantua, the Imperiali of Genoa, the Estes of Ferrara, were all great collectors. In Mantua at least Veronese's work was well represented.

Moreover, at the time Rudolf returned to Prague in 1571, his father was busy trying to obtain a Veronese through his agent in Venice, Veit von Dornberg. On March 31 of that year, the ambassador had written to Maximilian, saying that, on His Majesty's orders, he had examined a painting by the master. This appears to have been a *Venus with the Satyr,* which Veronese had in his studio and which, according to the ambassador, had been "universally praised." The Emperor replied from Prague on May 2, requesting that the ambassador inquire the price of the picture. This particular deal came to nothing, and the painting remained in the Caliari family. But it shows that Veronese's work was sought after by the Habsburgs as early as 1571 and that their ambassador in Venice was in contact with him.

Another piece of circumstantial evidence concerns Rudolf's religion. In matters of the soul, the Emperor was very eclectic. Though a Habsburg bearing the title of Holy Roman Emperor, he was by no means put off by those who came into conflict with the Inquisition. On the contrary, according to one Czech scholar, "He rather approached those against whom the council's policy had been directed." For example, the astronomers whom Rudolf invited to Prague after he was crowned Emperor were Protestants: Kepler and Tycho Brahe, both Lutherans. According to one account, it was Rudolf's proxy who saved the goldsmith Paul van Vianen from the Inquisition in Rome when he was accused of blasphemy. This last fact especially helps us to imagine how Rudolf would have responded to the news, which the imperial ambassador in Venice would surely have reported to Maximilian, that Veronese had been arraigned before the Holy Office in 1573 on a not dissimilar charge, but had been conditionally let off. This would have made Veronese and his work more, not less, intriguing to the future Emperor, who was just turning twenty-one.

Still further circumstantial evidence may be found within the paintings themselves. In *Wisdom and Strength,* for instance, two crowns may be seen at the foot of the canvas. The presumed resemblance of one of these crowns to the Habsburg crown, together with the letters *R* (reversed) and *o,* half-lost in the folds of drapery at Hercules' feet, led many scholars to assume that this confirmed the Rudolf version. But then it was pointed out that the Habsburg crown to which Veronese's bears so close a resemblance was not made until 1602, well after Veronese was dead. In fact, the crown in *Wisdom and Strength* is probably nothing more than a roughly drawn coronet which resembles any number of ducal headpieces in use in the sixteenth and early seventeenth centuries. At the same time, the presence of two crowns could easily be symbolic of the fact that Rudolf was for a while the ruler of two kingdoms.

Rudolf was crowned King of Hungary in 1572 and then King of Bohemia in 1575. These coronations, took place while his father was still alive *(vivente rege)* to ensure there would be no squabbling when the ruler did die. Now, assume that the spur to Rudolf's commission to Veronese was not his coronation as Emperor but Veronese's own appearance before the Inquisition. We know from our reading of the man that, just as he helped rescue Paul van Vianen for much the same offense, he would have been drawn to Veronese. The news of Veronese's arraignment would have reached Prague sometime in 1573. We know from the exchange between Maximilian and his Venetian ambassador in 1571 that negotiations over paintings could take months. It is possible therefore that by the time the commission was sorted out, and certainly by the time the paintings were completed, Rudolf was either already crowned King of Bohemia or well aware that such a coronation was to take place. Thus the two crowns could refer to these two kingdoms, Hungary and Bohemia. Add to this the Hercules figure in the painting. In keeping with classical tradition he wears a lion's skin. But the meaning is enhanced because the symbol of Bohemia was a lion. Thus the Hercules figure is doubly appropriate.

There is still further supporting evidence for the case. In *Vice and Virtue,* the companion picture to *Wisdom and Strength,* the young man torn between two women, and two paths, is dressed in fine silk, though his hose are torn. In the Venice of Veronese's day all the fashionable young men belonged to a club known as the Company of the Hose, since the club's hallmark was the fine stockings its members liked to wear. The garb was all the more colorful because, according to Venetian law, the men did not achieve their proper majority until they were twenty-five, when they had to abandon their finery and don the more sober, somber robes of the Senate. Since Rudolf was born in 1552, he would have been twenty-three when he was crowned King of Bohemia and a year older when he became Emperor. In other words, he too was about to make the transition from frivolous youth to responsible manhood.

There is also the fact that the inventory of Rudolf's collection, compiled in 1612, shows that it contained many paintings by Veronese, seven of which (including the Frick pictures) seem to "hang together" in the sense that their themes overlap and complement one another. Yet there is no suggestion that the five others ever belonged to Albrecht. And surely if he *had* possessed seven works by the master it could never have been said of him, as it was, that he had no works by Italian artists of note.

The six pictures takentogether feature Hercules, Mercury, and Venus particularly strongly. Hercules filled a special slot in the Habsburg self-image at the time. So, surely, Albrecht or his historians would have made something of the Hercules in Veronese's pictures, had he possessed any. Other Habsburg monarchs, Ferdinand, Charles V, and Maximilian II, all shared a preoccupation with the figure, as did Rudolf.

Mercury and Venus were common in all court art in the sixteenth century, but even so Rudolf was especially attracted to them. Like many other rulers of the age, he equated art with virtue and in this scheme of things Mercury embodied moral superiority as much as inventiveness and skill. The same is true of Wisdom, for it is based not only on talent but above all on knowledge and diligence. In Rudolf's pictures Wisdom is frequently shown triumphing over indolence and envy, not just over ignorance.

Finally, all of the Veroneses possessed by Rudolf suited his personality. The Emperor was immensely interested in mythological subjects but also relished "highly erotic, mythological canvases, depicting primarily the amorous adventures of stylized, contorted couples who are usually—like Hercules and Omphale or Vulcan and Maia—ill-suited in age and appearance." Nothing could better describe *Wisdom and Strength* or *Vice and Virtue* or any of the other allegories. A German scholar on Rudolfine affairs, Jaromír Neumann, once wrote that the Emperor was attracted by "a combination of monumentality and precise observation of detail," again a description which, though not applied specifically to the Veroneses in Rudolf's possession, could not fit them better.

Nor should it be overlooked that there were a great many links between Venice and Prague and that Rudolf was in touch with the art available on the lagoon. Giangiorgio Trissino, the patron of Palladio, was well known in the Bohemian capital. Rudolf actually tried to persuade

Jacopo Bassano to settle in Prague. Ottavio Strada, the Emperor's agent and Jacopo Strada's son, negotiated on Rudolf's behalf the purchase of some crystal vessels in Venice. And another time the Emperor was so taken with Dürer's *Rosenkranzfest* that he organized its transportation across the Alps from Venice, with four bearers to hold it upright all the way.

None of this proves that *Wisdom and Strength* went straight from Venice to Prague and short of Veronese's account book turning up or some unknown Habsburg papers coming to light, this particular mystery is unlikely to be solved. The view taken here, in the meanwhile, is the Frick's own: that the balance of circumstantial evidence, despite the undated inventory, points to the paintings, all seven of them, being directly commissioned by Rudolf.

But what exactly would "commissioned" have meant in the second half of the sixteenth century? What arrangement would the Emperor have had with Veronese and how much, for example, would the paintings have cost?

In one sense Rudolf was lucky. Certainly, many rulers have inherited paintings and other works of art, as he did. But Rudolf also inherited two other things: a number of painters and other artists who were present at his father's court, people like Giuseppe Arcimboldo, Hans Mont, the medallists Alessandro and Antonio Abondio, father and son, and Wenzel Jamnizter, though it is doubtful if he ever went to Prague; there was also a network of ambassadors, agents, and talent scouts who were experienced in the acquisition of works of art for an Emperor. Thus, on his accession, Rudolf had a ready-made collection *and* the infrastructure to go on collecting.

He also had enormous personal zeal. He made great efforts to secure the Isenheim Altarpiece by Grünewald and worked equally hard to acquire Holbein's altar in Freiburg. Later on in his reign an important politician, Rudolf Coraduz, spent four weeks in Rome negotiating for paintings on his behalf. Rudolf admired Dürer and chased down works by this master in his home town of Nuremberg. The Fuggers, who lived in nearby Augsburg acted on the Emperor's behalf. Arcimboldo himself acted as an agent more than once, acquiring pictures, jewels, and curios.

Rudolf had agents in four places at least: Rome, Madrid, Burgundy, and Venice. In Venice there was more than one person acting on his behalf, including Ottavio Strada. His official correspondence shows him always alert for the chance to acquire something: when Philip II died in Spain, Rudolf wrote immediately to his ambassador in Madrid urging him to acquire what he could of Philip's collections, especially paintings by Titian, Bosch, and Parmigianino. He sent Hans van Aachen to the Netherlands to acquire the works of Lucas van Leyden. And he offered ten thousand gulden to the city of Frankfurt for Dürer's *Assumption,* which he did not get. Rudolf was the first collector of art who *systematically* sought to collect old masters by manipulating, even coercing, the market.

Rudolf was aware that his father had an agent in Venice in 1571 and that the agent had met Veronese to discuss business. Rudolf was drawn to people like the painter, who had come into conflict with the Inquisition. It is easy to imagine therefore that, on hearing the news about Veronese's appearance before the Holy Office or, on the death of his father and with a coronation imminent, Rudolf would have sent word to his people in Venice to offer the controversial master a commission.

Whether the commission was for just two paintings, the two pictures now in the Frick Collection, or for seven is not known. None of the early accounts of art of the period makes any mention of it.

By the mid-sixteenth century, contracts between artists and their patrons, at least in Italy, had become fairly sophisticated documents, even to the point of having the rather dry and convoluted legalistic flavor of modern documents. These contracts, besides specifying price, usually detailed the contents of a particular painting and even, in certain cases, the materials to be used. For example, Michelangelo's contract with Cardinal di San Dionisio, for the *Pietà,* involved a third party, a wealthy Roman banker called Jacopo Galli. He acted as a kind of trustee, guaranteeing that Michelangelo would in fact complete the work and, at the same time, that the cardinal would actually pay.

The contracts for Veronese's commissions are not as well preserved as those of some other artists, but one which has survived shows that he received up to five ducats ($330) for preliminary drawings. The records for his work at San Sebastiano also survive and show that, in 1556, he received 1,029 ducats ($67,914) in fourteen separate installments. His contract with the Monastery of San Giorgio for *The Marriage at Cana,* dated June 6, 1562, specifies the dimensions of the work (it was to cover the wall in the refectory), the subject (the miracle of turning the water into wine), and that there were to be many figures in the composition, as well as many colors and other devices to make the picture interesting. It was unusual, however, to give Veronese the freedom to invent. The price agreed was 324 ducats ($21,384) and Veronese was paid a deposit of 50 ducats ($3,300). In return he agreed to have the picture completed by the Feast of the Madonna in September 1563. Veronese was also to receive wine and food on the days he was actually working on the picture in the refectory.

Another contract, dated March 24, 1584, and signed by both Veronese and Giacinto Rosello di Cividal del Friuli, is, again, typical. Not only is the theme specified in the contract but Veronese agreed to make the figures "in large proportions," the figures being the Virgin with the baby in her arms and angels holding a crown above her head. Veronese even agreed to put his signature in a particular place, which probably implied that this work was in fact by his workshop.

Such arrangements were not out of the ordinary for the sixteenth century. Painters were more respected than they had ever been but, at the same time, their patrons were used to laying down stringent requirements and were used to being obeyed. Painters—Veronese included—did not demur.

If Rudolf was lucky in what he inherited, Veronese was lucky to have lived and painted in one of the world's most thriving economies so that he could enjoy the benefits of a strong currency, the Venetian ducat. The Mediterranean world had by then seen four dominant currencies: the Byzantine solidus, the Muslim dinar, the Florentine florin, and, from the late fifteenth century on, the Venetian ducat. All these coins were similar, theoretically, in that they consisted of between 3.5 and 4.5 grams of fine gold. Working out actual values in 1576, or even the latter half of the sixteenth century, is fraught with danger since for one thing gold then had rather greater purchasing power than it does now and already different economies attached different values to things. Any calculations designed to show what people earned or spent at today's values must therefore be highly tentative.

But applying a straight calculation, at the time of this writing, 4.5 grams of fine gold costs roughly $67.* So if, in 1555, Veronese was paid 150 ducats for painting one large and four smaller works for the ceiling of San Sebastiano in Venice, this translates at today's prices, using gold simply as the base for the calculation, as $9,900. As the years went by, Veronese's prices rose steadily: in the late fifties, when he was doing his last works for San Sebastiano, he charged 200 ducats ($13,200) for the organ shutters. From these figures, and being conservative, it would appear that Veronese could command fees up to 350 ducats ($23,100) for a work—say 250 ducats on the average over his lifetime.

Referring now to the official record of Veronese's complete oeuvre, there are 307 works definitely attributed to him, with 42 mentioned in the documents but now lost and another 117 attributed but doubted by many scholars. Assuming that all the lost works were genuine, and that

* Gold = £395 per ounce; 28.35 grams = 1 ounce; therefore 4.5 grams = $420/28.35 × 4.5 = approximately $67.

none of those attributed to him are, this gives a total oeuvre of 349 pictures, say 350. Roughly speaking, therefore, Veronese's total income during his Venice years (1553–88) was somewhere in the region of 87,500 ducats ($5,775,000), or $165,000 a year at current prices.

These figures are so tentative that all we may really allow ourselves to say is that Veronese was comfortable. He certainly made enough money to buy a small farm on the mainland. But he was not a fierce negotiator and, like most painters of his time, he never became truly rich.

This background at least enables various assumptions about Rudolf's commission to be made. Sometime in 1574, 1575, or most likely 1576 (Rudolf was crowned later that year), Veronese was approached by the Emperor's agent in Venice. This may have been a special emissary or it may have been the ambassador. The painter would have been aware that the Emperor knew his work and he may have met the emissary before. This man would have made it his business to know what prices Veronese charged. There would have been quite a bit of discussion about what the paintings might contain: the next two chapters will explore what those discussions would have amounted to.

Finally, a contract, now lost, would have been drawn up, almost certainly specifying subject matter, dimensions, and when the pictures were to be completed. The ambassador would have paid a deposit of about a third of the commission. And he would have left an additional sum of about a quarter or a third with a mutually respected third party.

3.
The Theme:
The Secret Meanings
of Allegory

Allegorical paintings look rather strange and are generally unpopular these days, except among art historians. Scantily clad women, dancing or dashing about among classical ruins, small chubby cupids holding bows and arrows, swords or ribbons, men who are half beast, or goats with fish's tails, do not fit easily into the taste of the postphotographic generation. It is important to remember, however, that Veronese lived at a time when allegorical painting was at its height. It was as fashionable then as Impressionism is now. One reason was that, in an allegory, especially where the patron of a picture is shown as a god or as a moral quality, the directness of portraiture is blunted or avoided altogether. The picture's avowed aim is to flatter and everyone knows it. But the approach at least let the artist and the sitter off the hook.

Classical allegory in painting first became popular around the early 1480s, about the time Botticelli completed his *Primavera*. *Primavera*, now among the most famous paintings in the world, is rich in complex Christian and mythical allusions, including among its nine figures Mercury, Cupid, the Three Graces, and the most famous figure of all, Flora, decked in hundreds of flowers. Allegory grew in popularity during the sixteenth and seventeenth centuries but by the end of that period the heavy symbolism which had such an appeal to begin with had become so fragmented that mythology, as a way of presenting a particular message, had been fatally weakened.

At the time Veronese lived, however, the fact that allegory not only held its own during the Renaissance but actually flourished, as much as religious painting, is a fact of great significance. This is because the deities never went totally underground. Instead, many of them were adapted to the Christian tradition in hybrid form; this, despite the efforts of the Church in medieval Europe to establish itself as the only true belief. That pagan ideas of gods and of astrology still retained a fascination for many people raises a question all too often glossed over— namely, whether, in medieval times, people were actually as convinced of Christianity as the Church has always maintained.

To begin with, of course, Christianity itself contained astrological elements such as the names for the days of the week and the timing of Christmas. In the ninth century, the relationship between the planets and the virtues was codified, producing an alliance of sorts between Christianity and astrology, since both identified the heavens as the seat of virtue and power. (The planets were presumably regarded as powerful because the sky was more interesting at night.) During the great flowering of Christian art in the thirteenth and fourteenth centuries, astrologers in Italy directed the lives of whole cities. And by the early fourteenth century, the pagan gods commonly appeared not just in literature but on monuments as well. In Venice they were used on the Gothic capitals of the Doges' Palace, and they appeared contemporaneously in Padua, Florence, and Siena as well. It was a bishop, the Bishop of Meaux, who argued in his mammoth poem, *Ovide Moralisé*, that Christian instruction could be found in many of the myths of Ovid. That would prove very important later.

In the early fifteenth century, getting nearer our period, the use of pagan mythology and astrology became even more open. In the Old Sacristy of San Lorenzo in Florence, just above the altar, there is a cupola containing mythical figures and a constellation of the heavens which coincides with the sky above the city at the time of the Council of Florence. Later equivalent decorations were to invade even the palaces of the Popes (the list of St. Peter's successors in the Borgia apartments is surrounded by celestial symbols, including Jupiter and Mars).

As the fifteenth century wore on, mythology grew to be more and more complex as first this author then that sought to find contemporary significance in the pagan gods. And the complexity was part of the point. Men of learning loved to think that they possessed the key to the mysteries of the universe and the decoding of allegories and myths was one way to achieve this (the decoding of hieroglyphs was another).

Thus the survival of the pagan gods—Greco-Roman mainly but Egyptian too—was an important element in the Renaissance. By itself, however, that would not have explained the blossoming of allegory. The other important change was the development of Humanism, the realization, in the fourteenth century, that both classical Greece and then ancient Rome had been highly developed civilizations in their own right, with their own intrinsic values. That changed the way men looked at themselves.

Humanism and Ideal Beauty

Padua and Verona were the two earliest centers of Humanism in Italy. Both had fine libraries. And in Verona, about 1300, the works of the Roman poet Catullus, who had been born in the city, were rediscovered. Padua was the birthplace of the historian Livy.

As Humanism grew, so antiquarianism, the study and often veneration of ancient objects, became very popular. At times antiquarianism acquired almost religious overtones of its own: Alfonso the Great (1416–58), King of Naples, went to great lengths to obtain relics, such as an arm bone of Livy, his favorite author. In Mantua, birthplace of Virgil, a statue was removed from public display in 1397 because it had become an object of superstitious reverence.

Francesco Petrarca (Petrarch, 1304–74) is generally regarded as the first great figure in Humanism. For him, pagan antiquity was to be seen in strong contrast to the intervening Dark Ages, as a shining civilization all but extinguished by the barbarians of medieval times.

Petrarch prepared the way. But the reincarnation of the ancient deities in all their dazzling classical splendor, which really came about in the second half of the fifteenth century, occurred as a result of several other interdependent events.

Artists, caught up in the wake of the Humanist movement, were inevitably drawn to the Roman ruins. Sculpture from that time tended to survive, whereas painting or fresco fared less well. The sculptures were often classically proportioned nudes. It is also true that around this time it became popular for families to decorate their *cassoni,* or bridal chests, which had long front panels that were well suited to narrative scenes with moral messages. Petrarch's *Trionfi* and Boccaccio's *Decameron* were popular early sources for the narratives and this appears to be how Greek and Roman myths were popularized in the first place. On the *cassoni,* however, the pictures were not classical but contemporary retellings in modern dress, with nude scenes sometimes used on the insides of the lids. In this way, however, the stories of the ancient gods became more widely known even if their classical appearance did not. Then, in 1435, in Florence, Leon Battista Alberti published *Della Pittura.* Alberti was a Humanist, with wide learning in both scientific and classical studies. But he also pursued painting, sculpture, and architecture. In his book he encouraged artists to become men of letters themselves and to look for illustrative subject matter in classical writers. Though this book was first published in Latin, and therefore intended for learned scholars, not painters, it was later translated into Italian.

Another factor encouraging interest in the classical period was the fall of Constantinople to the Ottoman Turks in 1453, soon to be followed by the conquest of all Greece. The Turkish advances swelled the number of Greek scholars who found refuge in Italy and their presence naturally fueled the Humanist appreciation of ancient Greek culture. At the same time, the works of Latin and Greek classical authors were now being produced in ever greater numbers thanks to the invention of printing. As a direct result, a knowledge of written and spoken Greek became not uncommon among educated people.

In 1439 an institute for the study of Plato was set up in Florence at the instigation of Cosimo de' Medici the Elder. The institute soon became a center for a group of illustrious Renaissance poets and philosophers, including Cosimo's grandson Lorenzo the Magnificent and also the leader of the group and its most influential member, Marsilio Ficino.

Ficino was a philosopher, a priest, and a physician. He translated Plato and other Greek authors. But Ficino's cast of mind was also mystical and this is important in understanding how one strand of Humanism developed. Ficino adopted and developed the ideas of the Neoplatonist Plotinus. In essence, Plotinus argued that there are "universal forms," entities created by God and which exist as entities only in the upper world. These entities, he said, are known to us only through partial examples which we see about us on earth. Ideal beauty was one of these ideal forms taken over by Ficino, and it was of obvious importance to artists. No one on earth had ideal beauty, said Plotinus/Ficino, but God showed what it was by endowing various individuals with bits of it. Therefore one aim of artists, in fact the highest aim, was to improve on earthly beauty. The successful artist was the one who could combine the right mix of earthly features to create a beauty never before seen, indeed a beauty that by definition was impossible to see in living form on earth. As a measure of how influential the Humanists were, it is enough to say that both Raphael and Michelangelo sought to create this ideal beauty.

Ficino's second achievement was to found a whole school of exegesis in which it was accepted that wisdom could be sought in classical allegory. Ficino also added a mystical element which attracted many people. To be able to decipher an allegory conferred a kind of insider status which appealed very much to the mood of the times and was adroitly developed by one of Ficino's followers, Pico della Mirandola (1463–94). According to him the ancient myths were a kind of code which concealed a secret wisdom: this wisdom was veiled by allegory which, once deciphered, would reveal the secrets of the universe. He cited the teaching of Moses who, after all, had communed with God for forty days on the mountain and yet returned from Sinai with but two tablets: much more must have been revealed to him which he kept secret. Jesus himself confessed as much when he said to his disciples: "It has been granted to you to know the secrets of the Kingdom of Heaven; but to those others it has not been granted." To Mirandola, and many others like him, all religions shared mysteries. And only to a select few—philosophers—could the secrets be revealed through the deciphering of ancient myths. One way of trying to do this was to explore the links and the similarities between classical myths and Christianity.

Allegory thus achieved two different, but intertwined ends. It was an attempt to sort out the meaning of the universe but (because even in the Renaissance, Humanists were only human) it also became a deliberate way for the educated to show off their knowledge. At the same time that allegory was supposed to clarify matters, it also clouded them.

As the fifteenth century drew to a close, Humanist ideas were influencing all of the arts and were also extending beyond the narrow confines of the intelligentsia. On the one hand, academies like Ficino's were established in other cities and, on the other hand, at a more popular level, the ability to understand an allegory, or even to decipher a conundrum, became a desirable accomplishment of the courtier and helped set him apart from the lower ranks of society. As part of this general broadening of interest in the allegorical approach, emblem books and what were known as *impresa* became fairly common.

The first book of emblems appeared in 1531. Each entry contained an illustration of the emblem in question, which concealed a hidden, symbolic meaning. There were also a few lines of verse explaining in a brief, pithy way the moral underlying the picture. There would be Janus looking both ways, teaching prudence; Bacchus, reminding of the evils of alcohol. Venus, standing in a pillared hall with one foot on a tortoise, teaches that woman's place is in the home and that she should know when to hold her tongue.

The *impresa* was rather different. It also consisted of an image and text but was devised specifically for a single individual for whom it had a wholly personal application. It usually commemorated a particular event or some trait of character and appeared not in book form but on a medallion or as a sculpture on the ceiling of a prince's palace so that he could reflect on its message as he lay in bed.

And so allegory and the allegorical understanding of the world became increasingly familiar. Against such a background it was only a matter of time before a number of mythological manuals became available to artists and it is these which would have appealed to, and exerted an influence on, Veronese. Between 1548 and 1556 there appeared no fewer than three manuals of great importance, both in terms of their intellectual content and their publishing histories. In 1548 *The History of the Gods,* by Lilio Gregorio Giraldi, was published in Basel. In 1551 *The Mythology,* by Natale Conti, was published in Venice. In 1556 *The Images of the Gods,* by Vincenzo Cartari, was published also in Venice.

Conti explains best the purpose of these works. He wrote that, from the earliest times—first in Egypt, then in Greece—thinkers deliberately concealed the great truths of science and philosophy under the veil of myth in order to withdraw them from vulgar profanation. He therefore organized his own book according to what he thought were the hidden messages to be revealed: the secrets of nature, the lessons of morality, and so on.

What makes these manuals particularly relevant, apart from the fact that two of them had just been published in Venice when Veronese began painting there, is that each one was specifically addressed to poets and artists to provide models and themes for inspiration. The foreword of Cartari's *Images,* for instance, specifically mentions that it is "of a nature gladly to be welcomed by painters and sculptors, providing them with themes for a thousand inventions with which to adorn their statues and painted panels."

If this seems strange to us now, with our conception of the artist as someone jealous of his creativity and originality, it was not at all unusual in the sixteenth century. In a book published in 1587, the year before Veronese died, Giovanni Battista Armenini even enumerated those authors who, in his opinion, should be in every artist's library. At much the same time, Giovanni Paolo Lomazzo, in his *Treatise on Painting* (Milan, 1584), exposed what he felt were the limitations of culture and imagination among many painters.

Veronese was, therefore, surrounded by attempts to educate him and to "civilize" his work. Jean Seznec, author of *The Survival of the Pagan Gods,* sums up the spirit of the time when he says that allegories came to be regarded as a means of "rendering thought visible." Just how successful the three manuals were may be judged from their publishing history. Conti's book appeared in Venice in 1551, 1568, and 1581, as well as in Frankfurt four times and in Paris three times (in 1605 it was issued by three different publishers simultaneously). It was also published in Geneva, Rouen, Padua, and Lyon. Cartari's *Images* appeared in Venice in 1556, 1566, 1571, and 1580 but was also published in Padua, Lyon, Rothenburg, Mainz, Frankfurt, Tournon, and London. By the standards of the day, they were bestsellers.

We may be certain then that Veronese was well aware of the mythological tradition as reflected in these manuals. Very likely he possessed at least one of the books himself. Veronese was compiling his pictures for Rudolf at the very height of the fashion for allegory.

Christianity and Allegory

One other quite different factor contributed to the popularity of allegory: the Reformation and the Catholic reaction led by Rome.

While Humanism was growing in Florence, Rome was recovering from the Great Schism of the West, when theological and political divisions among rival contenders for the Papacy had led to one set of Popes ruling from Rome and another set from Avignon. The Great Schism lasted from 1378 to 1417. From then on, however, Rome began to recover until, by the beginning of the sixteenth century, she was again living in a golden age so far as art was concerned. True, this was to be short-lived, for the city was sacked in 1527 by the mutinying troops of the Holy Roman Emperor; eight days of turmoil once again left Rome in ruins. But by that time both Michelangelo and Raphael had made their impact.

For the purposes of this narrative, these men were significant for two reasons. First, they did more than anyone to raise the social standing of the artist in Italian society. The concept of the "learned painter," as opposed to the artisan painter, was born. Second, both of them succeeded in combining classical themes and forms with their Christian beliefs. Michelangelo did this most spectacularly in the Sistine Chapel ceiling in the Vatican, where his nude figures recall the classical statues of ancient Rome. Raphael did it most notably in the Stanza della Segnatura, also in the Vatican, where he depicted allegories of theology, philosophy, and justice at the same time as he featured Apollo, Dante, and various saints, including Peter. No one thought either of these great works odd or blasphemous in any way.

In helping to raise the status of artists, Michelangelo and Raphael (and others, of course) also helped to free them from being quite so dependent on the Church for their livelihoods. In the fifteenth century personal patronage began to replace the guilds as a source of commissions. For a time artists had a relatively free hand in compiling what they liked, subject only to the taste of their patrons. Around the middle of the century, however, when Veronese was just coming into prominence and moving to Venice, new influences were felt. The Church once more started to dictate stricter rules as to the form and content of paintings.

The religious reform movement, which spread through northern Europe from the 1520s on, was partly aimed at correcting abuses and corruption of the priesthood. It also reflected a growing conviction that an individual might receive God's grace without the mediation of a priest. This new view was based in part on a reevaluation of the early Christian texts, a method which, ironically, had been developed by the Humanists in Italy and then spread north. Thus the Humanists themselves played a part in bringing about the Reformation.

One of the main targets of the reformers was what they saw as the growth of idolatry in the Roman Church. The Catholic Church responded in two ways. It became clear that the more austere the Reformed Churches were the more ostentatious the Roman Church needed to be, in order to appeal to that part of man's emotional makeup that loves pomp and ceremony and mysticism. So the Virgin was glorified anew and new saints and themes were encouraged. Second—and more directly linked to the appearance of *Wisdom and Strength*—traditional theology was reasserted in a variety of ways. New, idealistic religious orders sprang up in the 1520s followed, in 1534, by the most famous of all, the Jesuits. Freedom was strictly curtailed; for instance, the more erotic poetry was banned or bowdlerized. But the most important moves of the Counter Reformation were the revival of the Inquisition and the Council of Trent, which first met in 1545. The council met off and on for nearly twenty years, instituting a number of measures to maintain the appeal of Catholicism and the central authority of Rome. And, in one of its last sessions, it laid down broad guidelines for sacred art. The council was careful to avoid any accusations of idolatry that might be made against it. Images were to be allowed in churches but it was to be made plain that their prototypes only were objects for veneration. Otherwise, paintings and sculpture were for instruction in the faith and it followed that they had to be accurate, so far as matters of doctrine were concerned. There must be no superstitious elements, no lasciviousness, nothing lacking in decorum. Allegory was allowed, but as a cloak for Christian instruction.

Subsequently, there appeared a number of books which set out to interpret the council's guidelines, their aim being to instruct artists in the correct choice of subject matter and in the way images should be represented, thus ensuring that Catholic art was safe from Protestant criticism. One of these books was published in 1570, two others in 1584. The author of one of them, Cardinal Paleotti, conceded that many scholars were drawn to the pagan gods quite legitimately, since these were proper aspects of antiquity. He therefore allowed that such images could be kept but for study only and therefore *out of sight.* This was a strict ruling, and he made it clear that he regarded the public display of mythology as dangerous, "filthy and criminal." Other authors went even further. It was now that ideas about "decorum" surfaced, with the argument that art should always be suitable to the place it was to occupy. In other words, scenes of death would be fitting only in a cemetery, or the decorations on fountains should always allude to water.

The years Veronese was in Venice were therefore exactly the time when this controversy over allegory and "suitability" was raging. While Veronese was in full flood, the Council of Trent concluded its deliberations and books on both sides of the argument were published in Venice. Nudity and mythological subjects continued to appear in painting, but there were as many zealots to oppose this as there were Humanistic supporters. This adds a twist of understanding to Veronese's appearance before the Inquisition and to the meaning of *Wisdom and Strength.*

The Singular Situation of Venice

The Reformation and the intellectual landscape surrounding Humanism had their own particular coloring in Venice. This is no surprise when the difficult relationship that existed between the Popes and the doges, the elected rulers of the city-state, is recalled. But there were other factors.

Venetian painters, in contrast to Florentine ones, were much more likely to be only that. Unlike their counterparts in central Italy, they were rarely involved in other branches of the arts, in literature or poetry, for example. There was no equivalent of Vasari, Leonardo da Vinci, or Piero della Francesca. Apart from Titian, painters in Venice did not become Humanists, like Alberti, or form fast friendships in other walks of life, like Raphael and Baldassare Castiglione, author of the influential book on courtly manners, *The Courtier.* There was much less writing of poetry in Venice than elsewhere and what there was was not sought out by her painters. In fact, the high point in Venetian painting, when Veronese was active, occurred when the city was commercially decadent, just ceasing to be the chief link between the Levant and Europe. In Rome, Florence, and Siena, by contrast, economic, military, and artistic successes had gone together.

An important element was the (relative) weakness of the Church in Venice. This was partly due to the republican system of government, which had helped to set Venice against Rome for so long. That colored every aspect of life in Venice, painting no less than anything else. Any artist of standing in Venice would have been aware of the differences between painting in the city and elsewhere. But in Veronese's day this rivalry was particularly sharp. This was because, when he arrived in Venice in 1557, Lodovico Dolce published his *Dialogue on Painting.* This was a treatise in the form of a dialogue between Pietro Aretino and Giova Francesco Fabrini, a grammarian from Tuscany who occupied the chair of eloquence in Venice for thirty years, starting in 1547. In their dialogue,

Dolce makes the two men discuss the rival merits of the Roman, Florentine, and Venetian schools of painting.

Dolce's book was in part a rejoinder to Giorgio Vasari's *Lives of the
Most Eminent Painters, Sculptors, and Architects.* This had appeared in 1550
and, besides arguing for the supremacy of Michelangelo over all other
artists, had put forward the general view that *disegno* (form or line) was
significantly more important in art than color. This implicitly subordi-
nated Venetian painting to that of central Italy. Vasari's preferences were
also made explicit in his choice of painters to write about: he did not
neglect the Venetians entirely but gave them much less space than the
Florentines and the Romans.

Dolce—using the voice of Aretino, born in Arezzo, found fame in
Rome, and settled in Venice—argued that color was as important as line
and went further, adding that invention, sheer imagination, also mattered. He argued, too, that it was important for art to *move* people and he
said that color was all-important in this. Just as Vasari had cloaked his
admiration for Michelangelo and Raphael in a general argument, so
Dolce did with Titian.

Dolce was not as close to the artists he wrote about as Vasari was but he
still had an effect: his book was one factor which stimulated Vasari to
come to Venice in the late 1560s. The latter was preparing a new edition
of his book and wanted to visit Titian's studio. The age-old debate of line
versus color was thus raging anew in Veronese's Venice. In the context of
Humanism the controversy also played a part in helping to change the
status of the painter.

The Changing Status of the Artist

The intellectual changes overtaking Europe not only affected the *appearance* of pictures, but they eventually affected the social standing of painters also. To begin with, in the early 1400s, painters, sculptors, and architects in Italy had been no more than craftsmen, their disciplines classed as
the mechanical arts. This was an important distinction for, as Anthony
Blunt points out, the liberal arts were practiced by freemen whereas the
mechanical arts were undertaken by slaves. Although this began to
change as the fifteenth century came to a close, it was a slow business: to
take one example, Bernardino Pinturicchio, who had assisted Perugino
with his frescoes in the Sistine Chapel, ignored painters, sculptors, and
architects in his main work, a series of frescoes showing the liberal arts,
which were painted for the Borgia apartments of the Vatican in the last
decade of the fifteenth century.

As the 1400s wore on, however, certain painters tried hard to disassociate themselves from the idea that they were merely craftsmen. In this they were particularly helped by the controversy over perspective. The principles governing this had been discovered in the fifteenth century when it was known as *costruzione legittima* (literally, "legitimate construction"). Perspective was important in this context because it involved an understanding of mathematics, which at that time *was* included in the liberal arts. So if painters could show that their art depended on mathematics, this would further their claim for painting to be regarded as one of the liberal arts.

This was just one of several similar controversies of the day. Gradually painters, sculptors, and architects got their way: by 1500 or thereabouts, the visual arts came to be accepted by the Humanists as liberal.

These debates were then replaced for a while by equally serious (and to us equally irreconcilable) disputes over, for instance, the rival merits of painting and sculpture. No matter that these disputes were never settled; they succeeded in achieving for painters and sculptors recognition as men of learning, educated souls. And that is what they were after— membership in Humanist society.

This was an important development for it eventually produced the concept of "fine arts," a single phrase which we take for granted today but which was not used until the middle of the sixteenth century, the very moment when Veronese began working in Venice. In turn the concept of fine art led to the idea of the "work of art." Until that time painting and sculpture had been commissioned by patrons. Now, but only now, art became a thing that was beautiful in its own right, without necessarily having a decorative function or purpose. Only now did the modern idea of "art for art's sake" come into being. It was not until this time, either, that artists themselves showed any awareness of the public, that a painter or sculptor might serve the mass of people at large rather than a particular master or patron.

This development gives added significance to that exchange between Rudolf's father, Maximilian II, and his ambassador in Venice. He was negotiating in 1571 to buy a picture of Veronese's, a picture that *already existed.* This was a state of affairs that would not have made sense a few years earlier, when painters worked only on direct commission. The fact that painters did this meant also that they could afford to do so: they could take off some weeks to invest time in a painting they had not yet sold. Even in this, then, Veronese lived at a crucial time for painters, when the whole nature of the business of art was changing. It also confirms that he was fairly prosperous.

There was also a more practical aspect to these changes in the status of artists. In the fifteenth century painters were organized into guilds which exercised tight control over what they might and might not do. By 1500 many of the more successful painters had shaken loose of the guilds. Then, in the later part of the sixteenth century, a new type of organization grew up: the academy. The difference between guilds and academies was that the former had the dual function of maintaining technical standards and operating as closed shops, whereas the latter sought to look after the teaching of painting and to safeguard the traditions of fine art.

The Venetian painters' guild was founded in 1271, so it may have been the oldest in all Italy. But unlike the guild in Florence, however, the Venetian guild never exercised any political power: that was available only to patricians, as we have seen. A painter, if he was successful, would progress through the various grades recognized by the guild, from *garzone* (boy apprentice) to *maestro dell'arte* (master) which gave him the right to open a shop, employ assistants, and sell objects. Apprentices usually entered shops in their early teens and the apprenticeship lasted from a few months to several years. (Cennino Cennini, the fourteenth-century author of the earliest Italian treatise on painting, provides us with most of what we know on tempera techniques; he recommends six years as a minimum.) The master in a workshop agreed not only to train the apprentice but to provide for his safety and, sometimes, to pay him a wage. In a city the size of Venice there would have been about two hundred members of the painters guild.

During the fifteenth century there were several divisions of the guild, which reflected the fact that painting was not yet considered one of the liberal arts. At the top came the figure painters; then came the gilders, textile designers and embroiderers, leather workers, makers of playing cards, mask makers, sign makers, and illuminators. To begin with, the *figure* or figure painters had no special status in the guild over and above the others. When Veronese appeared before the Inquisition in 1573 he identified himself: *"Io depingo et fazzo delle figure."* (I am a painter inscribed in the first column of the guild.) But as early as 1511, for example, Cima da Conegliano, a follower of Bellini in Venice, attempted to weight the membership of the *Banca,* the governing board of the guild, by giving two seats to figure painters instead of one.

The change that Titian went through in this context is revealing. In 1511, for example, the young artist signed himself *Tician depentor,* that is, master in the *Arte dei Depentor.* Two years later, however, a new note is sounded and in a petition to the Senate he declared that, from childhood, he had dedicated himself to painting "not so much out of a desire for profit as to seek the acquisition of some small fame," a Venetian paraphrase of Alberti's Humanist arguments. Later still, the artist signed himself differently again, as *Titiano Vecellio pittore.* The use of the word *pittore* meant that Titian was giving himself more status than that of a mere *depentor,* and describing himself as a serious artist rather than a decorative one.

These varied self-descriptions by Titian, which clearly underline the conflicts of painters of the time, were paralleled in the similar growth of the self-portrait. The tradition of the artist inserting a self-portrait into an altarpiece or into a fresco dates back only to the fourteenth century. Veronese sometimes put himself in his pictures, which is not quite as vain as it appears. Rather, it was professional pride as much as anything.

The life of the Venetian artist also differed from the life of the artist elsewhere in that it generally consisted of family workshops. Whereas Florentine art was produced by individuals—and individualists—in Venice, artistic production was more of a communal enterprise. The phenomenon of the family workshop was one of the most distinctive characteristics of Venetian painting. It lasted more than four centuries and the famous names run from Paolo da Venezia in the fourteenth century, through the Vivarini, Bellini, Vecellio (Titian), Robusti (Tintoretto), Caliari (Veronese), and da Ponte (Bassano) in the fifteenth and sixteenth, to Tiepolo and Guardi in the final years of the Republic, and on into the nineteenth century.

In Veronese's case, he worked with his brother Benedetto, his son Carletto, and occasionally with a nephew. In such a workshop everybody actually worked on a picture which was set out in a style established by the master. The workshop technique does, however, pose certain problems for the modern connoisseur. To the Renaissance Humanists, artists were born not made. Yet the workshop tradition to some extent goes against that: it affirms that painting is a craft that may be learned. Here is another factor which probably helps account for the late arrival and acceptance of Humanist ideas among painters in Venice.

Nor should it be overlooked that it takes time and money to establish a workshop. It was a significant event for a son to be bequeathed his father's workshop. Drawings, which today we regard as works of art in their own right, were then tools of the trade, books of instruction as it were, to offer inspiration and technical solutions to problems. They too were usually passed from father to son.

From tax returns it is clear that most painters were not wealthy. Their list of creditors usually exceeded their meager assets. Wills and court documents show that patrons were often very lax in paying for commissions and bitter legal battles would ensue. The changing social standing of painters eventually led to better financial circumstances for some of them. For example, da Vinci, Vasari, and Titian all had houses that were palaces compared with those of more ordinary painters.

Veronese was not as well off as these three, but came on the next rung down. Like many artists he had interests outside his workshop from which he sometimes made money. Giotto rented out rooms but a more common occurrence was for an artist living in the city to own a small farm in the countryside which provided him and his family with wood, olive oil, and wine. Sometimes it would be rented to a tenant farmer. Later in his life, Veronese had just such a small holding, of some forty *campi* (about forty acres), on the mainland. This is a measure of how much Veronese's personal social standing improved in his lifetime.

The Form and Meaning of the Picture

Wisdom and Strength cannot be looked at in isolation from the other paintings which Veronese painted for Rudolf. They may have been part of the same commission and they certainly contain overlapping and intertwined meanings. The inventories of the time were far from perfect, so it is impossible to be certain how many Veronese canvases the Emperor owned. But there were at least six other, similar, allegorical or history pictures which Veronese executed for Rudolf. (In addition, four other Veronese allegories, now in the National Gallery in London, were ceiling pictures and therefore somewhat different.) Rudolf's seven pictures, with their current whereabouts, are:

Wisdom and Strength	Frick Collection, New York
Vice and Virtue	Frick Collection, New York
Mercury, Herse, and Aglauros	Fitzwilliam Museum, Cambridge, England
Venus and Adonis	Stockholm National Museum
Mars and Venus United by Love	Metropolitan Museum, New York
Venus and Love	Private collection, Switzerland
Mars and Venus, Cupids, and a Horse	Lost but with a copy in a private collection in Florence

All of these paintings were executed between 1576 and 1584, though in what order is not clear. They are all allegorical and mythological scenes. Venus and Mars appear in several, as do the Virtues, cupids, dogs, and horses.

Given that Rudolf may have suffered from some form of mental illness which later in his life deteriorated into schizophrenia, one is tempted to find something obsessive in this list of six pictures. In each of the compositions, the women are either undressed, partially nude, or frankly seductive. Rudolf had unusual tastes and a love of paintings with voluptuous naked women was foremost among them. However high-flown a painting's meaning might be, it also performed a very different and much more down-to-earth function.

The figures which Veronese put into his pictures for the Emperor convey an unmistakable message, though not one that is immediately obvious today. The figures in the seven pictures also act as an excellent introduction to a general understanding of allegory. The individual components of the paintings reveal Veronese's intentions a step at a time.

VENUS

Venus was the Roman goddess of love and fertility, the equivalent of the Greeks' Aphrodite. She is the mother of Cupid and is generally attended by Three Graces. Among her attributes are a pair of doves or swans, which may draw her chariot, a scallop shell, dolphins (which, with the shell, recall Venus's birth from the sea), a magic girdle, a flaming torch (which kindles love), a flaming heart, and myrtle, which, like love, is evergreen.

Venus, who was widely known through statues of her which had survived from antiquity, appears in many guises in painting and is sometimes simply a synonym for the nude, without any mythological symbolism at all. She is often painted in the likeness of the wife or the mistress of either the artist or his patron. One depiction was of the theme "Sacred and Profane Love," in which twin Venuses were shown to express the two ideas of love first formulated by Plato and resurrected by the Florentine humanists. Celestial Venus symbolizes love aroused by contemplation of the eternal and the divine, whereas the common or earthly Venus stands for both the beauty found in the material world *and* the procreative principle. The humanists regarded both as virtuous, *Venus vulgaris* being a stage on the way to *Venus coelestis*. In art the two Venuses are distinguished by their clothes: earthly Venus is richly dressed and bejeweled to reflect earthly vanities, whereas heavenly Venus is naked, since during the Renaissance, nakedness in art signified purity and innocence. This is perfect allegorical thinking. The heavenly Venus is the higher form, but her nakedness can be admired in a very down-to-earth way.

MARS

Mars was the god of war and one of the twelve Olympians. He was so brutal by nature that he was hated by nearly everyone. The exception was Venus, who fell hopelessly in love with him. There is no fixed type for Mars, but in general, he is not a popular figure in art, except as a warlike figure who is tamed by love. He is usually shown in armor of some sort and accompanied by a wolf, which represents his aggressive nature.

VENUS AND MARS

Homer first wrote about the affair between Venus and Mars. In his account it was little more than an episode of adultery punished by the jealous husband. The allegorists of the Renaissance, however, made much more of it. In some ways, this subject is the most moral theme of all: love has conquered, having overcome the god of war. Mars is usually shown in anything but a warlike state. Sometimes he dozes, usually his armor is put to one side, and in many cases he is fettered. This may be nothing more than a love knot tied by a Cupid, but it is enough. Mars, with his warlike nature refined if not exactly tamed, becomes therefore a lover as well as a warrior and this was a combination that the Renaissance courtier set out to follow; it was the basis of chivalry, as developed in the Middle Ages.

HERCULES

In contrast to Mars, Hercules (Greek: Herakles) is one of the most popular figures in art. He represents the personification of physical strength and courage. And his Twelve Labors, in which he triumphs over evil at great odds, are part myth, part saga and may well be based on some events in ancient history. His story overlaps with those of both the biblical Samuel and the Sumerian Gilgamesh.

In art, the Twelve Labors of Hercules lend themselves especially well to frescoes and to sculpture. His main attribute, itself sometimes a symbol of virtue, is a lion's skin won in his first Labor. In allegory, he is often accompanied by Minerva, his protectress, who personifies the complementary virtues of moral strength, or Wisdom.

Wisdom and Strength is immediately recognizable here. Hercules wears a lion's skin, appears strong but not ferocious, and is accompanied by a woman who looks away from him and up to the heavens. On one level, then, the message of the picture is clear: wisdom is better than strength.

Hercules at the Crossroads, another popular theme, is also the theme for the companion picture to *Wisdom and Strength* in the Frick. Though this is called *Allegory of Vice and Virtue* the elements are also readily recognizable. Typically, in this subject Hercules is seated under a tree with two women standing over him. They personify Vice and Virtue respectively and each invites him to follow. The fable was invented by Prodicus, a friend of Socrates and Plato. Virtue's way is narrow and rocky but leads upward, often to a plateau where Pegasus, the winged horse and a symbol of fame, stands. The easy path of Vice leads to sunny pastures where naked figures dally in a pool. Virtue is usually properly clothed whereas Vice is naked, has her bust uncovered, or is in a state of *déshabillé*. The attributes of Vice include masks, symbolizing deceit, playing cards, symbolizing idleness on which lust thrives, and fetters, a consequence of wrongdoing. Virtue's attributes, significantly, are fewer. There may be a poet by her side, wearing a laurel crown and reading a book of Hercules' Labors; she may take the form of Minerva, goddess of Wisdom and Hercules' mentor; an owl may be present. The overlap in meaning between the two Frick paintings is immediately obvious.

LOVE

Venus takes many forms but she is by no means the only representation of Love in allegory. Cupid was one of the lesser figures in Greek and Roman mythology though in Renaissance painting he makes a symbolic appearance very frequently. He rarely plays a direct part in the story but he serves in paintings as a reminder that the theme concerns Love.

When Adonis takes his leave of Venus, for example, Cupid dozes in another part of the canvas, reminding us that Adonis's thoughts are elsewhere. Or he may be shown toying with Mars's weapons, typifying Love's power to disarm the strong. Sometimes he is blindfolded, not simply to prove that Love is blind but also as a reminder that darkness is associated with sin. In the Renaissance he was usually shown as a winged boy, although Baroque and Rococo painters often turned him into a more sentimental, chubby infant. His attributes include the bow, arrow, and quiver. An extinguished torch shows that earthly pleasures burn out, and a globe shows that Love is universal. In the classical "Punishment of Cupid" paintings, Venus is shown taking Cupid's arrows away from him, since they cause so much mischief.

VIRTUES AND VICES

The idea that human figures might represent psychological or abstract qualities was very common in antiquity and this appealed to the early Church, which saw in it a way of teaching the illiterate certain moral lessons. In general, in art, the Virtues and Vices are pitted against one another with Virtue, usually female, treading on Vice, her human or animal opposite.

The canon of Virtues was made up of three that were theological—Faith, Hope, and Charity—and the four that were cardinal—Justice, Prudence, Fortitude, and Temperance. Plato, and, much later, the Humanists, thought that these were needed for the ideal city-state. The fathers of the Catholic Church sanctioned them for Christians and they were the benefits to be derived from the Eucharist.

Whatever developments there were in the Church the combat of the Virtues and the Vices continued, very largely unabated, presumably because the rivalry answered some inner psychological need. Thus Apollo, Diana, or Mercury, representatives of Reason, might be pitted against Cupid or Venus as representatives of the passions.

Wisdom is a Virtue, of course, sometimes shown with a book and sometimes a snake, which together are the attributes of Prudence, which may replace Wisdom in cycles of the Virtues. Wisdom too may be represented by Minerva.

Vanity is one of the minor Vices and is generally represented by a naked woman on a couch combing her hair and looking at herself in a mirror. Here again we have an overlap, this time with Venus. The idea of Vanity is also commonly conveyed by the presence of jewels, gold coins, a purse, or, more bluntly, the figure of death himself. An inscription on a scroll reads *Omnia Vanitas*—All Is Vanity.

Hercules, Wisdom, Minerva, Vanity: each of these entities appears in *Wisdom and Strength,* overlapping, reinforcing, and refining each other.

MERCURY

Mercury was also one of the twelve gods of Olympus; he had the power to induce sleep. His attributes included winged sandals for speedy travel, a winged hat, a caduceus, or magic wand, also winged, with two snakes entwining it. He was young, athletic, and graceful. He was also the god of commerce and so was shown, from time to time, wearing a purse. He invented the lyre.

In allegory, Mercury usually represents Reason and Eloquence; he is a teacher. One of his most common scenes is of Mercury and Herse, taken from Ovid's *Metamorphoses* and one of the themes Veronese painted for Rudolf. This recounts how three sisters, returning from the festival of Minerva, were seen by Mercury, who immediately fell in love with the most beautiful of them, Herse. Aglauros, another sister, was so consumed with envy that she tried to stop Mercury from entering Herse's room. Mercury touched Aglauros with his wand and she was turned to black stone, the color of her thoughts.

ADONIS

Adonis was the child of an incestuous affair between King Cinyras of Cyprus and his daughter, Myrrha. He was exceedingly beautiful and Venus fell hopelessly in love with him after being accidentally grazed by one of Cupid's arrows. But Adonis was killed by a wild boar while out hunting one day. Venus heard his dying groans and flew off in her chariot to help him. She was too late: where Adonis was slain and the ground was stained with blood, anemones grew. This myth formed part of the annual fertility rites as practiced by many civilizations in the ancient world and in some cases the sprinkling of sacrificial blood on the ground was believed to fertilize it. The classical image of a woman with a dying man in her arms may be an early precursor of the *Pietà*.

ANIMALS

In the seven pictures which Veronese painted for Rudolf, there are a number of horses and dogs. Horses are the mount of warriors and also an attribute of Europe, one of the four parts of the world (Europe, Asia, Africa, and America), which, in Counter-Reformation art, symbolized the great expanse encompassed by Catholic Christendom. The equestrian painting or statue also has a long tradition as a means of commemorating a great leader.

In ancient times the dog was not revered: it was regarded as a scavenger and a thief. Even in the Bible it is rarely mentioned except in an unfavorable light. To Pliny the Elder, however, the dog was, with the horse, the animal most faithful to man and it is this virtue which it usually represented in medieval and Renaissance art. A dog accompanies the hunter, Adonis or Diana; it may lie at the feet of Judas in the Last Supper. In portraiture, on the lap or at the feet of a woman, it alludes to marital fidelity. Dogs then are not unlike cupids: they are reminders, reminders that love and honor require fidelity.

The Secret Message in the Paintings

All the paintings Veronese carried out for Rudolf were secular allegories or history pictures. This may seem like an obvious point, but it is not without significance when one remembers that Veronese's work was often executed for the great monasteries of his day or that the commission was carried out for a man whose official title was Holy Roman Emperor.

Beyond that, it should now be clear that *Wisdom and Strength* is only part of the commission: since the contracts have been lost, no one can be certain. If that is true, however, then the picture contains only one seventh of the message. To understand fully what Veronese was saying in response to the Emperor's commission, the sweep and range of all seven pictures need to be examined. At a later date, a much later date, the seven paintings were dispersed in different directions as tastes changed and the appreciation of allegory weakened. But a proper grasp of Veronese's intentions can be acquired only by, in a sense, bringing them back together again.

The paintings were fashionable. Not only did the subject matter flatter Rudolf, because by implication he was a learned man who could decipher the secrets of allegory, but at the same time Veronese was hinting that he too was learned. In painting allegories he was showing that he too had read or was acquainted with the necessary books which explained the "secrets" of the gods, that he too appreciated the civilizations of the past and the lessons they had for his times.

Veronese had probably been told about the fantastic nature of Rudolf's court. He would have known that the palace in Prague was a center for the pursuit of secret knowledge in all its many guises and he would have guessed that allegories fitted perfectly into that setting. A secular subject also gave Veronese the opportunity to paint certain aspects of contemporary Venetian life, such as the rich clothes and fine tapestries. Equally significant, so far as Rudolf's tastes were concerned, each of the six pictures shows a woman who, if not totally naked, is in some way seductive or in a state of *déshabillé*. Veronese could not have done this if he had painted religious subjects for the Emperor. The Counter-Reformation might never have been very strong in Venice but Rudolf *was* Emperor and was obliged to set an example. But nudity, provided it was set amid a secular and morally uplifting theme, was acceptable. The women in the two Frick paintings, though one represents Vice and the other has her breast exposed, are, in fact, more covered up than the women in the other five pictures. At one level then, and by the standards of the day, the pictures were a form of pornography—high-class pornography perhaps but pornography nonetheless.

Nudity apart, and if it is true that the pictures reflect a single commission, the moral messages in the seven paintings form a series of overlapping meanings. Mars is overcome by Venus, Strength is tamed by Wisdom, Hercules chooses Virtue over Vice, Love triumphs over Envy. For Rudolf, who had just become Emperor, the message was clear: Veronese was depicting the kind of moral choices facing a man in such a great position and saying what kind of Emperor the world would admire. Rudolf was pleased to show that he attached more value to the qualities of peace and love than to Mars's warlike attributes. At the same time, the inclusion of Hercules, Mercury, and Adonis implied that Rudolf was courageous, intelligent, and physically attractive. In fact, if the themes of all the canvases are followed closely, Veronese's reasoning is cleverly circular. Rudolf is a godlike warrior (Mars) who appreciates the qualities of love and peace (since Venus tames him); but the Emperor is also courageous (Hercules) and this part of him appreciates that wisdom is better than brute force; he is Reason personified (Mercury) with power over women so that he is an object of jealousy rather than jealous himself; yet he is not merely tamed by love, but tames it too, as Adonis tamed Venus.

Even the minor attributes of the paintings, horses, dogs, and cupids, show that Rudolf had conquered the passions, was faithful (in this case to the Catholic Christian religion), and well versed in the various forms of love, as a civilized courtier should be. He was the envied center of the world, Europe personified. He was to beware the vanities of the world, the jewels, the crowns, the baubles, if he wanted to be remembered after his death as an honorable and virtuous man.

A final point. In *Vice and Virtue,* the companion picture to *Wisdom and Strength,* Vice also has some of the attributes of death. There is a sphinx and a knife. The artist is boldly reminding the Emperor of the ultimate peril for those who are too uneducated to understand allegories. Those who cannot understand the riddle must die. But of course Rudolf could and it comes all the way back round to flattery.

The seven paintings therefore convey several layers of meaning not immediately apparent to the modern eye but which would have been clear to the Emperor. They are a mixture of tribute, flattery, moralizing, a gentle sexual titillation (not as obvious as in Bronzino, say, or Titian), intellectual pretension, travelogue, and social commentary. Finally, it is important to remember that the gods and the goddesses enacting this theme were dressed in ways that recalled the extravagance and sophistication of Venice, the beauty of her women, the lifestyle she had to offer. The six paintings illustrate perfectly the ways in which allegory was used in those days to convey more than one meaning. As time went by this came to mean less and less to the owners of the pictures. *Wisdom and Strength* and the other paintings remained objects of great physical glory but their "internal beauty" was lost.

4.
The Overall Appearance: Color, Canvas, Painting Technique

There were, however, more down-to-earth matters that would have concerned Veronese almost as much as the gods and goddesses he had to choose. What models should he use for his figures? How much would he have had to pay them? What pigments did he prefer? What sort of canvas and brushes? What drawings should he make? Once again, one of the reasons *Wisdom and Strength* is such a significant picture is because in this time of great changes the very *appearance* of the painting is a reflection of the Venice of the late sixteenth century.

Venetian painters of the sixteenth century, Tintoretto and Veronese in particular, used enormous canvases. For one thing both men, having worked so much in fresco, were used to covering huge areas of wall. Furthermore the public buildings of Venice and the churches and monasteries presented large surfaces to be covered.

Canvases may be woven from the fibers of flax, cotton, hemp, or jute. Flax is the most commonly used for a good canvas, with the warp and woof woven at right angles. Cotton is usually suitable only for small canvases of not more than a meter square. Jute, or Bengal hemp, is regarded as an inferior material. However, the large paintings of the Venetians were woven out of coarse hemp fiber which, as is the case with *Wisdom and Strength,* was not woven at right angles but with a twill or herringbone pattern. For a large surface this is stronger. Hemp fibers are very long (from one to two meters), which also makes them especially suitable for large canvases. Even so, *Wisdom and Strength* is made up of several pieces sewn together. This too was not unusual.

Prior to 1500, oil painting, now the most common form for a masterpiece, was by no means the dominant medium for pictures. Tempera was. Strictly speaking, tempera refers to any kind of binder which will "temper" powder color and render it manageable. In practice, however, the term tempera almost always applies to egg tempera. In the classic manner, the pigment was mixed with fresh egg yolk thinned with a little water. The resulting paint was spread on a wooden panel covered with a ground made of gesso (gypsum, or chalk, mixed with either size, a glue, or water). This produced a hard, brilliant color which dried very quickly. Tempera was suited to small, delicate, but complicated pictures with lots of fine detail. Because it dried so quickly, however, three-dimensional effects could be produced only by cross-hatching. And so, to overcome this, pigments mixed with oil were used in the later stages of a painting. The oils also covered the picture with a unifying film.

Toward the end of the fifteenth century, as the advantages of oil as a medium became more and more apparent and its flexibility more and more appreciated, it became the technique of choice. Oil had the added advantage that it was suitable for use on canvas, and canvases could be rolled up and carried; this was more difficult with wooden panels and impossible with walls. Therefore, during the late fifteenth century and the early part of the sixteenth century, painting underwent a major technical revolution as oils and canvas replaced tempera and wood. By Veronese's time, however, oil painting was barely a hundred years old and new developments were still taking place. Moreover, and more important so far as the appearance of *Wisdom and Strength* is concerned, oil painting was developing differently in different parts of Europe. Venice was different from Florence, for example, and they were both different from Flanders and Germany to the north.

From the wills, shopbooks, and other documents which belonged to artists of Veronese's time, it is possible to reconstruct what would have been in his workshop. That workshop was above all a place of work so it is likely to have had less the atmosphere of a bohemian garret and more the feel of a small factory. There would have been ledger books recording commissions (Veronese's is lost); there would have been heads and bodies fashioned in terra-cotta for modeling and heads and hands of wax, also for modeling. There would have been books of drawings, although these were not regarded as works of art as we think of them now. Rather they were regarded as tools, providing solutions to awkward problems of composition, exercises, and first drafts.

On the shelves would have been jars of pigment. The preparation and the availability of pigments has changed over the years. Sometimes this is due to fashion, sometimes to extraneous factors such as politics, which affect the availability of raw materials. In Veronese's day, the pigments he used would have included white lead, black chalk (lamp black, coal black, black of vine charcoal), lac, vermilion, English brown, yellow ocher, yellow lake, massicot, smalt, cendre, ultramarine, umber, green earth, verdigris, minium, indigo. By the second half of the sixteenth century, many colors could have been bought ready-made from the apothecary or *speziali*. But that was a skilled job and as part of his training an artist would have been taught how to make his own pigments so that they would remain vivid. Veronese, for example, would have learned to sub-lime, or rapidly heat, sulfur and mercury in a covered crucible. This was a process not without danger but when it was carried out successfully the solids went straight to a gaseous state, then distilled into red crystalline chunks, which is cinnabar, the basis for vermilion.

Vinegar was a useful material for a painter. Its vapor, acting on metal-lic lead, produced white lead, known to artists as flake white. Alterna-tively, when copper was immersed in it, dissolved, and the solution al-lowed to crystallize, verdigris was produced. This was dangerous in a different way for an artist, although in Veronese's time not all artists appeared aware of the problem: verdigris turns black with age and, worse, invades other colors. It is the cancer of old masters.

Ultramarine was one of the most complicated colors to make, though in many people's eyes the most beautiful. It comes from lapis lazuli, a complex silicate containing iron pyrites. The stones were pummeled in a mortar which was covered over to prevent any loss of this expensive raw material. It would then be put on a slab of porphyry and ground further, sifted through a strainer, and ground again. The powder would then be mixed with resin, mastic, (another resin used in the manufacture of var-nish), and wax in carefully measured proportions. This mix would be melted in a pipkin, or small pot. The melt would be strained through a piece of linen, allowed to cool and then a paste would be made up with linseed oil. That mixture was kept for three days and kneaded regularly. To it would be added a small amount of lye, a strong alkaline solution. The lye absorbed the blue and could be poured off. The lye process could be repeated several times, on each occasion yielding a weaker blue. These different densities were obviously useful for painters and they were kept separate. Lapis lazuli comes from the East and also from Ger-many, which had strong trading links with Venice. This benefited Vero-nese and the other Venetians for it meant that ultramarine, the most expensive color (and for that reason usually costed separately in con-tracts), was cheaper in Venice than anywhere else. Even so, a painter like Veronese probably did not always make up his own ultramarine; certain monasteries became very well known for its manufacture and he would have got it from them.

The use of pigments has varied over time, too. As the figure on page 67 shows. Many substances in use in Veronese's lifetime have since died out, while new ones have been invented. (This changing picture is some-times the way fakes are spotted: the forger uses a pigment which had not yet been invented at the time the picture was supposed to have been executed.) Because no later pigment is quite the same as an earlier one, in looking at a Veronese, the reds and yellows, the greens and blues are,

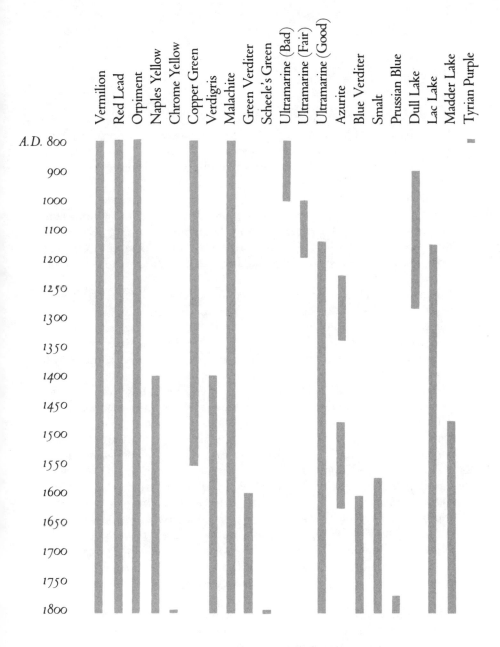

DATES OF USE OF VARIOUS PIGMENTS

Adapted from *The Pigments and Medicines of the Old Masters,* A. P. Laurie, Macmillan, London (n.d.).

in a manner of speaking, a visual experience that can never be fully re-created.

The Composition Begins: Veronese's Drawings

Titian, because of his facility and his overriding concern with color, liked to compose directly on the canvas. Veronese, Tintoretto, and Bassano, on the other hand, returned to the earlier tradition of making drawings in order to try out ideas or seek solutions to problems.

Practice was not the only reason for drawings. More finished drawings, to which wash and perhaps chalk are added to the pen outlines, were often used as part of a contract, to show the patron what to expect. These were known as *modelli*. The *modelli* were then worked up into cartoons from which, in the age of tempera and fresco, the design would be transferred to the wall.

Drawing in Florence and Venice really developed in the 1400s and, from what we know of plaster, it is easy to see why. Since it dried so quickly and allowed no chance of second thoughts, it made sense for the artist to do his thinking on paper first. When he had a satisfactory design, he would divide it into squares: this made it easier to transfer the design to a large wall. Or, if the cartoon was full-size, he might prick the outlines of the figures with fine holes, place the cartoon against the wall where the painting was to go, and transfer the outlines by scratching marks on the white plaster ground. However, this practice was more true of Florence than of Venice, where artists were more likely to go straight from a preparatory drawing to the picture and leave out the intermediate stages.

Drawings were usually made in pen and ink and in Venice red chalk was often added to suggest body. Chalk was much easier to use, once it had been mastered. It corresponded more to a brush than did a pen, which soon ran out of ink and where the line could not be varied so much. It followed that pen and ink were more likely to be used for the preparatory drawings, whereas chalk was used for the *modelli* or cartoons. It is for this reason that fewer *modelli* or cartoons survive than preparatory drawings: they were likely to be damaged or destroyed, in effect "used up."

If Veronese differed from Titian in the plentiful use he made of drawings, he also differed from Tintoretto in not having any wax models in his studio. This is because he preferred to work from drawings in which he had used real people as models. He liked the use of dramatic foreshortenings, and these would have been easier to work out by experimentation with the pen than by tipping wax models this way and that. This is confirmed by the fact that Veronese once expressed the wish to have all his drawings pulled together, perhaps in a book to be printed at the end of his life.

Veronese's drawings are some help in dating his work. His later drawings show a much freer handling, with bolder figures, a greater use of white chalk heightening the figures, and more wash. Later still, in the 1580s, his drawings became even freer, abstract almost, with many of the individual lines showing a clumsy quality not evident in his paintings. The drawings also show that he worked in two ways, that is, ideas occurred to him by two processes. In some cases Veronese prepared sketches in which all the poses, all the configurations, were laid out at once on a single sheet of paper. At other times ideas occurred gradually, evolved over a period, and were then all pulled together in one composition. With *Wisdom and Strength* the second of these two processes was used.

Elements of the composition occur in no fewer than five different drawings, most of them done on blue or gray-blue paper, mostly with pen and wash and mostly heightened with white. Because of this stylistic similarity they are all dated to the master's middle years—that is, the late 1550s and early 1560s.† In one, *Allegory of Fortune,* the "Habsburg-shaped" crown is prominently displayed at the foot of the composition, exactly as in *Wisdom and Strength;* in a second, *Triumph of Temperance over Vice,* Veronese shows a woman with her foot raised and her body twisted in a manner that anticipates Wisdom's in the Frick picture, and this is repeated in a third drawing, *Allegory of Victory,* which also shows a strap placed diagonally across the woman's bosom, as in Wisdom. In *Study of a Standing Woman,* he extends the woman's arm and hand across her breast; although it is a different hand, the graceful lines of Wisdom are hinted at. But it is Veronese's *Study of St. Margaret* which offers us the best insight into the master's mind. This drawing is one of a group of eight saints, all of which are now in the Hermitage in Leningrad. Nothing is known of their purpose except that some of the eight saints are framed by a thin oval line; this echoes the shape of the panels which contain the four evangelists surrounding the *Coronation of the Virgin* in San Sebastiano, the church Veronese so loved when he moved to Venice (see page 24, above).

The *St. Margaret,* however, is not framed; she stands against a shadow, indicating a niche. More important from our point of view, her stance is precisely that of Wisdom in the Frick picture, *except it is reversed.* Where Wisdom looks to her left, Margaret looks right, where Wisdom raises her

† These dates are adduced by Richard Cocke, author of the standard work on Veronese's drawings.

right foot, Margaret raises her left, where Wisdom's left breast is exposed, Margaret's right is. But the figures are otherwise the same: the folds in their dresses are identical, their necks are turned in the same way, the amount of breast exposed is the same. Margaret also has a globe at her feet. Her foot does not actually rest on it but Veronese did not have to make many changes for the Rudolf painting.

Only one of these drawings, the *Triumph of Temperence over Vice,* has a counterpart among Veronese's paintings and even here the finished work is rather different from the study. It may well be, therefore, that *Wisdom and Strength* is an amalgam of several earlier ideas come together to give us the figure we now see. The new elements are the man and the fact that Wisdom looks up to the sun.

The slumped and very distinctive pose of Strength, or Hercules, is found nowhere among Veronese's drawings and may have been taken from a classical statue. The long, dangling arm—of a man or a woman— was a favorite motif of Veronese's and presumably it acted as a useful frame to a composition, just as did his fake architectural devices, such as the one in *Wisdom and Strength.* This device serves to give depth to the painting since the landscape beyond is both brighter and much smaller in scale.

Faced therefore with a commission that needed to flatter an Emperor, that needed to convey an uplifting moral theme which also showed female flesh *and* some of the legendary Venetian finery, Veronese opted to adapt his earlier *Study of St. Margaret.* This had the added bonus that, in the twisting of her figure, he could introduce movement into the painting without needing to tell a complex narrative in what was, for him, a fairly confined space. Somewhere, though, a proper pen and ink study for the Frick picture may be lying unrecognized. Veronese certainly did one for another of Rudolf's pictures, *Venus with a Mirror.* (This drawing is now in the British Museum.) Thus, there is an extra mystery connected with the painting: Where is the drawing Veronese did when he was planning the composition?

That the situation is always changing may be seen from a packet received by the Frick Collection in April 1973. It had been sent by the head of the Western European arts department of the Moldavian Museum of Arts at Kishinev in Russia. It contained a photograph of a drawing in the museum's possession, which had been sent to Kishinev from the Hermitage in Leningrad in 1956. Drawn in oil on paper, it showed a detail of *Wisdom and Strength,* the small Cupid which cavorts at the foot of the canvas and looks upward. No one quite knows whether this is a study or a copy. But, if it is a study, it confirms that, in the case of *Wisdom and*

Strength, Veronese adapted figures from several compositions rather than dream up something entirely new for the Emperor.

The Venetian Manner of Painting

By now it should be clear that Venice was different from the other Italian Renaissance cities in many respects. This difference also translated to the style of its art. The fact is that the grandiose Venetian canvases, which were such a dominant aspect of the city's decoration, demanded a different mode of painting from the much smaller, more intimate Flemish works which were preferred farther north and the strongly religious art further south. Because of the scale of the canvases in Venice, small areas of the picture were not usually meant to be viewed close up. Instead, the vast picture, conceived as a whole, aimed at striking effects with light spreading over the entire area.

Starting with basics, the Venetians did not, for all these reasons, begin with white grounds to their works, like the Flemish, say, or the Florentines. Her painters preferred darker grounds: red, black-red, or, in Veronese's case, gray-green. On to this dark ground the broad outlines of the composition were drawn, often in red. The light areas were picked out in white chalk and this is where Venetian painting began to take on its distinctive quality. For in classic Venetian art there are two main characteristics: the dark areas and the shadows are thin, with a minimal amount of paint. The light areas, however, have a lot of pigment. This gives Venetian pictures two advantages. It makes them very vivid because the white under the color makes the color stand out and creates that unique "Venetian lighting" effect which is so beautiful. Second, it also makes the pictures look more realistic because it actually corresponds to reality: as in real life, light was distributed *unevenly* over the canvas.

A second important characteristic is that Venetian paintings, in contrast to art elsewhere, have far fewer sharp outlines. Painters, following Titian, used glazes—thin, translucent layers of paint, one on top of another, to create body and gradations of color and tone and indicate different surfaces. Titian once made a celebrated remark: *"Svelature, trenta o quaranta."* (Glazes, thirty or forty.) The intention was to create a mysterious effect. Indeed for a long time, Titian was believed to have used a secret medium which played a role in this, but it has been proved by chemical analysis that he used linseed and walnut oil like almost everyone else. It is probably the glazing of Venetian paintings that makes them so appealing to the modern eye. In painters' studios, although the apprentices would help in all sorts of ways, only the master was involved with drawing, at the very beginning, and with glazes, at the very end.

Veronese was not entirely typical of the Venetians. His technique varied from that of the other masters in that he used blue colors *a guazzo,* in glue or tempera, which counteracted the yellowing of many oil colors. This is why his paintings of daylight scenes have not darkened much with age. Not technically perfect, he had a tendency to make his gypsum grounds too heavy, which caused flaking on his pictures. According to a technical report in the Frick Collection archives, *Wisdom and Strength* shows no trace of the dark grounds usually associated with Veronese and scrapings reveal an unusual, almost transparent ground that may be Bolognese chalk. The picture is also coated with resin (mastic or dammar) which has yellowed over the years. However, this is not a serious problem and today, more than four hundred years on, the painting is in good condition, its lighting effects as fresh as ever.

Verona itself was an influence here, too. Taste there tended to prefer the silveriness of Lotto, the "morning freshness" of Moretto, the "lunar coolness" of Savoldo to the vivid polychromy of Titian or the turbulent draftsmanship and dramatic perspectives of Tintoretto. You have only to look at any paintings of Veronese to see this immediately: bold crimsons disappear, for the most part, in favor of silvers, light blues, pale yellows. Whereas much Venetian painting seems set in the sultriness of late afternoon, Veronese's pictures convey more of a dewy, silvery morning freshness. Both Frick pictures have, for the most part, retained that morning glitter.

The intervening years since 1576 have seen *Wisdom and Strength* undergo some remarkable adventures, in wars, revolutions, and in the company of some remarkable people and objects. After it left Venice it never again returned to the city and perhaps that is appropriate. For Venice herself was into the decline that has now reached crisis proportions, with the entire city threatening to sink into the very lagoon that gave *la Serenissima* her unique appeal and her unrivaled glory. Moreover, not long after he completed his commission of six paintings for Rudolf, on April 19, 1588, Veronese died.

II

PRAGUE

5.
Rudolf's Magic Court

Prague at the end of the sixteenth century was a pleasant, grandiose, and spacious city of fifty thousand people. It occupied both banks of the Vltava River (the Moldau), the Lesser Town on the left (the west) bank, with the Old Town opposite. The city's roofs were steep, mainly red, sharply pointed and very graceful. A fine, low bridge of many arches linked the city across the wide river. A crenellated wall encircled everything, extending to the Petrin slope, the main hill in the vicinity of Prague, so that even some fields came within its protection. The city itself was dominated by the Hradčany, the royal palace, which included a castle and the cathedral among its buildings. Parts of this, which rambled down a hill, were five stories high—impressive in those days—with the spire of the cathedral rising above everything else. The castle/palace was surrounded by its own wall and most of the town lay between this and the main crenellated wall. In general the buildings of the town were two or three stories high, laid out along fairly wide streets, with several large squares, arcades, and formal gardens. A third, smaller wall was built beyond the main one.

Just as the Hradčany dominated the town physically, so the court was the natural social, cultural, and intellectual focus of Prague life. The court naturally reflected the fact that Rudolf was Emperor, and therefore the obvious point of reference for almost any political development in central Europe. Rudolf's singular personality also colored court life. It was utterly different from anything we know now; it was fantastic even by the standards of the day. It was different in its assumptions, its attitudes, its appetites, and its ambitions. Different above all in its understanding of the world. Yet it was thoroughly typical of its time and a perfectly natural destination for *Wisdom and Strength* and the other Veroneses. Rudolf was not only a great collector but he followed assiduously the dominant intellectual fashions of the day and sought to acquire Wisdom (and therefore Strength) through any means: through art, philosophy, astronomy, even through magic. In those days there was a marked link between magic and art.

Rudolf's court and capital had not always been in Prague (the very concept of "capital city" was not strong then). He had moved there from

Vienna after his coronation because the Turks, an ever-present menace in the sixteenth century, were occupying much of Hungary and were a mere hundred miles from the city. Bohemia at that time boasted a population of four million and was the most densely peopled, the richest, and the best developed region of central Europe. These riches, and the strength of population, meant that besides being farther from the Turks, it was a good political base: armies could be raised and paid.

History has taken a hard view of Rudolf as a politician, however, and his long reign of thirty-six years ended in disgrace. But there can be no doubting his achievement as a patron of the arts and as a collector: he was the greatest connoisseur of the whole house of Habsburg. By current standards his tastes were strange, but by any standards they were magnificent.

He was a rather haughty man, stiff and dignified. His education in Spain had something to do with this because the Spanish Habsburgs were notorious for their stuffiness. Rudolf's portrait busts, whose purpose admittedly was to flatter him, show a strong head with full hair and beard and a prominent Habsburg jaw. His eyes were large, almost bulbous, his nose broad, and his lower lip fleshy. Physically, his head was strong; and as revealed by those sculptures he looks self-conscious and slightly ponderous.

His time in Spain, however, left him well informed, well-read, and curious. He spoke German and Spanish, was familiar with Italian, Latin, and French and he had some knowledge of Czech. His wide education, however, could not disguise one of Rudolf's other inherited characteristics. The Emperor was showing signs of mental disturbance as early as 1578 and in 1598–1600 he suffered a serious mental collapse. This illness, which would lead indirectly to his dethronement in 1608, was inherited from his mother and grandmother, both of whom showed its signs. Rudolf may have been the most overtly mad in the house of Habsburg, though he was not alone.

His madness was only part of the picture. By far the most interesting side to Rudolf's nature, and one that was of immense importance to his collecting, was his religious tolerance. This may not seem like much nowadays but at the turn of the seventeenth century it was not only psychologically important but politically crucial. This tolerance extended not only to Protestantism (he was, after all, Holy Roman Emperor) but to the occult as well.

Rudolf's interest in all forms of "secret knowledge"—astrology, alchemy, kabbalah—affected whom he invited to Prague and his tastes in art. It attracted him to allegory and it meant that his collections took on a particular shape, unfamiliar now but very typical then. For Rudolf did not have an art gallery as we would recognize it: he had a *Wunderkammer,* literally "wonder chamber," though a better translation is "chamber of curiosities."

The mysticism that Marsilio Ficino had introduced to Humanism in Florence suited Rudolf perfectly. He loved the idea that there was "secret knowledge" and he yearned to know its mysteries. Besides alchemy, astrology, and the kabbalah, he pursued clairvoyance, Hermetism, hidden codes—the whole "magic universe." This Prague mysticism had an important consequence in the history of art and it helps to explain the movement known as Mannerism.

Veronese, Mannerism, Prague

Mannerism, with its values so different from our own and the resultant art so strange and unsympathetic, is especially difficult for us to appreciate today. Put simply, Mannerism was a style of art carried to *excess*: it valued difficulty for its own sake, it valued distortion as creativity, it liked complexity, artificiality, surprise, variety, and, above all, "ostentatious ingenuity." Its most characteristic form was the *figura serpentinata,* like the twisting of a live snake in motion, a waving flame, the letter *s.*

The term Mannerism itself was not used until the 1920s. Until then much sixteenth-century art had existed in a kind of limbo; it was neither High Renaissance nor Baroque. Nowadays, Mannerism is regarded in part as a development out of the High Renaissance, particularly as it was practiced in Rome. Over the years the term High Renaissance has been used by art historians in an ever-narrower way, until it has finally come to mean that period, mostly in Rome, between 1500 and 1520 when Leonardo, Raphael, and Michelangelo were all alive and at the peak of their powers. The High Renaissance was "the moment of equilibrium," with clarity and fitness of purpose on one side and elegance, grace (but never without proper motive), and unobtrusiveness on the other. Mannerism, which began around the time of the Sack of Rome in 1527, was an extension of this achievement.

The term itself derives from the Italian *maniera,* the broadest English equivalent of which is "style," in the sense that we describe a person or the interior of a house as having "style." *Maniera* became a desirable attribute of a work of art. Vasari included it as one of the five qualities which separated the sixteenth century from the fifteenth. It also came to be a desirable quality of life in general.

A parallel development which helped the growth of Mannerism was the increasing awareness of the creative process which showed itself in a number of ways. First, there was the concept of the "work of art," already discussed. People wanted to own *a* Raphael, *a* Titian, *a* Veronese. Art was equated in this way with being civilized, being on the inside: the idea of a work of art as an enduring virtuoso performance was born. Another development was the very concept of the old master itself, first encountered in the sixteenth century and showing itself by way of a continuous demand for *copies after* Leonardo, Raphael, Veronese, and so on. And finally there was the use of prints. The medium was well established but in the early sixteenth century it was used in a new way; to bring the creative process of an artist to a wider public. Prints were published, not just of finished works, but of works in progress, showing the public's interest in the workings of an artist's mind.

It was this changing psychology, or this concern *with* psychology, which, as much as anything else, was to usher in Mannerism. It makes it easier to understand Mannerism and why it valued artificiality and ostentatiousness, which are so frowned upon today. In the sixteenth century the word *artifizioso* was entirely complimentary. It was felt that paintings and books *should* contain artifice.

A painting was esteemed if, even while being a faithful imitation of nature, it was also obviously artificial (that is, natural-looking people or animals were shown doing what was impossible in nature). That was the *point*. The same was true of *difficoltà*. The point, in Mannerist art, was to *overcome* difficulty. An artist, to be regarded as such, needed a facility of technique which enabled him to address difficult subjects and to treat them with an easy, graceful, artificiality: the virtuoso performance was admired for itself. Castiglione, in *The Courtier* invented a word—*sprezzatura*—for the kind of well-bred, easy confidence and self-possession that was to be valued by English gentlemen centuries later. But it was used long before then in relation to the arts.

Given this background, and the cast of mind that helped create Mannerism, it is not difficult to see how it developed into a love of complexity rather than of economy, into the very opposite of what the "modern" twentieth century has come to value. Arts other than painting were affected, too. In architecture, for example, embellishment of a purely decorative kind became the embodiment of this trend, partly helped by the rediscovery, around 1520, of stucco. This was used with a new enthusiasm, on fireplaces, doorways, and staircases which became the main attractions in many buildings of the period, notable for their virtuoso performances. In such an atmosphere it is no wonder that curiosities, natural ones as well as weird mechanical automata, provided they were complicated, obscure, and elaborate, became objects of veneration quite as much as art works. Such curiosities were to be just as much a part of

Rudolf's *Wunderkammer* as *Wisdom and Strength* and Veronese's other allegories.

Mannerism was never a major element in Venetian painting. The system of state patronage in Venice and the many family workshops meant that the concept of the virtuoso took longer to catch on there. Also, Mannerism was a court art; it flourished in Prague, Florence, Mantua, and Rome, where its obscurity could be applied more easily to a single ruler. Mannerism was in addition an art which was concerned with details, the parts, of a composition. Given the sheer size of much Venetian art, concern with detail was not practical. Titian had a very brief Mannerist period in the 1550s, El Greco spent time in Tintoretto's studio in 1570, and Tintoretto, in the energy reflected in his pictures, is generally regarded as the most Mannerist Venetian painter.

Nonetheless, Veronese had his Mannerist elements. His foreshortenings, with their debt to Michelangelo, his massive compositions with more detail than most other Venetian works, were each designed to show, among other things, his facility and his virtuosity. Veronese delighted in overcoming the difficulties posed by these dramatic perspectives. His treatment of banquets and brocades is ostentatious; his architectural references are conceits that could not exist in nature: they are entirely artificial.

Yet, equally important, there is no strain in Veronese's pictures, no distortion. The settings may be fantastic—but only slightly so. The figures are all natural, the color a perfect match. Veronese did not need to go over the top; he could produce great paintings without giving way entirely to distortion and ostentation as many Mannerists did. Nevertheless, the fact that Veronese was brought before the Inquisition for having contravened the rules laid down by the Council of Trent (". . . images shall not be painted nor adorned with excessive elegance . . . there shall be nothing dishonest or profane"), the fact that his paintings were highly esteemed by Rudolf II, patron of the greatest Mannerist court, and that he was imitated by other great Mannerist painters points to the conclusion that he was seen by others as leaning that way.

In *Wisdom and Strength*, the figure of Wisdom shows a number of Mannerist elements. The twist of her body is a textbook *figura serpentinata,* snaking in a graceful spiral from the goddess's raised foot, up through the folds of her gown, on through the way her arm and breast are held, through the curve of her neck to her head and the gaze which she directs to her left and up. The way Veronese contrived to give such grace and fluency, such sinuous movement, to a stationary figure, would have been especially admired in Prague.

.   .   .

Prague Mannerism, the art Rudolf loved and encouraged with his patronage, is perfectly illustrated through the artists whom the Emperor acquired from his father and those others he attracted to the court. In painting particularly, but in sculpture too, it is easy to see how well *Wisdom and Strength* and the other Veroneses fitted in.

The three most important Mannerist painters at Rudolf's court were Bartholomaeus Spranger, Giuseppe Arcimboldo, and Roelant Savery. Spranger (1546–1611) was the founder of Rudolfine art. He did not arrive in Prague until 1580. Until that time he was very happy in Vienna where he had worked for Maximilian. But he was close to Rudolf, who would spend days watching him work and engaging him in private conversation. Spranger became chiefly known for his mythological and allegorical works, including a long series on the loves of the gods and the heroes. In Spranger's pictures it is as if the principles underlying Veronese's various allegories have been taken one step further. The central figure is always a woman. She is always nude, her nakedness presented frontally to the spectator and with a sexuality which is much more open than in Veronese's work. Her pose always fits the *figura serpentinata;* she is entwined, often with a man, a god, or cherubs. Frequently, her stance approaches distortion. The canvases are always crowded, usually with subsidiary allegorical paraphernalia: other figures, animals, and devices like books, orbs, or wands. The couples are contorted, ill suited in appearance and in age. There are plentiful references to astrology and alchemy. The sumptuousness of the cloth in which the figures are (almost) dressed and the fantastic artificiality of the backgrounds is very Veronese-esque.

Giuseppe Arcimboldo (1527–1593) stands apart from anyone else in the history of art and yet he was entirely characteristic of the Prague milieu. Born in Milan, he was invited to Vienna as early as 1562 by Ferdinand I. He is known today chiefly as the creator of a series of extraordinary—grotesque—portraits, composite heads made up of animals, vegetables, books, and kitchen utensils, with titles like *Summer, Fire, The Seasons.* Some of the heads are double portraits, illusions which look like one thing one way up, and something quite different from the other. Arcimboldo's *Cook* looks like a piece of roast meat from one angle, a man in armor from another. Extraordinary as these appear to us now, at the time they were taken very seriously and were regarded as legitimate examples of philosophical speculation allied with social criticism and satire.

Arcimboldo pictured Rudolf in a famous portrait entitled *Vertumnus* where the Emperor's likeness is made up from a variety of fruits and vegetables; his nose is a pear, his eyebrows are ears of corn, his beard is a

bunch of ripe blackberries, and so on. The aim was to suggest that a time
of peace and plenty would return under Rudolf. Arcimboldo had no
stylistic predecessor in art and no real followers. But it did not worry
Rudolf that this extraordinary man was one of a kind. He thoroughly
enjoyed his work, so much so that Arcimboldo was ennobled by the
Emperor. Note too, the obvious symbolism of Arcimboldo's allegory, to
our minds there is nothing really "hidden" in these pictures, though he
was thought by some to possess the answers to many "secrets" at the
time. This underlines the fact that some allegories are more open than
others. *Wisdom and Strength,* never forget, contains an inscription: *Omnia
Vanitas.*

The other truly great painter attached to Rudolf's court, and in many
ways the most fantastic, was Roelant Savery (1576–1639). Educated in
Holland, like so many of the others, he arrived in Prague as a follower of
Pieter Bruegel, whom Rudolf also admired immensely. Savery was the
greatest exponent of Rudolfine landscape painting. His precisely executed woodland scenes are among his most distinctive works, but as time
went on he occupied himself more and more with painting great numbers of animals. In his compositions, scores of birds, horses, cattle, deer,
goats, dogs, and lions crowd into a glade or clearing, often constituting a
Paradise Lost motif in which Savery combines the symbolisms of Neo-
platonism and Christianity. In Savery's paradise, Humanism and Mannerism coexist like Adam and Eve.

Other painters/engravers in Prague at that time included Hans von
Aachen, who had received some of his education in Venice where he
came under the influence of Veronese. He too was close to Rudolf and
was sent by the Emperor on a number of diplomatic missions. His art was
more restrained than Spranger's. He painted more portraits and genre
scenes but there was no shortage of allegories, including a series on the
Turkish wars.

Josef Heintz, another artist, was in terms of style, more influenced by
Titian than by Veronese but he too painted a wide range of mythological
and allegorical works. He too was sent on buying expeditions for
Rudolf's collections. He was a superb portraitist, the faces in his allegorical paintings showing a lightness of touch, and a sense of irony and
humor that looks forward to French Rococo painting of the eighteenth
century.

The greatest sculptor in Prague during Rudolf's reign was Adriaen de
Vries (ca. 1545–ca. 1628) who came from the Hague and was a disciple
of Giambologna in Florence. He arrived in Prague in 1593 where he
executed a *Mercury and Psyche* (now in the Louvre) and a *Psyche Carried to
Olympus* (now in Stockholm Nationalmuseum). In 1602 he was appointed

Rudolf's court sculptor. More than anyone, De Vries's work was founded on the *figura serpentinata,* emphasizing the naked human form, attractive in all situations and from all points of view.

A major preoccupation of each of these artists, and of the rest of Rudolf's court, was the acquisition of wisdom. Wisdom, intellect, and skill were more highly valued at Rudolf's court than inspiration. This is why, in Rudolfine art, Minerva (Wisdom) and Mercury (Reason, Skill) are often shown triumphing over ignorance, indolence, and envy. Again and again we find the belief that a preoccupation with art (and science) leads to a kind of "insider" status and to the secrets of the universe. This is why even the painters in Prague believed in the purposes of an academy; they shared the view that art could be learned and that with it came greater wisdom. It followed that an interchange with other artists was crucial.

A second theme of Rudolfine art concerned love and here it is important to add that the erotic art at Prague was erotic in two senses, one of which is almost lost to the modern viewer. One sense is the straightforward, familiar one: art as titillation. Insofar as titillation succeeded, it often only emphasized the second form of eroticism: namely that love blinds reason. This *ambivalence* toward love was important in Prague (Rudolf himself never married). Many works glorified love: Venus in many cases was made the equal of Minerva and Mercury. On the other hand, Spranger painted pictures in which Amor shackles Mercury at the command of Venus or, elsewhere, Phyllis rides Aristotle as if on horseback. Other popular works showed the superiority of wine over love, and Rudolf's own apartments were decorated with *nodi d'amor,* scenes showing the "knots of love," in which the problems of the romantic heart—lovesickness, unattainability, jealousy, arrogance—were spelled out in dramas that, as often as not, had three figures, not two. One of Veronese's allegories for Rudolf, *Mercury, Herse, and Aglauros,* fits exactly into all this. It shows three figures and its theme is romantic jealousy.

A third thread running through Rudolfine art is related to the first and is shown clearly by the works of Arcimboldo and Spranger. These works are *concetti,* conceits, attempts to perfect nature, to create by virtuosity and by hidden codes, languages and symbols, an earthly beauty that does not exist in the natural world. This was, so to speak, a self-conscious twist over and above what the Humanists and the Renaissance masters like Raphael and Michelangelo had sought. The Renaissance artists were seeking to uncover a beauty that God had created but the Mannerists were intent on creating their own, man-made kind. It was an attempt to elevate the status of the artist even further.

The Prague court was concerned not only with visual beauty. The city was equipped with a botanical garden and a zoo. Every type of rare and exotic plant or beast was housed there including, if we are to believe a likeness compiled by Savery in 1608, the now-extinct dodo bird from Mauritius. Whereas Savery concentrated on animals in his paintings, Joris Hoefnagel did the same for plants, portraying them in fine detail but at the same time stressing their symbolic and mystical powers.

All the applied arts at Rudolf's court attempted to mix natural observation with artifice, to exercise Mannerist virtuosity in the search for deeper meaning. Objects in gold, silver, glass, enamel, mosaic, and much more unusual materials became famous well beyond the court. Prague craftsmen, whose names we still revere today, included the Jamnitzer family, Paul van Vianen, and Jan Vermeyen. They all lived and worked in Prague in the first years of the seventeenth century when the finest objects of all were produced, namely, the new imperial crown jewels— scepter, orb, and the crown which scholars at one time thought were reproduced in *Wisdom and Strength.* Combining gems, pearls, enamels, and fantastic reliefs on its gold surfaces, the crown showed, among other things, the creation of the world. After this, the standard of goldwork and gem cutting remained remarkably high at Prague for some time.

The Mannerist obsession with the artificial led to a natural fascination with mechanics and, at Rudolf's court, there was a lively concern with fountains, water machines, pumps, flight machines, automata, clocks, scientific machines in general, and perpetual motion machines in particular. There was even a "perspective lute" which was used in an attempt to pin down the relationship between musical tones and colors. Among the clockmakers who came to Prague was Joost Bürgi from Kassel who invented logarithms while he was at the court.*

Although the allegorical art which appealed to Rudolf contained "secrets" which only the learned could fully fathom, these secrets were by no means as obscure as some of the other mysteries Rudolf was obsessed by. For the Emperor was equally embroiled in what have been called the occult arts.

The occult arts were a final, but equally important aspect of the intellectual life of Prague. In fact, the intellectual preoccupations behind them were virtually identical. This was because the "occult" in Prague did not necessarily mean "black" magic. It was magic, in that it was not science or Christianity, yet its aim was not glorification of the devil. It was simply another way of trying to understand the secrets of nature. And this was what it had in common with art proper, especially symbolic or allegorical art. Kabbalah, together with the occult arts of alchemy and astrology,

* John Napier also claimed to have invented logarithms.

were also striving to penetrate that other reality which, it was believed, lay beyond the world of experience. It was part of the Renaissance idea that there were a number of hidden laws governing everything, if only man could discover them.

Rudolf was extremely interested in the occult. He believed he was possessed, prey to the devil. "I know that I am dead and damned," he once said. This may have been an awareness of his mental illness and the effect it would have on him eventually. But it accounted for his fascination with the occult so that anyone who appeared to have special powers was welcome in Prague—people like Giordano Bruno, for instance. Bruno was a philosopher, a Dominican friar who had doubts, became involved in a murder in Rome, but escaped to Geneva where he turned to Calvinism at first but then attacked his new colleagues and was imprisoned there. Bruno found fame as a believer in the mystical power of numbers and he took part in celebrated intellectual debates in Paris and Oxford as well as Prague. He was eventually denounced to the Inquisition by the Mocenigo family, who had invited him to Venice, and was burned at the stake.

In Prague, all manner of ideas, however magical, were worth exploring, whether it be squaring the circle, the elixir of life, or transmutation. But this atmosphere of magical intellectuality which pervaded everything was shown best by that trinity of alchemy, astrology, and Kabbalah.

In central Europe alchemy was the great obsession of the age. Prominent alchemists were very famous men and not all of them, especially in Prague, were charlatans. Alchemists believed that, at base, all matter was derived from the same source. The search for the philosopher's stone was hardly new but at the turn of the seventeenth century it reached a climax. It was not only the regeneration of metals which was sought but also the moral and spiritual rebirth of all humanity. There again we see the linking of everything, in metaphorical or allegorical terms, with morality. The famous alchemists in Prague during Rudolf's reign included Hájek, who was also an astronomer, and Martin Ruland from Bavaria, who took part in the controversy over one of the miracles of the day, a Silesian boy born with a golden tooth. There was Mardochaeus de Delle, one of the leaders of Rudolf's secret laboratory, who wrote accounts of his experiments in verse. And there was the famous Pole Michael Sędivoj, or Sendivogius, who was one of several men at court believed capable of turning copper into gold or lapis lazuli into silver (he *was* briefly imprisoned for quackery). One of the exhibits in Rudolf's collection was the Gemma Augustea, plundered from Paris in 1591 and to which a variety of magical properties were attributed.

Among the astrologers was John Dee, the Englishman who had been at the court of Elizabeth I. He was not a charlatan either, being one of the most learned men of his day and the teacher of Sir Philip Sydney. In his séances, astrological predictions—or horoscopes—were made.

Kabbalah, a popular subject in Rudolf's court, was a form of Jewish mysticism stemming from thirteenth-century Spain. It is essentially a set of beliefs about creation: divine emanations, plus a mystique of numbers and letters. It includes a form of messianism or an apocalyptic message. Many influential non-Jews in Prague studied Kabbalistic literature; again it was its preoccupation with codes and hidden languages that was especially popular and provided a link with Mannerism. The influence of the Kabbalah in Prague was partly a result of the fact that the ghetto there had many commercial and some financial contacts with the rest of the city, proving that Rudolf's religious tolerance did not extend only to Protestants.

Just as Christianity and mythological gods existed side by side in the art at Rudolf's court, so, in the occult world, did charlatans and serious intellectuals work cheek by jowl. This is an important point to grasp in understanding the intellectual spirit of the times. The best illustration of all is the fact that, alongside this preoccupation with alchemy, horoscopes, hidden languages, and numerology, there were two very famous scientists at Rudolf's court. These two, Tycho Brahe and Johannes Kepler, made major discoveries in Prague.

Brahe settled in Prague in 1599. His time there was short but while he was in Bohemia he began his detailed astronomical calculations which helped Kepler, after him, make some of his most important discoveries. Johannes Kepler was a Lutheran though not an orthodox one, always avoiding the wrangles over religious dogma. Like Brahe, Kepler had a number of mystical friends but he confined his own activities to science. He arrived in Prague in 1600 and shortly afterward was appointed imperial astronomer to succeed Brahe. The twelve years Kepler spent in Prague were the most productive of his life, during which he produced his three laws on the movement of the planets. Despite this, Kepler, who had a complex and enigmatic personality, was imbued with mystical ideas about universal harmony and he had an astrological world view of cosmic power. The Kepler story is a perfect example of the life in Rudolf's Prague. Here was the greatest scientist of his day, and one of the greatest astronomers ever, who at the same time was a mystic. Although scarcely a mix that could exist today, there was nothing unusual about it then.

Only when we fully grasp that almost symbiotic mix of intellectual life in Rudolf's world can we fully appreciate his collections. Painting, botany, jewelry, alchemy, astronomy, numerology, mysticism were all part of the same *universal* aim at complete knowledge: they were merely different ways to explore and understand the hidden secrets of nature. In Rudolf's day there were not two cultures, merely different ways of capturing one wisdom.

Rudolf's collection was described by contemporaries as a *Wunderkammer*. It was an appropriate word since, although he followed his uncle, Ferdinand of Tyrol, in being one of the first true collectors in the modern sense, and although his collection represented a first stage in the evolution of the modern permanent display, it was nevertheless very different from the collections assembled in more recent times. It was, in effect, an encyclopedia of the visible world. Besides paintings, there were, in the Spanish wing of the Hradčany, which housed the collections, cabinets of curiosities, and cabinets of virtue—objects showing some sort of obvious technical mastery—the whole designed as an encapsulation of the mysteries of the world. The gardens, stables, and menageries were also included in this overall scheme.

The Emperor was very secretive about his possessions and a complete inventory was not drawn up until after his death. Despite the secrecy, however, Rudolf's collection was regarded as one of the miracles of the age and was valued in 1612 at seventeen million gold pieces. At today's rates, that would be $2.56 billion.

The collection was divided into three sections, *naturalia* (natural objects), *artificialia* (works of art), and *scientifica* (scientific objects). The inventory was written in a delightfully casual style, a few examples of which will convey the flavor:

—First of all half a cake, as though eaten by a catfish, by Arcimboldo;
—An Indian organ and several Indian seeds, and together with these several uninteresting objects;
—Several boxes of various kinds of painted Indian quills;
—22 pieces of Indian pottery of various kinds, some of which are empty and some filled with tiny items.

According to the inventory, many things were shut away into what must have been a huge cupboard with three sections. Still other things were stacked on shelves or on the stairs, including pictures attributed to Titian, Tintoretto, Spranger, and Leonardo da Vinci. Many of the best pictures were kept in the Spanish wing, some on the walls, some on the ground, such as a Holbein portrait and works by Arcimboldo and a Bosch copy. On the walls were displayed two Tintorettos, four Sprangers, two Bassanos, and four Veroneses itemized thus:

1193 Mercury and Two Female figures
1201 Venus and Adonis
1212 Virtue and Fortitude
1216 How Vice converts to Virtue

Rudolf had numerous maps, several pictures of unusual fish, statues made of seashells, a coconut carved into a fool's head, medals, naturally formed coral decorated with jewels, glass engravings, and musical instruments.

Life at Rudolf's court was magical, in all senses of the word. But it is relatively forgotten now, in contrast to the courts of Mantua, Madrid, the papal courts, the equivalent life in Venice, or the Versailles of Louis XIV. It thus shows better than they do how values, assumptions, and beliefs have changed in the intervening years. The pendulum may be swinging back. In 1988/89 the Kunsthistorisches Museum in Vienna and the Museum in Essen staged an exhibition "Prague Around 1600," devoted to Rudolf's court. And *The School of Prague,* a scholarly glossy work, also devoted to Rudolfine art, was published by Thomas DaCosta Kaufmann only a year or so before.

But we can now see how *Wisdom and Strength* and the other Veroneses fitted perfectly into the Emperor's collection. The whole raft of meanings which Veronese had given to his pictures was complemented by the company they kept on the walls of the Spanish wing in the Hradčany. The central subject of the six pictures was Wisdom and Love so it is no wonder that they had pride of place.

The Emperor's first mental breakdown occurred in 1578 when he was twenty-six. One effect of this instability was to prevent him from marrying, although he did have a number of illegitimate children by Ottavio Strada's daughter, Catherine. He later had a much worse breakdown, which lasted from 1598 to 1600. He was so withdrawn that he was not seen in public for three years and eventually had to show himself at a castle window to prove to his subjects that he was still alive. As time went by, however, he became progressively more secretive and this, combined with the superstitions of the age, fueled his obsession with allegory, hidden codes, and mysticism. An extra factor was the end of the century.

"End of century fever" set in as early as 1588 when, according to one set of Christian apocalyptic beliefs, the world would end. The year 1597 was another black date, being a powerful magic number. The year 1600 was important for obvious reasons. The heavens were in turmoil, as anyone with a telescope could see, and had been since the appearance of Haley's comet in 1577. A nova, an exploding star, appeared in the heavens in 1604. To this, Rudolf was able to introduce his own, personal gloss; he was worried that, like his father, he would die before he reached the age of fifty—which would occur in 1602.

Whether his schizophrenia was involutional, causing him to turn in on himself, or whether he was truly affected by his intellectual and superstitious concerns, or whether politics caught up with him, the fact remains that, as the sixteenth century came to its close, a crisis approached for Rudolf. There is no doubt that the Emperor's strangeness became more marked after 1600. Suddenly, for example, he ceased to show the religious tolerance that had characterized him all his life; overnight he embraced the cause of the Counter-Reformation. This was popular in the powerful but distant courts of Rome and Madrid but the immediate lands governed by Rudolf were not used to it and did not like it. This about-face led, eventually, to revolt.

There were other pressures. There was, for a start, the problem of the succession. By the time the seventeenth century was born, Rudolf was no longer a young man by the standards of the day and he could die at any moment. He had always refused the brides suggested for him, such as the Spanish infanta, and that set him against the other Habsburgs. He was divided between a wish to preserve the majesty of the family tradition and a dislike of his relatives. He became indecisive and inaccessible as time went on, which further exacerbated the situation. The most important crown which Rudolf wore, the Imperial one, was naturally a source of particular concern. Like his other crowns, succession to this one was not necessarily hereditary and a clear heir, known in advance, would have helped the family. Rudolf's children by Catherine Strada, who would have been known to his relatives, did not help either: it meant there were bastard heirs complicating matters, but no legitimate ones.

An alternative heir might have been Rudolf's younger brother Ernst but he died suddenly in 1595. The next brother in line after Ernst was Matthias, five years his junior. Matthias had political ambitions early on and he and Rudolf hated each other. In 1577 Matthias, on his own initiative, tried to take over the government of the Netherlands. He did not succeed and from the 1580s on the two brothers had little contact. Matthias might have remained in Rudolf's shadow but for the Emperor's extraordinary mishandling of the Turkish war.

The renewed Turkish wars were fought on Hungarian soil and lasted for fifteen years. To counter the Islamic threat, a huge pro-Catholic propaganda effort was carried out across the country. This coincided with Rudolf's turnaround on religion and made sense from his point of view because it advanced the Habsburg case as the hereditary rulers of Hungary. But Hungary by then had a number of very powerful Protestant estates which did not welcome such an offensive. On top of that, since Rudolf had no immediate heirs, it seemed to the Hungarians as though the ultimate beneficiaries of the Turkish wars would be the Spanish Habsburgs whose lands were at the other end of Europe. As a result, in 1604 the Hungarians rebelled against Rudolf.

Two things followed. In April 1606, several members of the Habsburg family, now thoroughly alarmed by Rudolf's strange behavior and his incompetent opposition to the Sultan, declared him incapable of ruling Hungary and recognized in his stead his hated brother, Matthias. Matthias immediately made peace with the rebellious Hungarians but he did so by giving away large portions of the kingdom which Rudolf still regarded as his. Later the same year Matthias also managed to conclude a treaty with the Turks which left the two brothers more implacably opposed than ever.

Rudolf responded by trying to renew the war. It was a tactical mistake because Matthias countered by enlisting the aid of the Hungarians. They were already sympathetic to him because of his gifts of land and they did not want fresh blood spilled on their soil. As a result, in 1608, Rudolph was forced to cede Hungary in its entirety, as well as Austria and Moravia, to Matthias.

Rudolf tried to fight back again but he had few reliable allies. And before long, it was the turn of the Bohemians to strike out for greater religious freedom. Rudolf was still King of Bohemia and rejected this claim at first. Increasingly isolated, however, he was eventually forced to yield to the opposition even in Bohemia and this led, in 1609, to the famous Letter of Majesty. This was effectively a royal charter that guaranteed religious freedom to many non-Catholics and made other concessions which further weakened the Habsburg hold over Prague.

The Letter of Majesty bought peace but only for a while. Rudolf was next let down by another member of his family, Archduke Leopold, who used the unrest in Bohemia as an excuse to invade. The Bohemians, in view of what had gone before in Hungary, turned not to Rudolf for help but to Matthias. Matthias gathered an army and expelled the archduke. As a result of that, in 1611, the Emperor, still Emperor but now a virtual prisoner in Prague, was forced to cede yet another kingdom to his brother: Bohemia. He was even subjected to the humiliation of witnessing Matthias being crowned King of the country.

It was the final blow. The best years of Rudolf's court had been in the 1590s. By now Jamnitzer, Arcimboldo, Heintz, Hoefnagel, and Mont were all dead. Spranger, Savery, Vries, Vianen, and Aachen were still there but the mood, the ambience, had changed. The joy had gone. The dead hand of politics and religious rivalry had spoiled Prague and it was no longer the intellectual, artistic, and magical firmament it had once been.

On January 20, 1612, still Emperor, still unmarried, but no longer the glorious and glorified center of an artistic *Wunderwelt,* Rudolf died.

6.
Forgotten for Thirty Years

After Rudolf's death, his collections remained in the Hradčany for many years. *Wisdom and Strength* was probably more neglected then than at any other time in its life because Rudolf's two immediate successors as Emperor, Matthias and Ferdinand II, were more interested in politics than culture. As a result, Bohemia came to an end as a national entity and Europe was plunged into the bloody Thirty Years' War, which meant that *Wisdom and Strength* and the other Veroneses were on the move again.

The Thirty Years' War was initially sparked by Rudolf's signing of the Letter of Majesty. Carried out in 1609, this did no more than reflect the very real religious differences in Bohemia. Even Matthias, who was less tolerant than Rudolf, recognized this and, after he became Emperor on Rudolf's death, he did little to change it. Like Rudolf and Ernst, Matthias had no legitimate heir and it became apparent that on his death the various crowns he wore, including that of Emperor, would be fought over. Foreseeing this, he tried to prevent a conflict by helping to ensure that the crown of Bohemia went to the Habsburg Ferdinand of Styria. However, in May 1618, a dispute arose over the rights of Protestants to build on the royal domains. The Protestants suspected two Bohemian advisers of Ferdinand's of influencing him against their case since the two men were staunch Catholics. At a meeting in the Hradčany the pair were thrown out of the windows, an event which became known as the famous "Defenestration of Prague." The two advisers were not seriously injured and escaped to Vienna, where Ferdinand had his court. But the following March, Matthias died, the Bohemia rebels established a provisional government in Prague and chose Frederick, Count Palatine of the Rhine, as their King in Ferdinand's stead.

Ferdinand, however, was not prepared to be tolerant; he, after all, was the man who had extirpated Protestantism from Styria. He had been educated by the Jesuits and had become a Catholic zealot who once said he would rather "take a staff in his hand, gather his family around him, and beg his bread from door to door than tolerate a heretic in his dominions." He now amassed an army with Maximilian of Bavaria, another zealous Catholic, and this Catholic league advanced on Prague to put down the revolt. At the White Mountain, just outside Prague, the battle took place on November 8, 1620. It was over in less than two hours, two hours that were crucial for Bohemia. The Bohemians were routed, Frederick was driven into exile, and Ferdinand and his Jesuits took command of the country and started exacting revenge.

Ever since the Council of Trent, the Jesuits had taken it upon themselves to foster the Counter Reformation whenever they could in northern Habsburg lands. Now, in Bohemia, the Jesuits gave the people a simple but brutal choice; either they must return to Roman Catholicism or leave the country.

They were vicious in the force they used. Twenty-seven leading rebels who had not fled after the Battle of the White Mountain were executed in the marketplace of Prague. But that was just a beginning and the scale of the havoc wreaked by the Jesuits almost staggers belief. Prior to the battle, Bohemia, "which was practically Protestant before any other European country" and was one of the most culturally advanced, numbered around two million inhabitants. In a remarkably short period of time, however, the Jesuit persecution reduced that to fewer than eight hundred thousand. Some were executed, many were thrown into prison for life or almost as long, and thousands went into exile. The Bohemian schools were closed and the national language was suppressed. The Jesuit Antonín Koniáš became known as the greatest book destroyer ever, claiming to have burned no fewer than sixty thousand volumes.

It was a disaster for Bohemia and, in such straitened circumstances, one might have expected the fabulous art collections in the Hradčany to have been looted by Ferdinand and transferred bodily to Vienna. That this did not happen when the Bohemians were so routed means that much of what was in the castle did not appeal to the new Emperor. As a staunch Catholic, Ferdinand did not share Rudolf's obsession with rival belief systems: the occult worlds, the Humanistic concerns, the scientific approaches. Certain works *were* taken to Vienna but a great deal was left, including *Wisdom and Strength* and the other Veroneses. The nudity in the paintings may have been a factor, as was their allegorical form, which would have been too complicated and convoluted for Ferdinand who was a much more straightforward, political animal. As we have seen, an inventory of Rudolf's collections, drawn up in 1621, provides the first undisputed mention of the *Wisdom and Strength* in a historical document. In that document, probably completed before Ferdinand decided what to move to Vienna, the painting is described as *Virtue and Fortitude.* At one stage the rebels had plans to sell all the collections—especially the nudes —but nothing ever came of it.

Although Ferdinand did not share Rudolf's unusual tastes, he was still a Habsburg and so not without some culture. This must account for why what was not taken to Vienna was not destroyed either. It appears simply to have remained in the castle which was now used infrequently. Ferdinand preferred to make his court in Vienna and, until his death, was busy fighting elsewhere. This must account for why everything in the Hradčany remained untouched for so long.

After the Battle of the White Mountain, the focus of the Thirty Years' War shifted away from Bohemia. The first decade, broadly speaking the 1620s, saw the Habsburgs successfully reestablishing both themselves and the Roman Catholic faith throughout the southern half of Germany. Indeed, for a time it looked as though the Habsburgs would overrun the entire country and all of Germany would be lost to the Protestants. And so the outside powers that encircled Germany on three sides stirred. They included Holland, Denmark, and Sweden, together with Spain, France, and for a while even the Papacy. The 1630s therefore saw a general Protestant retaliation. An important element in this, and a dominant one in the Protestant fighting machine, was the might of the Swedes, under their magnificent warrior King, Gustavus Adolphus.

In 1629 Gustavus Adolphus alerted his council to what he said was a danger from the Holy Roman Emperor, whom he pretended to believe had designs on the Baltic. By this time Sweden was already the dominant power in that area, though Gustavus's troops, who had defeated the Poles, had yet to beat the Danes. Gustavus Adolphus claimed that the campaign he intended to wage in Europe was to free Protestants from Habsburg domination but, emboldened by his successes elsewhere, he clearly had designs on northern Germany which would give him a toehold in the very heart of Europe. He left Sweden in 1630.

He led a brilliant campaign. Unlike most armies of the time, the Swedes did not suspend operations during winter and, in rapid succession, Gustavus Adolphus took Pomerania, Brandenburg, and Saxony, where the Swedes destroyed the imperial army, killing eight thousand men and taking six thousand prisoners. So convincing were his victories that Gustavus moved on quickly, ever deeper into Germany, to Frankfurt am Main and even to Bavaria.

This daring was his undoing. The Swedish king was killed in 1632, shot in the back at the Battle of Lützen. His successor was a baby girl, Christina, and so the country was ruled for some years by a regency council headed by Axel Oxenstierna. The latter pursued the same policies as his king but with less energy and effectiveness and the Swedes never reached farther South than they had when Gustavus Adolphus had been at their head. Still, they held on in the North and in 1635, when France finally entered the war, renewed a treaty with that country. This produced a measure of stability in northern Europe. Further, when Emperor Ferdinand II died in 1637, his successor, Ferdinand III, did not have the same appetite for war. Looking around him, he could see that France was still Catholic. If the South of Europe could remain that way, then perhaps they could put up with a Protestant North. Ferdinand III began to think about peace. That took another decade but the Peace of Westphalia was signed in 1648. It left Europe forever changed: Germany was divided, with a Catholic Austria separated from the largely Protestant northern part of the empire.

France had done well and culturally this would be important. France's literature and eventually painting would take over from Italy as the leader of ideas in Europe. The Papacy had not done so well. Insofar as politics and religion had become separated, the Papacy as a political force was weakened, marking its decline. Sweden was still dominant in the North.

Bohemia, where it had all begun, was in limbo. The economy of the country was devastated by the population decline and during the peace negotiations, which had begun several years earlier, the Swedes tried to arrange for the safe return of many Protestants and for the reintroduction of Protestantism in Bohemia. But Ferdinand III said he would fight, rather than give way in the country where the conflict had started and which was, even now, one of the mainstays of his power. All sides had had enough and the Swedes gave in. Still, while the negotiations to end the war were under way, the Swedes launched one final thrust into Bohemia to plunder what they could. They were very successful. They stole Rudolf's treasures, including *Wisdom and Strength*.

7.
Down the Elbe

The Swedes were used to plunder. In their campaigns they had had the pick of Riga, Pskov, Braunsberg, Würzburg, Bremen, Goslar, Olmütz, and, above all, Munich, where they had captured the elector's Dürers, Holbeins, and Cranachs. But what they found at the Hradčany must have astounded even the most war-weary marauders.

The storming of the castle took place on July 26, 1648. As an indication of the speed of news in that part of the world at that time, Queen Christina heard about the sacking on August 5, ten days later. There is some evidence that plunder, and artistic plunder at that, was the object of the attack in the first place. The Swedish troops, under General Johan Christoph, Count von Königsmark, seized that part of the capital which lies to the west of the Vltava: the Kleinseite and the Hradčany. But instead of striking out directly for the right bank of the river as would have been natural had they intended to sack the whole city, they turned instead to plunder. For this reason the Swedes never took all of Prague. By the time Karl Gustav, who had replaced Gustavus Adolphus as commander, reached the city, the Bohemians had organized their defenses and the stalemate was prolonged until November, by which time the Peace of Westphalia had been signed, and the Swedes hurried home.

According to one individual, "It was impossible to describe the plunder that went on all day without respite." A Swedish officer, whose letters home survive, wrote boastfully that seven million (kronor) worth was pillaged that day ($1,075 million at modern day prices) and that he was unable to comprehend how the Swedes could have got away with so much gold and other precious items. Presumably, he meant to imply that the citizens of Prague were taken by surprise.

Given the turmoil that reigned during the sacking, it is amazing that Rudolf's collection remained intact. That probably had something to do with Dionysio Miseroni, originally a stone carver who had become superintendent of the collection. When he realized that an attack by the Swedes was imminent, he hid away as many of the precious items as he could. Equally important, he hung on to the keys of the royal palace and only revealed their whereabouts under threat of torture. The delay caused by this brave action may have ensured that more responsible authorities were on hand when the collection was finally captured; and this, in turn, helped keep the imperial collection together.

Even if the marauding Swedes could not fully appreciate the many fine things they found in the royal palace, they must have been impressed by the sheer scale of the treasures in the Hradčany. Right at the entrance to the castle, in a passage or corridor leading to the inner chambers, they found a hundred paintings, including Veronese's *Mars Disarmed by Venus,* probably the same painting that now hangs in the Metropolitan Museum, New York, with the title *Mars and Venus United by Love.* Beyond this entrance area, there were four large chambers and several galleries of which the Spanish wing and the New Hall were the most important and impressive. The corridors connecting these halls were themselves lined with paintings, no fewer than 158 according to one list.

The first chamber contained twenty cabinets and nine tables, but paintings and clocks seem to have dominated, the latter laid out on an exquisite round table in the center of the room. The second chamber was smaller, containing just six cabinets with ceramics. Around the walls were sculptures, including a bust of Rudolf, a horse, and, next to a window, a grotto made of coral. The third chamber, about the same size as the second one, also with six cabinets, contained the church silver from Prague Cathedral, the great altar silver, and an ebony crucifix and candelabra. The last chamber contained items of natural history and a weapons cabinet.

Moving farther into the castle, the next area was the Emperor's own study or writing room. This was quite large, containing twenty bronzes and fifty paintings. But the Spanish wing was the most exquisite room in Rudolf's collection. It contained musical instruments and two hundred of his most beautiful pictures. Among these, according to the Swedish historian Olof Granberg, were "nine of Veronese's colourful, mythical and allegorical scenes" which included *Wisdom and Strength, Vice and Virtue,* and the four ceiling allegories now in London's National Gallery. From later documents drawn up in Stockholm, it appears that some canvases by Veronese and possibly by other painters too were cut rather carelessly from their frames by the Swedish troops. This could account for the change in their measurements over the years.

The New Hall, which was the last part of the collection reached by the Swedish troops, may not have been finished, or else it also may have been used as a storehouse. It contained five bronzes (among them ironically, a bust of the Swedish king) but also about 120 paintings, not hung, but leaning against the walls. Another explanation is that Dionysio Miseroni had tried unsuccessfully to make off with these.

Despite the fact that the booty from the imperial collection in Prague was huge, several masterpieces known to have belonged to Rudolf were missing. Some had been moved by Ferdinand II: these, such as Giovanni Andrea's beautifully carved lyre, Kaspar Lehmann's engraved glass portrait of Rudolf, and an unusual drinking cup made of rhinoceros horn are now in the Kunsthistorisches Museum in Vienna. Some had presumably been removed by Miseroni or a predecessor as a precautionary measure when the Swedes first invaded Bohemia in 1637. Some may have been stolen earlier during the thirty years of neglect and today may lie unappreciated in a European attic.

Though the sack of the Kleinseite of Prague occurred in the summer, it took some months for the booty to be organized and packed up. Königsmark knew that his young Queen was very eager to see the treasures but there was still the matter of the rest of Prague, which had still not been taken. And while the Swedes remained in Bohemia this gave them an extra bargaining ploy in the peace negotiations at Westphalia.

Königsmark put his secretary, J. Hertwig, in charge of the transport of the booty north along the Elbe River. A captain of the cavalry was given charge of the live lion from the bestiary. The cargo was crated up and loaded onto five barges and towed off down the river on November 6, 1648, thirteen days after the peace had been signed but three days *before* the news reached Prague. Only broken statues and old frames were left behind.

The convoy moved slowly down the river. Immediately to the north of Prague, the Elbe cuts a tight course through hilly terrain but from Dresden on it makes wide sweeps in level countryside, flowing at a stately pace. The barges moved slowly, so slowly in fact, that in the end the river was blocked by ice. The bad weather forced a stopover at Dömitz. But as soon as Queen Christina heard that the booty was held up, she decided she could not wait and sent word to the commandant at Wismar, on the Baltic shore of northern Germany. He was instructed to get the treasures overland to Wismar and then, via open water, to Sweden. The order was carried out with difficulty and the treasures did not actually reach Stockholm until the end of May 1649—a trip of nearly six months, as compared with the ten days the original news of the sack of the Hradčany had taken the previous summer.

Until the Prague pictures arrived in Stockholm, the court in Sweden had been adorned mainly with about a hundred works by minor German, Flemish, and Swedish painters. The Queen was therefore very excited and ordered that everything be brought to her right away. She was particularly enchanted by the Italian pictures Rudolf had either inherited or collected, and those of the Venetian school pleased her the most. The Queen had her own *chambre des arts* in Stockholm Castle and the great

Venetians were given pride of place there. They were to remain among her favorites all her life.

Just how many of Rudolf's pictures were lost on the journey down the Elbe and overland to the Baltic is not known. However, in the inventory of Rudolf's collection, drawn up in 1621 and repeated in the account by the Swedish historian Olof Granberg, 571 pictures of all kinds are listed as having been in Prague. And then, in an inventory of Queen Christina's collection, compiled in 1652, 472 items are shown as having arrived in Stockholm. The possibility thus remains that roughly one hundred works were lost on the journey. Conceivably, a number of these survive, unrecognized for what they are, in the great houses of Germany, modern Czechoslovakia, or just possibly in Sweden too.

Interlude One:
The Dispersal of Art
in the Seventeenth Century

The distribution of art in the developed nations of the world is not simply a question of random buying and selling every now and then: it is the result of systematic historical changes, in religion, in economics, in politics, and particularly in war. It is taken for granted these days that most of the major cities of the world will have museums which contain great paintings and other works of art. Few people are curious as to why great Italian art is to be found in Vienna or Paris, or that great French or Spanish paintings are to be found in England or Scotland, or that some of the greatest Dutch and Flemish masterpieces are in New York and Washington. And yet how this came to be raises interesting and vital questions that must be addressed if we are to understand fully the history of Western art.

Wisdom and Strength is a perfect example of a work of art which has moved around the world. There have been three great movements in the history of art which have shaped our cultural world and Veronese's masterpiece has taken part in all three. The first of these great movements was, as Hugh Trevor-Roper so aptly puts it, "the plunder of the arts in the seventeenth century."

The religious, political, and philosophical factors which led Rudolf II to become a great patron of the arts did not apply only to him. In stressing the importance of antiquity, the Humanists had made *nonreligious* art, including allegory, much more popular. As a result, this increased the amount of art patronage outside the Church and during the Renaissance collector-princes grew up everywhere, from Burgundy and Bavaria to Mantua and Madrid.

Then, in the hundred years after the Renaissance ended, when the divisions between religious Reformers and the Counter-Reformers grew, painting and sculpture also became divided into a Catholic art and a Protestant art. It was inevitable that the hatred which the two religious groups felt for each other was also applied to art so that treasures were now regarded as legitimate spoils.*

---

* It also bears repeating that only after the Renaissance and the invention of oil painting were most pictures done on canvas. Before that time, with frescoes, it was much harder, if not impossible, to steal paintings.

By the time the seventeenth century began there had already been a certain amount of movement. Nonetheless, across wide stretches of Europe the first two decades of the seventeenth century constituted the last period of peace and prosperity for a long while, when many collections including Rudolf's, were consolidated. In the next decades many of them were destroyed or looted.

The Assyrians, the Egyptians, and the Romans had all looted art, though this had mainly been sculpture. (Venice herself boasted her share of booty after the Crusades.) The seventeenth century was, however, the first period of wholesale plunder in modern times and, equally important, was the first time when paintings were moved around on a large scale.

The first attempt, appropriately enough, was made on the collections in Prague. In 1619, when the Protestant nobility in Bohemia rebelled against Ferdinand, they proposed to sell off Rudolf's treasures to finance the revolution. The Protestants were incensed by the "statues and paintings, many of them shameless representations of naked bodies, apter to corrupt than to enlighten men's minds." All these, and the fountains and clocks and silver writing tables, the rebels said, should be pawned in Nuremberg. An inventory was drawn up but the sale did not go through. The Battle of the White Mountain forestalled it, just as it forestalled everything else the Protestants were hoping to do in Bohemia.

This meant that the first major cultural victim of the Thirty Years' War was not a Habsburg Catholic collection but a Protestant one, that of Frederick V, the elector palatine. The Palatine was invaded in 1620 by Ambroglio di Spinola, the Italian general in Spanish service and a specialist in sieges; the capital, Heidelberg, was stormed two years later by Count Johan Tilly, general of the Catholic league. Frederick was forced to flee and, in his absence, the treasures of Germany's great university city were pillaged shamelessly. Culturally, this was as great a blow to the Protestants as the sale of the Prague treasures would have been for the Catholics. For just as Catholics rejoiced in picture galleries, the Protestants, who disliked such popish or pagan pomp on principle, gloried instead in their libraries. And the palatine library in Heidelberg was quite simply the best. Founded in the fifteenth century, it had been added to by a succession of Humanist princes and improved still more after the sacking of various German monasteries during the early stages of the Reformation. Numerous distinguished scholars, by their gifts and bequests, had also contributed to its glory.

The sack of Heidelberg was supervised by the Duke of Bavaria, a lesser Habsburg and a descendant of Albrecht's, who invited the then Pope, Gregory XV, to cannibalize the library. The Holy Father was eager to do so. Bindings and wrappers were removed to reduce the weight (and to remove traces of ownership) and borrowed books were traced and the borrowers forced to return them. Then, in February 1623, 196 cases were loaded onto a vast mule train, which set off up the Rhine and over the alpine passes into Italy, not arriving until the following year. The great majority of the palatine loot is still in the Vatican library.

This example was soon followed.

The removal of the Gonzaga collection from Mantua was, in theory, perfectly legal. But to many it was plunder just as much as if it had been a victim in war. Its eventual fate reinforced that view.

The first installment in this saga took place between 1627 and 1630 by which time the Mantuan collection had been famous for more than a century. Leonardo, Perugino, Correggio, Raphael, Giulio Romano, Titian, Veronese, Mantegna—all these artists had works in the collection and helped to make Mantua a small but polished jewel among the city-states. At the beginning of the seventeenth century, however, the city hit hard times. The silk industry, the basis of the Mantuan economy, failed in 1612. Worse, financial misfortune coincided with weak leadership: the dukes who ruled in Mantua in the early part of the 1600s were not the strong men who had created the Mantuan court and formed its fabulous collections but corrupt ex-cardinals, sensualists who were less interested in creation than in procreation, whose passion was for curiosities not canvases. The Countess of Arundel, wife to one of England's greatest collectors, and Sir Anthony Van Dyck, the painter, who were both at the court in Mantua in 1623, were told that the pictures might be available for the right price.

Some time later a certain Daniel Nys appeared in Mantua. A merchant, he was known there as a supplier of mirrors, perfumes, and furs—all the vanities. But Nys had another purpose: he was on a secret mission for the Earl of Arundel, the Duke of Buckingham, and even King Charles I of England. He had arrived to negotiate the sale of the Gonzaga pictures.

A year later the agreement was announced. In exchange for £15,000 ($1.42 million at today's values), Nys took Titian's *Twelve Caesars,* Raphael's *Holy Family,* Giorgione's *Pastoral Concert,* Correggio's *Virtue and Vice,* Caravaggio's *Death of the Virgin,* and works by Mantegna, del Sarto, and many others. Rumor of the impending sale had already been circulated and fierce objections had been raised on the part of the Mantuans. When the announcement was formally released the furor was such that the duke even thought of raising a loan and buying back what he had sold. But just then an unusual she-dwarf came on to the market in Hungary, he had to have her, and the Nys deal went through.

This sale had both immediate and long-term political consequences. Because of it Charles I was unable to provide proper financing for the expedition he was then planning to send, under Buckingham, to relieve the Huguenot citadel of La Rochelle, which was under attack from Richelieu's forces. Starved for funds, Buckingham's expedition was a disaster. The long-term effect of the sale was even worse, for the fate of the collection was tied to the fate of the King. Like Rudolf, Charles I was not a great politician and, also like Rudolf, his one undisputed success as a monarch was the formation of his art collection. He was the best collector the British royal family has ever known. But Charles was executed in 1649 as a result of the civil war in England. And, just as his collection had been built up through political sacrifice, so the collection itself now became part of the political sacrifice the crown had to pay.

Protestant Reformers all over Europe had looked upon religious works of art of all descriptions as symbols of a hated social system. As a result, they had (albeit in an orderly fashion) destroyed organs, smashed stained-glass windows, decapitated statues, and sacked whole monasteries as repositories of dead images which, they said, enslaved men's minds. To an extent this religious/political hostility was transferred to secular princes and it was no real surprise that once Charles I had been decapitated, the rebels turned their attention to his collection. But this time they did not destroy the King's pictures and sculptures or throw them into the river. They put them up for sale.

The Commonwealth sale, as it was called, was an extraordinary affair in its way. Every monarch in Europe was represented, secretly or otherwise, despite the fact that many of them officially deplored Oliver Cromwell's act of regicide. Philip IV of Spain, through an intermediary, bought the Titians. Cardinal Mazarin, through the French ambassador, got his share. Queen Christina of Sweden, through her agent Michiel le Blon, bid for the jewels. Archduke Leopold William, the Habsburg governor of the Spanish Netherlands who was a first cousin once removed of Rudolf's, was also represented.

The two sales that dispersed the Gonzaga pictures around Europe were both legal. Nonetheless, the forces that brought about these events were just as much a result of religious bigotry as the episodes of more obvious plunder which split up other collections.

The third collection to suffer in the seventeenth century was that at Munich. The date was 1632 and the course of the Thirty Years' War was changing. The Protestant powers, which had done poorly in the 1620s, now began to hit back. And the very same Duke of Bavaria who had helped the Pope to loot the palatine library now became a victim himself. The elector Maximilian I had built up his collection over many years, paying little attention to cost. His holdings were important because he was one of the first collector-princes to break with the prevailing fashion for Italian art. He was fond of German and Flemish masters and especially favored the works of Dürer.

He fell to the Swedes. Munich was only the start but the plunder was especially bad there. The elector had fled when the Protestant forces appeared and when he returned it was to find that his *Kunstkammer,* his art chamber, had been pillaged. The Dürers, the Holbeins, Cranach's *The Payment* were all gone and could never be replaced. Munich today has a fine art gallery, the Alte Pinakothek, with some beautiful Cranachs. But its collection of Dürers and Holbeins is sadly lacking what Maximilian's collection could have provided.

The Swedish armies moved on. They stole Russian icons from Riga and Pskov, altarpieces from Stargard and Braunsberg, pictures and books from Würzburg and Bremen, altarpieces by Grünewald from Mainz (lost at sea on the way back to Sweden). They stole gilt silver crosses from Halle Cathedral, reliquaries from Goslar. They looted the Jesuit and Capuchin churches at Olmütz.

The effect of the Thirty Years' War on art was permanent. As a result of the war, politics and religion became separated in many countries, which meant that iconoclasm never again had the force it did in the seventeenth century. Art never again stimulated the same hatred, never again had the same blatant propaganda value in such a divisive way, was never again part of the great intolerance.

But there was another sense in which the plunder of the Thirty Years' War had an effect on art as we know it. The great collections that existed after the Peace of Westphalia ultimately became the great national collections of Europe. The collections of Richelieu and Mazarin were first joined together under the roof of the Sun King, Louis XIV, then became the nucleus of the Louvre. Philip IV's collection, including the Titians he bought in London, became the Prado in Madrid. And the pictures of the Archduke Leopold William, who went back to Austria in 1656 and bequeathed his collection to the Emperor, helped to create the Kunsthistorisches Museum in Vienna.

Only one of the great collections created in the sixteenth and early seventeenth centuries, and which changed hands during the Thirty Years' War, did not become immobilized in its entirety in a museum. That collection was Rudolf's.

III

QUEEN
CHRISTINA

8.
Christina's Stockholm

In May 1649, when the booty from Prague arrived, Stockholm was a bustling town, the hub of the Swedish-Finnish state, though not yet on the scale of either Venice or Prague. In the early part of the century, Stockholm had been known as a "green town," because its houses were thatched with green turf. Almost all its buildings were one-story wooden structures. The prominence of numerous long white chimneys also gave the town a distinctive appearance. About 1620 the population was ten thousand but by 1660 that had risen to thirty-nine thousand. One of the reasons for the city's transformation was Sweden's successes in the Thirty Years' War, which made it a world power.

But with Sweden's military achievements, there also went responsibilities, and these particularly affected the lives of the nobles. They could no longer spend as much time on their estates, as their presence in the capital was required more and more to meet the expanding needs of the administration. As a result, a number of fine palaces were built in Stockholm after 1620. A drastic fire in the center of the city also helped to change the landscape for when the center was rebuilt afterward, King Gustavus Adolphus, Christina's father, ordered that the rebuilding should include "some very large and beautiful houses." This rebuilding was begun around 1637 and involved the demolition of no fewer than two thousand blocks of buildings. The Stockholm of 1649 was, therefore, a fairly new town in many ways and in that sense not unlike the Venice Veronese had found when he first arrived on the lagoon.

Stockholm was not without some claims to civilization in those days, although it was not as cosmopolitan as the Italian, French, Spanish, or Habsburg towns. Not having the same cultural advantages, or valuable trade routes which went via her towns or shores, not being at the geographical center of things, Sweden was more provincial and lacked the international flavor of those countries farther south. Stockholm was administered by a governor and a Council of Regents and the citizens of the capital enjoyed certain privileges, in the form of tax exemptions and customs advantages. Families even had the right to be looked after by the city if the breadwinner died.

The city was divided into several areas. Stadsholmen was the most

fashionable district, where the wealthy nobles had their houses. Kungs-
holmen, by the lake, was the industrial area where most of the craft and
artisan workshops were. Across the bridge was Gamla Brogatan, where
the orphanage was, and in the southern suburb of Södermalm lay the
Rusche Bodar, or privileged trading center of the Russian merchants.

The castle in Stockholm, where Queen Christina lived and where *Wisdom and Strength* and the other Veroneses were to be housed for the next
few years, was made of white stone and built on three floors, with a much
taller round tower in the center. It was known as the Tre Kronor (three
crowns) and had been extended and enhanced by Gustavus Adolphus.
This work was continued under Christina, who paid particular attention
to the interior.

All her life Christina was a controversial character. That controversy
dogged her from the moment of her birth and it continues today. To
some people she is one of the most extraordinary figures in history,
romantic and tragic, the young girl who, even while she was crowned
Queen of a powerful Protestant nation, had already made up her mind to
convert to Catholicism and abdicate. Along with Catherine the Great of
Russia, she was the only female art collector who can rank with Richelieu, the Duke of Orléans, Rudolf II, or Charles I of England. But to
Hugh Trevor-Roper she was a "dreadful woman," a "vulturine queen,"
a "crowned termagent and predatory blue stocking," a woman whose
callousness helped to kill the great philosopher René Descartes.

She was born on December 6, 1626. The astrologers had predicted a
boy and so, when Christina was born covered in hair and with a caul (or
membrane) which enveloped her from head to knees, the King was told
he had a son. When the mistake was discovered, no one had the courage
to tell him. "Eventually it was [the King's] sister who carried the infant
to the King: the baby was naked so that he could see for himself what no
one dared say to his face. In the event Gustavus Adolphus bore the
reversal with some wit, saying: 'She should be clever, since she has
deceived us all.' "

Christina's parents were no less remarkable than she. Gustavus
Adolphus, even today, is revered as Sweden's greatest hero, the most
distinguished of the Vasas, the historical line of Swedish kings, and the
warrior who, through the Thirty Years' War, turned Sweden from a backwater into a world power. Military matters were his chief intellectual and
emotional concern and he invented new battle formations. Though Gustavus Adolphus was killed in action when Christina was only six, his
influence lived on.

Christina's mother, Maria Eleanora, was a Hohenzollern and daughter
of John Sigismund von Hohenzollern, Elector of Brandenburg. Her

daughter was the third child she had given birth to but the first to survive. In those days women in Sweden were very definitely regarded as inferior beings and although the Swedish law was firm and clear and guaranteed Christina's succession, her mother had badly wanted a boy. For this reason, Maria Eleanora took absolutely no interest in her daughter for several years. Indeed, Christina later found out that her mother could not stand the sight of her because she was "a girl and ugly."

Another problem in Christina's psychology almost certainly arose from the fact that Gustavus Adolphus had left instructions that his daughter was to be raised as a boy. She was, therefore, instructed in athletics, horsemanship, and hunting and she excelled in all three. She was also given a more intellectual education than she might otherwise have had. Here too she did not disappoint. She was soon able to speak and even to write French, German, Italian, and Dutch, as well as Latin and she was familiar with Greek, Hebrew, and Arabic. No less accomplished in the sciences, she displayed preferences for classical philology, philosophy, theology, mathematics, and anatomy.

The Queen reached her majority at eighteen, when she was old enough to govern in her own right. That happened in 1644, at which time, according to Pierre Chanut, the French diplomat, she made a dazzling impression. Apart from being well-read in poetry, literature, and the sciences, and besides her proficiency in languages, he found her "quick witted, with a supple mind, wise and restrained." She expressed her desire to govern her kingdom herself (interesting, in view of what was to happen later) and spent a year sitting in on the Privy Council, taking in their deliberations.

The booty from Prague arrived in 1649 when Christina was twenty-three. When she had first heard news of the Prague loot, on August 5, 1648, the Queen immediately had plans drawn up for an extension to her castle, to house the art collection. The architect Nicodemus Tessin the Elder was commissioned to design an annex, a whole range of buildings, to display the magnificent pictures but nothing ever came of this plan. Instead, after the collection arrived, it was displayed in an art and curio chamber on the second floor of an extension built in the 1620s by the architect Kasper Panten, in the east wing of the castle.

Prior to this massive influx of pictures and other objects, Sweden was not overburdened with art, and taste in Stockholm was dominated mainly by German and Dutch fashions. The Vasa kings had acquired a valuable collection of woven tapestries which had been augmented by the purchases of Gustavus Adolphus's grandfather, Gustavus Vasa, who acquired a number of northern schools' paintings—mainly landscapes, still lifes, and flower arrangements, with some portraits. There was, by Christina's time, wooden paneling in the castle and there were carved doors ornamented with marquetry and ceilings painted with flowers. There was also magnificent plate of silver and vermeil.

At first the young Queen was more a passive recipient of fine gifts than an active collector: when her father was abroad in the wars she had sent word to him to "bring me back something beautiful." She was never very keen on the northern style. In her early years she was supplied with art by Pieter Spiering Silfvercrona, who eventually became Swedish minister in the Hague. For instance, he sent her a series of genre paintings by Gerard Dou but they did not appeal to her and were returned to him. Art from the south and particularly from Italy was another matter: she particularly cherished some drawings by Raphael and Michelangelo.

More than anything it was to be Christina's reign which changed tastes in Sweden. Portraits of the young Queen painted during her minority were stiff and formal, likenesses recorded for posterity rather than for enjoyment at the time. The change to a more lively, secular style, more appealing to our modern eye, reflected Christina's appetites exactly.

An embassy to France in 1646, led by Magnus de la Gardie, had something to do with it. This directed her attention to French art, which in turn led to an appreciation of the art even further South, in Italy. An unintended dividend of the young Queen's classical education was that it had prepared her for the pagan and secular highlights of Italian Renaissance and Mannerist paintings just as much as for religious works. A second man who helped to influence the Queen's taste was Michiel le Blon, a Frenchman living in Amsterdam who served as a spy for Sweden, under cover as an art dealer. Le Blon started buying sculptures for the Queen (she had planned a museum of sculpture in Sweden at one point) but he soon moved on to antiques in general. It was Le Blon who bid on Christina's behalf for the jewels at the Commonwealth sale.

A third agent of Christina's who helped to fashion her taste was Matthias Palbitzki. He was despatched to the Mediterranean countries with instructions to purchase marble sculptures. He was given enough funds to travel as far afield as Asia Minor and Greece. And it was thanks to Palbitzki that Christina had her first sight of the Eternal City, Rome: he brought back a number of veduta panoramas showing the city as it then was and clearly depicting recognizable buildings and landmarks.

The booty from Prague arrived, therefore, just as Christina was developing into a confirmed classicist and a lover of the warm, Italianate south.

After they had been unpacked, only some of the paintings were displayed on the second floor of the castle. The lesser pictures were kept stored in a room in the state archive on the floor below. The art chamber proper was divided into two sections: the "rarities" (i.e., curiosities) were kept together in one place, and the paintings, including landscapes, were on view in an adjoining square gallery. The pictures were grouped according to school: Italian, Spanish, German, Flemish, Dutch, and French. There were more Italian and German-Flemish paintings than anything else and the quality of the Italians was the most impressive, with the Venetian school the most notable of all. Among individual masters, however, Rubens, Giulio Romano, and Veronese dominated. Christina owned no fewer than thirteen Veroneses which must mean that she acquired some from a source other than Prague, since Rudolf had but eleven. Or perhaps during the turmoil of the Thirty Years' War and the northward journey, certain pictures came to be attributed to Veronese that were not in fact by him. One remarkable fact about Christina's Veroneses is that she owned no religious pictures or banquet scenes: they were *all* allegories. In addition to those already encountered, a *Rape of Europe* is listed and *Wisdom and Strength* has the slightly different title of *Strength (Hercules) Accompanied by Wisdom*.

Although the lion's share of the booty which General Königsmark and the Swedes amassed as a result of the Thirty Years' War went to the crown, Sweden in general benefited greatly. For one thing the nobles who had fought in the war had seen for themselves how well their counterparts in other countries lived, and there was no going back. The traditional Swedish style of interior decoration was essentially sober, though in many cases the workmanship was excellent. But now the lush, more colorful, more exuberant objets d'art of the warmer south began to fill the castles and manors of the nobles: painted or gilded leather from Spain, German or Italian furniture inlaid with jewels, ornate gilt chairs, and stuccoed moldings for ceilings, crystal chandeliers, and gilt torchères. As a result of the Thirty Years' War, the taste of Sweden changed: Christina was temperamentally ready for it and her enthusiastic espousal of everything Italian or French probably hastened and crystallized something that was already under way.

The arrival of the Prague booty was as important a lever in this change as any. Certainly, as the Queen became more interested in and knowledgeable about foreign countries, so she started to pursue more actively the works of art produced abroad. Her fluency in languages was a great help in this respect. She began to make particular use of Matthias Palbitzki, whom she sent back to Italy. On his earlier trip, Palbitzki, a skillful draftsman as well as everything else, had made drawings for the Queen of such things as Cleopatra's baths in Alexandria. He was now instructed to go to Venice and Rome, charged with the task of buying drawings and antique marbles. He was not successful in this particular regard for the Italians forbade him to take anything out of the country.

But his travels paid off with other dividends. On his way south he stopped off in Florence and, through the Grand Duke of Tuscany, was introduced to Paolo Giordano Orsini, Duke of Bracciano. This proved to be an important friendship for, as a result, the duke, who had himself traveled as far afield as Norway, wrote to Christina. In her replies to him her attitudes and views about art were clearly set out.

By this time the Queen was beginning to feel rather claustrophobic in Sweden and she seems to have used her correspondence with the duke to obtain all the news she could of the exciting south. The most revealing of her letters is one written in May 1652, although the views expressed in it were not new to her. She says: "I will send you my portrait when it is finished, also a miniature of a Titian, and if you like will send you other copies of Italian pictures from Prague which include Veronese, Polidoro, Correggio, Tintoretto, etc. All the Prague gallery is here and is very beautiful, there are Albert Dards [Dürer] and other German masters of which I do not know the names; which anyone but I would admire very much. I swear to you that I would give them all for a pair of pictures by Raphael, and think that I was doing them too much honour. I would like to know if there is any composer better than Carissimi or anyone who approaches him? What are the best Roman and Italian poets? They say that Balducci is good, I don't think so. Is Guarini good? He seems so to me, and would seem wonderful to anyone who has not read Tasso or Ariosto, but I only read him after them; what is the judgement of your academies on him? Please excuse my curiosity. . . . This is the only amusement I have, to nourish my spirit with these beautiful things in the hours from which my other occupations allow me breathing space, and I would rather lose my life than give up these innocent pleasures."

In his replies Orsini provided information about other painters, musicians, and intellectuals in whom the Queen had expressed interest. To judge from his references, Christina was especially taken with Pietro da Cortona, Guercino, and the musician Horatio Benvolo.

After the better pieces seized in Prague had been properly installed in the Queen's art chamber in the castle, Johan Holm was entrusted with the care of the collections. This was a step up for Holm, who had started out as Christina's tailor. As perhaps might have been anticipated, it was not an entirely successful appointment. He was ordered to catalog the existing collection and was responsible for adding future acquisitions to the list. He also had to keep an account of "what is taken out and to whom it is delivered." To help him he had his young brother-in-law, the colorfully named Polycarpus Crumbugel, who was master of the royal household. Neither man seems to have been much good as a curator: the inventories drawn up at this time were very poor and in fact Holm was replaced after three years.

The arrival in Stockholm of the Prague collection was a major event of 1649 and was to have a lasting effect on Christina. That same year, however, there were other visitors, each very different. They too had an effect on the young Queen's psychology and played a part in causing her, eventually, to abandon her country.

In August, Nicolas de Flecelles, Count of Bregy, and his wife Charlotte, stopped off in Stockholm on their way back to Paris after a diplomatic posting in Poland. The impact of this couple was out of all proportion to what anyone might have expected. In the first place, such a visit in itself was rare: most visitors to Sweden at that time went solely for business or diplomatic reasons and were therefore of a serious caste of mind. The Bregys were not. The count was tall, handsome, and distinguished, and immediately appealed to Christina, who appreciated men with some sort of presence. Charlotte was famous, or rather notorious, in Paris society for her frivolity. On the surface the couple might not have been expected to suit Christina's court but in fact they were the hit of the year. In the Bregys the Queen met for the first time the polished product of the Parisian salons and, although the couple made no secret of the fact that they found her court, by comparison, very simple, the enchanted Christina tried every wile she knew to keep them. She suggested the count become court chamberlain or command a corps of French guards. In their honor she gave the grandest ball ever seen in Sweden. All to no avail: the Bregys always had every intention of returning to the sophisticated world they knew. Their physical presence in Stockholm was fleeting but their effect on Christina, on her yearning for the world they came from, was to endure.

The third important arrival in that year of 1649 was another Frenchman. But there was nothing frivolous about him: it was the philosopher René Descartes. Christina had been corresponding with the great man for some time and his visit had been arranged by her old friend, the French diplomat, Chanut. It was an extraordinary encounter. The difference between her response to his presence and to that of the Bregys was shocking—and very revealing.

Descartes expressed the same enthusiasm about meeting the Queen as she had expressed about meeting him. So keen was he in fact that he arrived in Stockholm, not in spring or summer as would have been wise given the traveling conditions of the time, but toward the beginning of Sweden's arctic winter. Moreover, friends who watched Descartes embark for Sweden from Holland were astonished to find that he had prepared himself for the meeting by dressing as a courtier, with curled hair and lace-trimmed gloves.

Descartes certainly had some expectations of Christina. In this, no doubt, he had been prepared by Chanut, the man who had found her so "quick witted, with a supple mind, wise and restrained." By the time the philosopher arrived in Stockholm, however, Christina was rather different from how Chanut remembered her. The great intellectual whom Descartes had expected, the "Pallas of the North" as she had come to be known, was at that time besotted with the ballet (in which she herself played a part) and much taken up with the sophisticated trivialities and frivolities of the Bregys from Paris.

Christina received Descartes ceremoniously enough but took an instant dislike to him. So involved in the ballet was she that she actually suggested he take part (he was fifty-four). When he declined she suggested he write the libretto. "Not even Descartes could refuse two royal requests so Europe's most famous philosopher was set to work writing verses for the *Triumph of Peace,* as the queen's ballet was called (it was to be performed on her twenty-third birthday)."

From then on Christina neglected Descartes. Once the ballet was over she suggested that the Frenchman take five or six weeks' holiday to get to know Sweden. Her behavior was quite disgraceful. Only after the new year had come and gone did the Queen finally consent to start their meetings. But even now Descartes must have been more than a little shocked when he was told they would take place in the library, under the art chamber in the castle, *at five o'clock in the morning.* He must also have been surprised to learn, as he wrote back to France, that the young Queen actually knew very little philosophy. For a while they met fairly frequently and she asked him to draw up plans for the creation of an academy of intellectuals. But nothing came of that for, as January turned into February, Descartes's lungs filled with congestion: the arctic winter got to him. On February 11, barely four months after he had arrived in Sweden, he died.

Christina appears to have been grief-stricken, as well she might since it was her coldness, as much as winter, which had killed him, and she had great plans for a statue to commemorate him. But nothing came of that either and the whole encounter stands as a disturbing episode in her career.

Christina never took to Descartes because he was not physically attractive. But a more important reason lay in the fact that he believed the young Queen would treat plainspokenness as a compliment. Instead, Christina could not bear to be contradicted: she had been the center of the court and the center of attention for too long. When Descartes was confronted with her mind, which was lively but, to him, untutored, he failed to realize that the most important thing about the Queen was her "boundless self-esteem." Once Christina realized that the great Descartes thought her accomplishments were meager, she was bound to have turned against him. The long-awaited encounter between them was worse than a catastrophe: for both of them it was a disappointment.

The Descartes episode is important because it is an early sign of the less attractive side of Christina, the side that has drawn the fire of historians such as Hugh Trevor-Roper. Yet the fact is that this aspect of the Queen, which preferred the ballet and frivolity to philosophy, was to play just as much a role in her decision to abdicate and to move south as did her religious feelings. All her life Christina was two people and, like many others both before and after her, she was to find that the two people inside her added up to less than a whole. For many years yet she would be a restless soul, an unfulfilled woman. And it was this restlessness that led her to collect and to try to find fulfillment in that way. It helped lead her to Rome, taking her favorite art with her.

After Descartes died, Christina's thoughts were taken up with her coronation, set for October 1650. Her actions at this time suggest that the philosopher's presence, though very different from that of the frivolous Bregys, was not wholly dissimilar in its effects on the young woman. The lifestyle, the arts, the intellectual fads and fashions of the warm south became increasingly attractive to her. So did the certainty and rich coloring of the south's religion (despite his philosophizing, Descartes was a devout Catholic). These changes in the Queen help explain the fact that, less than a month before her coronation, on September 25, Christina suddenly proposed to the Riksdag, the Swedish parliament, that her cousin Charles Gustavus should not only succeed her but that he should be officially appointed her heir, and that his male children should succeed *him*. It was a final ploy in what had been a running battle with the nobles since the regency. The aristocracy had seen Christina's minority as an opportunity to curtail the power of the monarchy, and the Queen's action was a device to reassert the hereditary power and position of the crown. She won, and less than two weeks before the coronation, on October 9, Charles Gustavus became her heir. At that point, Christina alone was aware of what was to come.

Her coronation, as befitted a Queen who so loved the arts, was a fabulous affair. Apart from anything else, the succession of the "daughter of the mighty Gustavus Adolphus" attracted the attention of all Europe. Prior to coronation day, Christina had withdrawn to the house of one of her ministers, intending to make her state entry into the capital from there. She did so attended by pages, guards, heralds, and trumpeters and with members of the Rad preceding her in their carriages. The Queen rode on horseback, with a saddle decorated in silver, enamel, and diamonds and swathed in black velvet patterned with gold. She was surrounded by halberdiers and footmen and followed by her mother. After that, curiously, came six camels, with saddles and canopies over them, and a dozen mules covered in swags of rich gilded decorations. Most of the accessories—saddles, costumes, coaches—had been commissioned in France, which was now replacing Italy as the leader of fashion in the decorative arts.

As she arrived, everyone else was already in place: the Rad, the Grand Treasurer carrying the golden keys, Oxenstierna carrying the orb, and the high steward—last—with the crown. The Queen, as she descended and entered the Storkykan, or Great Church, was wearing a gown of crimson velvet embroidered with gold. She was received by the archbishop, Johannes Lenaeus, bearing the gold and enamel anointing horn. She then entered the church with a canopy above her, decorated with designs based on Botticelli. The church was lined—and no doubt warmed—by a number of tapestries. Christina had ordered no fewer than forty-six of them from Holland in 1647 and, if a 1650 inventory is to be believed, more than two hundred hung in the throne room of the castle and in the Queen's own apartments. It was some of these which had been transferred to the Great Church for the ceremony. There was a sermon and then Christina took the oath. She was anointed, crowned, and invested.

After the ceremony was over, she left the Great Church and mounted a golden triumphal chariot, pulled by four white horses, and returned in procession to the palace. The treasurer walked before her throwing gold and silver medals to the crowd. As the procession arrived at the Tre Kronor, an 1,800-gun salute was sounded from forty men-of-war in the bay. It lasted two hours.

The coronation celebrations continued for several months, with banquets and other festivities and with the Queen receiving the oath of fealty from all the estates of Sweden. At one of these banquets for which there are records a roasted ox was filled with turkey, geese, and chickens and the wine flowed from a statue.

With hindsight, however, Christina's coronation must be seen as more notable for what was going on beneath the surface rather than above it. For the Queen faced a psychological dilemma found nowhere else in history. This extraordinary woman was crowned having already made up her mind to abdicate.

·   ·   ·

Queen Christina ruled as a crowned queen for just under four years, from October 20, 1650, to June 6, 1654, and during that time her life can be divided into two aspects. Her public life was made up of politics, the court, the arts; her secret life had but one dimension, her conversion to Catholicism. Although these two aspects will be considered separately, the Queen's love of the arts and her religion were in some respects different sides of the same coin: her longing for Italy.

Christina always preferred the company of men, so the court was a male affair. Indeed, she seldom spoke to women, unless they were visiting the court on a special occasion. The only exception to this was Ebba Sparre, *la belle comtesse,* with whom Christina was very intimate. Ebba Sparre was the daughter of Lars Erikson Sparre, a member of the Rad who had died in 1644 and left his daughter in the Queen's charge. She had "a melancholy beauty" which, for once, appealed to the Queen, and she became lady-in-waiting, known to Christina as Belle.

The court itself was made up of two types of person. There were the foreign ambassadors and diplomats who were obliged to be there; and there were the scholars whom she drew to her (as Rudolf had done in his court) from all over Europe. Among this number there were several painters.

Foremost among the diplomats was Pierre Hector Chanut (1604–1667). He had been French minister, resident from December 1645 until 1649, and had then returned in 1653 as ambassador. Chanut had a lot to do with the Queen's decision to lure French philosophers and artists to her court, and it was this early interest in French life and culture that led her to look south and, eventually, to Catholicism. Chanut's description of Christina has become famous: "During the past three weeks, when I have had the honour of being in her presence for more than eight hours a day, I have perceived more strength and brilliance in her intellectual faculties than I would have believed possible. She manages to combine learned studies and innocence with sound judgement and dignity in a manner that one cannot help admiring."

Don Antonio Pimental de Prado, the Spanish ambassador in Sweden, was on his very first diplomatic mission when he arrived in Stockholm in May 1652. He headed a brilliant retinue. Indeed it was this retinue which helped Christina decide to model her court on that of Spain. Pimental soon gained Christina's confidence and helped organize the entertainments at court. Though he was recalled to Spain in 1653, Pimental met up with Christina after she had abdicated and he was present at her secret acceptance of the Catholic faith. He then traveled with her to Rome.

But the ambassadors at Christina's court—important though they undoubtedly were for the trade which Sweden needed to maintain, and crucial as one or two of them were to be in her conversion—very definitely took second place to the scholars who the Queen sought to attract to the Tre Kronor from the rest of Europe.

Traditionally, Uppsala had been the center of academic life in Sweden. But now Christina was ensconced in the castle, surrounded by the spoils of the country's successes in the Thirty Years' War. Thus Stockholm became for a while the center of attention not only in Sweden but in all Europe. Christina once wrote: "I shall do my utmost to set aside a few hours in my study for conversation with the dead, who grant me life, whereas the living at all times bore me to death." Neat, but by no means true since the Queen very much enjoyed her conversations with the living and sought to bring some of the most interesting minds of the seventeenth century to Stockholm.

Among the first men to have an influence on Christina was Johannes Freinshemius, who came from Strasbourg in 1642 to occupy the Skytte chair in political science and rhetoric at Uppsala. Through Freinshemius the young Queen became interested in the syncretists, whose aim was to level the differences between the various branches of Protestantism. Significantly the syncretistic attitude to Catholicism was markedly conciliatory. Later, the Queen became interested in Stoic thought and shared the general adulation of the heroic ordeal. This entailed an almost obsessive concern with the concepts of honor and virtue and with the classical qualities of Hercules. It is obvious why she was drawn especially to the paintings of Veronese and a few other Italians, such as Correggio.

Her encounter with Descartes, in many ways the most typical example of her dealings with scholars, has already been described. But, at more or less the same time, due to the sack of Prague and some wise purchases from Cardinal Mazarin of France, Christina's library began to be one of the most impressive parts of her collection. To go with the books, she succeeded in luring Gabriel Naudé to Stockholm for a while. Regarded as Europe's foremost librarian, Naudé served three cardinals, was famous for being a skeptic and was a forerunner of the Enlightenment. He brought with him to Sweden a number of Mazarin's most valuable books.

The best-known Swedish intellectual at that time was Georg Stiernhielm, who was involved in one of the most pressing intellectual problems of the day: the quest for the purest language, the original tongue spoken before the confusion of Babel. Stiernhielm's contribution was to argue, perhaps not surprisingly, that Swedish was in fact closest to the original. The Queen took a lively interest in this matter, though whether she found Stiernhielm's thesis in any way convincing, is not known.

Blaise Pascal, the famous mathematician who had developed Euclidian geometry, never actually went to Sweden, but in 1652 he sent an example of his famous calculating machine, the first entirely mechanical one, to the young Queen, together with a long, admiring letter. Christina may have had it in her mind to persuade him to come north, but shortly afterward Pascal underwent a spiritual crisis of his own and disappeared into strict retreat. That such an eminent scientist could suffer a change of belief may have affected her too.

But by far the two most controversial and influential scholars at Christina's court were Claude de Saumaise and Pierre Bourdelot. Saumaise (also called "Salmasius" by contemporary faddists who liked to latinize names) was a Dutch philologist and known as the "Prince of the Erudite," a formidable debater who, it was said, set his dogs onto anyone who refused to acknowledge his right to the title. He included among his intellectual achievements a defense of Charles I against Oliver Cromwell.

Saumaise was instrumental in bringing the erudite French doctor Bourdelot to Sweden. The latter arrived in Stockholm in 1652 and stayed for more than a year. During that time he transformed the court, an achievement due in no small part to the fact that, shortly after his arrival, he won the Queen's eternal gratitude by curing her of a lingering fever. This, Bourdelot achieved through skillful psychology and a prescription for healthier living on Christina's part. It may also have had something to do with the doctor's nature. Though erudite, he was in fact a coarse man and he lured the young woman (still some years from her thirtieth birthday) away from the drier scholars at court and she seems to have enjoyed and benefited from the change.

Bourdelot's arrival and success at court also injected new impetus into Christina's plans for an academy. The Frenchman became the academy's first president, a not altogether wise decision on the part of the Queen for it made the doctor very unpopular. Like Saumaise, he hated competition and it did not take long for Bourdelot to abuse his position. For example, he compelled scholars with no singing voice to sing. And Naudé, the librarian, was forced to give an exhibition of Greek and Roman dancing. Everybody enjoyed the spectacle of others being made fun of but secretly they all grew to hate Bourdelot. It was said that the muses had been banished from the court in favor of frivolity.

Frivolity is perhaps too strong a word and it may well be that, for all their learning, the scholars at Christina's court were a fairly dull bunch. The world—the Swedish world at any rate—was just emerging from a bleak period of long wars and lugubrious taste in the arts. As in so much, Christina merely reflected and probably crystallized, this change. The truth is that, like many people, she was actually drawn to the arts more than to scholarship. Her real love was less philosophy, philology, and mathematics than the theater, music, and painting.

Christina was especially lucky with the theater. On January 28, 1638, just after her eleventh birthday, she watched a play that was brand-new in Stockholm. The French court ballet had just been developed and for Sweden, as for most places, it was quite revolutionary in tone. Hitherto, the theater had been didactic and instructional. Now, suddenly, it was fun—irreverent, haphazard, serving to provide pleasure and delight rather than anything else. It was burlesque but it was still theater: there was a concern with artistry for its own sake, for the effects it could produce. Important elements of Mannerism survived in the theater.

In this way the Queen acquired a lifelong interest in the stage that had a special affinity with with her interest in painting. This was because, by the time she ascended the throne, there had been a further change in theatrical fashion. Allegory and mythology were now very much in vogue in the theater. It had become popular to liken Swedish heroism to the gods of classical Greece. By 1649, when Christina's own theater opened, there had been another twist: until that time the story line in any theatrical entertainment had been rather haphazard, subordinate to the dramatic effects that could be produced. Now plots became stronger and more important. Later on, before the Queen abdicated, Italian opera came to Sweden and so, in a very real sense, the range of theater available in Stockholm was much wider than ever before and changing all the time. Underlying it all was the same mode of allegorical thinking that was to make Veronese's pictures so popular with the Queen.

Christina and Art

After the arrival of the pictures from Prague, Christina's taste for Italian works was enthusiastic. But it had not always been that way. In 1647, for example, David Beck, a Dutch painter, arrived in Sweden and was appointed court painter. He received an annual salary of 600 riksdalers (approximately $77,000 at 1987 values) plus a fee for every picture he painted. As court painter, he not only executed several portraits of the Queen, but he was sent abroad on missions to paint important personages of whom Christina wanted likenesses. On this basis he went to Belgium, France, Italy, and England.

Beck painted four portraits of the Queen while she was in Sweden, all of them showing her right profile. The second of these, painted in 1650, a year after Rudolf's gallery had arrived in Stockholm, offers an interesting comparison with Veronese's allegories. Christina is shown dressed in a rich white silk dress, with sumptuous folds more than reminiscent of the

Venetian ladies in Veronese's paintings. She wears flowers in her hair much as Virtue has a laurel crown in Veronese's *Vice and Virtue.* The Queen also has a globe under her hand, in which she holds a letter. It is too much to say that these images are derived solely from Veronese's art, for such symbols were very common at the time. But it may well have been that Christina showed her enjoyment of Veronese's pictures and that Beck was moved to emulate some of his strongest elements.

The arrival of the Prague pictures was one of the most important elements which caused Christina to look South for her inspiration. Another was Raphael Trichet du Fresne. He was a Frenchman who had come to Sweden with Gabriel Naudé and, when Naudé was appointed librarian, du Fresne was appointed his assistant. However, du Fresne was also known as the man who had published Leonardo da Vinci's *Treatise on Painting* in France. Because of this, and because Holm and Crumbugel were doing such a poor job, in 1652 Christina made the Frenchman *garde des medailles* (keeper of medals) and *garde des tableaux* (keeper of pictures). He recataloged the collection and while he made some definite improvements over his predecessors, he was still far from perfect. He gave the provenance of most of the works and a description but he never made any mention of the artists' names and he often counted several items as one. For example, he grouped no fewer than 8,658 medals as one item.

Whatever the drawbacks, du Fresne's inventory was typical of its time. And in any case it is the only record there is of what was in Christina's possession in the early 1650s, before her move to Rome. It therefore becomes vital for an understanding of how Christina's taste, and that of a seventeenth-century Protestant court, differed from Rudolf and a late-sixteenth-century Catholic one.

The total number of items in the collection was in the region of 40,000, of which 35,000 were medals and 750 were paintings. Several things stand out. One, there were a large number of portraits, either as paintings or as medals; the Queen was always very interested in what people *looked* like. Two, she had many more books than Rudolf. Three, the collection was just as rich as the Emperor's in clocks and mathematical and scientific instruments. The occult was not such a major concern (though Christina was interested in alchemy): instead she was fascinated by the Enlightenment and the beginnings of the scientific revolution. This meant that her taste ran to practical instruments rather than to clever but pointless automata. The amount of jewels in her collection was not large, reflecting the fact that Christina's interests were intellectual and artistic rather than materialistic. Finally, the Queen had a large collection of "Indian objects"—over fifty pieces.

If this conveys the overall shape of Christina's collection, what of the detail? When she came to leave Sweden later on, she chose to take certain things with her to Rome and was prepared to leave others behind. The inventory helps understand her thinking.

Among her Italian paintings, and in addition to the Veroneses, Christina had Jacopo Bassano's *Adoration of the Shepherds* (now in the Barodo Museum), three Palma Vecchios, including a *Sybil* now in Hampton Court, and *Venus and Cupid in a Landscape,* now in the Fitzwilliam Museum in Cambridge. She had Tintoretto's *Young Women Making Music,* now in Dresden, and about forty pictures from Prague said to be Titians (i.e., both originals and copies). Among the more notable Titians was *L'Esclavonne,* which had been given to Rudolf II as a gift in 1599 by Cesare d'Este, grandson of Laura de Dianti, whom many believe to be the model in the picture. This work is now in the Kisters Collection in Kreuzlingen, Switzerland (another version exists in the National Gallery in London).

Christina had a modest collection of the Bologna school—the next stage, as it were, from Veronese. There were five works by Annibale Carracci, four by Guido Reni, and one by Domenichino. The Bologna school was to become much more fashionable later on. And finally, among her Italian paintings, Christina had Correggio's famous pair of compositions, *Danaë* and *Leda,* depicting how Jupiter transformed himself into a shower of gold and a swan. In the du Fresne inventory these pictures had the letters *NB* (for *nota bene)* written in the margin opposite them. This was how she indicated, when the time came, which paintings she wanted to take with on her momentous journey to the south.

Among the northern works of art which she had in Sweden were Hans von Aachen's *Diana with Two Nymphs, Hounds, and Game.* Of the fifteen known paintings by Aachen which were taken from Prague, this is the only one whose whereabouts is known (it was apparently given away by Christina before she left). That points to the others perhaps still being in Sweden somewhere, unrecognized. About twenty of Giuseppe Arcimboldo's paintings were also taken to Sweden, and far more of these survive. She also had Pieter Bruegel's *Peasants Attacked by Robbers* and six Cranachs, all from Prague. The Queen also had many sculptures by Adriaen de Vries. No fewer than seventy-six bronze statues and six bronze reliefs by him had come from Prague. A dozen of these still stand today in the park at Drottningholm.

The Queen's love of the south, its warmth, its sensuality, its light, was therefore reflected in her collection. The Italian pictures, especially the Veroneses, were sunlit, cheerful, sensual. Whereas Rudolf looked inward for his answers, she looked outward for her entertainment. The more she considered her collection, the more she longed to go where such art was created.

To satisfy that craving she began by trying to bring the south to her. If her first court painter, David Beck, could not really stand comparison with the great names in her collection, her second was a far more serious talent. Better still, he was also from the south, from France.

Sébastien Bourdon had been born in 1616 in Montpellier in the South of France and he worked at first in Paris and Bordeaux. He traveled to Rome, where he was influenced by Claude but then returned to Paris via Venice. While he was in Veronese's city he emulated the master by executing a number of huge canvases with both religious and classical subjects and with a Venetian richness of handling that was particularly reminiscent of Veronese. All this made him not just any Frenchman. When he arrived in Stockholm with his wife in October 1652, he was an immediate success. He stayed in Stockholm for about a year and painted a great many portraits. While there he produced two types of picture for the Queen. The first, which he seems to have completed almost as soon as he arrived, shows Christina with her hair hanging freely, a pose that agrees very well with the literary descriptions of her at the time. (Chanut, for instance, wrote that the Queen never bothered with her appearance and that she took only fifteen minutes to dress.) But the most famous portrait Bourdon did of the Queen was the one he executed in June 1653. Pimental, the Spanish envoy, acting on behalf of Philip IV, had requested an equestrian portrait of Christina. In this picture she is shown riding sidesaddle and wearing a riding coat over her ordinary clothes. The motif of a rearing horse had previously been planned by Leonardo da Vinci and executed by Velázquez (of Philip IV), by Rubens, and by Van Dyck (of Thomas of Savoy). The idea can be traced back as far as Phidias's frieze on the Parthenon. Once again Christina's taste for and knowledge of classical themes from the south are apparent. This picture is now in the Prado.

Du Fresne's inventory gives a good idea of the shape of Christina's collection and explains how, at that stage of her life, her tastes and attitudes differed from Rudolf's. There is, however, one question left to answer. Why was du Fresne asked to compile the inventory in the first place?

Early inventories were always compiled for a particular reason, either because a collection was being sold or because, at someone's death, a proper stocktaking was necessary for the purposes of inheritance and/or tax. There was undoubtedly a specific reason on this occasion, a very unusual reason, and one that introduces another twist in the story. The inventory was the first move in deciding what Christina would take with her when the time came to abdicate.

Abdication

The ostensible reason for Christina's abdication, the catalyst, was her religious crisis. But there were other factors. The Queen stood at a crossroads, not unlike Hercules as she would have loved to have it put. She was faced with conflicting ideals in three very important areas: marriage *or* celibacy; the crown *or* freedom; Protestantism *or* Catholicism.

As early as 1646, when she was twenty, Christina told her two most obvious suitors, her paternal cousin Charles Gustavus and her maternal cousin Prince Frederick William of Brandenburg, that they should not expect to marry her, *ever*. Several theories have been put forward for this: her childhood and adolescent tomboyishness, her known aversion for mirrors—"because they have nothing agreeable to show me"—and her marked affection for Ebba Sparre-Belle, who came into her life as a lady-in-waiting but was soon much more intimate; all this points to lesbian tendencies in the Queen. This issue has been thoroughly aired by historians but the Queen's later life, as will be seen, did not exclude strong attachments to men. Aware that she was not sexually attractive, the Queen may have relegated her hopes on that score beneath her intellectual pursuits. But none of the theories entirely squares with what is known about her later life.

There can be little doubt, however, that more than religion led Christina to vacate the throne. Her personality was such that she found the affairs of state irksome. She was by nature an intellectual, yet she had no real discipline even for things that she liked. The burdens of political office, at least for a while, soon became too much.

Ironically enough, the actual encounter which led directly to her acceptance of the Catholic faith, which propelled her conversion on its irreversible course, was an accident. This was her meeting with Antonio Macedo. It arose through the arrival of Pinto Pereira, the Portuguese ambassador, who was concluding a trade agreement in Stockholm. It was Christina's habit sometimes to take part in the negotiations herself. Pereira, however, spoke no language but his own and so he invariably had with him an interpreter. In the spring of 1651, not long after the coronation, the official Portuguese interpreter fell ill and Pereira took with him to one of the meetings his chaplain, a Jesuit, who was a good classicist and Latin scholar. This was Macedo.

Although Macedo started off discussing trade questions, the Queen soon asked him about other things. These were mainly literary matters to start with but, eventually, she got around to religion. Christina always spoke very respectfully of the Pope in these discussions and showed herself very curious about, and not at all hostile to, Roman Catholicism. Intrigued at first, Macedo soon began to see that the Queen was showing a more than passing interest: she might even be a possible convert. As it was then illegal to be a Swedish Catholic, the significance of this can hardly be overstated and were not lost on the Jesuit.

The trade negotiations came to a close at the end of the summer and Macedo was due to return home. Consequently, the Queen made arrangements with him to have certain Italians sent to her court. These individuals, disguised as tourists, would give her further instruction. Macedo, who could not tell his ambassador what was afoot, had Christina's help in being spirited away via the back door of the castle which opened directly to the sea. He went first to Hamburg and then on to Rome, where he alerted the general of his order.

The impatient Queen could not wait for Macedo's efforts to bear fruit and on August 7 that year she summoned the Rad to inform them of her intention to abdicate. She gave three reasons for her decision: that a man was needed to lead the army; that Charles Gustavus was a ready alternative; and that she herself wanted peace and privacy. She said she had been thinking of abdicating for four or five years and hinted there were other reasons for her decision, which she could not mention.

The Rad, this time anyway, reacted rapidly and firmly. Fourteen members signed a document pointing out to the Queen the responsibilities that had been imposed on her by her birth and begging her, in the strongest terms, not to abdicate. The idea that anyone should want to give up the throne of such a powerful nation as Sweden was beyond the politicians. None of this truly changed Christina's mind, although in November she withdrew her threat.

For a while, life seemed to proceed as before. Christina's lifestyle was so flamboyant at this time that the expense of the royal household began to exacerbate Sweden's economic problems. During the regency Christina's expenses, together with the court's, absorbed 3.1 percent of the national income. By 1652 they were over 10 percent.*

But while all this was happening, Macedo *had* reached Rome and alerted the acting head of the Jesuits there, Fra Goswin Nickel. He was not slow to act on Macedo's momentous news. Nickel selected two men for the difficult and very secret task of pursuing Christina's conversion. These two were given their orders in November 1651 and very specific

---

* For comparison, the British Queen in 1987 is voted by Parliament a sum that is 0.00352 percent of the national budget.

orders they were. Besides traveling in "plain clothes," as we would say today, one was instructed to let his hair and beard grow. Both assumed false names. The two men were further instructed that in any correspondence with Rome, they were to use code: the Queen was "Don Teofilo," Nickel became "Amiano," and Macedo was "Apollonio."

A winter crossing of the Continent was not to be recommended but the mission was so important that speed overrode every other consideration. The two men traveled on horseback via Innsbruck and then to Hamburg. The weather turned bad and one of them fell from his horse, which kicked him. From Hamburg they made their way to Schleswig-Holstein and Copenhagen. They arrived in Stockholm on February 14, 1652.

They had a hidden letter for Christina, to prove who they were, but it seems that she figured out who they were despite their disguise. At a supper party one of her generals happened to remark to her that he had traveled back from Germany with two Italians who did not seem to be afraid of the appalling cold. That seemed particularly un-Italian and the Queen, alerted, conveyed that she would like to meet them.

After the initial meeting a further—secret—one was arranged and the final act in Christina's long-running abdication drama began. The Jesuits reported back to Rome that the Queen had admitted to them her dissatisfaction with Protestantism and that she had explored other religions—Judaism and Islam among others—in her quest for peace of mind. She had also admitted that one of the reasons she had invited so many foreign scholars to her court was to explore their *beliefs* as much as their scholarship or scientific conclusions. At one point the Queen asked if she might be a sort of part-time Catholic, taking Lutheran communion once a year, for the sake of appearances. She was told, firmly, that this was not possible.

By May (having arrived in February), the two Jesuits felt confident enough of the Queen's change of heart for one of them to leave Stockholm for Rome to report that she *would* convert. He took with him a letter from Christina to Nickel: she had already decided she wanted to live in Rome afterward.

In retrospect it is extraordinary to think that the Queen was taking secret instruction while on the surface everything seemed so frivolous. Diplomats from abroad, although they were anxious to see the court, were actually more worried about being posted there for the expense it would inevitably involve.

Amid this frivolity the Queen's own behavior grew more and more extraordinary. Her academy—the one for which Descartes had drawn up the rules—met every Wednesday and discussed "dangerous" ideas, such as whether there are demons. The Queen was believed to be searching for unconventional books, like Bodin's *Heptaplomeres,* which put Judaism in a more favorable light than Christianity. On top of everything, she swore regularly and appeared in a state of *déshabillé* in public. It also became clear about now that her taste for "the noble and nude" in painting, especially when done in the Rubens style, was, like Rudolf's, not simply a platonic concern. Rumors ran around Europe concerning Christina: one minute she was having an affair with Pimental, the next with Ebba Sparre. It was so bad that even her mother taxed her with her irreligiosity. A more paradoxical background to conversion can scarcely be imagined.

Still, in November 1652 the Queen learned that the Jesuit general in Rome had approved her conversion and, as the new year was ushered in, close observers would have noticed that from this time on Christina really did lose interest in her own country and in being a Queen. Maybe it was her anticipation of this that led to her libertine behavior.

However, she made no outward move in 1653; her promise to the Rad had to last for some while. She made secret preparations for departure, however. Among them, she had du Fresne's inventory, unsatisfactory as it was, marked up to indicate which items she wanted to take with her. These included *Wisdom and Strength* and the rest of her Veroneses plus tapestries, manuscripts, and books to the value of 500,000 livres. The valuables were packed into a hundred chests and loaded onto a ship, the *Fortuna,* in August 1653.

An inventory drawn up later in Antwerp shows more fully what she actually sent onto the *Fortuna.* She selected 19 bronze sculptures, 72 tapestries, about 50 geometrical, astronomical, mathematical, and other instruments, and 70–80 paintings, roughly 45 of which had come from Prague, almost exclusively Italian masterpieces. She also took a large number of books: 3,700 printed works and 2,150 manuscripts.

As 1653 turned into 1654 the wider public in Sweden may have had no inkling of Christina's intentions but those close to her began to sense that she had lost her will to govern, that she was set on conversion, and that she had been making plans to leave the country, taking with her some of her most treasured possessions. There was, therefore, no real resistance when she announced her decision publicly to the Rad in February. One or two tried: besides the constitutional crisis it threatened and the religious hatred such a move could generate, the psychological impact would be extraordinary. Christina's father, Gustavus Adolphus, had died fighting the Catholics, Sweden had grown rich and powerful as a result of the religious wars, yet Christina was going against everything and she was still not thirty. It was no use: the Riksdag was called for May 1.

The intervening months were taken up with financial discussions, discussions which were never really sorted out to Christina's satisfaction. She should have anticipated this: as the Duke of Windsor was to find out 280 years later, abdication does not endear a monarch to his or her people. By the time the abdication took place, on June 6, 1654, her financial problems had still not been settled.

On that day, according to one observer, she looked "beautiful like an angel" as she entered the great hall of Uppsala Castle in her coronation robes of purple velvet and wearing all the other state regalia. The sword, scepter, orb, and golden keys were ceremoniously laid down on as many cushions on a table beside the throne. Before laying aside her crown the Queen made a short speech in which she wished every happiness to Gustavus. No one wanted to take the crown from her, and more than one man refused. But finally it was done and she took off her robes. Then, divested of all the trappings of royalty, she curtsied to her cousin and retired.

Straightaway he walked in procession to Uppsala Cathedral and was crowned.

9.
South, to Rome

None of the journeys which *Wisdom and Strength* has made was as colorful as the one south to Rome. To begin with, the fact that the *Fortuna* set sail well before Christina announced her final intention to abdicate the second time raises the thought that she was worried she might be denied the objects which the ship contained. Because there was not in those days the same distinction as now between goods belonging to the state and those belonging to the monarch personally, presumably someone could have made trouble for her. Otherwise, why would the Queen have made the arrangements she did?

Among the paintings she took with her were twenty-five portraits, kept by the Queen as photographs would be kept today, mementos to remind her of her friends. The others included works by Bassano, Correggio's *Leda* and *Danaë*, three Palma Vecchios, including the *Sybil* now in Hampton Court, a Parmigianino Cupid, several Titians, including *Venus and Adonis* (now in the Galleria Nazionale d'Arte Antica, Rome), and several works today regarded as copies. She took at least a dozen Veroneses, including *Wisdom and Strength*, its Frick companion, *Vice and Virtue*, and the Metropolitan and Fitzwilliam pictures.

The *Fortuna*, after it left Stockholm with this precious cargo, encountered some very heavy weather before reaching Ostend. There the art collection was unloaded except for thirteen cases containing books, mathematical instruments, pictures, and certain curios which Trichet du Fresne, who had traveled aboard the *Fortuna* with them, considered his own in lieu of wages. Christina was now a confirmed classicist and the objets d'art of amber, ivory, coral, and mollusk, which were so typical of the princely *Kunst-* and *Wunderkammer* of the courts of northern Europe (as in Prague), no longer interested her. When du Fresne reached Le Havre, however, these objects were impounded: Christina, in the middle of all her other troubles during the abdication, nevertheless still found time to report these objects as stolen. Du Fresne protested his innocence, saying that however costly these items might seem to ordinary people, they no longer corresponded to the "exalted taste of their former owner." He was right and once more we glimpse Christina as a petty and ungracious person.

The Queen herself encountered as much adventure as her collection. At first she had intended to follow the same route as the paintings and go by sea. No fewer than thirty warships were drawn up at Uppsala for her departure, but at the last minute she dismissed them and decided to travel overland. That journey, too, added to her legend.

She left Stockholm on June 10, 1654, three hours after sundown, so as "to avoid seeing the people's sorrow and mourning at the loss of so great a queen." It is no exaggeration to say that the whole of contemporary Europe took an interest in her journey south to Rome. Everyone wanted to know what Christina would do, expecting fireworks. She did not disappoint them.

For the first few days she traveled quickly by the standards of the seventeenth century. She went first to Nyköping, where she met her mother for the last time. Then on the same night to Norrköping. From there the road took her south to Halmstad, where she dismissed her Lutheran preacher and several officials who had accompanied her from the capital. After that her retinue consisted of her doctor, four ladies-in-waiting, nine young gentlemen, and some forty servants. In Laholm, however, Christina decided on an even smaller entourage. She cut her hair short and dressed herself as man. She passed into Denmark, crossing from Hälsingborg to Elsinore in a small boat. Then it was on to Hamburg, which she reached on July 13, five days ahead of her retinue, carrying her own baggage. She was still dressed as a man.

Her stay in Hamburg was an eventful affair, the first of several on her way south. She was famous, not to say notorious, and many people wanted to see her. She received visits from civic leaders, the princes and princesses from all around, as well as from Swedish diplomats who included none other than General (now Field Marshal) Königsmark, who was then the Swedish governor of Bremen. The city of Hamburg provided the Queen with several barrels of beer, Rhenish wine, and some costly silver pieces as gifts.

Moreover, the stop in Hamburg was not accidental. It was the leading commercial center of the area (the second bank of northern Europe, after Amsterdam, had been established there). Abraham Diego Teixeira, a banker and one of the leading Portuguese Jews in Hamburg, was a friend to the Queen and was to play an important part in her negotiations with Sweden over funds. On this first visit they set up the infrastructure to enable her to support herself in exile.

On the Queen's last night in the city there was an extravagant banquet which went on very late. Afterward, the Queen moved on quietly in the small hours, a departure reminiscent of that from Stockholm. She was again dressed as a man and was now accompanied by only five other people. For this reason she managed to pass through all of Holland without being recognized and in doing so avoided many tokens of honor that the authorities had planned for her. She did, however, take the time to visit two scholars. The first was the renowned theologian, Johann Friedrich Gronovius, professor of history and oratory, who dedicated his edition of Seneca to Christina. She also visited the no less famous Anna Maria van Schurman, known as the "Minerva of the Netherlands," who was equally prolific as an author, painter, and engraver. The Queen had not yet caught up with *Wisdom and Strength* and her other treasures, which awaited her in the Spanish Netherlands (now Belgium).

The intelligence services of several governments were following the Queen's movements since so many rumors were running around Europe at that time. Besides the intriguing fact of her abdication, it was said that Philip of Spain had considered giving her the Netherlands to govern and that Cromwell was worried she might marry Charles II, then in exile in northern Germany; and the Netherlands press reported that she was going to marry an envoy of Philip's. None of it was true.

Christina was to remain in the Spanish Netherlands for more than a year and it was here that she was reunited with *Wisdom and Strength* and her other treasures. Several of her Italian masterpieces were unpacked because it seems that the Queen, now more than ever, had a need to be surrounded by beauty and splendor and by familiar things.

She led a very social life in the Low Countries. In a letter to Ebba Sparre in Stockholm, she wrote: "I occupy myself with eating well and sleeping well, studying a little, talking, laughing, and going to see French, Italian, and Spanish plays and spending the time in a pleasant manner. In short, I no longer listen to sermons, I despise all preachers; as Solomon says, all else is just stupidity, since everyone should live happily, eating, drinking, and singing." Hardly the words of a pious convert approaching her acceptance into the Catholic Church. She was still as paradoxical and perplexing as ever.

While she was in Antwerp, Christina stayed with her business representative, Don Garcia de Yllan. He, like Teixeira in Hamburg, was a wealthy Jewish banker from a Portuguese family. Christina's finances were already giving cause for concern—she was forced to send word home to John Holm-Leijoncrona, her business manager in Sweden, to send her services of gold and silver plate to the mint to be melted down. In Antwerp, too, she was forced to pawn a large part of her jewels for 46,000 ecus and never saw them again (46,000 ecus would now be roughly $7 million). Her 200,000-crown appanage existed only in theory: she rarely, if ever, received it in full.

Yllan lived on the Rue Longue Neuve, where his house may still be seen today. A painting of Antwerp at this time, by Erasmus de Bie, which is said to portray the Queen's coach in the middle, shows the city to be well built, with the familiar Low Countries' crenellated architecture, houses of three or four stories, much traffic, and plenty of well-dressed people. It was at that time one of the richest trading cities in northern Europe, even though the Peace of Westphalia had curbed some of its success by closing its harbor.

It was also, as it had been for some time, a center of the art trade. Oil painting was discovered in Flanders. In the late fifteenth century, Quentin Massys (Metsys) had opened the city's first great period and during the early sixteenth century no fewer than 694 artists were registered in the guild of painters. These included Pieter Bruegel, Jacob Grimmer, Mabuse, Lucas van Leyden (who met Dürer there in 1521), and Josse de Momper. Holbein and Erasmus had visited the city in the first years of the sixteenth century when the discoveries by Vasco da Gama of the sea route to India changed trading patterns permanently: the Portuguese brought spices direct to northern Europe as early as August 1501. Indeed, as the fortunes of Venice declined, those of Antwerp rose.

It was, however, the second "golden age" of Antwerp that Christina entered. This was mainly due to Peter Paul Rubens. He had been born in Westphalia in 1577 but he came of an Antwerp family and returned there by 1589. Rubens's glittering career rivaled Titian's and his travels exceeded even those of Dürer. Appointed court painter to Vicenzo Gonzaga, Duke of Mantua, he accompanied an embassy to Philip III in Madrid. Later he became court painter to the Spanish governor of the Netherlands, the Habsburg Archduke Albrecht and his bride, the infanta Isabella. He also continued to work for other monarchs such as Charles I of England and Philip IV of Spain.

Rubens was dead by the time of Christina's arrival in Antwerp. So too was Anthony Van Dyck, his chief assistant who also visited Italy (including Mantua where he was told the Gonzaga pictures were for sale). Like Rubens, Van Dyck had been very popular with European royalty, especially in England where he received a knighthood. The influence of these two masters lived on and their colleagues and followers, Frans Snyders and Jacob Jordaens, were active in Antwerp. Snyders had studied under Pieter Bruegel the Younger (Hell Bruegel) and he, Paul de Vos, and Jan Fyt specialized in majestic paintings of animals. Snyders, with his wife, was painted by Van Dyck: this pair of pictures, which shows the couple as rather prim and bourgeois, is now in the Frick Collection; they hang in the same room as *Wisdom and Strength.*

David Beck was also in Antwerp but the artist who most suited Christina's taste was Jacob Jordaens. Jordaens was strongly influenced by Rubens. He was popular with the King of Spain, who had chosen him over Van Dyck to complete various commissions. He also painted several pictures for the King of Sweden, including some large ceiling compositions for the castle in Uppsala, so he would certainly have been known to Christina by reputation. He would also have been of interest to the Queen because he was making a religious journey that was the opposite of hers. Having renounced the Catholic faith, he had become an orangist (Protestant).

Christina displayed her paintings while she was in Antwerp and they became a major attraction, almost as much as she was herself. *Wisdom and Strength* and the other Veroneses were among the pictures unpacked. Insofar as Veronese was a forerunner of Rubens, whose color and allegorical subject matter emulated the Venetians, there would have been a close interest in his painting.

The Queen also had her portrait painted in Antwerp. She was portrayed twice by Justus van Egmont, a pupil of Rubens. Christina is shown as Diana and as Minerva, dressed in armor, surrounded by swags of cloth, and with long ringlets. Several other likenesses were painted and it seems she used them as gifts of thanks to those who had shown her hospitality.

The Queen's next stop after Antwerp was Brussels which she reached on December 23, 1654. The archduke at the time was Leopold William, and he went to meet her at Wilbrach, where they dined in state. They entered the city together on a golden barge as the centerpiece in a quite fantastic reception. All of Brussels was illuminated for the entrance and more than 460 pounds of gunpowder, 500 firecrackers, and 2,000 boxes of other fireworks were used.

For the first seven weeks of her stay, Christina was the guest of Leopold William. The archduke, brother to the Emperor, a cousin of Rudolf's, was a bishop, commander in chief of the army, and at that time was serving as governor of the Spanish Netherlands. He was also a great connoisseur of art. Christina had not seen the archduke before but she did know what he looked like: a portrait of him by Frans Luyckx had hung in the castle at Prague and was part of the booty looted by Königsmark. Her visit also took place five years after the great Commonwealth sale in England where Leopold William had been one of the main buyers. Some idea of his fabulous collection may be had from David Teniers the Younger's painting of the archduke in his gallery. Teniers had worked in Antwerp until 1651 when he moved to Brussels and became court painter to Leopold William and keeper of his pictures. His output was prodigious. More than two thousand works are attributed to him, many of them scenes of peasant life and curiosities, such as witches' Sabbaths or apes and cats dressed as people. Teniers was a great copyist too and 244 of his copies were engraved in a book that was given to the Queen as a gift. She gave him a gold medal in return.

But he also specialized in painting the interior of picture galleries in which many of the masterpieces are recognizable. In the Teniers picture of Leopold William's gallery, the paintings are shown crowded in on one another, stretching from floor to ceiling, as was the style of the time. Many of the paintings are recognizable, including works by Giorgione, Titian, Dosso Dossi, Tintoretto, and Veronese's *Adoration of the Magi* and *Christ Healing the Woman.*

In all, Leopold William acquired 1,300 paintings, 542 sculptures, and 343 drawings. The shape of his collection reflected the taste of a Habsburg brought up in the spirit of the Counter-Reformation. Like Rudolf, he had spent his youth at the Spanish court and had come to enjoy and revere the great Venetians. He bought comparatively few works by Rubens but owned a couple of Van Dycks. As a Catholic he acquired almost nothing by Rembrandt or the other geniuses of Protestant Holland who were working only a few miles away. The archduke returned to Vienna in 1656 and, on his death, bequeathed his collections to the Emperor, Leopold I. With the additions made by successive Emperors, those collections eventually formed the bulk of the Kunsthistorisches Museum in Vienna. Nearly all of them may be found there today, including a copy of *Wisdom and Strength.*

Within twenty-four hours of her arrival in Brussels, on Christmas Eve 1654, Christina was received into the Catholic faith. The ceremony was carried out in secret, as a public conversion was planned for later. The witnesses who heard her abjure Lutheranism were Leopold William, Pimental, and the two highest-ranking Spanish officials in Belgium. The act took place shortly before midnight mass and was carried out by the Dominican, Fra Guemes, who had been with Pimental in Sweden and who subsequently accompanied the Queen on part of her journey farther south. The conversion was accompanied by a full salute from the city, although neither the authorities nor the general public were told why the guns were going off.

Christina stayed in Brussels for several months, until the following September. After her seven weeks as the guest of the archduke she moved to the Palais d'Egmont, enjoying herself and seeing the sights. One of the people she visited was the Jesuit scholar, Jean de Bolland, who, with the institute named after him, was compiling a vast anthology of legends of the saints, the *Acta Sanctorum.* Having begun the *Acta* with the saints whose feast days were celebrated on January 1, by the time of

Christina's visit, the Bollandists had reached only as far as February 1.*
Christina was not merely a tourist, however, for she was able to make
available to the Bollandists a number of medieval manuscripts which she
had collected and brought with her from Stockholm. The Jesuits found
these documents so remarkable that publication of the *Acta Sanctorum* was
suspended for a time to permit incorporation of the new material.

It was in Brussels, however, that the Queen was to find that in abdicating she may have left her irksome responsibilities behind but not politics.
The question of adequate funds still hung over her and to that were now
added other political developments that threatened to complicate her
financial situation still more. One factor was the evident intention of her
cousin Charles Gustavus to attack Poland. This was dangerously near
Pomerania which at the time belonged to Christina, at least in theory,
and was a potential source of revenue. Another factor was the election of
Cardinal Chigi as Pope Alexander VII. Since the Thirty Years' War, the
Vatican had been divided, much as the rest of Europe was divided in
those days, into Spanish factions and French factions. Chigi inclined more
to the Spanish side than the French, just as Christina was being aided in
her conversion by the Spanish and the Portuguese. This meant that it
would be better for her if she arrived in Rome while Chigi was there as
pontiff.

On September 22, therefore, she quit the Belgian capital. Her financial
affairs were still precarious and the day before she had signed an IOU in
favor of Don Garcia de Yllan for 136,437 riksdalers ($21,800,000 at
1987 prices), more than half of which (88,000) were to pay for her
journey, including the onward passage of her works of art. The rest was
to be held in reserve for further expenses.

Having arrived in the Low Countries with a very modest retinue,
Christina now moved on in a quite different style (which accounts for the
fantastic cost of the remaining leg of the journey). She was accompanied
by nearly 250 people and as many horses. At least half the retinue traveled at her expense, yet only two people, Lilliecrona and Appelgren her
page, remained of those who had accompanied her from Sweden, a striking statistic which reminds us of how solitary the Queen's position was.
She also had Fra Guemes, who had received her into the Catholic
Church, who was disguised as her chaplain. David Beck had rejoined
her, once again as court painter. She had left her paintings and other
treasures behind; they would catch up with her in Rome. But Beck's
presence in her party nicely shows where this hard-up Queen placed her
priorities.

* The complete work was not finished until 1794.

The much larger entourage traveled far more slowly compared with the earlier rapid crossing of Denmark and Holland more than a year before. It took Christina nine days, for example, to get from Cologne to Frankfurt, a distance of some 150 miles. In Frankfurt she met Charles II, where nothing came of the rumors that once sought to join these two. From there the retinue traveled south, to Augsburg. At the end of October, she reached Innsbruck.

Christina's hosts during her week there were the governor of the Tirol, Archduke Ferdinand Charles, his wife, Anne Medici, and his brother, Cardinal Sigismund Francis. The two princes were cousins to Emperor Ferdinand III and to the governor of Belgium, Leopold William. Ferdinand Charles received Christina with apprehension, as the Queen's massive retinue called for extensive preparations. The roads were repaired, quarters had to be arranged for everybody, and silver was borrowed from nearby courts for the inevitable banquets.

Wherever she went the Queen enjoyed inspecting art and antiquities, but the main business at Innsbruck was her public conversion which took place in the Hofkirche, on November 3, 1655. Christina was dressed simply for the occasion, in a black silk dress and a diamond cross. Her conversion was received by Fra Malines, whom she knew, and Lucas Holstenius, a clever, considerate choice by the Pope for Holstenius was himself a northern convert, famous for his learning and at that time librarian of the Vatican. He was a man with whom the Queen must immediately have felt at ease; and indeed she and he became lifelong friends.

Christina, now twenty-nine, confessed her faith in a "clear, distinct and loud voice"; she was absolved and blessed and so received publicly into the Church. A mass and a Te Deum followed, accompanied by a salute of cannon and musketry. She wrote to the Pope immediately, humbly asking for his protection, and to Charles Gustavus. Lilliecrona probably summed up what a good many ordinary Swedes must have felt when he wrote home professing his surprise and relating how he had asked to be dismissed from the Queen's service. (She persuaded him to stay, however, at least until Rome.) Five days after the conversion, on November 8, the Queen signed four printed copies of the Profession of the Tridentine Faith: one for herself, and one each for the Pope, the Vatican Library, and the Innsbruck Archive.

And then it was off again, on the final stage of her momentous journey. She crossed the Alps, possibly taking the same road as *Wisdom and Strength* had done in the opposite direction some eighty years before. Then she traveled to Trent and on via Venetian territory to Mantua, now denuded of its magnificent pictures, some of which she had seen in Brussels at Leopold William's court. She was honored and feted wherever she stopped but the real welcome was reserved for the moment she entered the papal states.

It was an extraordinary occasion. Traveling in winter, the weather was very bad. It had poured with rain throughout the crossing of the Alps and when the Pope's representatives met her, they were standing *up to their knees* in mud. Graciously, the Queen stepped down from her carriage and stood with them in the mire. From then on she traveled in one of His Holiness's own carriages, specially sent out from Rome for her use. She was also provided with two beds, two canopies, a complete table service in silver gilt plate, and a chef. She herself did not appear as elegant as all this sounds. Even when she entered Ferrara, she was still dressed as a man.

The conversation on her first night—made against a background of the Pope's chef's sumptuous food, which included marzipan gilded with real gold leaf—revolved around Pietro da Cortona and Bernini. There was also mention of an opera dedicated to the Queen, which was to be performed on her arrival in the Holy City. Christina was at last part of the warm, the cultured, the sophisticated south she so desired.

From Ferrara she traveled to Bologna, Imola, Faenza; then Pesaro and Senigallia where she met the Santinellis, a troupe of acrobats, comedians, and jugglers whom she invited to join her party. The weather continued bad as she crossed the Apennines to Foligno, from where she visited Assisi. It was raining when she was met by Paolo Giordano Orsini, the same Duke of Bracciano with whom she had corresponded and in whom she had confided her admiration for Raphael. It had been arranged for her to spend that night, the last of her journey, as the duke's guest at Bracciano Castle, overlooking the lake. The duke and duchess, out of consideration for her, displayed all their art treasures and arranged a concert. It was a Sunday, December 19, almost a year since she had been secretly converted and her last night on the long and emotional road to Rome. She was at last content.

Next day, a few miles out from Rome at the Villa Olgisata, the four nuncios who had accompanied Christina since she had entered the papal states, were replaced by two cardinal legates, who came out from the city to meet her. The facade of the villa was decorated according to the fashion of the time, with allegorical figures painted in trompe l'oeil, not unlike Veronese's own allegories at the Villa Maser almost exactly one hundred years before. The cardinals were accompanied by soldiers, trumpeters, and drummers and, after a ceremony of greeting, the swollen party set out on the final leg.

That day the Queen's arrival was purely informal and so, as she reached Rome after dark, it was arranged for her to enter the Vatican via a shortcut through the gardens. Christina was dressed in a gray smock with her usual black shawl around her shoulders. She was led up through the Vatican's back staircase, torchlit and lined with pictures. The corridors, as it happened, were also lined with scores of people interested in catching an early glimpse of the celebrated convert. There were so many people that the Queen was moved to remark: "Is this the usual way of entering Rome incognito?"

The Pope, Alexander VII, was a small, delicate man of fifty-six who, like the Queen, preferred the company of poets and scholars to any other. Unlike the Queen, however, he was a skilled diplomatist. He was also a circumspect man and on this occasion granted Christina a private audience of just fifteen minutes. According to contemporary accounts, the Italian Pope was struck by Christina's vivacity, the constantly changing expression on her face, and the beauty of her eyes. The Italian fashion was for more expressionless faces among women.

Artistic concerns cropped up in a most unusual way at that first encounter between Pope and Queen. After her abdication, Christina continually posed problems of etiquette and protocol, in the Vatican as elsewhere. There simply was not much precedent for a grand Queen who no longer ruled. In this instance, Vatican protocol dictated that only *ruling* monarchs were allowed to sit in a chair with arms in the presence of a Pope. Alexander got around this by having the great Bernini himself design a special seat for the Queen. It was appropriately magnificent but the important thing about it was that the back was low and the arms rounded. Therefore, so far as the Vatican bureaucrats were concerned, it was a *stool.* Protocol was not disturbed and the encounter took place without a hitch.

But if the Queen was ever so slightly demeaned by her first audience with Alexander, the Pope conferred honor on her in another way. For the first time in the Vatican's recent history a woman was to be lodged for a few days *inside* the walls (officially, that is). The apartment was not actually in the palace itself but located in the Torre dei Venti, up the hill at the top of the gardens. But it was known as the tower of winds for good reason and, since it was the dead of winter when Christina arrived, she was welcomed with braziers burning and even with a silver bed warmer. A motto in the tower to the effect that "all evil comes from the North" was hurriedly erased.

In her first few days in Rome the Queen went sight-seeing. This was made all the easier by another honor bestowed by the Pope—the provision of a carriage, litter, and sedan chair. The sedan had been designed by Bernini and the carriage was to become one of her most cherished possessions. She still had it at the time of her death more than twenty years later.

Three days after her "incognito" arrival, Christina made her official entry into Rome. This time she was met just inside the gate by the entire college of cardinals, each man mounted on a mule. Cardinal Francesco Barberini, the senior cardinal, read the welcome and as she listened, Christina was able to survey not just the college but all the Roman nobles dressed in their finery. Most notable of all was Prince Pamphili who, although still in mourning for his uncle Innocent X, was dressed in black velvet decorated in diamonds valued at 100,000 scudi.

Christina could not have matched these niceties: after all, half her own jewels had been pawned in the North. She appeared that day dressed in a simple gray dress with a black scarf and a plume in her hat. She wore no jewelry save a single gold ring.

Thus, surrounded by cardinals, Christina moved on through the gate, which had been decorated by Bernini, and made her way to St. Peter's. Arriving at the basilica, Christina dismounted and knelt on a golden cushion to kiss the cross. Inside the church the Pope had the entire area lined with the marvelous tapestries which belonged to his family, showing that he had been alerted to the Queen's tastes. In addition, over the central door there was a painted allegory of a royal crown and the Vasa sheaf of corn adrift in a stormy sea.

The climax, however, at least so far as Christina was concerned, came two days later, on Christmas Day itself. She received the sacraments of confirmation from no less a person than the Pope himself. She took Alexandra as her second name now, in honor of her "father." Her wandering was finally over.

On St. Stephen's Day, the day after Christmas, the Queen had to vacate her apartments in the Vatican and set up in the first of her residences in Rome: the Palazzo Farnese. But before she could do so His Holiness accorded her another singular honor: he invited her to dine. According to Vatican protocol, no woman may eat in the presence of a Pope and this was a rule that had been broken only twice in the hundred years preceding Christina's dinner with Alexander, in each case on the occasion of a royal or imperial wedding. The dinner itself was a work of art. Protocol was, as ever, a problem. The Queen and Alexander had to sit at different tables, with the Pope's raised a few inches higher than Christina's. The dishes placed in front of them were fantastic: aspics, jellies, and blancmanges, gilded and molded into wonderful shapes. Bernini's assistants had designed sugar sculptures, allegorical statues which represented abundance, with the Vasa sheaf worked into them and, as a reference to Christina's learning, Minerva was shown surrounded by the liberal arts.

There was music and a sermon and then, the dinner over, the Queen was accompanied by a cavalcade of ambassadors, nobles, and others to the Palazzo Farnese, which was the most sumptuous Renaissance palace in the city. In the piazza outside the palazzo that night there were bonfires and torches of welcome and the entire frontage was covered with paintings of Old Testament virtues and classical allegories.

The palazzo had been placed at the Queen's disposal by the Duke of Parma, who was not entirely disinterested in making it available to her. He had hopes that Christina would help him in his ambitions to have certain restrictions on Parma lifted by the Pope. But Christina was not bothered by that on such a night. A Renaissance villa in her beloved Rome, works of art to her taste all around her, an attentive, intelligent, and highly cultured Pope. Her journeys had taken her as far from Sweden as she would ever be. Yet she was home.

10.
Christina in Baroque Rome

The Rome which Christina found was very different from Stockholm. It was not just the capital of a small country; it was in some senses the capital of the world. Vienna, Madrid, and London were, for all their power, on the periphery of Europe. Venice had had her day and Paris's was yet to come. In one important respect, however, Rome had something in common with Venice. Like her northern Italian sister, she did not yet perceive that her glory was waning, her artistic preeminence especially. Throughout Christina's time in Rome that decline continued.

In 1655, however, it was not yet apparent; the glory that was Rome was there for everyone to see and for the Queen to take part in. One factor was that Rome had escaped the ravages of the Thirty Years' War. But the main reason for Rome's shining brilliance was a rare mix: a decisive shift in the religiopolitical mood, a superb artist (Bernini) available to interpret that shift, and an enlightened, energetic, and rich Pope (Urban VIII), who had acted as a patron and encouraged the artist to the best of his abilities.

The shift in mood was of course the Counter-Reformation. This had crystallized since Veronese's day. The more the Protestants of the North stressed the puritan aspects of religion, the more the Catholic Church responded by emphasizing the mystical. In art this produced the movement known as Baroque, which should be regarded not simply as an attempt to record, or report, the mystical experiences of biblical or Christian figures, but also as an attempt to *create* mystical experiences in the spectator, in the worshippers of the day. Baroque art concerned itself overwhelmingly with religious ecstasy, the cults of images, the experience of the Immaculate Conception on the positive side, and with the images of purgatory (which Protestants denied existed), penance, and death on the other. It was a time when relics were again venerated, when images of the Virgin were believed to possess mystical properties, when indulgences were widely bought and sold.

This is also why the Baroque, as an art form, consisted more than most artistic movements of architecture, sculpture, *and* painting. Churches built at the time, in Rome especially, were an attempt to *overwhelm* anyone who entered them. The scale, the ornateness, the sheer virtuosity of the work was designed to make people wonder and marvel at the creative powers of religion, as if God himself were interceding, via the artist, who became—almost—a recruiting agent for the faith.

The very fact that the dominant artist of the Baroque was a sculptor and not a painter highlighted this. Sculptors of the Baroque did things with stone that could normally only be done in paint. That fact reflected their brilliance, as agents of God, and contributed to the mystical experiences in churches. Whereas Veronese and the other Venetian painters of his day had celebrated the glories of the state, the artists of Baroque Rome did the same for God, although this did, of course, reinforce the position of the Pope.

The dominant artistic figure of the Baroque was Gianlorenzo Bernini. This man, who was to become a good friend of Christina's, had been born in Naples in 1598 and was the son of a sculptor. Bernini was twenty-five when Maffeo Barberini was elected Pope as Urban VIII. Giovanni Battista (Giambattista) Passeri, a contemporary writer about art, put it this way: "When Urban VIII became pope it really seemed as if the golden age of painting had returned . . . his nephews all protected the fine arts." Barberini was to become a great—a magnificent—patron. Perhaps he was one of the greatest of all Popes from this point of view. But his election did not take place in a vacuum: his immediate predecessors had completed St. Peter's and had also set a fashion for building huge family palaces in Rome, a villa in the countryside, and a luxurious family chapel in one of the great Roman churches. By the time Urban VIII was elected, this was something all the great families aspired to do. At the same time, many religious orders had been created as a result of the Counter-Reformation and they too were eager to build churches in the city, churches that had to be designed and decorated. This was a fertile period for building, like Venice when Veronese first arrived there, and a period of wide patronage both within the Church and without.

Since Veronese's day, the status of the artist had changed again. As a result of the revised notions of the religious experience stemming from the Counter-Reformation, artists were no longer seen as persons who could help unlock the mysteries of the universe. Rather, they were merely mortals who could *add* to God's work by their virtuosity. And that was all. Not until the eighteenth century would the cult of the genius be revived. Together with this decline in the status of the artist, there were also many foreign artists in the Holy City who also had an impact on attitudes. For the first time in seventeenth-century Rome we read of a group of what we would today call bohemian painters, artists who lived as groups, producing art not to commission but on a prospective basis.

Along with all that, it was increasingly accepted that such a thing as the "artistic temperament" existed, that a degree of eccentricity may be necessary and desirable in an artist. This was shown in two ways at least. One was the recognition, very different from the perceptions of Veronese's Venice, that artists were born, not made, that art was not necessarily learned in a workshop. Workshops in seventeenth-century Rome became instead identified with craftsmen, not artists. The other was the greater tolerance shown for artists with "difficult" personalities, people like Caravaggio, Guido Reni, and particularly Salvator Rosa, with whom Christina certainly came into contact.

To understand the Baroque fully, and Barberini's Papacy in particular, one other fact needs to be taken into account. The Counter-Reformation, successful as it was in keeping Protestantism at bay, also faced a more subtle and perhaps more insidious opponent: science. After Galileo, science was beginning to make its mark. It did not matter that some of the science consisted mostly of those by-now familiar standbys, astrology and alchemy. The important point was that they were all alternative explanations to religion. The effect this had was to make orthodox Catholicism assert itself even more strongly, in as optimistic and confident a way as possible. This gave the Baroque its exuberant gloss.

By the time of Christina's arrival, Rome was more Bernini's creation than anyone else's. His first commission, for the magnificent baldachino of twisted columns above the tomb of St. Peter, had come less than a year after Barberini's election. It was a great success and from then on Bernini never looked back, at least not while Urban was Pope. Architectural achievements followed those of sculpture. Rightly has it been said that it is impossible to see Bernini properly outside Rome and few people have left such an impression on one city.

If Bernini was the greatest sculptor of the Baroque, his equivalent (if not quite his equal) in painting was Pietro (Berrettini) da Cortona. Cortona was a Tuscan but he spent much of his life in Rome, where he too benefited from the reign of Urban VIII. Born in 1598 he would have been fifty-seven when Christina arrived. He would have a number of dealings with her. (She had corresponded about Cortona with Orsini even before she left Sweden.) Cortona was known for his docile character. He liked his patrons to choose for themselves the themes they wanted painted. His greatest work was a ceiling for the Barberini Palace, now in the Galleria Nazionale in Rome, which is a complicated allegory, representing Divine Providence and Barberini power. The central part of the picture, which is a huge illusion, is open to the sky with the figures all seen from below in dramatic perspective. The identification of the roof of a church or building with heaven was obvious enough and certainly not new: Veronese had done it at the Villa Maser. But what was new in the Baroque age were two new themes making use of heaven.

These were the Assumption of the Virgin into heaven and the apotheosis
of saints in heaven. The main reason for these developments was the
Counter-Reformation, which reasserted the Church's traditional doctrine, denied by Protestants, that the Virgin and the saints could inter-
cede with God and therefore could be invoked by the faithful on their
behalf. Veronese, among others, had painted a good number of Assumptions of the Virgin, but the many heaven/sky images in Baroque art
highlight the intercession implied by this. The saints pictured were the
founders of religious orders and it was thus appropriate for them to be
seen as having a direct line to the Lord. It was, to put it plainly, good for
business.

Urban VIII died in 1644. He was followed by Innocent X (Giovanni
Battista Pamphili, r. 1644–1655). Under Innocent, the entire Barberini
clan was forced to flee Rome because an investigation of their finances
revealed the extent of their excesses. Many artists patronized by Urban
VIII fell from favor and received no papal commissions for several years.

Urban's profligacy with the papal funds, though bad for Italy overall,
was good for the arts and artists. The Pamphili parsimony may have been
better for the country but it did not endear Innocent to the artistic community and there were many arguments. The change in patronage was
apparent immediately. In 1645, for instance, barely a year after Innocent
had been elected, Poussin, who was then living in Rome, wrote to his
patron in Paris: "Things in Rome have greatly changed under the present papacy and we [artists] no longer enjoy any special favor at court."

Not until Innocent's death, when Fabio Chigi was elected Pope, as
Alexander VII, did things change again. Alexander was a direct descendant of the very rich Agostino Chigi *(Il magnifico)*, who had been an
intimate of Raphael and had written his biography. The new Pope had
always preferred the company of intellectuals, poets, and artists and right
from the moment of his election he set about resuming the plans of
Urban and eradicating, if not the memory, then the style of Innocent. On
the very day of his election, Alexander summoned Bernini and told him
what he wanted done with St. Peter's. The master was reinstated fully as
a virtual dictator of the arts. In this sense, it was a perfect moment for the
Queen of Sweden to arrive.

Christina's time in Rome falls into two parts. From the time of her arrival,
in 1655, she at first went on a number of travels that were linked with
her political ambitions. It was not until these adventures were over that
she decided to bring *Wisdom and Strength* and the rest of her collection to
Italy from Brussels, where it was still in storage, and to settle down
properly to enjoy the south she said she adored so much.

It may sound surprising that Christina should have any political ambitions at all. Yet however much the Queen may have *said* that she wanted to give up the trappings of state in favor of a private life, which would enable her to enjoy the arts to the full, the fact remains that by the time she got to Rome, she had discovered what countless others, grand or not, have also discovered in their lives: that resignation brings with it symptoms of withdrawal. Put quite simply, she missed power. On top of everything, her finances were still a problem and she soon realized that one way to solve that would be to acquire another country.

And so, during her first period in Rome, Christina traveled a lot, trying to secure for herself two *new* crowns, first that of Naples, then a Spanish dominion, and second that of Poland.

It was only after Christina's attempts to capture a new crown for herself had failed that she felt free to follow the only course available—the enjoyment of culture. There is surely something more than a little pathetic about a Queen who had spent so much time and energy in abdicating, and going on so much about wanting to be free, then finding that she wanted to be a reigning Queen after all. As soon as she set foot in Rome, the full enormity of what she had done came home to her.

Christina's first home in Rome, the Palazzo Farnese, was exceedingly handsome, exactly the sort of place she must have dreamed of when she was still ensconced in the cold North. The building was begun by Antonio da Sangallo the Younger, for Cardinal Alessandro Farnese, later to become Pope Paul III. Work was continued by Michelangelo and completed by Giacomo della Porta. At the time that Christina occupied it, the palazzo still contained the famous Farnese collection of sculptures, cameos, and engraved gems. In addition to all this, tapestries and pictures were sent from Parma to help the Queen enjoy her stay. Parts of the palace that had fallen into disrepair while not in use were covered up by canvas painted in clever trompe l'oeil. Some of the rooms overlooked the Tiber, where there was a garden terrace. Christina enjoyed one of the greatest settings in all Rome.

Christina's household was now run by the marchese Giandemaria, major domo for the Duke of Parma. His dispatches home provide an interesting account of the Queen's behavior at this time. He says, for instance, that she changed bedrooms almost every night. He was also surprised by the fact that Christina would wander from room to room solely in the company of men. This was always likely to lead to rumor and in time it did. But Giandemaria also wrote that the Queen never forgot who she was and there was never any sign of liberty. He noticed too that Christina was different in her relations with cardinals. Whereas with others, diplomats and nobles, she would invariably stand on her dignity as a Queen, with the cardinals she was much more likely to be on intimate, informal terms. This was especially true of the relatively young group of cardinals who made up the so-called *squadrone volante,* or "flying squadron," which had helped to ensure the election of the new Pope, Alexander VII. Among this group one man was especially sought out by the still-young Queen. He was Cardinal Decio Azzolino.

Azzolino came from a Fermo family, lesser nobles but still distinguished: they had already produced two cardinals. According to some reports he was very handsome and had early on shown a gift for diplomacy and administration so that, by early 1656, he was very much a personality in Rome. Moreover, at thirty-three he was very close in age to Christina. Bernini was to sculpt Azzolino in the years to come and in that bust the feature which stands out is his mouth, which shows wit and charm. It may have been this, rather than his overall looks, which made him attractive to women.

Azzolino was very flattered to be singled out by the Queen whose arrival in Rome had created such a sensation. Christina was also a political asset to the flying squadron in which Azzolino was a dominant influence. More than this, however, they shared many genuine interests. As an intellectual elite, the members of the flying squadron had an interest in art, literature, and learning, and Azzolino was also well informed about such things as engineering. (He was one of those who wanted to make the Tiber navigable.)

There can be no doubt about how well the two got on. Indeed, Rome began to buzz with rumors, so much that Azzolino found it necessary to write to the Pope's confidant saying that his relationship with Christina was entirely innocent.

Christina lost no time in entering the intellectual and artistic milieu of Rome. Early on she founded an academy similar to the one with rules drawn up by Descartes which she had initiated in Stockholm. This met every week to discuss such questions as whether day or night was more suitable for composing poetry (night won) or whether a woman's apparent indifference to a man, even her cruelty, was often a sign that she really was in love with him. As well as the academy, the Queen soon had her own carnival. The high point of the festivities was an opera dedicated to her. It was called *The Triumph of Piety* and the libretto, together with the music, was especially composed for the occasion by Monsignor Giulio Rospigliosi—a future Pope. It was the custom in those days for separate performances of operas to be mounted if women were to be present but in Christina's case she was given a special box with its own entrance so that she could watch the version for men without being seen.

Other allowances were made so that the young convert could enjoy herself. A number of papal decrees were issued which enabled the Queen to visit certain sites that otherwise would have been barred to her. She was allowed to visit any monastery or convent in Rome; and she was allowed to see the relics of St. Peter.

Of course, the other leading lights of Rome all arranged entertainments in her honor. It was at one of these—a performance of Corneille's *Heraclitus* at the house of the French ambassador—that Christina's political ambitions in Rome first became clear. Until then the Queen had been identified with the Spanish Habsburgs and against the French in the political divide which dominated Europe after the Thirty Years' War. It was Pimental, after all, who had masterminded her conversion and she had traveled south through (and actually converted in) the Spanish Netherlands. Her public conversion had taken place at Innsbruck, another Habsburg-ruled territory. The ongoing hostilities between Spain and France were mirrored in Rome: the Spanish and French factions invariably had different candidates in any papal election. In Rome the Spanish had a right, or *thought* they had a right, to expect Christina to promote their interests. They were mistaken, for the Queen now began to align herself with the French and her visit to the Corneille play was the first hint.

That the Queen should have wanted to see a French play at all was a disappointment for the Spanish faction in Rome. But the fact that she was prepared to go to the French ambassador's residence, rather than have the play performed in her own palace, was seen as a double blow. Matters were made even worse by the hat business.

Seventeenth-century Rome was incredibly protocol conscious and one of the most important diplomatic issues of the day was whether an ambassador could wear his hat in the presence of a reigning monarch. Christina complicated matters, of course, because she was not a reigning Queen. She had always insisted that the Duke of Terrenova, the Spanish ambassador in Rome, take off his hat in her presence. But now she allowed Hugues de Lionne, only a chargé d'affaires so far as the Vatican was concerned, to keep his on! The Queen was humiliating the Spanish in the most ridiculous way.

This breach with the Spanish appears to have been Christina's doing. It was, in fact, related to her long-term plans. At this time Christina's financial situation was once again precarious (the money from Yllan had run out) and she had dispatched someone to Sweden to try to improve matters. She was not, however, hopeful and this is where her realignment with France came in. What she had in mind, quite simply, was to secure the backing of the French for an incursion—led by herself, the daughter of Gustavus Adolphus—into Naples.

The kingdom of Naples was ruled by the Spanish but there was a strong rebel movement, some members of which contacted Christina. If she could pull it off and become Queen of Naples, she could solve her financial problems once and for all *and* satisfy her reawakened craving for power and influence. It gives us a revealing glimpse into this extraordinary woman's mind to know that she, who gave up one crown in 1654, should want another in 1656.

The plan turned into a deadly fiasco. She visited France twice to discuss an invasion of Naples with Cardinal Mazarin. All went well initially and it was while Christina was in France on the first of her visits that the duc de Guise, the King's representative who met her at Lyon, wrote his celebrated description of Christina. His letter, which was later read aloud to Louis, runs as follows: "At a time when I am dreadfully bored I would at least like to amuse you by sending you a portrait of the queen I am accompanying. She isn't tall but has a well-filled figure and a large behind, beautiful arms, white hands, but more like those of a man than a woman; one shoulder is higher than the other, but she hides this defect so well by her bizarre dress, walk and movements, that you could lay bets as to whether it exists or not. Her face is large, but not to a fault, also her features are marked: the nose aquiline, the mouth big but not disagreeably so, teeth passable, her eyes really beautiful and full of fire; in spite of some marks left by chicken pox her complexion is clear and quite good; the shape of her face is fair but framed by the most extraordinary coiffure. It's a man's wig, very heavy and piled high in front and at the back there is some slight resemblance to a woman's coiffure. Sometimes she wears a hat. Her bodice, laced up cross-wise at the back, is made practically like our *pourpoints,* her chemise shows all round between it and her skirt, which she wears badly fastened and not very straight. She is always very heavily powdered over a lot of face cream, and practically never wears gloves. She wears men's shoes and her voice and nearly all her actions are masculine. She loves to show off her mastery of horses and she glories in it and is quite as proud of it as her father the [great?] Gustavus might have been. She is very civil and full of flattery, speaks eight languages, but mostly French and that as if she had been born in Paris. She knows more than all our Academy and the Sorbonne put together, understands painting as well as anyone and knows much more about court intrigues than I do. In fact she is an absolutely extraordinary person."

Mazarin was keen on her Naples idea at first but soon cooled to it. And he dropped it completely after Christina, in an extraordinary act of brutish callousness, had one of her advisers (whom she believed to be a spy for the Spanish in Naples) hacked to death in the apartments which had been made available to her as a guest of the French government. It was hardly an advertisement for her judgment. She went so far as to have uniforms designed for her guards—violet, trimmed with crimson and white—but they were never needed. She never got the French backing she sought.

Her next plan, to gain the crown of Poland, did not fare any better. The throne had become vacant because of another abdication: that of King John II Casimir, the last male of the Vasa line. The King of France had two candidates, the Emperor had two, and the Pope had two. None of them appealed overly much to the Poles and in fact Christina's case rested primarily on the fact that she was a Vasa. The decision to try for the Polish crown was very revealing. Already she had changed her mind over being a Queen. Now it turned out that Christina's love of the warm south was not that rock-solid either: Poland scarcely qualified as a warm southern country.

Her candidacy might have looked good on paper. But in practice she never stood a chance. When the Pope's nuncio put forward her name to the electors, he was told never to let her name pass his lips again "for fear of general derision."

And so it was back to Rome where, once she had narrowed her horizons, everything was perfect. In June 1667 Giulio Rospigliosi had acceded to the Papacy as Clement IX. He was universally acknowledged as a good man and was a close friend of both Christina and Azzolino, who was now appointed Secretary of State. The Queen was now as close as she could be to power. More, Rospigliosi shared Christina's love of pictures, music, and theater. He even paid her the honor of visiting her and awarding her a pension.

It was now 1669. Her abortive political adventures had taken more than a decade of her life. The Queen was forty-three but looked a great deal older, partly because she had developed a double chin and partly because she had the unbecoming habit of combing her hair straight back and with a center part. From now on she would never leave Rome and instead started to take a more positive role in the cultural and intellectual life of the city. She was never fabulously rich, as some Queens have been, but, with the Pope's pension and the more stable circumstances in Sweden, her finances were at last coming under some sort of control and she was able to indulge her interests.

By now she had also found a permanent home. This was Azzolino's doing. He found her the Palazzo Riario, and it was to be her residence for the rest of her life. Now called the Palazzo Corsini, it was located in the Lungaro, near Trastevere, almost opposite the Farnesina. It was here that *Wisdom and Strength* and the other Veroneses were to be exhibited in one of the finest displays of Venetian painting ever assembled. The palace dated from the fifteenth century and was one of the earliest examples of the Renaissance suburban villa in Rome. Suburban was not then the derogatory term that it has become now. Villas like the Riario were a retreat for cultivated people and so were objects of admiration and envy. Just before Christina took up residence there, the villa had been let to a variety of people and it was somewhat run-down. Christina returned it to its former glory. Its one truly lovely feature when she took possession was its garden which was, and still is, very large, extending right up the Janiculum, the hilly park in the center of Rome overlooking St. Peter's.

The palace was not, strictly speaking, a royal residence, but it was quite large (it is now the French school). The garden still dominates the building, though it is not as well cared for as it was in the seventeenth century. In the Queen's lease it was specified that the parterres filled with spring bulbs must be maintained. The garden also contained pergolas of jasmine and "secret gardens" filled with orange and lemon trees. Beyond those there were groves of flowering trees and ilex and beyond that it stretched up the hill, with shady, winding paths and fountains in the most surprising places.

At first, while the main palace was made ready for her, the Queen lived in the casino at the top of the hill. The casino had its own enclosed garden but only nine rooms, a space not nearly large enough for Christina's treasures. So these, which had arrived in 1659 from Garcia Yllan, were kept packed up until the main palace was ready.

All was well for a while but it did not last. Clement IX had been an old man when he was elected, his health was not good, and in December 1669 he died. Unfortunately, Christina's beloved Azzolino was only forty-eight, too young to be the next Pope. He would be a likely candidate for the not too distant future, however, unless there was a long reign by a Pope hostile to him and to what he stood for.

The conclave that followed was a very long one and Christina moved into the Palazzo Colonna in the Borgo so as to be nearer Azzolino. She had taken it upon herself to provide him with intelligence and sometimes wrote him three long letters a day which were smuggled in. The conclave stretched on, lasting for more than four months. The upshot was that Azzolino, or rather the candidate he had supported and schemed for, was defeated. Equally important, the election of Cardinal Altieri, as Clement X, was a victory for Azzolino's enemy, Cardinal Chigi, who assumed the power and influence which Azzolino had enjoyed under Clement IX. It was more than a setback but Christina's reaction to the news was not atypical: she swore, but then ordered her carriage and dashed off to show her obedience to the new man.

Clement X reigned for six years as a kindly and devout but essentially unexciting Pope. During this time Azzolino's political influence waned, as did Christina's. Then, in 1676, when Clement X died and Cardinal Benedetto Odescalchi was elected as Innocent XI, the final seal was put on any hope that Christina or her still-beloved Azzolino would ever regain the positions of influence in Rome which they had once enjoyed. Odescalchi came from a family of rich merchants from Como in the north. Traditionally, northern Italians, especially merchants, have little sympathy for the slower, easier life in Rome: they were instinctively opposed to all the things that had attracted Christina to the south. Innocent XI was humble and puritanical. He sold all his family furniture and gave the proceeds to the poor. He himself went about in old clothes. And he quickly set about reforming the gaiety of Roman life: he granted few, if any, favors, reduced the carnival to a minimum, cut the number of theaters, and barred women entirely from the stage. He had the breast of Guido Reni's Madonna painted over because he thought it too exposed and very quickly earned himself the nickname *Papa minga* or *mingone,* "Papa no," since *mingone* was the word for "no" in his native dialect. As a result, Christina took less and less interest in politics and instead sought peace of mind and influence through the arts, culture, and the intellect.

Christina's True Realm

In the arts, change was in the air in Rome. The city had become a magnet for artists. Christina was not the only person to come from the North and settle in the city. Among the great names who traveled south to live and work in Rome at the time Christina was there were both Poussin and Claude.

Neither of these fellow exiles appealed to her, however. She preferred native Italians, among whom probably the most colorful was Salvator Rosa, who was forty when the Queen arrived. Born in Naples, he was precocious as a painter of battle scenes and landscapes. He moved to Rome but left it twice, first because he caught malaria and second because he wrote a lampoon of Bernini. Around 1649 he finally settled in the city. Although he was very popular in the nineteenth century, Rosa was never that much of a success in his own time. He seems to have been continually at odds with many of the artists of the day and with the fashions favored by the patrons in Rome. He railed particularly against the fashion at that time for *bambocciata,* domestic genre painting. He longed to be given some major public commission but never was, instead being confined to small romantic landscapes, which he painted extremely well. Rosa had talents for poetry, music, and mime and was a clever conversationalist, making him much in demand as a companion or guest. However, this still did not bring him any great commissions. He remained a prickly personality and there are many stories which show this side of his nature, one of the best being his behavior during an exhibition of paintings at which *Wisdom and Strength* was shown.

One exhibition was always held in March at the Pantheon, and another in August in the cloisters of San Giovanni Decollato. Rosa always made full use of these exhibitions to show off his talents but in 1668 the Rospigliosi family organized the August exhibition. Rospigliosi was then Pope so it was bound to be a grand affair and the family decided that only old masters would be included and all contemporary work excluded. Being a good friend of Rospigliosi, Christina was persuaded to exhibit some of her Venetian paintings, including *Wisdom and Strength* and some other Veroneses, which were then fabled throughout Rome. Rosa was incensed by the exclusion of contemporary work and, being Rosa, merely took the embargo as a challenge. He plotted and schemed and, in the end, he was the only living artist with any pictures in the exhibition. A lesser man might have been content with that but not Rosa. He now induced a band of his supporters to go around Rome announcing: "Have you seen the Titian, the Correggio, the Paulo Veronese, the Parmigianino, the Carracci, Domenichino, Guido, and Signor Salvatore? Signor Salvatore is not afraid of Titian, of Guido, of Guercino, or anyone else." It did not endear Rosa to others.

Christina seems not to have been a close acquaintance of Rosa's and never owned any of his major paintings. However, she did own a few sketches so she appreciated his talent even if she still preferred her old masters.

Whatever his faults at the time, Rosa is at least still remembered today. This is much less true of Carlo Maratti and Michelangelo Cerquozzi. These two illustrate as well as anyone the vagaries of taste. Famous and well paid when they were alive (Maratti numbered among his patrons two Popes and several English lords making the Grand Tour in Rome), they enjoyed the Rome of Christina's day. Yet their names and reputations have sunk steadily since then. Christina owned a few things by each of them yet she was never very enthusiastic. Only two figures in the contemporary art scene meant much to her. These were Pier Francesco Mola, her court painter (who also specialized in sugar sculptures at her dinners), and Giovanni Pietro Bellori.

Mola was very highly regarded in his day: he had commissions from the Pamphili family and, at one point, Innocent X himself handed Mola a canvas, a gesture then regarded as equal to Charles V picking up Titian's brushes. Christina certainly liked Mola, even taking him in her carriage. What probably appealed to her was that his style—he was a great colorist —which was almost Venetian.

Giovanni Pietro Bellori was not a painter but a scholar, a librarian, the most important critic of his day and a man who, like Vasari before him, wrote an important book on the lives of the painters. Born around 1615, he was the nephew of an antiquarian collector, who became his guardian. It was in that setting that Bellori met Domenichino and acquired his taste for the antique. He was an early member of the Accademia di San Luca but as a writer and critic, not as an artist. Like Christina, he studied antiquity but he was also interested in the contemporary scene: he cataloged several Roman collections and, in 1672, published his *Lives,* short biographical pieces about a number of important painters. Bellori was a great friend of Poussin's, many of whose ideas he took over. In this he was helping to prepare the way for Neoclassicism.

In time, Bellori's influence grew so that in 1671 he was made secretary of the Accademia di San Luca and not long after he became librarian and antiquarian to Christina. The Queen was not always guided by Bellori, although with their shared love of Raphael and the antique, they must have got on well. At the least Bellori persuaded the Queen to patronize some contemporary painters, among them Domenichino's pupils.

Patronage in Rome

Bernini, Cortona, Algardi, Poussin, Claude, Rosa, Maratti, Mola: one reason why the artistic life of Christina's Rome was as fertile as it was was because there had been changes in the system of patronage. Just as the nature of patronage was changing during Veronese's own time, so it had now changed again. There were, of course, still wealthy individuals who bought pictures. But to them were added two new factors. This was a time when the new religious orders that had been set up to further the cause of the Counter-Reformation were commissioning a lot of work; and second it was also a period when, for the first time, it was becoming fashionable for the general public to collect. As well as being important in terms of art history, Christina's Rome was equally noteworthy in the history of collecting.

The Jesuits, the Oratorians, and the Theatines were prominent in seventeenth-century Rome. Their churches, all built and decorated at that time, were respectively the Gesù, the Chiesa Nuova, and San Andrea della Valle. The Gesù had been decorated by Bernini and Gaulli, the

Chiesa Nuova had Rubens and Caravaggio, and San Andrea della Valle had Lanfranco and Domenichino.

Three private individuals were patrons on a grand scale, the equivalent of the Barbaro and the Contarini families of Veronese's Venice. The first was Paolo Giordano Orsini, Duke of Bracciano, the same person Christina had corresponded with in Sweden, and with whom she had stayed for a night on her journey south. Orsini was a most cultivated man who had traveled to Scandinavia and soldiered in Germany. He was a dandy who wore his hair long and commissioned many famous artists—Bernini among them—to record his likeness. He was a member of the Spanish faction in Rome, however, which meant that his fortunes declined during Urban's Papacy. This culminated in the 1690s, when his nephew was forced to sell the castle of Bracciano to the papal nephew of the day, Don Livio Odescalchi.

The most important private patron in Rome during the time Christina was there was Cassiano dal Pozzo. Although they only overlapped by two years—he died in 1657—his collecting habits had a great effect on her, on everyone. He was a Tuscan, a friend of Galileo, and was himself as interested in scientific thought as in art. He was also a friend of Orsini and admired by scholars all over Europe. He collected rare birds and plants, anatomical drawings, medals, prints, precious stones, and accounts of curious events (such as reports from Spain that vegetables had been found growing out of a man's stomach). If his friendship with Orsini was one reason why Christina would have been drawn to him, his collection of antiquities, especially Roman antiquities, was another. A third was that he was one of several Roman connoisseurs who helped foster an interest in Venetian painting. He was also friendly with Gabriel Naudé, the librarian, who had been with the Queen in Sweden.

Despite his fondness for Venetian art, dal Pozzo's most important act of patronage was the fact that he owned fifty Poussins. These included the series of the *Seven Sacraments,* which the master had begun in the second half of the 1630s. The subject and its treatment were revolutionary and dal Pozzo may well have had a hand in the design of the series.

The other major patron in Christina's Rome was Camillo Massimi, who came from one of the Holy City's most distinguished families. He owned a number of works by Poussin, but he also admired Claude and had his portrait painted by Velázquez, who visited Rome in 1649. Massimi collected books and superb antiquities as well as paintings.

The long-term achievements of these patrons, of whom Christina was one, were twofold. They had an interest in antiquity which kept alive a tradition which, in the next century, would provide the foundation of the Neoclassical movement. And dal Pozzo and Massimi recognized the genius of Poussin and Claude, which the Church, with its devotion to the Baroque, did not.

Around these patrons the infrastructure of art was changing. The production, marketing, and appreciation of pictures was all in flux. The chief effect was to extend the appeal of art outside the circles of the rich and beyond the Church. Rome was increasingly attractive to tourists (another new development) and this was one of the reasons why the number of art dealers began to grow in Rome.

They were very unpopular. At first the dealers were mainly involved with new or young artists, who were unable to fit into the established system of patronage. The dealers had a poor reputation mainly because they were middlemen, who came between the artist and the patron, and no one liked that. Furthermore, they often sold copies as originals. Claude, for instance, was forced to keep a set of drawings as records of all the works he had actually done. Yet a third reason for the unpopularity of dealers was that they also sold pigments and frames and this was regarded as demeaning to the liberal arts.

Despite all this the number of dealers in Rome continued to grow and by 1674 there were about a hundred of them, mostly in and around the Piazza Navona. The Flemish were prominent among them, one reason for their preeminence being the success of the art market in Antwerp. But the vagaries of papal patronage was another. Urban VIII had stimulated the demand for artists, but then, when Innocent retrenched, a lot of them were left high and dry. On top of that the tourists now flocking to Rome found it easier to go to the dealers than to tour all the studios.

Apart from art dealers, art exhibitions also began to extend across Rome and were flourishing by 1650. Originally these were associated with the celebrations and processions which took place on certain saints' days, which were a major feature of seventeenth-century life. The most famous exhibition was that held in March. It was there that Velázquez first showed the sensational portrait of his servant, Juan de Pareja. The other important one was the exhibition held in the cloisters of San Giovanni Decollato in August, under the auspices of a different patrician family each year. Owners of private galleries lent masterpieces and it was to this show, in 1662, that Christina lent some of her pictures, including *Wisdom and Strength* and the other Veroneses, not long after their arrival from Brussels. Azzolino himself started an exhibition in the Church of San Salvatore Lauro in 1669 and by the end of the century there were four art shows in Rome every year, in March, July, August, and December. As time went on they became more and more commercial, with as many as two hundred pictures for sale at any one time.

Naturally, this changed attitudes toward art still more. Its sheer accessibility meant that pictures were coming to be appreciated as objects for pleasure and decoration rather than records of some higher (religious) truth. This was important so far as the appreciation of a painting like *Wisdom and Strength* was concerned. It was now that the old divisions of painting—religious, secular, mythological—began to give way to a new aesthetic: more and more people were prepared to judge a painting *as* a painting. This aesthetic was to become widely apparent only in the next century but the origins were in Rome in Christina's day.

It accounts, too, for the popularity of the still life, of landscapes, and other subjects that had not, hitherto, been regarded as suitable material for art. Notorious among these was the *bambocciata,* the genre of little pictures that represent scenes from everyday life. They were named after Pieter van Laer, a deformed Dutch painter, another exile who had moved south to Rome some time before Christina—1627–1639—and who was the leader of a group of painters producing pictures that were regarded as opening "a window on life": the cake seller, the water carrier, the tobacconist. This fashion was well established by Christina's arrival.

In time, this concern for everyday pictures that showed only the good side led to a vogue for the picturesque, paintings in which the subject matter, usually a landscape, was artfully arranged to please the eye. A century later, these landscapes influenced garden design in France and England, explaining numerous attempts to re-create Italianate landscapes around the great country houses. The same impulse also led to the worship of nature, which was such a feature of the nineteenth-century Romantic movement. However, a more immediate effect of the popularity of *bambocciata* lay in the wider availability of art. The subject matter, much less daunting and elevated than religious or allegorical art, was more popular among the middle classes. It was smaller, less ambitious, and above all cheaper. It boomed. Giulio Mancini, the Pope's doctor who was also a *marchand-amateur,* wrote a treatise for "buying, hanging, and preserving pictures," in which he identified two markets, the rich and aristocratic on the one hand and the *huomini di stato mediocre e di stato basso* (people of a middle or lower class) on the other.

The trend to *bambocciata*-type painting was deplored by the better-heeled connoisseurs but that did not stop it. Genre pictures were here to stay and artists like Cerquozzi and even Rosa were, to an extent, affected by it.

Pieter van Laer is relevant in another context too. In Rome he naturally mixed with a group of northern painters who kept themselves together to resist dues levied by the Rome academy. Known as the *bentveughels* (or flocks of birds), they were rowdy and eventually banned by the Pope at the beginning of the eighteenth century. Their Protestantism and their foreignness, their desire to be in Rome but to be outside the normal range of patronage and outside the reach of the academy, were important factors in changing ideas about art and artists. Together with the greater tolerance of painters with difficult personalities, and the realization that, perhaps, an artist actually *needed* an element of eccentricity, the *bentveughels* helped to create the notion of the bohemian painter which has become so familiar. Linked to this was another new development, the oil sketch, or *modello,* which people now began to collect. The existence of *modelli* was related to the mystical origins of the Baroque and the broader range of patrons now available. Artists were required to sketch for their customers what they planned to paint, but at the same time, the sketches were collected in much greater numbers because they were felt to be "spontaneous" in contrast to the more highly finished works of art and in that sense more in keeping with the Counter-Reformation's ideas about the artist being a sort of mystical intermediary between God and this world. The sketch marked the artist's first inspiration; it was the hand of God at its purest.

Added together, these various aspects of the Rome art world had one vitally important consequence for Christina. Exciting as the Eternal City was in the second half of the seventeenth century, and however different the Queen found it, compared with Stockholm, artistically and culturally speaking it was *not* the Rome she had been expecting. It was not the Rome of her beloved Raphael: his cool, calm, restrained art could not have been more different from the frenzies of the Baroque or the wild behavior of Rosa and the *bentveughels;* its lofty aims could not have been more different from the *bambocciata.* During her time in Rome, Christina collected *some* contemporary works, but her main acquisitions were old masters and antiquities. She was consistent enough in this at least to keep to what she had always liked. But, to an extent, she was a fish out of water.

Christina's Collecting in Rome

Wisdom and Strength and the other treasures which the Queen brought with her from the north were not unpacked until 1662–1663, at which time another inventory was drawn up. This one was compiled by Sebastiano Bevilacqua, the master of her household at the time, and a much better document it was. He listed both the dimensions of all the works *and* the names of the artists. This was fortunate because it makes it easier to identify what the Queen acquired after she arrived in Rome.

Her first serious purchase must have been a wonderfully satisfying occasion for her. It came in 1663 when she bought no fewer than five small paintings by Raphael from a convent in Perugia. They formed a predella, the strip that went under the main altar. Part of the deal was that Christina had to replace them with modern reproductions. The pictures had all been produced around 1505 and when the Queen bought them they were to be found in the Colonna family's altar in the convent. They included: *S. Francis: S. Anthony of Padua,* now in the Dulwich Gallery; *Agony in the Garden,* in the Metropolitan Museum, New York; and *Christ Carrying the Cross,* in the National Gallery, London. They were so fine a group that when Alexander VII heard of the sale he was very angry and ordered an investigation, which resulted in the nunnery being given a sharp reprimand.

An equally important acquisition made by Christina in Italy was the purchase of more than twenty items from the Imperiali family's collection in Genoa. (The Imperiali were the grand family of Genoa, an Italian-speaking city-state ruled by Spain.) This purchase took place in 1667 and was negotiated for Christina (who was away on her travels) by Azzolino. Among the Imperiali pictures were included works by Rubens, Tintoretto, and Caravaggio, as well as *The Three Ages of Man* by Titian, now in the National Galleries of Scotland in Edinburgh. Thus, whereas the booty from Prague had contained about forty Titians, or copies of Titian —and only about a quarter of them were thought good enough to bring to Rome—in Italy Christina was able to add about a dozen pictures by this master, most of which were originals.

Her collection of pictures by Titian at the Riario were much admired and Nicodemus Tessin, a Swedish architect who visited the Queen in 1668, wrote that in one room alone there were "seventeen pictures [by Titian] each one more beautiful than the last." The other Titians she acquired in Rome included: *Salome with the Head of John the Baptist* (now in the Galleria Doria-Pamphili, Rome); *Young Woman Combing Her Hair,* attributed to Pordenone in Christina's time; *Venus with a Shell* (National Galleries of Scotland, Edinburgh); *Diana and Actaeon* (National Gallery, London); *Venus and the Lute Player* (Fitzwilliam, Cambridge); *Christ and the Woman Taken in Adultery* (Corporation Art Gallery, Glasgow); and the famous *Portrait of Baldassare Castiglione* (National Gallery, Dublin.) Though Christina may be criticized today for missing the chance to acquire some great works by her contemporaries in Rome—Poussin, Claude, Bernini, or Cortona—the old masters which she did add to the Prague loot are beyond reproach.

DRAWINGS AND STATUES

Christina received at least one book of drawings from Prague. This was compiled by Hendrick Goltzius, who sketched antique marbles in Rome. Another series of volumes, which she had acquired before she left Stockholm and brought south with her, comprised a number of Italian masters of the fifteenth and sixteenth centuries, including works by Raphael and Michelangelo.

Once in Rome, she continued to collect but now added the drawings of contemporary artists. Her collection eventually covered three centuries, the fifteenth, sixteenth, and seventeenth, and was made up almost entirely of artists who were Italian, or who lived and worked in Italy. She had drawings by Reni, Rosa, Domenichino, Claude, and Guercino. And she had, as well, at least seventeen works by Bernini, including a sketch for the *Fountain of the Four Rivers* in the Piazza Navona and his famous *Time Revealing Truth,* the original of which is now in the Galleria Borghese in Rome.

A new interest in Rome was archaeology. The vast amount of ancient ruins in the Holy City would eventually inspire the Neoclassical movement right across Europe, but not for nearly another century. Christina managed to obtain the Pope's permission to excavate the ruins of Decius's palace near the Church of San Lorenzo on the Viminal Hill. This turned out to be one of her more worthwhile ventures and Christina's sculpture collection was to become famous even in her day: at the time of her death she had more than 160 items.

Most of the sculptures were exhibited on the ground floor of the Riario in a suite of vaulted rooms and, as was the practice of the times, the Queen employed her own sculptors to restore any damaged antiquities and make them "whole." The most important works in her collection were classical Greek or early Roman copies of Greek originals dating roughly from the third century B.C. All of which is not surprising, since until the nineteenth century, Greek sculpture was known to the West only through Roman copies (with a few, very rare exceptions), it is clear that Christina's taste was far ahead of its time, or she was lucky in what she dug up.

Her collection included a Venus with a Dolphin, dating from the first century A.D., a work similar to the Venus Pudica in the Piazzo del Campidoglio in Rome, and a bronze head of a Greek athlete, dating from 300 B.C., which stood on a table in the Sala dei Quadri in front of a mirror which Bernini designed especially for Christina, and showed Truth being unveiled by Time. Christina believed that the head was a portrait of her hero, Alexander the Great. She also had an entire classical gallery on the ground floor of the Riario. Known as the Stanza della Muse, this gallery was devoted to a well-known theme from classical mythology: Apollo leading the choir of the Muses. The eight goddesses, all classical Greek copies of Hellenistic originals dating from about 300 B.C., included Clio (history), Urania (astronomy), Polyhymnia (lyric poetry), and Thalia (comedy). Symbolism was strong in Rome, so the parallel must obviously have been drawn between Apollo surrounded by the Muses and Christina's position at the center of cultural life in the Holy City.

THE RIARIO

Today in Rome the Palazzo Riario is a run-down and anonymous building. Known as the Palazzo Corsini, it is the home of the French school, as well as being an art gallery and is overshadowed by the much better-kept Farnesina on the other side of the Lungara, the narrow street which runs from the borders of the Vatican toward Trastevere.

However, it was the hub of things in Christina's time. Festooned with great art, the palazzo was a regular meeting place for some of the great intellects of the day. They entered by the ground floor, which contained a large number of rooms and a wide stone staircase. The Queen's sculpture was on this floor in rooms lined with tapestries.

On the second floor the rooms were more intimate, though they still had high ceilings. There was a long gallery, connecting the different wings of the building and a terrace with magnificent views of the Janiculum. It was on this second floor that most of the Queen's pictures hung. Some of these rooms were also lined in tapestries. The main gallery was known as the Sala dei Quadri, with the Sala dei Valetti, the Anticamera delle Lancie Spezzate, and the Anticamera de Cavalieri adjoining it. The Queen's own bedroom was also here, near the pictures but opening on to a side street.

For the best part of twenty years the Palazzo Riario housed what was probably the best collection of Venetian painting ever assembled by a private collector and probably the best anywhere at any time, save for the collection housed today in the Accademia Museum in Venice. The collection contained two Bassanos, a Bellini, a Paris Bordone, a Giorgione, a Palma Vecchio, a Palma Giovane, three Pordenones, two Schiavones, three Tintorettos, thirteen Titians, and eleven Veroneses. To this must be added the non-Venetian masters, five Raphaels, seven Correggios, two Caravaggios, and four Carraccis. At the same time, it contained at least a score of pictures which featured women who were either totally naked or else *déshabillé*. Such pictures appealed as much to Christina as they had to

Rudolf and, perhaps, bearing in mind some of the rumors, for much the same reason.

Christina's books were housed on the top floor of the Riario. Her library of printed books and manuscripts was every bit as extensive as her collection of pictures. The fact that she was able to help the Bollandists in the preparation of the *Acta Sanctorum* on her way south is an indication of the quality of her library. She had nearly 4,000 printed books and 650 manuscripts and among the rarer works she owned was Descartes's *Discours de la méthode,* Saumaise's *Defensio regio pro Carolo I,* Francis Bacon's *Novum organum,* and Hobbes's *Elementa philosophica de cive.* The Queen also owned the *Opera omnia* (complete edition) of many scholars and some lives of the early Popes.

All this made the Riario a perfect setting for the intellectuals of Christina's day. The scholars would mount the great stone staircase and enter the Sala dei Quadri, with its thirteen Titians and eleven Veroneses, its five Raphaels, and its Correggios. When the group was assembled, Christina, who always liked theater, would enter from the opposite direction.

Scholars and Academies in Rome

Academies, popular in Veronese's own lifetime, were just as widespread in the seventeenth century, especially in Italy. Almost every town of any size had one, which served as a meeting place for the educated gentry. Having had her own in Stockholm, and having visited a number of others on her way south, Christina quite naturally wanted one in Rome. However, the Queen's intellectual interests, at least during her early years in Italy, were somewhat different from those she had had in Stockholm. Conceivably she was a no less serious person than she had been in the north but for a while in Rome she was taken up with a number of issues that sound facile. She was no longer content with the rich diversity of the study of languages, philosophy, poetry, and the arts. Instead she became embroiled in the mysteries of alchemy and astrology. Even though she lived three quarters of a century after Rudolf, the boundary between chemistry and alchemy and that between astrology and astronomy was still far from clear. The Catholic Church was, at least in theory, opposed to alchemy and astrology but that did not stop many clerics from experimenting (including Azzolino himself), in search of universal medicines or synthetic gold.

In the Riario the Queen had two laboratories. One was a distillery which probably produced perfumes. The other was an observatory where she received instruction from Jean Dominique Cassini, not as famous a scientist as Kepler, but one of the foremost astronomers of the time and the man who discovered, among other things, the four moons of Saturn.

Among the varied crowd of scholars who assembled in the Sala dei Quadri, there were some remarkable men, for the Queen was undoubtedly au courant in all intellectual matters. Her academy included Lucas Holstenius: born in Hamburg, he studied medicine and philology at Leiden and classical manuscripts in England and Paris. Becoming a Catholic in 1655, it was he who received Christina's confession of the Catholic faith at Innsbruck. He subsequently traveled to Rome and became the Queen's librarian. There was the alchemist and heretic Francesco Giuseppe Borri whom Christina first met in 1667. As well as being interested in universal medicines, Borri was a flamboyant adventurer. He had been educated by the Jesuits in Rome and founded a secret religious order, whose adherents had to obey him unquestioningly. He also claimed that the archangel Michael had revealed to him how to make gold. In 1660 he was convicted of heresy and ended his days in Castel San Angelo, allowed out now and then to treat important figures. There was Johann Rudolf Glauber, who discovered Glauber's salt, sodium sulfate, a genuine medicine. There was also Giovanni Alfonso Borelli, the physiologist and mathematician whose most important work was published at Christina's expense. This book, *De motu animalium,* concerned the movement of muscles and the circulation of the blood.

In addition to the members of the Academy, there was the seer of Lyon. Christina never actually met this man, Lazare Meysonnier, but she corresponded with him and he distinguished himself by correctly predicting her death. "These bad tidings," he wrote on January 21, 1689, "are such that you could not know of anything more terrible if you love this life, for I declare that you, according to my supposition, are to depart from it this year, and that in the coming spring a part of the earth will be opened for the burial of your body; you are to die this year, and my reason for informing you of this lies only in my desire and Christian longing that you prepare yourself in a befitting manner." Some idea of the Queen's reputation abroad at this time can be gathered from the fact that Meysonnier also advised her to make a public bonfire of all her "lewd" pictures and to break up those of her sculptures which were "a trifle naked."

Christina formed a second academy in 1674, after she had completed her travels and had reconciled herself to the fact that she was not going to acquire another crown. Reports of the meetings were written down in a book bound in red and showing the Queen's coat of arms. There were seventeen volumes in all. The Accademia Reale met in the Sala dei Quadri. Other academies patronized by the Queen also met in the

Riario. Just after her death, a group of poets founded perhaps the most famous of all in the gardens of her palazzo: an academy called the Arcadia.

Whatever failures she may have had in other areas, the Queen was successful in turning the Riario into the center of Rome's intellectual and cultural life.

Theater, Opera, Music

Christina maintained her interest in the performing arts throughout her years in Rome. There were at least two performances in the Riario during Christina's time—taking place on the top floor of the palazzo where the library was.

It was a no less interesting time in the theatrical arts than in the visual ones. Not only was the opera a relatively new and very popular development but the very concept of the modern theater was evolving in Italy at the time. This was true despite the fact that theater in the Holy City was always dependent on the attitude of the reigning Pope. (In some ways, this stricture helped, since it gave the theater a somewhat raffish air that made it appealing to certain types.) Christina always wanted her own theater and these plans began to materialize toward the end of the 1660s when she bought a building near the Tor di Nona prison and commissioned the Baroque architect Carlo Fontana to design the auditorium. This was financed in the Venetian way by inviting individuals to subscribe to boxes. Fontana's theater consisted of six tiers, each with twenty-one boxes. Christina kept five for herself in the middle of the second tier, with the center one surmounted by a crown. Thus to Christina goes the honor of having invented the concept of the "royal box."

Performances in those days generally comprised what we would now recognize as opera-plus-ballet-interludes, often with spectacles such as fireworks thrown in. The quality of Christina's taste may be gauged by her appointment as musical director of none other than Alessandro Scarlatti. Although a Neapolitan, Scarlatti was the most important figure in the late seventeenth century in the Venetian style of music. He worked for the Queen for four years and dedicated a number of works to her. The Queen also employed Arcangelo Corelli, the violinist and composer. He led the orchestra in concerts sponsored by the Queen and, like Scarlatti, dedicated a number of works to her.

Over the course of the last twenty years of her life, once her political ambitions had finally been laid to rest, Christina seems to have come to terms with her predicament, that of being a Queen without a country to govern. She was able to settle down to find what was perhaps her true "realm": as a leader in the intellectual, social, and cultural life of Rome. Not for nothing was this period referred to as *"il seicento Cristina."*

Christina's life drew to its close steadily and peacefully. In 1688, when she was more than sixty years old, the Queen was described as "very small of stature, exceedingly fat and corpulent. Her complexion, voice and face are those of a man; she has a big nose, large blue eyes, blonde eyebrows and a double chin from which sprout a number of isolated tufts of beard. The upper lip a trifle prominent, the hair light chestnut, a palmsbreadth in length, powdered and standing on end uncombed over her forehead." Never the most attractive of women, the Queen seems finally to have given up any attempt to soften her appearance. In any case, by now her health was failing.

From 1686 Christina suffered from an ailment known as the Rose, or St. Anthony's Fire: what we now call erysipelas. This was accompanied by fever and swelling of the legs. In general the attacks were worse in springtime, but in the winter of 1688, as the old year turned into the new, Christina seems to have had a premonition that she did not have long to live. At the end of the year she ordered what was, for her, a very unusual dress. It was wonderfully feminine, made of white silk, embroidered with flowers, and trimmed with a golden fringe. Christina tried it on on Christmas Eve. Besides her ladies-in-waiting, another woman, known to the Queen as Giulia, arrived. She was an alchemist, a concocter of potions and stories, a sort of seer. Asked by the Queen what she thought of the new dress, Giulia replied, "Your Majesty will be buried in that dress not long from now."

With the onset of spring, the attacks of St. Anthony's Fire became much worse. On February 13, the Queen had a fainting fit: her health was now critical, bad enough for her to receive the sacraments and to draw up her will. There were messages sent from the Pope, who was not well himself, and a number of people in Rome competed to put their physicians at her disposal. She hung on for a few weeks but finally, at six o'clock on the morning of April 19, 1689, in the presence of her beloved Azzolino, Christina died.

After the postmortem, the Queen's body was embalmed, as was the practice with royalty. Her face was covered with a silver death mask, which even today conceals the cranium in her coffin. A crown of gilded silver was placed on her head and a silver scepter put in her hand; all three articles were the work of the papal goldsmith, Giovanni Giardini. In death she received one final honor: Christina is the only woman buried in the Vatican.

The Queen's will stipulated the arrangements to be followed at her funeral and it also provided for a large number of legacies. However, her sole heir was Azzolino and the great majority of the Queen's treasures, including *Wisdom and Strength* and the rest of her beloved paintings, now passed to him.

History is left with two distinct views of Christina. One is that she was a romantic, tragic, and ultimately lonely figure, a courageous convert and a high-minded woman. The other is less charitable, best summed up in Hugh Trevor-Roper's words: "this tyrannical spinster," "that eccentric anachronism," "the most famous and most predatory of royal blue stockings . . . a glutton for culture."

Undeniably, the Queen was at times headstrong, willful, more than a little foolish. Her learning and her religion were not as deep or as dedicated as they might have been. The motives for her abdication and her conversion were mixed and Trevor-Roper is almost certainly right when he says that Christina wanted to have her royal cake and eat it too—she wanted the privileges of being a Queen without the onerous responsibilities that go with governing.

But whatever her intellectual shortcomings, she enjoyed art. She developed her own tastes and was, by the standards of the day, well informed. It is arguable perhaps whether she had the right to take with her the pictures and other treasures which had been looted from Prague in the name of the Swedish crown but there can be no disputing the fact that Christina enjoyed and appreciated the pictures more than any of her contemporaries in Stockholm. The Palazzo Riario was a more interesting, lively, and therefore more suitable home for them than the Tre Kronor. And in removing them as she did, legally or not, Christina added immeasurably to the interest of *Wisdom and Strength* which, otherwise, would probably still be in Stockholm. As it was, after her death, its adventures were far from over.

In traveling to Rome, Christina believed she was moving from the edge of the world to its center, both in spiritual terms and in cultural and material ones. In a sense, she was. The spirit of the Counter-Reformation, the genius of Bernini, and the patronage of Maffeo Barberini together created a peak of civilization which, if not as great as the Renaissance itself, was certainly better than anything else at the time.

But it didn't last. Politically, the center of Europe was already elsewhere. The Peace at Westphalia, in 1648, confirmed this. It took the crusading element out of the Counter-Reformation and the world became set, if not yet settled, into Protestant and Catholic camps. The standing of the Papacy changed permanently, aided ironically by the financial extravagance that had helped Barberini create the Baroque. Rome did not turn into a backwater overnight, but its decline had definitely begun. Tributes from abroad, on which Rome relied to some extent, were drying up, since less and less of the world was Catholic. Trading patterns were changing as even other allegedly loyal Italian states, like Genoa, took to getting their grain from the Adriatic countries instead of from Rome.

The shift in trading produced social changes in Italy. For instance, some of the older, grander families were impoverished and a new class of rich entrepreneurs was created. This produced two related effects for the arts. In general patronage declined, hitting its lowest ebb after the mid-1660s. In 1665 Salvator Rosa wrote: "As for commissions, I haven't had any, even from a dog, for a full year . . . I might as well plant my brushes in my garden . . ."

A second effect was the "Italianization of Europe." Because there was no opportunity in Rome, the Italian style, including Italian painters and Italian taste, was exported to other countries, not unlike the fashion for European culture in America today. This was very successful. Within a few years of his complaints that he had no work in Rome, Rosa could write to a friend that "every day I have to turn down commissions (and important ones at that) from all over Europe." Nonetheless, that spirit, that amalgam of politics, economics, and individualism that had created the Baroque had moved north, and in the late seventeenth century neither Rome, nor all of Italy for that matter, could boast a painter who was the equivalent of Velázquez, Rembrandt, Vermeer, de la Tour, or Watteau. That, more than anything, sums up Rome's decline at the end of the seventeenth century.

Christina's death thus occurred at a point of change in Europe's fortunes, a change that was faithfully reflected in art. Italy would never again be preeminent in art, just as the Papacy would never regain *its* ability to govern men's minds. Political power, creative energy, and civilization in general had all moved north and the embodiment of that new spirit, that new force, was the preeminence of France.

Though this was partly the result of the Thirty Years' War, it also owed a lot to three extraordinary men, men who were brilliant politicians and formidable personalities as well as being great collectors. These were two cardinals, Armand Jean du Plessis Richelieu and Giulio Mazarin, and one King, Louis XIV.

Cardinal Richelieu was a very able connoisseur who collected old masters (he had acquired works by Perugino, Mantegna, and Correggio which once belonged to Isabella d'Este), and modern French and Flemish works by Poussin and Rubens. He was followed by his protégé, the equally able Giulio Mazzarini, Cardinal Mazarin. Mazarin, a very cultured man, was a friend of the Barberini and the other leading families of Rome. His mistress was Leonora Baroni, probably the first operatic "diva." Mazarin was one of the chief bidders at the Commonwealth sale.

Louis XIV shared the cardinals' arrogant nationalism and developed a state Catholicism in France, as independent of Rome as possible. This independence encouraged a marvelously productive period for French literature—it was the age of Corneille, Racine, Molière, Fontaine, Fénelon, and le Rochefoucauld. Louis moved the French court to Versailles, where his dominance and his tastes were more apparent than they might otherwise have been. The King was also fortunate in that Jean-Baptiste Colbert, Marquis de Seignelay, his minister, was a discerning man who achieved a virtual dictatorship over the arts. Whatever the King's shortcomings, at the least French art, architecture, and literature were provided with a single dominating theme—glorification of the crown. These combined forces helped to fashion "the classical moment" in French civilization and it was against this background that *Wisdom and Strength* made its next journey.

11.

The Papal Nephew

After Christina's death, her collection passed to Azzolino. He, however, survived her by only a few months. His effects, including the Queen's paintings and other treasures, passed to his nephew, Marchese Pompeo Azzolino. This Azzolino was not a rich man, nor was he very cultivated and he soon derived profit from his good fortune by opting to sell the paintings. For reasons that were perfectly natural and which reflected the times, he looked north, to France. The Queen of Sweden's pictures constituted the finest collection of old masters available and included the best gallery of Venetian paintings ever assembled. The Italianization of Europe was in full flood, France was asserting herself. The pictures and all the other things were offered to the French King, Louis XIV.

In normal circumstances, the Sun King would probably have jumped at the chance to acquire such booty. At that time, however, he was defending himself against the League of Augsburg and was already in debt when the collection was offered to him. The King therefore replied to Azzolino through Cardinal d'Estrées, his ambassador in Rome: he sent his good wishes but added candidly that the affairs he was obliged to pursue at that time were "more pressing" than the acquisition of pictures and furniture, however distinguished.

After this setback, Pompeo Azzolino did nothing for a while. An inventory of the collection was drawn up but the weakening economy in Rome meant that there were few buyers there. The academy of the Arcadia had started to meet in the Riario even though Christina was dead so it is entirely possible that the pictures remained where they were.

In 1692, however, Pompeo eventually found a buyer, who turned out to be an Italian after all. This was Don Livio Odescalchi, none other than the nephew of Pope Innocent XI, the Pope who had no interest in art whatsoever and had closed down the opera, the theater, and the carnival, much to Christina's distress.

Livio was a typical papal nephew in that he was immensely rich, a colorful personality, and relished secular pursuits. But his experience was also atypical in that his uncle did not indulge in any of the corrupt practices of his predecessors and did not promote his relatives to cardinalates and positions of power within the Vatican hierarchy. Don Livio was never made a cardinal, nor did he receive any appointment from his uncle. Worse, while his uncle was alive he was forced to live modestly, allowed only the minimum number of servants and a single carriage. The Romans were stunned at such treatment of a papal nephew and, according to one contemporary writer, "When they wanted to curse someone, they would wish him to suffer the fate of Livio Odescalchi."

Like Innocent, Livio grew up in Como in the North of Italy. The Odescalchi had for centuries been a wealthy patrician family of bankers in Lombardy. Livio was the only son of the Pope's elder brother, Carlo, and a Milanese noblewoman, Beatrice Cusani. Livio's father died early on and after that he was adopted by his uncle, Benedetto, who was then a cardinal. Benedetto summoned his nephew to Rome.

Although Livio was given no preferential treatment, he did work with his uncle and distinguished himself in the process. Their main venture was the Catholic League against the Turks, to which both Benedetto and Livio made large financial contributions. For Livio had by now become the recipient of the immense family fortune.

Livio's contribution to the fighting was not only financial, however. He fought bravely in a number of campaigns, most notably during the defense of Vienna in 1683. He clearly had a disposition different from that of his uncle, the Pope. In 1678, Livio bought the dukedom of Ceri (Cereveteri in Latium), although he was at first prevented by the Pope from carrying the title. In 1687 he was made a grandee of Spain, with the title of "Don." His exploits as a military man had won him many friends who wished to show their gratitude—but it was only after Innocent died that Livio came into his own.

A few days after the death of the Pope in 1689, Emperor Leopold I decided to honor Livio in recognition of his deeds against the Turks all those years earlier. He made him a hereditary prince of the empire, with the title of *altezza*. The same year Don Livio was also given the kind of job many nephews might have enjoyed under their uncles: he was appointed commander in chief of the papal army and made governor of the Roman state. His appetite for titles was healthy. Not content with what he had, and perhaps because he had been denied so much power when Benedetto was alive, in 1695 he bought the prestigious dukedom of Bracciano from the Orsini. It was with Paolo Giordano Orsini that Christina had corresponded and it was in the Bracciano castle that she had spent the last night of her journey to Rome.

Two years after the Orsini purchase, Don Livio was again honored by the Emperor and made Duke of Sirmio and Duke of Sava, both in Slavonia, which at that time belonged to the Kingdom of Hungary. The Hungarian branch of the Odescalchi were a prominent family until the twentieth century. Don Livio reached the peak of his prestige as the century came to a close: in 1697 the Polish aristocracy nominated him for the crown of Poland, the very same crown that Christina had tried so hard to obtain thirty years before. He did not become King of Poland but he did entertain Maria Casimira, the widow of King John III Sobieski of Poland when she came to live in Rome, lodging her in his palace until she found one of her own. As part of the privileges conferred on him by the Emperor, Don Livio was allowed to coin money and bestow academic degrees.

Like his uncle he remained a bachelor but, once the Pope had died, he no longer felt the need to emulate Innocent in other ways and he spread his wings. He was thirty-six and the wealthiest prince in Rome. He found himself a palace more in keeping with his rank and he started to collect art. He was not unmindful of the fact that the other great papal families in Rome—the Pamphili, the Chigi, the Barberini, the Rospigliosi, and the Altieri—each had great collections. But he surpassed them all at a single stroke with the purchase from Pompeo Azzolino of Queen Christina's collection. He got the "medals, paintings [275 in number, 140 of them Italian], statues, columns, tapestries, furniture, weapons, etc.," gems, and drawings for 123,000 scudi, a very reasonable price.

Two years later Don Livio moved into a palazzo at the Piazza SS. Apostoli (where the Odescalchi still live today). This had been built by Stefano Maderno for the Colonna princes but had been acquired in 1661 by Cardinal Flavio Chigi, himself a famous banker. Chigi had commissioned Bernini to erect a new facade, the seven bays of which became very famous in Rome, though they have since been added to. The building was "among the most remarkable of the palaces in Rome" and an appropriately sumptuous home for Don Livio's new collection.

The Palazzo Odescalchi consisted of three ground-floor apartments, two *appartamenti nobili* on the second floor, a top floor, extensive utilities, a garden, and the adjacent palace (facing the Via del Corso, opposite the Church of Santa Maria in Via Lata), which housed the servants. The paintings and the drawings were exhibited in the *appartamenti nobili,* including the bedrooms, where they were hung according to the fashion of the time, from floor to ceiling with no space at all between the frames. The effect was crowded but the high ceilings offered relief.

Don Livio was not a great patron of the arts. The painters associated with him are scarcely household names today. In earlier days he had commissioned works in the north, in Milan and Como, from the young painter and architect, Andrea dal Pozzo. Maratti did a number of paintings for the family, Don Livio included, and other works were commissioned from Francesco Monnaville, a painter of landscapes (who had worked for the Queen), and Pierre Monnot, a sculptor. Perhaps the most distinguished artist patronized by Livio was Mattia de'Rossi, Bernini's favorite pupil, who remodeled the Church of San Galla, below the Capitoline hill, where Livio and the other Odescalchi are buried. Don Livio was also responsible for a sumptuous tomb in St. Peter's; designed by Maratti and executed by Monnot, it was completed in 1701.

Don Livio was also the subject of no fewer than seven medals struck in his honor, mostly commemorating his appointment as commander of the papal armies. These all had mottoes, one of which read: *non novus sed novitur,* "not a new family but action of a new kind." The medals, and other contemporary portraits agree in showing him to have long hair, a long, hooked nose, heavy-lidded eyes, and fleshy lips. His face was pleasantly open and not at all haughty.

Don Livio's wider significance in the history of art and taste lies more in the fact that he was a great collector of drawings. Livio's estate inventory, preserved today in the family archive, runs to eight hundred pages. When it was drawn up at Livio's death in 1713, it took the notary and his assistant more than four months to complete the task. Whereas Livio had bought from Pompeo Azzolino some 275 paintings and about 2,000 drawings, at his death the prince owned six times that number of paintings and five times that number of drawings—more than 10,000 in all.

Collections of drawings have, in general, a different history than those of paintings. Some people, like Christina, Rudolf, and Everhard Jabach, a German banker who lived in France, collected both. But most great collectors of drawings other than these—Pierre Crozat, Nicodemus Tessin, Vasari, Pierre Jean Mariette, Sir Joshua Reynolds, Padre Sebastiano Resta, Francesco Rapantino—did not amass great picture collections as well. Several reasons account for this. Cost was one but a more interesting reason stemmed from the very nature of drawings. Throughout its history, painting, or rather painters, have been divided as to which is the higher aspect of their art: line or color. Obviously, those who valued line valued drawings. At first drawings were kept as technical aids: they were not regarded as works of art in their own right. Only after the concept of "fine art," art for its own sake, came to be accepted, was the way open for drawings to be appreciated as beautiful in themselves.

In the fifteenth and early sixteenth centuries, collections of drawings were kept together, even after an artist (like Leonardo) died and began to have historical, if not yet a proper artistic, interest. Giorgio Vasari was an early collector of drawings, as was Joachim von Sandrart, the painter and biographer, who visited Prague, Venice (where he copied the Titians and the Veroneses), and London, where he came to the attention of Charles I. But it was not until the seventeenth century that a lively trade in drawings started to develop and collectors and dealers started to hunt down drawings on their trips abroad. One reason for this was that recent developments in art, notably Mannerism and the Baroque, were complicated and ornate, so that preparatory drawings were more necessary. Another was the idea, sixteenth century in origin, that drawings could actually represent a *higher* form of art, namely the conceit or *concetti,* by which was meant the very first apprehension an artist had of an idea, the idea in its pure, unadulterated, unfiltered form. If the artist was divine in some way, the drawing was his first message from God, before he put "human" trappings around it.†

Many of the great drawings collections were first formed in the seventeenth century and Livio Odescalchi's perfectly fits into this development. The British Royal Collection, for instance, really started with Francesco Rapantino, the assistant to Domenichino (1581–1641), in Naples. He collected 3,600 drawings which subsequently passed to Maratti, then to Pope Clement XI Albani, and then to the Royal Collection. Everhard Jabach compiled two collections. The first, which consisted of 5,542 drawings, he sold to Louis XIV in 1671 and that forms the basis of the Cabinet des Dessins in the Louvre today. Padre Sebastiano Resta (1635–1714) collected 2,638 sheets of drawings which he sold in 1710 to John Talmann, an Italian. From there they passed to Lord Somers who sold them off in diverse directions, some to Christ Church, Oxford, for example, and many to the Duke of Devonshire, at Chatsworth. Only two collections outstripped Don Livio's: (1) the collection of Pierre Crozat (1665–1740), the French "amateur," described as the "all-time 'king of drawing collectors,' " who assembled no fewer than 19,000 sheets; and (2) the Medici drawing collection in Florence. However, Don Livio's 10,000-plus sheets prove that he was a ravenous collector by any standards.

His drawings were kept in his private apartments in thirty-nine books that were stored in specially crafted walnut cabinets. They included 800 landscapes by Grimaldi, 228 caricatures by Mola, 128 pages showing drawings of snails and shells, works by Rosa, Guercino, Allegrini, and Maratti. There were 525 drawings of curiosa, including monsters and foreign costumes. The most distinguished part of his collection, however, was that acquired from Christina. This was made up of 2,998 drawings, mostly by established artists. She in turn had acquired them through and from Pieter Spiering van Silfvercrona, the Swedish ambassador in Hol-

---

† Not all art historians accept this, however. Indeed many are now divided, generally speaking, into those who subscribe to such interpretations and those who believe that, in the development of the discipline, many pictures and the motifs within them have been loaded with far more meaning by scholars than the original artists ever intended.

Allegory of Wisdom and Strength, the Frick Collection, New York.

Rudolf II by Adriaen de Vries. A
strong head by the artist has
captured well the melancholy nature
of the first owner of *Wisdom and
Strength.*

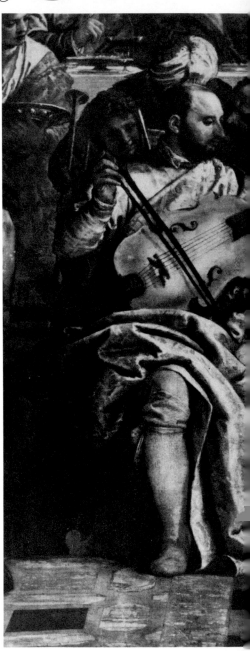

Veronese's house in the parish of
San Samuele in Venice.

Veronese by Veronese. Along with Titian, at right on the bass, Bassano on the woodwind, and Palladio in the middle, Veronese pictured himself, at left, in this detail from *The Marriage at Cana,* now in the Louvre.

Queen Christina of Sweden as a young woman by Jacob Henrick Elbfas.
"Bring me back something beautiful," she instructed her warrior father.

Christina's Abdication by Willem Swidde. Christina took about forty works of art with her when she left Sweden. *Wisdom and Strength* was one of them.

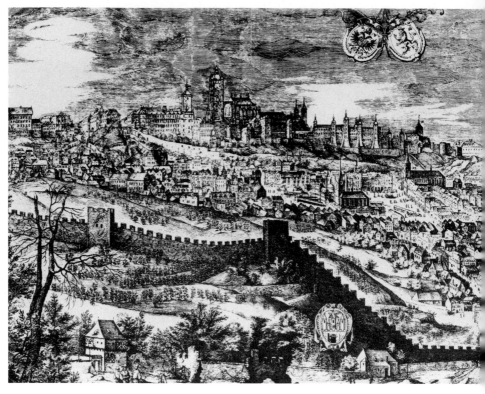

Hradčany Palace, Prague. The palace/castle/cathedral complex was so vast that one Veronese painting, lost after Rudolf died, was rediscovered there in 1962.

The Storming of Prague by Carlo Serata. It was here that Christina's army looted Rudolf's vast collection, including *Wisdom and Strength*.

Beſtürmung der Prager Stätte.
1648.

Christina in later years
by Wolfgang Heimbach.

Cardinal Decio Azzolino by
Gian Lorenzo Bernini. It
was Azzolino who found
the Queen her palace in
Rome and it was to him that
she left her collection when
she died. Bernini was also
a close friend.

land. Two other books had been acquired by Christina from Sandrart in 1644. Christina's collection also consisted of the Goltzius book that had belonged to Rudolf.

The extent by which Don Livio expanded Christina's collection and the fact that he appears to have been concerned as much with quantity as quality may indicate that he was somewhat profligate in the prices he paid. Certainly, he was extravagant in his appetite for titles and this may have been repeated in his appetite for art. Whatever the reason, when Don Livio died, in 1713, he was no longer the extravagantly wealthy man he had once been. He had improved the family's prestige: his honors in the material world had almost equaled Benedetto's in the spiritual. But at what cost? The change in his fortunes must have been widely known for, no fewer than two weeks after his death on September 7, 1713, his heirs were approached to see if they wanted to sell his collections.

Remaining a bachelor all his life, Don Livio had identified as his successors the son of his sister Lucrezia, Baldassarre Erba, who took his name, and Benedetto Cardinal Odescalchi, another nephew who was archbishop of Milan. They did indeed want to sell: both were short on cash and neither shared his uncle's passion for art. The sale, however, was not to prove easy.

IV

THE
HOUSE
OF
ORLÉANS

12.
Pierre Crozat's Hard Bargain

"As the last letters from Rome tell, that Don Livio is dead, and that he leaves a successor charged with debt, I have no doubt that the furniture, bronzes, pictures and statues which he had from the Queen of Sweden, will now be sold. I ask you, sir, to give attention to the disposition which will be made, so that I may know what ideas his inheritors have, to sell altogether, or in detail, and what accommodation can be made about payment, if the pope permits that they may leave Rome. Which are the ones that His Holiness will allow more easily to be transported abroad and which, on the contrary, he will forbid exit. You will give me great pleasure if you will give me these clarifications."

This letter was written on September 23, 1713 by Philippe II, Duke of Orléans, to the French consul in Rome, Pierre Claude Nivelle de La Chaussée. Not only was the duke's letter written only sixteen days after Odescalchi's death, but it was clearly a reply to one by La Chaussée, who must have communicated with Orléans immediately following Don Livio's demise. The consul clearly knew that Orléans would be interested in Don Livio's death and that the duke was knowledgeable about Queen Christina's collections.

The Duke of Orléans was to be the next owner of *Wisdom and Strength,* as well as all the other Prague and Stockholm Veroneses. Like Rudolf, and like Christina, he was an extraordinary personality. Like them he was an intellectual and passionate about the arts. And he was also sexually unconventional. His father, Philippe I, was the younger brother of Louis XIV, which meant that, at his birth on August 4, 1674, only the Dauphin and his own father stood between Philippe II and the throne of France. This had its disadvantages, since it meant that some members of the Sun King's immediate family looked upon Philippe as a rival. At the same time, Philippe's difficult position, in being so close to the throne yet so far from it, made him react against the King and the court. It was a reaction that would shape his personality and tastes and have far-reaching effects on the arts in France and the rest of Europe.

Since he was at first denied a role in political affairs, Philippe soon turned to artistic, cultural, and intellectual concerns. He painted, he composed an opera which was actually produced, and he dabbled in alchemy just as Rudolf and Christina had. And, like them, he collected art. Indeed, Philippe was to amass the finest collection of paintings ever assembled in France. He emulated Rudolf in this matter also, for like the Emperor he maintained a number of agents all over Europe ready to look out for works coming on the market. This meant that he was forewarned about the Odescalchi family's financial dilemmas, probably even before Don Livio died. It would also explain the French consul's prompt missive.

La Chaussée, to begin with, was not able to provide the duke with the clarifications he needed and nothing happened for some months. The following year, therefore, Philippe asked his friend Pierre Crozat, who was leaving for Rome, to see for himself how an approach could best be made to Don Baldassarre, the heir who was handling negotiations. Crozat was second only to Philippe in his importance to the history of art and occupied a very crucial position in the France of his day. His own collection was to become legendary, and his drawing collection (of 19,000 sheets) was probably the finest, and certainly the largest, ever assembled.

Crozat's family was originally from Toulouse and it was there that he was born in March 1665. He was the second son of a functionary of the town and it seemed that he and his brother would continue in that tradition by sharing the post of treasurer of the estates of Languedoc. Not much is known about what happened next. But in 1699, at the age of thirty-four, Pierre Crozat was in Paris and already an "amateur" in art. This concept, as it was then used, was close to the modern meaning of "connoisseur." Being an amateur involved the pursuit of culture, but not as an active or professional artist, as someone who painted, or carved, or drew, or even as a patron. Rather it involved the pursuit of culture as a collector, as someone who could show his learning, his taste, and refinement—his *virtue,* as Rudolf would have put it—through the kind of art he associated himself with in his collections. Amateurs might occasionally deal, but their taste and social position implied that they were incorruptible and exchanged works more for the pleasure of owning something new than for profit. This fashion reached its apex in the 1740s (when Crozat died), when the Academy devoted an entire session to the contributions of the collector.

Pierre Crozat was in some respects the typical younger son. His elder brother, Antoine, was also a banker, but a far more conventional character. Antoine lived in the fashionable Place Vendôme, was very much in the social swim, was often cited in the memoirs of the day, and received a number of titles and honors. To distinguish the two, Antoine became known colloquially as "the rich" Crozat and Pierre as "the poor"—ironically so, of course, since they were both exceedingly well-off.

While "the rich" Crozat interested himself in economic and political matters, Pierre became, not bohemian exactly, but he familiarized himself with art, the doings of the academy, and the private affairs of the Duke of Orléans. The French Academy of Painting was both similar to, and different from, the Italian and Swedish academies that have been encountered so far. It was to play an important role in art in eighteenth-century France and had something to do with Orléans's acquisition of Christina's pictures.

At the end of the seventeenth and the beginning of the eighteenth century, the Academy was split, ferociously divided in fact, into the "color" camp and the "line" camp. It was the old battle but this time the protagonists had new names: Rubénistes and Poussinistes. The division had begun in 1671–72, but it was of course essentially the same argument as had featured in Italy in Veronese's day, when Vasari and Dolce had contested similar rival claims (see page 27 above). This time it was the Poussinistes who argued that color was a mere decorative device, an adjunct, whereas drawing and design were all important. To this camp the strictly formal works of Raphael, the Carracci family and Poussin were supreme. The Rubénistes argued that painting was an imitation of nature and that color was the true essence of the natural world—that there was no such thing as a contour, except in artifice. There were also overtones of chauvinism in the debate this time, for the inclusion of Poussin in the "line" camp made it into France *versus* "the rest of the world."

Charles Le Brun, a painter-politician who was rector, chancellor, and director of the Academy, and who had been a virtual dictator of the arts in France under Louis XIV, tried to impose his will on this issue before he died in 1690. He had written: "The function of color is to satisfy the eyes, whereas drawing satisfies the mind"—the classic theory of *disegno*. This time, however, Le Brun's dictatorship and French chauvinism did not work. In 1673, the critic Roger de Piles published *Dialogue sur le coloris,* putting forth the Rubéniste view. Four years later he published a life of Rubens which, in 1699, earned him election as an honorary member of the Academy. This marked the final victory of the Rubénistes. Piles himself, having started with Rubens, mainly because the great cycle of the *Life of Marie de Médicis* was in Paris, then moved on to an enthusiastic appreciation of the great Italian colorists, especially the Venetians. And so, as the seventeenth turned into the eighteenth century, Titian, Veronese, and Correggio were regarded as *the* old masters to emulate and their canvases were especially sought after by collectors. This change in taste eventually led to changes in French art, to Watteau and the Rococo. But it also helps explain why, economic factors apart, Louis XIV was relatively uninterested in Queen Christina's collection in 1689, yet, from 1713 on, Philippe of Orléans went to great lengths to acquire it. *Wisdom and Strength* and the other Christina Veroneses and Titians were back at the center of fashion.

The change wrought by Piles (and others of course) appears to have suited the temperaments of both Crozat and Orléans. Both were sensuous men, attracted, as Christina had been, to the lusher reaches of Italian art. In the early part of the eighteenth century, Crozat attended the salons of Paris and came to know many of the intellectuals and artists who were living there at the time, including Antoine Coypel, Charles de Lafosse, and, a little later, Watteau himself. In 1704 Crozat had built himself a house in the Rue de Richelieu, right next to the Palais Royal, the Orléans's magnificent residence. He commissioned Lafosse to decorate the ceilings; the theme was the *Naissance de Minerve,* essentially the birth of the arts. And besides being a derivative of Veronese's style, it was regarded as the most modern, fashionable art of the time, and Crozat's house was looked upon by all as on a par with the duke's, where the new designs were by Antoine Coypel.

Crozat thus got to know the duke through their shared interest in the arts, but he was also chosen for the mission to Rome because he had good connections in the ecclesiastical world. He arrived in Rome in November 1714, just over a year after Don Livio's death, and was received by the Pope, Clement XI, in the company of the old French ambassador, Cardinal de la Trémoille.

The visit of 1714 was the first move in a drawn-out saga which was to last several years. What is known of the procrastinations comes from two sets of correspondence: one was that between Charles-François Poërson, director of the French Academy in Rome and Louis Antoine, Duke of Antin, the superintendant of arts in Paris; the other was between Crozat himself and Louis XIV's foreign secretary, the Marquis de Torcy.

During that first November, Crozat spent time acquainting himself with the sights of the Holy City, especially its beautiful churches. Because Crozat was rich, his reputation had preceded him: he was given introductions which enabled him to see the various private collections there. Nevertheless he was forced to wait in Rome for some weeks, until the arrival of Benedetto Cardinal Odescalchi Erba, the archbishop of Milan, before he knew whether anything would come of the proposed sale. To begin with, according to Poërson, things were not encouraging because "the prices appear very high." However, Crozat was eventually able to visit the collection sometime in January 1715.

Louis de Targny, an abbot and one of the guardians of the Bibliothèque du Roi, kept a record of the visit in his diary. "This cabinet," he wrote, "is composed of the most exquisite pictures and in very great numbers. There is an original so perfect that one estimates it is virtually priceless: it is St. John Visiting the Baby Jesus [this is the *Madonna del Passeggio,* by Raphael, now in the Sutherland Collection in the National Galleries of Scotland in Edinburgh.]" The abbott added, "This picture is to be sold for 20,000 Francs." Later, he went on to say that there were "many pictures by Correggio, Paul Veronese, Titian, Guido [Reni], Bassano, etc. There are beautiful nudes. The more indecent have been covered with *rideaux* [curtains]." The question of nudity often cropped up; the paintings had been covered over on the instruction of Cardinal Odescalchi during the year since Don Livio died. Quite apart from the art in the pictures, Crozat was aware of the Duke of Orléans's reputation as a sexual libertine, and so he wanted to see the paintings with any overpainting removed, as nature and their creators had intended.

Crozat was just as impressed by the collection of paintings as was Targny. Of the drawings, he wrote: "Messrs. Odescalchi have a very large jumble *[un très grand fratras]* of drawings, among which there are a hundred which I would be very happy to have and which I am hopeful they will give me." After the visit, and because neither of Don Livio's heirs was actually in Rome, Crozat took off for Naples to look for Salvator Rosas, Luca Giordanos, and Solimenas on his own account. In his temporary absence, he instructed the Marquis de Torcy to make all efforts to secure for His Royal Highness the pictures "which will form the most singular collection in all Europe."

The Odescalchis finally returned to Rome toward the end of February but it was a disappointment for Crozat. They drove a hard bargain and could not agree on a price for the paintings. Don Baldassarre pretended that the Emperor himself was interested in the collection, but this was just a ruse to force a higher price out of the French. On March 19, Crozat confided in Torcy just how much Don Livio's heirs were asking for their pictures and tapestries. He said they were not prepared to accept the 75,000 Roman ecus ($4,167,000–$10,000,000) he had offered even though, after much debate, Cardinal Odescalchi had contradicted his cousin Baldassarre and admitted they had no buyer other than Orléans. The Odescalchis' obduracy continued. Crozat told Torcy that if he had been negotiating with proper dealers who knew more about art, there would have been no problem in agreeing a price. He added that the only way forward was to bluff: shortly thereafter, Crozat prepared a much-trumpeted exit.

His bluff was called. Having announced his departure, he had no choice but to delay, hoping to force the Odescalchis' hand. By April 2 nothing had happened. Crozat finally did quit Rome, leaving no fewer than four officials with a watching brief: Poërson, La Chaussée, Cardinal de la Trémoille, and Cardinal Gualtiero, one of the French representatives to the Holy See. It did him little good.

Crozat returned to Paris via Venice, where he met Sebastiano Ricci and Rosalba Carriera. This visit underlines how important it was regarded in those days for amateurs to be personally acquainted with the artists of the day. It was assumed that if one knew the right artists, then something of their greatness and insight would rub off.

Sebastiano Ricci was the first of the band of itinerant Venetian painters —Canaletto, Bellotto, Tiepolo were others—who traveled abroad and worked in many cities. Ricci's work was much influenced by Veronese, so much so that his *Finding of Moses* in Britain's Royal Collection was for many years attributed to Veronese. In Venice, Ricci introduced Crozat to the great paintings from Venice's golden age, especially the Veroneses. Crozat's taste for Veronese was second to none and, in his later years, he possessed a very great number. When the Christina collection finally arrived in Paris years later, Crozat mentioned in the first breath a canvas of Veronese's that he admired above all others. This was probably the *Marriage at Cana,* for Crozat placed in the vestibule of his house in Paris a copy of this work, which Roger de Piles regarded as the "triumph of painting."

Rosalba Carriera, the other itinerant artist whom Crozat met in Venice, was notable not only because she was one of the first successful female painters but because she also had great success with her near-pornographic demi-vierges: these too caught the spirit of the regency.

On his arrival back in Paris, Crozat did not immediately have a chance to discuss his Rome visit with Orléans. In September 1715 he wrote to Gualtiero, making it clear that he had not yet had any chance at all to discuss art with the duke. The reason was understandable. On September 1, 1715, the Sun King died at last and Philippe II, Duke of Orléans, became regent of France.

13.
The Scandalous Regent

Philippe *did* get Christina's collection but it was not to be for another seven years. The Odescalchis drove a hard bargain, the Pope—or rather several Popes—interfered, and Philippe was equally inflexible as to price. The negotiations dragged on and on. Not until 1720 was Crozat able to go back to Italy and return with *Wisdom and Strength* and all the other works. By that time, Philippe's regency was in full swing. Thanks largely to him, France had changed its tastes in a remarkably short period of time; the Paris in which *Wisdom and Strength* arrived was very different from that of 1713.

Philippe's importance as a collector and as the person who acted as a catalyst of change within a whole nation owed much to the singular nature of his personality. But also significant was his constitutional position at the end of Louis XIV's long reign and the fact that he was regent with proscribed powers as opposed to an outright—and absolute—monarch. There were also a number of religious and political problems characteristic of the times.

Philippe's personality was formed early on by two factors, both of relevance to his taste in painting and art generally. His social and legal standing in relation to the crown has already been mentioned. This also went a long way toward shaping the style of his regency, which may be seen, in artistic matters as in everything else, as a revolt against the heavy, gloomy, excessively religious style of Louis XIV's later court, dominated as it was by his second wife, Françoise d'Aubigné, Marquise de Maintenon.

The second factor to form Philippe's personality and his tastes was the peculiar character of his parents, who were described by one historian as "an outlandish union, even in an age of ill-matched pairs." Philippe's father was also called Philippe but, as the king's brother, he was known as "Monsieur." This title was not short of ironic overtones, for Monsieur was an effeminate dandy, a homosexual who, for most of the time, was treated by his brother the King with a mixture of scorn and affection.

Philippe's mother, Elisabeth Charlotte, was Monsieur's second wife. His first marriage to Henrietta of England, sister of Charles II, had not been happy. Indeed, when she died in 1670, it was rumored that she had been poisoned. Elisabeth Charlotte was a sturdy German woman, daughter of the elector palatine, uncompromising and as devoid of female qualities as Monsieur was rich in them. From the start, she was so worried that her son might grow up to emulate his father in his sexual preferences that she allowed him to chase after women from a very early age.

But at the same time that the young Philippe, or Duke of Chartres as he was known while his father was alive, was making his reputation as a womanizer, it was also becoming clear to the court and those who knew him that he was a very exceptional man in many other ways, too. It became apparent, for instance, that he was far more intelligent than his Bourbon cousins in the senior branch of the family. Even as a child he had an agile mind and, like Christina, he showed a lively interest in history, geography, and mathematics. He was also a very capable linguist, with Latin, Spanish, Italian, and German all within his grasp.

He reached adulthood quickly. He fought his first military campaign in 1691, at the age of seventeen, under Marshal Luxembourg. He seems to have enjoyed being a soldier and was very good at it. At one siege he was reprimanded by the King for his recklessness. He was a lieutenant general at nineteen, and he performed magnificently against William of Orange in the Battle of Neerwinden, which was won and lost three times in a day. Philippe led the household troops in person and at one point was so far ahead of his men that he was captured by the enemy. He was actually on his way to the firing squad when he was rescued.

The duke returned home to find that he was the idol of Paris. But though he must have been gratified it was not all to his advantage, for none of this can have endeared him to Louis XIV, who was a jealous King at the best of times and hated any other member of the royal family being popular. When that figure came from the cadet branch, and his brilliance emphasized the utter nullity of the heir, Louis was vexed all the more. He decided that Philippe was to be kept out of the limelight for a while and a pretext was found to prevent him from fighting in the next campaigns. Matters were not helped when, in January 1692, Louis took it into his head that the duke would be the ideal husband for his natural— i.e., bastard—daughter, Mlle. de Blois, the product of the King's union with his mistress, Madame de Montespan. Both Philippe and his parents were against the plan, his mother especially. They took the view that marriage to a bastard, albeit a royal one, was a dishonor to the family. The duchess, in her memoirs, says she cried all night when the matter was settled, as settled it had to be, since it was a royal command.

Philippe's new wife also had a rather lofty opinion of herself, believing that although she was illegitimate, she was in fact grander than he because she was a daughter of France. As a result, she responded poorly to her husband's advances and, before long, he began to look elsewhere. Philippe's ineffectual marriage also shaped the regency.

Whatever problems and setbacks he experienced as a member of the royal entourage, Philippe continued to develop the intellectual side of his nature. Like Christina, he had an interest in Descartes, and he enjoyed philosophical debates with his friend Archbishop Fénelon (though not at five o'clock in the morning). He had a passion for chemistry, an enthusiasm that was to prove embarrassing a few years later. He acted, he sang, he became a painter and an engraver of considerable talent, he distilled perfumes. He researched the ancient musical system of classical Greece. A few years later, he wrote an opera, *Panthée,* which was at least good enough to be produced.

That may seem like too many interests for Philippe to have been truly serious about all of them but it would be wrong to imagine that he was something of a dilettante like Christina. He was sincere enough in his interests and, by all accounts, an omniverous reader with the happy knack of culling the core of a book very quickly. His wide range of interests probably reflects the fact that Philippe's main problem, which was to lead him into trouble, was boredom. All his life he tried to keep it at bay, but he never succeeded for long.

He was consistent in his love of fine pictures and first purchased paintings on his own account in the year he was married, 1692. The first serious work he purchased was a *St. John in the Desert* by Raphael (now known to be a copy). He bought it from the son of President Harlay, President of the Paris Parlement, and it cost 20,000 livres ($300,000). The death of Philippe's father in 1701 seems to have been the moment when he first thought about becoming a collector on a large scale. The King was so full of remorse for his past treatment of his brother that when Monsieur died suddenly, Louis instructed the new Duke of Orléans to look upon him, his uncle, as his father. He gave Philippe all the pensions of his late father, while enabling him to retain all those he had enjoyed as Duke of Chartres, plus the family estate at St. Cloud and other properties. After settling his father's debts, Philippe thus found himself left with an extremely comfortable income and could afford fine paintings.

But there was another reason why the death of his father produced in Philippe a desire to become a collector. He also inherited a small collection of pictures which contained one or two jewels of the first rank. The information about what Philippe inherited comes from two inventories. The first had been compiled in 1671 after the death of Henrietta, Monsieur's first wife. She had brought with her from England a number of pictures which passed to Philippe in 1701. These included Van Dyck's

Royal Family of England, Correggio's *Magdelen,* a couple of Titians, including his *Portrait of Titian and Aretino,* a Perugino, a Giorgione, a *Self-Portrait* by Annibale Carracci, and a Guercino. It was a small but impressive collection.

The second inventory was drawn up on the death of Monsieur. His things were much less distinguished than Henrietta's; in fact, Monsieur had appalling taste. There were, for instance, over 550 pictures left by him, either in the Palais Royal in Paris or out at St. Cloud or on the family's other estates, but the best ones were all by lesser artists. There was a *Finding of Moses,* by Francesco Salviati, the Florentine Mannerist and friend of Vasari, there was a Luca Giordano and a *Moses in the Bullrushes,* then attributed to Velázquez but now attributed to Honthorst. There were scores of miniatures, including a group of twenty-eight portraits of women, twelve paintings of "stormy seas," Chinese lacquer, porcelain, and a number of precious stones. Noting the difference between Henrietta's taste and that of Monsieur had a refining influence on the young duke and helped him develop a good eye.

Another important factor which stimulated Philippe's desire to surround himself with beautiful things was the Palais Royal, which he also inherited on his father's death. For here was the finest house in all Paris, in all Europe. It was, apart from everything else, a superb gallery, a natural home for a fine collection which Philippe now set about acquiring.

The first pictures to come his way after he moved into the Palais Royal were given to him by the Chevalier of Lorraine, who left them to Philippe in his will. These included a Domenichino, a Pietro da Cortona, and a Titian school painting. The chevalier's legacy came through in 1702 and in the next year Philippe bought two landscapes by Annibale Carracci. This was a revealing purchase so far as the taste of the day was concerned. Like Veronese, the Carracci family has come into and gone out of fashion more than most. But at that time Bolognese painting was very much in vogue: Philippe began his collecting in very conventional ways and only gradually did he acquire his own eclectic tastes. At the same sale he bought two pictures by Domenichino, a Parmigianino, a Ribera, a Teniers, a Dürer triptych, a self-portrait by Rembrandt, and a *Bal Champêtre* by Watteau. He also bought two Veroneses, a *Portrait of a Woman* and *Moses in the Bullrushes.* They were the first canvases the duke bought by a painter who was destined to be so marvelously represented at the Palais Royal.

Other paintings he acquired early on included works by Albani, Guercino, and Giulio Romano. These too reflect the same taste as the others: Italian, Bolognese, somewhat Mannerist. The duke had not yet developed an appetite for earlier works like Bellini, but that would change with his visit to Spain.

Philippe fought in several campaigns in Spain, beginning in 1707. It began well enough and Philip IV presented him with a gift, a *Rape of Europa* by Titian. While he was in Spain, Philippe also bought a Tintoretto and a pseudo-Michelangelo. His appetite was growing but his personality was also getting more complex and, like Christina before him, his judgment was called into question. On one occasion, for instance, Philippe was given permission to have one of the original masterpieces in the Escorial copied. Philippe however wanted to do more than have a copy made: he wanted to switch the copy for the original! It was a cheap idea and, when he was found out the religious authorities were rightly furious and wanted him brought before the Inquisition. They did not succeed but the whole sour episode only served as a curtain raiser to an even bigger scandal when Philippe nearly committed treason in Madrid by instructing an aide to sound out the Spanish about his rights to their throne. These were huge miscalculations that called into question his suitability for any real political role and are reminiscent of some of Christina's more high-handed actions.

About 1707–1708, Philippe's collection began to take on substance. In addition to what he had acquired in Spain, he was also given a number of pictures by the Duke of Gramont, among them a Dürer portrait and Giovanni Bellini's *Circumcision*. Gramont set a fashion that was to be followed a little later, when many of the nobles offered gifts to Philippe as it became apparent there could be a regency in France under Philippe. They were hedging their bets.

In contrast to his collecting, the notorious side to Philippe's character also began to emerge. He was faithful to his wife for a year, but no more, and even then it may have been just for form. After that they went their separate ways, with their own courts, each receiving different sets of visitors. During those early years of the eighteenth century, Philippe, with such a fine intellect, must have become more than a little bored by his position of being so close to the throne but with no other role than to wait for others to die. His rank was so exalted that for him to have indulged his intellectual interests and to have excelled too much at any one thing would, in those days, have smacked of bad form. The effect of this, undoubtedly, was to exaggerate his sense of being an outsider at the royal court and to hasten his adoption of both radical views and a radical lifestyle.

This meant that in the last years of Louis XIV's long reign, Philippe sought his pleasures more and more in Paris rather than at Versailles. And this no doubt had something to do with the fact that his mistresses were low women from the opera rather than the aristocrats who frequented the court. Another thing which drove him from the court was the heavy religious atmosphere that hung over Versailles during the last years of Louis's reign. This, as we have seen, was the doing of the King's second wife, Madame de Maintenon, and Philippe found it uncongenial and oppressive. Cynicism and irony were to be the order of the day during his regency and they reflected his own views entirely, in contrast to the piety and patriotic fervor of Versailles. Louis de Rouvroy, the Duke of Saint-Simon and diarist of the regency, encapsulates Philippe's attitude to his uncle's regime with the following anecdote, typical of those he specialized in: One Christmas Philippe accompanied the King to midnight mass. For the entire service he appeared to be engrossed in his prayer book. Given Orléans's character this impressed but puzzled everyone—until it was discovered that it was not a prayer book at all, but a volume of Rabelais.

The basic elements of a controversial and apparently contradictory personality were thus well and truly set out. However, before he took over the regency, two more scandals added to Philippe's notoriety. The first was the accusation of incest with his eldest daughter, the Duchess of Berry. Born in 1695, Marie Louise Elisabeth, to give the duchess her full name, was undoubtedly the apple of her father's eye, not least because she was as precocious and as ungovernable as he. She was a buxom young lady who was, from time to time, seen in public in her uncorseted nightdress and Philippe clearly relished her fiery, individualistic temperament. She was a lively relief from the tedium of the court. Though the rumors of their incest were widespread, there was never any firm evidence that Philippe's relations with his daughter were unnatural. The gossip may have started because she was such an unruly, difficult personality for everyone else to cope with and yet Philippe, usually so tart in his comments on others, was quite weak and indulgent where she was concerned. To the spiteful French court in those days, that meant they *had* to be lovers.

The second scandal arose out of Philippe's interest in chemistry and the fact that, on the top floor of the Palais Royal, he had equipped Willem Homberg, an otherwise respectable Dutch scientist, who had been a member of the French Academy since 1691, with a lavish laboratory. Inevitably, it was assumed that besides legitimate chemistry there was practiced in the Palais Royal some manner of devilry, alchemy especially. Then, when the Dauphin died in April 1711, there was no shortage of persons ready to suspect he had been murdered by Philippe, who had learned the black arts of poisoning in Homberg's laboratory. As a rival for the throne he was the obvious suspect. The rumors multiplied rapidly the next year when, within the space of three weeks, there occurred the deaths of, first, the Duke of Burgundy, Louis XIV's eldest grandson, and, second, the Duke of Bretagne, Burgundy's own son, aged five. That Philippe was the agent behind this crop of deaths gained wide currency despite the absence of any firm evidence and in spite of the fact that the future Louis XV, born in 1710 and next in line for the throne, was alive and, to all appearances, in good health.

While he was acquiring his reputation as a libertine and a poisoner Philippe nonetheless still followed his intellectual interests and still collected paintings. This was made easier for him because as the Sun King grew older, as his death got closer, so a regency became more and more likely and Philippe's position improved. More and more people followed the Duke of Gramont's lead and sought to please Orléans as a man who, one day soon, might wield ultimate power. Philippe was only too ready to be used in this way. He let himself be persuaded to visit the collections of many nobles. M. du Nacré, for example, had been the duke's companion at arms in Spain. He became captain of the Swiss guard at the Palais Royal, a fact not unconnected with his gift to Orléans of the better part of his collection which included four Albanis, three Annibale Carraccis, one Lodovico Carracci, a Mola, and a Valentin. This was, according to Casimir Stryienski, a Polish connoisseur living in Paris in the late nineteenth century and who wrote a history of the regent's picture gallery, a "pretty gift" for the age when it was believed that the Carracci had "said it all. . . . Beauty, like a Carracci, was a *dicton courant."* Others who benefited from Philippe's favoritism after he became regent, included Tambonneau, who became president of the treasury; de Launay, who became director of money; and La Ravois, who became receiver general of La Rochelle. Philippe became familiar with all the great collections of Paris and, in later years, he acquired pictures from some of the most illustrious names in France: l'Abbé de Mesainville, Derat, de Nossé, Seignelay, Paillet, Noailles, de Menars, de Vendôme, Corberon, de Bretonvilliers, du Cher, l'Abbé de Camps, Dorigny. Nor is that all. In this way the Palais Royal was enriched by many, many works which would eventually constitute the greatest collection in France. It was from other French families, who stood to benefit from his position as regent, that the Palais Royal acquired Raphael's *Holy Family,* Poussin's *Conversion of St. Paul,* and "countless Carraccis."

Not all paintings could be acquired in this way, however, as exemplified by the case of the Christina/Odescalchi collection in Rome. The successful importation of these pictures to France was to be Philippe's crowning act. That Philippe could wait so long and persevere so hard, even when he was regent of France with many political, economic, and administrative problems on his mind, says a good deal for his interest in art.

During his regency, Philippe showed himself as a competent ruler. Since France was his to govern only temporarily, he did not see it as within his remit to act adventurously. He believed his duty was to preserve the country and the crown intact for Louis XV. He survived an attempt to overthrow him, he tried hard to avoid the religious disputes of the day, notably the arguments over Jansenism, he saw the establishment of the Compagnie de l'Occident, set up to exploit the French colony of Louisiana in America. His one grave error was his support for John Law, a Scottish banker who had settled in Paris and who was obsessed with the use of paper money to restimulate the French economy, which had become moribund in Louis XIV's later years. Law's system fueled inflation. People hoarded gold. A devaluation was ordered. Ugly crowds gathered, baying for Law's blood and he eventually sought exile in Venice. In general, though, Philippe left France in better shape than he found it.

Not that Philippe's regency is remembered chiefly for its politics. Philippe II, Duke of Orléans, is nowadays remembered for one word above everything else, a word whose usage he himself helped to coin and which sums up better than anything else the scandalous, dissolute, debauched private life that he led, even when he was ruling France. That word is "roué."

Every evening at five o'clock, Philippe detached himself from the affairs of state. No one was allowed to disturb him. No one who was not invited was allowed into the *petits soupers* (little suppers), as his orgies at the Palais Royal were called. And although many of the men who were present were well educated, well connected, and highly intelligent, affairs of state were *never* discussed. One roué, Louis de Brancas, is chiefly known for the famous put-down he delivered to someone who had the nerve to seek a favor of the regent, by way of de Brancas. "I am very friendly with M. Philippe d'Orléans," he said, "but not at all with the Regent, therefore I can be of no help to you."

The men, the roués, who shared these evenings were all good looking, cultivated, cynical, and, like Philippe, sensualists. Whatever their occupations during the day, they devoted their evenings to their senses. The women, for the most part, were either aristocrats or actresses from the opera. Some were lesbians. All were extremely loose. Competitions were held to see which woman had the best-looking sexual organs, lovemaking was often carried out in public, and all manner of sexual devices were fair game, with Madame de Tencin's example perhaps being the best known.

Madame de Tencin, the *Canoness* de Tencin, was an extraordinary character herself. She had been sent to a convent against her will but, after five years, became pregnant and left. Her brother was a priest in Paris and she joined him . . . only to be accused of incest. Her troubles did not end there: later still, she was accused of murder, imprisoned in the Bastille, and only released after entreaties by the Abbé de Tencin. With such a background it was perhaps only appropriate that she should become the mistress of a highly placed man of the Church. In her case it was Cardinal Dubois, Orléans's lifelong friend and tutor, who had a strong influence on foreign affairs during Philippe's regency. Through Dubois the ambitious woman was introduced to Philippe but his attentions were engrossed elsewhere at the time and he did not take as much notice of her as she would have wished. Something special was therefore called for. She had more faith in her body than her speech and so, a few evenings later, at a *petit souper,* it was suddenly noticed that one of the marble statues in the room stirred ever so slightly. Everyone had been drinking and so at first no notice was taken, the movement was put down to alcohol. But no . . . eventually the regent could see that the figure above him, totally naked, was in fact a real woman. He approached the "statue" where the droll voice of Madame de Tencin said, "Monseigneur, help me down."

Her influence over the regent did not last long, but still long enough to introduce him to the "feast of the flagellants," nocturnal orgies copied from the days of Nero. Madame de Tencin also wrote a book, the "Scandalous Chronicle of Mankind." In this work, which the regent read, she described and evaluated all possible sexual combinations and related vividly the principal debaucheries in history.

Although Orléans went to extremes in his pursuit of pleasure and sensual gratification, in other ways he was exactly in tune with what was happening in the rest of France under him. He was both a cause and a symptom of that change, its most visible sign. His tastes in art were central to this for a distinctive, albeit short, phase in the arts known as the Régence style, is now recognized. It spanned Philippe's time in office and contributed to the development of the Rococo.

Rococo first emerged in France around 1690. It is noted chiefly for its freely handled S-shaped curves and its bright clear colors set in borders of gold and white. It is essentially exuberant, concerned, as was Philippe himself, with shaking off the deadening effects of the last years of Louis XIV's reign. Philippe was perfectly in tune with this change of mood in France. He found contemporary artists congenial, and at the same time as he collected old masters, like the Christina/Odescalchi gallery, he employed contemporary masters to refurbish the Palais Royal. Among the artists, four men stood out and between them typified the Rococo. These four were Antoine Watteau, Charles Cressent, Antoine Coypel, and Gilles-Marie Oppenord:

Watteau was born in 1684 in Valenciennes, a French town which had been Flemish until just before his birth. He moved to Paris around 1702 and a couple of years later became apprenticed to Claude Gillot, a painter of theatrical scenery. At that point Watteau had already contracted the tuberculosis that was to cut short his life.

Veronese was a great inspiration to Watteau, so it may have been in the Palais Royal that he first made contact with the Venetian's great masterpieces. The regent always kept open house in the palace for any serious artist or connoisseur who wanted to view his collection as this was before the age of public galleries. Even though *Wisdom and Strength* and the other Christina/Odescalchi Veroneses had not arrived others, like his *Moses in the Bullrushes,* had.

After he had worked for Gillot for a year or two, Watteau moved on to assist the decorative painter Claude Audran. Audran was also keeper of the Luxembourg Palace and this gave Watteau two advantages: one, he obtained easy access to the great Rubens cycle of paintings in the palace, the *Life of Marie de Médici* (the masterpiece which helped to divide artists in France into Poussinistes and Rubénistes.) These pictures had a profound effect on Watteau. Second, it gave him equally easy access to Orléans, since this was where the Duchess of Berry, the regent's eldest and favorite daughter, lived.

Around 1710–12, Watteau began to evolve his own form of Rubénisme. As with Giorgione before him, his concern was not so much to capture a likeness of a person or a place as to capture a certain *mood,* a fleeting sense of pleasure or a transitory moment of melancholy. That "mood catching" appealed enormously to the regent and he acquired what has become one of Watteau's more celebrated canvases, *Le Bal Champêtre.* In this painting, the image of a buxom woman, flimsily dressed, could almost be the Duchess of Berry herself.

Charles Cressent had been born in 1685 and was, therefore, like Watteau, a decade younger than the regent. He began as a sculptor but thereafter became the leading *ébeniste,* or furniture maker, in the Régence and early Rococo periods. His furniture was opulent, with elaborate bronze mounts which, against guild rules, he fashioned, cast, and gilded himself. Having been a sculptor his motifs were always more adventurous than those of the average furniture maker and he delighted in making his designs antifunctional. In his famous "dragon commode," for instance, the bronze motifs completely disguise the divisions of the drawers. For the Palais Royal he fashioned numerous opulent lanterns, in violet and rosewood, chests of drawers in all shapes (he may have invented the high-legged type, known as Louis XV), bookshelves, and consoles. And he specialized in superb cartel clocks (timepieces with elaborate cases designed to hang on walls).

Antoine Coypel may not be as famous today as is Watteau but at the turn of eighteenth century he was the official court painter under Louis XIV and remained in this position when Philippe became regent. He was the man who taught Orléans to paint and who told other pupils: "You are lucky in that Monsieur Philippe de Chartres [who was only seventeen at that time] is a person of so high a rank. Had he been an ordinary man, you should have feared a lot, for he would have surpassed you all." The Coypel family was a painter's dynasty which had begun with Noël and was to encompass Nicolas and Charles Antoine, who became first painter to Louis XV in 1743 and director of the French Academy in 1747. Antoine's sensualism is clearly what appealed to Philippe.

Gilles-Marie Oppenord was born in Paris in 1672 and was therefore the regent's contemporary. The son of a Dutch *ébeniste,* he went to the French Academy and started to design domestic interiors in 1714. He was very popular with Philippe and in 1715 became his accredited architect. It was Oppenord who, together with Philippe, had most to do with reorganizing and refashioning the Palais Royal.

Of all the buildings which *Wisdom and Strength* has occupied, the Palais Royal in Paris is without doubt the most historic. Today, it is difficult to see why, for the palace is as quiet now as it must have been when it was built by Cardinal Richelieu and when it was on the outskirts of Paris, at the city's northwestern tip. But from Philippe's time onward, the Palais Royal grew in importance and its role in the events leading up to the French Revolution in 1789 was vital.

As it existed in the seventeenth and eighteenth centuries, the Palais Royal was also regarded as one of the most beautiful buildings in Europe. Built between 1629 and 1634 by that other great collector, Cardinal Richelieu, from designs by Jacques Lemercier, it was first known as the Palais Richelieu and housed the cardinal's remarkable collection. After his death in 1642, when the collection and the Palais itself were left to the nation, Anne of Austria, mother of Louis XIV, moved there from the Louvre. It was not considered fitting for the Queen regent to live in a house bearing the name of one of her subjects and so it was changed to the Palais Royal. After Louis XIV came to the throne, the palace became a grace-and-favor (i.e., free) residence for his younger brother, Monsieur. Then, in 1692, at Philippe's controversial marriage to Mlle. de Blois, the King gave the Palais Royal to the house of Orléans.

When Philippe became duke on his father's death in 1701, his income jumped to an enormous sum annually ($77 million). Since his wife and mother were both wealthy in their own right, this gave him the opportunity to lavish an enormous sum on the Palais. He made no alterations to the facade but did make drastic renovations of the interior.

In those days, the Palais Royal was shaped somewhat like a capital letter "H" but with two crossbars instead of one. The southwest corner housed, as it still does, the Théâtre Français. This corner was where most of the life of the palace was located. The dowager duchess lived right next to the theater, overlooking the Rue St. Honoré and, because they did not get on, the young duchess lived at the other end of the palace, on the northern edge, overlooking the Rue de Richelieu. Both women lived on the ground floor with the household staff between them.

Philippe occupied three sets of rooms in the palace while he was Duke of Orléans. To begin with he had rooms opposite his mother, on the right-hand side, overlooking the Rue St. Honoré. Then he moved to the left side, where his *petits soupers* were first held. Finally he took the entire second floor of the left side when he revamped the whole building. Most of the private apartments of the palace were on the left side, with the public reception rooms in the center and on the right. The galleries in which *Wisdom and Strength* and the other Veroneses hung were all on the left side of the palace, on the second floor, where Philippe had his study or office.

The way in which Philippe redecorated the palace reflected his very negative reaction to the Louis XIV style that had dominated France at the end of the seventeenth century. That taste had been for heavy drapes and rich materials. Philippe wanted a lighter touch, more delicate, yet charming. This is what Coypel and Oppenord gave him. The heavy tapestries were removed from the seats and curtains of the private apartments and replaced by light gilding, softer fabrics in more cheerful colors with flower designs and Venus's attributes, such as ribbons. The great drawing room, which faced the Rue de Richelieu, was redesigned by Cartaud, another of Philippe's architects, so that it opened into smaller, more intimate apartments, ready for the supper parties.

The young duchess's apartments, which opened onto the Jardin des Princes, were decorated with magnificent boiseries—wooden panels—ornate gilt mirrors, and large fireplaces and adorned with brass fire dogs. The duchess had a passion for embroidery and her embroidery girls went everywhere with her. And when the duchess was not in residence, the embroidered hangings were folded up and put away. It was also the custom in those times for the upholstery and hangings to be changed with the seasons. The duchess had a beautiful set of gold and silver cutlery which, upon her death, was bequeathed to her ladies-in-waiting and maids. This followed the custom among the royal family and aristocracy: to bequeath things to the servants who had cared for them. So the head groom was given the horses, the butler got the silver, and so on. What started as a gesture for services rendered gradually became an obligation. The Orléans family kept up the tradition but when the duchess died in 1749 fights broke out among her staff over who should get what.

The regent's own apartments were no less sumptuous than the duchess's. The furniture was designed by Cressent and decorated with bronze figures inlaid with Philippe's favorite color scheme: purple and crimson. Crimson was in fact the dominant color throughout Philippe's apartments, although gilt, white, and walnut were also popular. Philippe's bed was of walnut and set into an alcove. The walls were decorated with panels of crimson silk, piped with gold trim, and surrounded by mirrors and sculptures. The chairs and stools were covered in crimson plush and there was a tomb-shaped chest of drawers also inlaid with purple wood and a folding screen with ten panels in crimson damask. Even his study was furnished in crimson.

The colors Philippe liked and the vanities—the mirrors, the ornate decorations—made the Palais Royal a perfect setting for paintings. Philippe's favorite painters appear to have been Titian and Van Dyck, whose pictures he kept in his bedroom, above the doors. The other paintings were hung in one or another of the galleries on the left side of the palace, on the second floor. The arrival of the Christina/Odescalchi collection was the crowning glory of the Palais Royal, just as it was the finest coup in all of Philippe's years of collecting. However, several years were to elapse between Orléans's renovation of the Palais and the arrival of the pictures. *Wisdom and Strength* and all the other pictures still had a few adventures left to experience before they made it safely to the Palais Royal.

After Pierre Crozat returned to Paris in 1715, he still maintained contact with the Odescalchi family but a solution remained difficult. The duke asked Crozat to choose the 110 paintings, out of 240, which he considered the best and to make an offer for them. It did not work. Next, the Odescalchis tried to pretend again that the Emperor was interested, hoping that this would force Philippe to dig deeper into his pocket. Very well, said Orléans, in so many words, I am really interested in only seven pictures: four Correggios and three Titians. All the paintings were of allegorical subjects and were a little "free" for the Rome of the day, so Philippe thought the Odescalchis might part with them for 20,000 ecus ($312,000). Unfortunately for the duke, Baldassarre Odescalchi had just become engaged and his fiancée was very rich. The Italians now felt no urgency and the tactic failed. Crozat tried again a year later, at the end of 1716, this time on his own initiative. He wrote to Gualtiero about the Odescalchis' jumble of drawings, hoping to dislodge a few. But no, the family was not interested in small deals. In March 1717 the negotiations broke down again.

Nothing happened for three years. Philippe was embroiled in government and John Law's controversial economic policies. And meanwhile the Odescalchi family enjoyed the funds of Baldassarre's new bride. Then, in 1720, as one contemporary observer put it, "the devil himself took a hand." The young duchess of Bracciano died in a distressing tragedy. Orléans moved swiftly, showing that he had never quite taken his mind off the collection. But, in view of the delicate situation, an approach was made in a roundabout way: the regent instructed Dubois, Dubois instructed Crozat, Crozat contacted Gualtiero, and Gualtiero contacted Bracciano's agent, abbé Calcaprina. The long way round, as it sometimes does, worked perfectly. The distraught Bracciano was receptive. Gualtiero even obtained a draft contract.

Now that a deal looked like it was on, Crozat charged an expert in old masters, Pierre Guilbert, to go and see the paintings and to draw up an assessment. Guilbert left for Rome immediately and produced his report promptly. It seems that the Odescalchi nephews did not share their uncle's passion, for the pictures were not hung properly, making it difficult for Guilbert to give a considered opinion. And he went on to say that many of the paintings were doubtful. Titian's *Sleeping Venus,* he said, was not a Titian at all, but by Palma Vecchio. Other Titians were not autograph works either but school pictures. But another painting, *The Departure of Adonis for the Hunt,* was an undoubted original. He had seen a very similar picture in Vienna, he said, which belonged to the Emperor and he considered that both were masterpieces. The Veroneses were in general admired and the "enigmatic" titles, such as *Head of a Man,* rather ironically regarded. Presumably, Guilbert meant to suggest that the Odescalchis were unaware of the classical allusions contained in Veronese's masterpieces. *Respect* was regarded as the best of the four ceiling paintings.

The Correggios were criticized in turn. *The Madonna with St. Jerome,* "on which one has seen engraved by Agostino Carracci, and of which the most authentic original is at St. Anthony's in Parma, is here of less grandeur, and I do not believe at present that it is an original picture, especially as it is retouched and disguised a lot." Another picture, *L'Amour qui taille son arc (Cupid Curving his Bow),* was, according to Guilbert, "a very beautiful copy by Parmigianino," the original being in Vienna "with the emperor." Correggio's three celebrated pictures representing the loves of the gods (*Danaë, Leda,* and *Io*) he said were excellent and indisputable originals but they had been damaged "and retouched by Carlo Maratti—there is much lost of their first lustre."

With all these caveats, Guilbert went on to say that "all the other precious pictures of this rare collection, all the famous masters—Titian, Parmigianino, Giulio Romano, Carracci, Guido [Reni], Rubens—seem to me to be original." His report is interesting not least for the fact that it is one of the first pieces of art criticism or connoisseurship that has a modern flavor. Guilbert was a professional. He had traveled across Europe and seen many undisputed autographed works, and was atuned to the fact that there were many copies around, masquerading as originals. And he was aware that there were people, like Maratti, who made a living out of "revivifying" old masters.

Guilbert's assessment concluded with some practical tips for the packing and transport of the paintings, but that proved still somewhat premature. Obstacles were now put in the way of a successful sale by the Holy See. There were not yet in the eighteenth century laws for the protection of masterpieces. But His Holiness's permission was nonetheless needed in order to export works of art from the papal states. (The experiences of Christina and her envoy Palbitzki show that this was not automatic even for grand persons, for Palbitzki was unable to take to Sweden certain drawings and sculptures which Christina wanted [see page 111 above].) The regent, therefore, had to write to Clement XI to persuade him to grant a license. He wrote from Paris on July 16, 1720 (in the middle of the crisis over Law's system), and reminded Clement that it had been some years since the negotiations had begun with the Odescalchis for Christina's collection. He informed the Pope that the affair was now near conclusion and said that Crozat was being sent to handle the matter.

What he did not say was that, at that stage, they had still not come to an agreement about a price for the collection. Orléans had offered 90,000 ecus ($1,400,000) but Bracciano wanted 95,000. For a moment it looked as though things might be stalled again, but then the Italian reduced his demands by 1,000 ecus, the toing and froing continued and, within a month, a price of 93,000 was agreed upon. Crozat, in the midst of everything, managed to look after his own affairs as well. He continued pestering the Odescalchis, via Gualtiero, about the drawings until he was told he could have some but that they would cost him "more than a few bottles of champagne."

All would therefore have been well, but for the fact that the Pope was now tardy in giving his permission for the export license. This was not simply diligence of course, or thoroughness, or because the Pope was reluctant to allow the pictures to go (although the latter was almost certainly true). The truth is that everyone, in an affair such as this, wanted a kickback of some kind, even the Pope. The Vatican representative who Gualtiero had to deal with was Pierre-François Lafiteau, and he had His Holiness's ear. Lafiteau opened this stage of the proceedings by telling Gualtiero frankly that there would be no problem over the export license, provided the license was paid for. Gualtiero passed this news on to Crozat, adding that he would be prepared to pay a small sum out of his own pocket but that if a large sum was necessary, "I shall have the honor of rendering the bill to HRH before it [i.e., the collection] passes abroad." At that point no one had any idea what the Pope would charge but a week later a commission of 3 percent was mentioned in another of Gualtiero's letters. This was an entirely arbitrary sum, however, there being no rules to govern a transaction of this kind. Gualtiero professed himself astonished by this demand, in view of Philippe's rank in France but the regent seems not to have minded. This commission was not all, however; it now transpired that the Pope also wanted a "souvenir" and this too was put to Crozat. Gualtiero's letters show him to be very embarrassed by this extra demand on the part of His Holiness. He wrote to Crozat, saying that the Pope coveted a book of Raphael's drawings: this is clearly the "souvenir" that the Pope had in mind. Gualtiero said that he had told the Pope that this was unfair, that if Philippe was buying something, it should belong to him. It did no good. The Pope was adamant and in his next letters Gualtiero, reluctantly, concluded that only if the Pope's wishes were honored would the paintings ever leave Rome.

This extra demand by the Pope seems to have stuck in Philippe's throat, too. Before acceding to His Holiness's demand, he now tried another tactic. While all this was going on, the abbé de Saint-Albin, an illegitimate son of the regent, arrived in Rome. He was charged with trying to find a solution to the chief religious problem in France: Jansenism. Orléans calculated that by showing the Pope his close personal interest in a religious matter, to the extent of sending his own son to deal with it, the way would be smoothed for the export of the paintings. But no, this was not to be. Now it was His Holiness's turn to try something different. He told Philippe that representations had been made to him by the Accademia di San Luca (the painters' academy) to the effect that the export of Christina's paintings would deprive Rome "of all that is most precious." The Pope therefore made the astonishing suggestion that Orléans might wish to take only the more obscene paintings among the collection—presumably he was well aware of Philippe's reputation. It was a misjudgment. Gualtiero called the Pope's bluff and in reply suggested that if—once a selection of nude pictures arrived in Paris—it became known that it was His Holiness who had had the idea in the first place and had a hand in the choice, it would hardly look good for the Church. The Pope dropped the idea and a short while later Gualtiero wrote, pithily, "He understood my thoughts."

This little maneuver being exhausted, the Pope once again reiterated his desire for a souvenir. He quoted a precedent concerning the Czar. His Holiness had sent the Russian a statue and, in thanks, had received a present in return. The Pope obviously saw the situations as similar, though Gualtiero, on Philippe's behalf, did not. Orléans would not budge.

Now the Pope fell sick, making him even more difficult to deal with. Across Europe, Orléans's minister, Dubois, found it in France's interest to conclude a treaty with Protestant England. This was obviously not going to be popular with His Holiness and, combined with his illness, would make him more obdurate than ever over the Odescalchi collection. Accordingly, Philippe gave permission for negotiations to be concluded in secret with Don Baldassarre and for the paintings to be smuggled out of Italy. The agreement was signed in January 1721, the contract stipulating that payment was to be made within four months.

This, in its turn, presented new problems. Philippe had put aside a set of jewels worth 120,000 ecus ($1,900,000) to pay for the pictures, but getting the money to Rome was difficult. (It was the financial crisis brought on by Law's system that obliged Orléans to pay in this way.) While Crozat, who had charge of the jewels, was in Lyon en route to Rome, a terrible outbreak of the plague appeared in Marseilles. All commerce between Italy and France was forbidden so Crozat had to turn around and make for Amsterdam, where he changed the jewels into cash at a Dutch bank. The delay brought Crozat dangerously close to the deadline stipulated in the contract. However, when Crozat did arrive in Rome, in April, the Pope was dead.

The problem now was different but no less awkward. With a conclave in session, there was still no sovereign pontiff, and therefore no one to give permission for the export license. Moreover, neither Gualtiero nor the other intermediaries, who were also cardinals, could communicate with the outside world. In these circumstances, Crozat decided to go ahead and smuggle the paintings out of the papal states while the conclave was still in session. His plan involved loading the collection onto donkeys, disguised as the belongings of the cardinal of Rohan, who had diplomatic immunity (and who of course was himself conveniently incommunicado in the conclave) and to ship them from the Odescalchi palazzo in the Piazza SS. Apostoli to the family home in Milan, which was outside the papal states. There the rest of the payment would be made and Crozat would ship them onward.

Before any of this could happen, however, Cardinal Conti was elected Innocent XIII. He might have brought about a speedy solution but in fact there were several turns of the wheel to go. Since one part of the payment had been made, Poërson, who was director of the French Academy in Rome, was allowed free access to the pictures. He took with him the chevalier Benedetto Luti, one of the best-known painters in Rome at the time, but also a famous restorer. He was to act as adviser and conservator. Now that he had a chance to see the collection close up, Poërson was divided in his opinion. "The more one sees these marvellous works," he wrote, "the more one admires them. But among these beautiful things there is much that is mediocre and a great deal that is worse than mediocre." The pictures were examined and a decision taken with Luti on which ones needed restoring.

Yet another obstacle appeared when the Odescalchi withdrew Poërson's free access because the balance of the money had not arrived. Everything got very awkward again. At long last, however, in June 1721, the new Pope finally allowed the collection to go. Philippe was told the news and the final installment was paid.

The next problem, given the traveling conditions of the time, was restoration. It was decided to do this *before* the journey rather than when they got to Paris, so Luti set about it, beginning in July and working through August. According to Poërson's letters, Luti carried out his task with great success: his repair of a *Virgin* by Raphael, for example, was admired "by all who have seen it." He had filled in holes, sometimes five or six layers deep and he had treated the wood of the stretchers and the panels so that they would be resistant to attack from insects. Luti was in the forefront of his trade, scientifically speaking, and Poërson was clearly telling no more than the truth when he confided to the Duke of Antin that "it was a stroke of luck that I have found this man."

By September the collection was ready to go. Immense pains were taken with the packing (the Odescalchi kept the frames since they intended to replace the collection with copies—they never did). Wooden cases were built for each canvas and then these were divided into fifteen caseloads, eight for the regent and no fewer than seven for Crozat.

That same month the cases were shipped to the port of Civitavecchia, northwest of Rome, where they embarked on a journey which, if not quite as momentous in personal terms as the one they had made south with Christina, was nonetheless equally colorful. From Civitavecchia, the cargo was shipped across the Mediterranean but not to Marseilles, as might have happened a few years earlier. Nor did the collection go through the Straits of Gibraltar, out into the Atlantic, and reach the north of France that way. The continuing wars between France and Spain had inspired a remarkable act of engineering in France which the paintings now took advantage of. The cargo was therefore unloaded, on November 4, at the small port of Sète.

Sète was the Mediterranean end of the Canal du Languedoc, also known as the Canal du Midi, which exited at the other end into the Atlantic Ocean at Bordeaux. At that time, the Canal du Languedoc was considered "the greatest feat of civil engineering in Europe" since Roman times. To Voltaire it was *"le monument le plus glorieux."* The joining of the Mediterranean and the Atlantic was not a new idea, yet it had been accomplished only recently, late in the seventeenth century. The 150-mile canal (linking seas 320 miles apart) had required eight thousand men to construct it and took fifteen years to complete. It was a phenomenal engineering achievement and Sète itself was built especially to be the Mediterranean end of the canal.

The building of the canal was not all plain sailing, though. The local taxes raised to pay for it were very unpopular and as a result there was a lot of violence, including several murders. A hundred locks had to be built to raise the canal 620 feet above sea level, as well as many aqueducts and cuttings and 139 bridges spanning it. It cost over fifteen million livres to build, or about fifty million gold francs (say $4.7 billion at 1989 rates), nearly twice the estimate.

When *Wisdom and Strength* and the rest of the Christina/Odescalchi collection traveled along it, the canal had been open for about forty years, having been finished in 1681. But it had not yet turned a profit. Revenues from the shipping tolls did not cover the original investments until 1724 and it was not until the wars with Spain, much later in the eighteenth century, that the canal became as profitable as had originally been anticipated by Baron de Bonrepos, who had built it. Then the valuable cargoes of wine from Bordeaux could get to the Mediterranean without running the risk of the Spanish coast.

Leaving Sète, the canal turned south to Agde (which is north of Narbonne), then inland to Béziers. After Béziers came the Malpas Tunnel, the oldest canal tunnel in the world. Next, the canal followed the Aude River through Carcassonne and Castelnaudary, where a *grand bassin* was built to provide a reservoir of water for the staircase of locks and which today is a very pleasant, small lake. Then it was on to Toulouse, where three canals joined up. From Toulouse the canal broadly followed the Garonne through flatter but still very beautiful countryside: Castelsarrasin, Moissac, Agen, Buzet, Meilhan, Castets, Bordeaux. From Bordeaux the better pictures, including *Wisdom and Strength,* went by road to

Paris while the rest went by sea north to Nantes, from where they traveled up the Loire to Orléans and only then by road to the capital.

And so, the affair which had opened on December 23, 1713, finally came to a successful conclusion during the early days of December eight years later. On the thirteenth of that month, the Duke of Antin was able to write to Pöerson that the pictures had arrived, to the great satisfaction of the regent, and he added his congratulations on the way they had been packed. Crozat, for his part, sent his thanks to Cardinal Gualtiero, adding that Orléans had found in the pictures "even more beauty than he thought he would. . . . Truly, there are sixty to eighty pictures which are marvellous. The satisfaction of HRH must augment the obligation to your eminence for having procured for him this superb treasure house of painting."

The rest of Paris had to wait awhile before it was apprised of the details of the collection now in its midst. The first account appeared in the newspaper *Mercury* in February 1722. The article was marked by so many mistakes, however, that it is questionable whether the writer actually saw the pictures. The size of the collection was doubled and the author also reported that Gustavus Adolphus *himself* had taken the treasures to Stockholm, "after having surprised the 'small town' of Prague in 1631." The list of masterpieces then given included a number of astounding inventions and several other pictures which had never been in the regent's collection at all. Other parts of the collection, especially the very popular Correggios, were described minutely and very accurately. This is not to be credited to the journalist, however, for these entries had been copied word for word from a guidebook to Rome published in 1700.

Orléans had just two years to live when the Christina/Odescalchi paintings arrived in Paris. By common consent, the pictures completed his collection, making it the best in the known world at the time and probably the best collection of Italian works in France in any age apart from Napoleon's temporary acquisitions (see pp. 254 ff., below). The collection also completed Orléans's galleries in the Palais Royal, where the fashions were rather different from those of Italy and Habsburg Europe.

There were at first three galleries in the palace, and later four, as Philippe's collections grew. All of them were on the second floor, on the left side of the building. Three of the galleries were, in effect, inherited from Cardinal Richelieu since they had hardly been changed by Anne of Austria or Monsieur. The first of these, the "Galerie des Hommes Illustres" ran the length of the inner wall of the palace and overlooked the courtyard. This gallery was an invention of the cardinal's and contained portraits of twenty-five illustrious French figures by such artists as Simon Vouet, Justus van Egmont, and Philippe de Champaigne. Each picture was accompanied by two marble busts, most of which were antiques. Among the people represented in this gallery were Henry IV, Marie de Médicis, and Gaston de Foix.

The gallery was separated from Richelieu's old chapel, now turned into an office, by the Chambres des Poussins, where the *Seven Sacraments* were displayed. Poussin's great masterpiece was Philippe's other great acquisition, made for him by Dubois in the Netherlands, when the cardinal went there secretly and undercover as an art dealer to negotiate with the English. (Christina's envoys had also used art dealings as a cover for secret missions.) Whatever political advantage came from Dubois's expedition, it is unlikely that it matched the enduring glory of the *Seven Sacraments*.

Beyond the chapel-turned-office was the second great gallery, the Mansart Gallery, which overlooked the Rue de Richelieu. This space was divided into several smaller rooms and in 1715 it was extended by Cartaud who created a salon known as La Lanterne because it had a glass ceiling to provide better light for the new pictures then expected from Rome.

At the northern end of the Mansart Gallery was the grand Salon d'Oppenordt which was probably the most impressive room of all. Oppenordt, who did the refurbishing just after Philippe became regent, decorated the salon mainly in gold. Its boiseries were picked out in gold leaf, there were gilt chairs and banquettes along the walls, which were partly hung with Gobelin tapestries. There were mirrors four meters high and a huge chandelier with twelve branches, made of rock crystal. There were two girandoles: carved mirrors with light brackets, which supported a bronze-gilt ship surrounded by nymphs and Tritons. There were also the inevitable crimson silk panels. In front of the windows looking out on the Rue de Richelieu there were two large, green, marble-topped tables laden with objets d'art, including a beautiful "Farnese lion and bull and the lion overwhelming a horse."

Twenty-seven pictures, including several Titians, hung in this room. But after the Christina/Odescalchi collection arrived, this was to be home for Philippe's considerable collection of Veroneses. The master's *Finding of Moses in the Bullrushes* which Philippe had acquired separately many years before, was now for the first time hung with *Wisdom and Strength* and the other Prague pictures.

Through the Salon d'Oppenordt, at the northern tip of the building and directly over the young duchess's apartments, was a gallery which Philippe helped to design. This was the Galerie d'Aeneas. It was furnished in much the same sumptuous way as the Salon d'Oppenordt: four sofas covered in Gobelin tapestries, no fewer than thirty-six girandoles with six branches each, twelve large torchères, carved and gilded, thirty-six footstools, and three large tables laden with ornaments. There was an enormous green marble fireplace and twelve windows. But the showpiece of this gallery was the group of fourteen pictures painted by Antoine Coypel on the architraves and paneling. It was Philippe's idea that they show the deeds of the heroes mentioned in the *Aeneid* and they made an impressive sight. Unfortunately, they disappeared at the end of the eighteenth century, when this part of the building was demolished.

Louis XV reached his majority on February 15, 1723, when Philippe's regency formally ended. He took over as Prime Minister but he did not last long. He died, aged forty-nine, on December 2 that same year. At the time of his death there was a quantity of pictures in his possession which he did not own; he had been negotiating their acquisition up to the end. These included a Titian, a Tintoretto, and a Zuccaro. His widow sent them back, however, since when the regent died the Orléans passion for acquiring fine paintings died with him.

This copy of
Wisdom and Strength
(by François Boucher)
was commissioned
by the royal family
of Portugal.

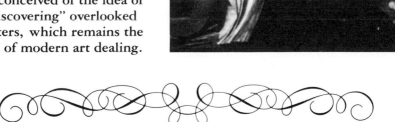

Jean Baptiste Pierre
Le Brun (self-portrait). The
keeper of Égalité's collection
also conceived of the idea of
"rediscovering" overlooked
painters, which remains the
basis of modern art dealing.

Francis Egerton, third
and last Duke of
Bridgewater.
Engraving by C. Picard
after J. H. Craig.

George Granville
Leveson-Gower, second
Marquess of Stafford,
by Joseph Nollekens.

Frederick, fifth Earl of Carlisle, by Sir Joshua Reynolds. These three acquired Égalité's pictures and then sold the ones they didn't want. Called the Orléans sale, this was one of the greatest auctions ever held.

The picture gallery in Thomas Hope's mansion in Duchess Street, London. The outline of *Vice and Virtue* may be seen on the left. *Wisdom and Strength* probably hung opposite.

Thomas Hope, shown in Egyptian dress. Painting by Sir William Beechey.

Lily, Duchess of Marlborough, who rented Deepdene at the end of the nineteenth century.

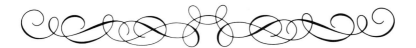

Deepdene, Hope's picturesque country house near Guilford in Surrey. After Hope Sr. died, his son Henry Thomas saw the house become the country headquarters for the Young England Party. It was here that Benjamin Disraeli's political novels were conceived.

LEFT: Roger Fry (self-portrait). It was Fry who advised Henry Clay Frick to buy *Wisdom and Strength*. RIGHT: Henry Clay Frick by John C. Johansen. One of America's fabled industrial titans, Frick created a collection at his home on Seventieth Street in Manhattan that the *New York Times* described as "Paradise."

A view of *Wisdom and Strength* in the West Gallery at the Frick Collection. "Paradise" was a fitting place for the masterpiece to end its adventures.

14.
The Palais Royal:
The Most Beautiful House
in Europe

The regent was a cultured and discerning man but it was the other side of his nature, his debauchery, which was to be his main legacy. Philippe was fond of his daughters, exceedingly fond in the case of the Duchess of Berry, but he disliked his son whom he regarded as a nullity.

Philippe's son, Louis, was known as the Duke of Chartres until the regent's death. He was twenty when his father died and somewhat delicate: the only exercise he allowed himself was dancing. This was quite the wrong sort of constitution for the times. Had he been a little older, or a little tougher, Louis could have followed his father as Prime Minister or played some other important part in the affairs of the day. As it was, however, he allowed himself to be elbowed out of the way and from that date, 1723, the importance and significance of the house of Orléans began to change.

The new Duke of Orléans changed in other ways, too. Like his father, Louis had been brought up to enjoy the same sensual pleasures: he was a young roué with no shortage of mistresses. All that now went. He dismissed his mistresses, canceled his orgies, and turned to religion. It was said that he had been shocked by the fact that his father had died unfortified by the last rites of the Church. He was also badly affected when his wife, Augusta, a princess from Baden, who had given Louis a son in 1725, died in August of the next year giving birth to a daughter. After that, his life became one of increasing austerity. Indeed, his austere, solitary nature became so intense that he decided to withdraw from the Palais Royal altogether and moved to Ste. Geneviève, an abbey in Paris, where he spent his time translating the psalms. He followed even the most minute devotional practices and studied so hard that he could read Chaldean, Hebrew, Syriac, and Greek. He never used a fire and he slept on straw. He personally distributed his alms, the only thing to earn him praise, for it was widely thought that his behavior was "unbecoming" for a prince of the blood. In 1749 his eccentricity turned into outright madness, following the death of his mother. Louis refused to attend her funeral on the unusual grounds that there was no such thing as death.

Louis believed that those whom one cared for did not die but merely disappeared from earth only to reappear a short time afterward. He was so convinced of this in the case of his mother that he continued to set aside her pension.

He also broke with his son that year because the then Duke of Chartres (known as Philippe the Fat) refused to sign a declaration stating that he and the duchess had no children—Louis having persuaded himself that the children had been bought and introduced secretly into the house. Louis refused to see his grandchildren. Only when he was on his death-bed were the two children admitted to his saintly presence, on which occasion he proceeded to bestow a curse upon his grandson, then aged five. This was none other than Philippe-Égalité.

To be fair to Louis, some of this may be exaggerated. After the French Revolution, many French historians were notoriously hostile to the house of Orléans and Louis was one of the most reviled. Yet could he have really been so mad given that he managed to restore the family's financial fortunes, which had been so severely depleted by the extravagances of his father, Philippe II? And in spite of his largesse in donating alms, he increased the Orléans' land holdings. Historians have certainly distorted some of his actions regarding the picture collection in the Palais Royal. When he inherited the palace, Louis did not touch the fabric of the building at all, or the decoration, since Philippe had left them in such magnificent condition. According to some sources, however, the pictures were another matter. In his piety he took such a fierce dislike to the more risqué Italian masters—particularly those from the Christina/Odescalchi collection—that he destroyed them in a bonfire. According to this ac-count, forty pictures were destroyed and it would have been more had not a boy saved some, including Veronese's *Leda*. If true, this would certainly count as the act of a mad philistine. However, the account contains a number of demonstrable inaccuracies, for example, that the Orléans collection was bought at an auction in Rome. Furthermore, com-parison of two catalogs of the collection, one compiled by Dubois de St. Gelais in 1723, on the death of Philippe, and the other in 1752, follow-ing Louis's own death, confirms that nowhere near forty pictures could have been destroyed. What does seem to have happened is that two pictures only, both by Correggio, were mutilated: Louis had the head of *Io* cut off and the canvas of *Leda* divided into three segments. It is cer-tainly possible that the suggestive nature of these compositions was the reason for Louis's action but that was the extent of the destruction. In both cases Coypel was able to repair the pictures and he succeeded in selling them to the King of Prussia.

Louis finally became convinced of the reality of death on February 4,

1752, when he underwent the experience himself. Ironically, he never received the sacraments which, lacking in his father, had helped bring about his own change of heart. Louis left his library and his medallions to the abbey but the rest, including the Palais Royal and the pictures, stayed in the Orléans family.

Louis Philippe of Orléans, Louis's son and heir, was born at Versailles on May 12, 1725. He was, therefore, never to know his grandfather the regent. He served with the French armies in the campaigns of 1742–44, during the wars of the Austrian succession, and at the Battle of Fontenoy in 1745. Like his grandfather he was very brave; he survived having his horse killed from under him at the Battle of Dettingen. After the campaigns, however, he retired to his country seat at Bagnolet where, now known as Philippe the Fat, he wallowed in pleasure. He liked the theater and gambling and was an inveterate hunter.

He married the young and beautiful Louise-Henriette de Bourbon-Conti and they indulged in a very public passion, Philippe-Égalité being its first fruit. Louise-Henriette would have been very popular with the regent for as well as being very beautiful she also loved scandal. Once, when the question of her son's legitimacy was being discussed, she laughed and replied, "When you fall upon a pile of thorns do you know which one has pricked you?" One widely circulated story about her related how, in order to recover her sexual appetite after her debauches, the duchess would plunge into a bath of human blood. Sadly, she died young, at the age of thirty-three, in 1759. The cause, the gossips said, was debauchery quite as much as consumption. After her death a large number of obscene limericks written by her were discovered by her bed.

Philippe the Fat was much more interested in the Palais Royal and in the arts than was his father. He began to refurbish the palace even before Louis died. In 1749–50, in collaboration with the city of Paris, he bought property adjoining the Opera so that he could improve access to it. He also introduced three important changes. He engaged Cartaud to build new rooms overlooking the Rue des Bons-Enfants at the north. Then, in 1752, Pierre Constant (later known as Constant d'Ivry) built a new facade for the second courtyard and extended the left wing. Finally, Jean-Michel Moreau rebuilt the facade on the Rue St. Honoré after the Opera had burned down in 1763. All in all, however, these were modernizations and refurbishments, not radical changes.

Under Louis Philippe, the collection also took on a new look. In keeping with the times, in which Oriental taste was very popular for interior decoration, the duke indulged a passion for collecting Chinese porcelain and lacquer. A new ironwork balustrade for the grand staircase was added and the staircase itself was decorated with bronze figures, which carried crystal vases to be used as lights.

To go with the Chinese flavor in the palace, the crimsons favored by Philippe were replaced by mint green, olive green, whites, yellows, pale blues, and pinks. The right-hand side of the palace, which had not really been occupied since Henrietta of England had been married to Monsieur, was now renovated: Constant d'Ivry gave it a white and gilded style, with plenty of glass and mirrors. The fireplaces were embellished with ormolu and girandoles. Corinthian pillars disguised the irregularities of the room and the ceiling was painted with mythological scenes. The overall effect was designed to counterbalance the Oppenordt salon in the other wing. Louis Philippe did not touch those formal galleries which had been decorated by Philippe but he did move the paintings.

During this time the duke also allowed a number of pictures, including *Wisdom and Strength,* to be copied. To the modern mind, copying has a negative air to it, probably for two reasons. In the first place, artists these days are so jealous of their originality that the very idea of using someone's else ideas or designs is anathema. Second, the overlap between copies and forgeries has been so shadowy at times that to many people they are virtually the same thing. An added reason, of course, is that since the invention of the photograph and the photocopier, the very notion of copying has become trivialized.

That was not always true, however. In Michelangelo's time, apprentices learned three types of copying. They copied other artists' work, they copied buildings, and they copied nature—in that order. Until the nineteenth century, when the individuality of the artist became paramount, copies were used as a means of reproduction, as a means of study, and as a source of solutions to formal problems.

Copies were also often a form of homage from one artist to another. Probably, in fact, the usual copy was an amalgam of homage and study. This would explain why so many first-rate artists copied the work of their peers. Michelangelo copied Raphael and Raphael copied Michelangelo; Bellini copied Mantegna and Mantegna copied Bellini. In his book *The Decline of the West,* Oswald Spengler argued that Manet's use of some of Raphael's figures in *Le Déjeuner sur l'Herbe* was indicative of decay in Western painting. If that is true, then all painting is in a state of perpetual decay and always has been.

Dürer was probably the most copied artist, mainly thanks to his many woodcuts, enabling artists as different as Pontormo, Ysenbrant and Baldung to benefit. El Greco was probably the most commercially minded copyist, in the sense that he and his studio produced a large number of nearly identical images for clients enamored of the same subject. Rubens was probably the greatest copyist, producing likenesses of the works of Raphael, Titian, Parmigianino, Caravaggio, Leonardo, Mantegna and Correggio. Second to him was David Teniers, who specialized in pictures of art galleries in which many of the masterpieces may be read (see the section above on Christina in Brussels, when she met the Archduke Leopold Wilhelm, page 133). Other artists who showed their homage in this way have included Delacroix, Poussin, Fragonard, Watteau, Degas, Van Gogh and Picasso, though in the case of many later artists their copies are more "paraphrases" than slavish likenesses. The only major artists who appear *not* to have been interested in the old masters were the "true" Impressionists—Monet, Sisley and Pissarro.

Probably the most extraordinary examples of copying in art historical terms were the decorations of a small room in Alfonso d'Este's castle at Ferrara. *The Feast of the Gods,* started by Bellini and finished by Titian, is now in the National Gallery in Washington. Poussin's copy of it is in Edinburgh. *The Feast*'s neighbor at Ferrara, Titian's *Andrains,* is in the Prado and Rubens's copy is in Stockholm. Van Dyck's copy of Rubens's copy, adapted to become *Amarillis and Mirtillo,* is in Gothenburg, and a version, once attributed to Poussin, of the sleeping Maenad taken from Titian's picture is to be seen in *Midas and Bacchus* at Munich.

Veronese himself copied Raphael in a lost version of the so-called *Madonna della Perla,* then in Verona, now in Madrid, and his own works have been copied by Guardi, Rubens, Tiepolo, Ricci, David Teniers, and Francesco Zugno. His pictures had little effect on the painters of the seventeenth century. And only about a hundred years after his death was he "rediscovered" by his fellow Venetian, Sebastiano Ricci. Ricci copied many Veroneses and through them Tiepolo flowered and Venice entered what has become known as its "silver" period, in terms of master artists. Cézanne recorded a debt to Veronese, in recommending that young Parisian painters copy Veronese and Rubens, "the great decorative painters."

No fewer than four copies of *Wisdom and Strength* are known, testifying to its popularity in the past, especially the eighteenth century, when at least three of them were made. The earliest copy is now in the Kunsthistorisches Museum in Vienna. Formerly in the collection of the Archduke Leopold William, it may have been made when Christina stopped in the Austrian Netherlands, now Belgium, during her journey south.

François Boucher was the second painter of note to copy *Wisdom and Strength.* Boucher was well known to Philippe the Fat, since he had painted the duke's wife. Boucher made his copy almost exactly one hundred years after the Vienna picture. The Frenchman was commissioned by the Portuguese royal family to copy three Veroneses, *Vice and Virtue* and *The Finding of Moses* as well as *Wisdom and Strength.* The Portuguese had no doubt heard of the regent's fabulous gallery and perhaps wished to emulate some of the grandeur of the Palais Royal. According to a note in the Frick archive, by 1929 the Boucher copy had passed to the collection of Baron Gui Thomitz, of Paris.

The third copy of *Wisdom and Strength* was made by Carle Van Loo (1705–1765). Carle was the brother of Jean Baptiste Van Loo, who had established himself as a portrait painter in the circle of the regent. Carle became principal painter to the King in 1762 and director of the Academy a year later. This picture is now in the Cambrai museum in France.

A fourth copy of *Wisdom and Strength* came to light in 1971 when the Marquess of Bute visited the Frick Collection and saw the original of a painting he had at his ancestral home in Rothesay, on the Isle of Bute in Scotland. The authorship of this version isn't known, but according to the Marquess's records it was bought by the third Earl of Bute and first shown in an exhibition of pictures at Luton Hoo, England, in 1799. This suggests that it too may have been made in the eighteenth century.

Each of the Dukes of Orléans allowed free access to their pictures for any serious artist, and Philippe the Fat was no exception. He took pride in his pictures and in the Palais Royal. Much of his work on the palace was done after his first wife died. It took him a while to get over her death and the work obviously helped, the more so since the Orléans were still seen as a threat to the main branch of the royal family and therefore were out of favor with the court. Moreover, his relationship with the court was not helped when he decided that he wanted to marry Mme. de Montesson, a writer of some repute. The King finally sanctioned the marriage but only if it was a morganatic union, since so many people at court refused to recognize her, and she was not allowed to use the title. In a morganatic marriage between a man of high rank, and a woman of low rank, any offspring would have no right to succeed to the man's possessions or title. The court's attitude was hardly conducive to happiness and Mme. de Montesson persuaded Philippe to move out of the Palais Royal and into a house on the Rue de Provence, which linked up with one he had given her in the Chaussée d'Antin. The houses were much less ostentatious and they could lead their separate-but-together lives far more easily.

Accordingly, in 1780, Philippe gave the Palais Royal to his son under one condition: that on no account could his heir sell off the Orléans collection. He could not foresee the Revolution that was just over the horizon, nor the dramatic and tragic part that would be played in it by that heir, Philippe-Égalité.

.   .   .

Égalité, as he is known to history, led a life that was every bit as tumultuous and controversial as that of his great-grandfather the regent. He was not as interested in art and he was not a collector. Indeed, rather the opposite was true. But the very events, political though they were, which led a Duke of Orléans to change his name to Égalité also had consequences for art in general, and *Wisdom and Strength* in particular. The French Revolution and the Napoleonic Wars which followed brought about the wholesale movement of art on a scale not seen since the Thirty Years' War. One reason for this lay in the fact that over the course of the eighteenth century the public perception of art was again changing, especially in France. Just as patronage was changing while Queen Christina was the owner of the Rudolf paintings, so was the infrastructure of the art world changing in France, while that same collection was in the Palais Royal. A brief account of those changes is needed in order to understand the next twist in the fortunes of *Wisdom and Strength*.

Besides the changes overtaking the art world, the political, economic, and social world was also in flux. No longer was it a world in which artists worked only for patrons, whether they were individuals or the Church. Now it was a world in which the *public* reception of a picture was what mattered most. Art, paintings especially, could generate great public enthusiasm and great scandal. Public comment on art became much more widespread than before, criticism was taken more seriously. Journals appeared to act as forums. Artists and painters became famous among the general public as never before, and, as the Revolution approached, began even to assume an overtly political role. It was a state of affairs which had never existed before and has not existed since in quite the same way. Although the *public* appreciation of art has continued to become more and more widespread, art has never again had such a sharp political role and painters have never been such tough—and effective—social critics as in eighteenth-century Paris. Both the regent and Pierre Crozat played an important role in these developments.

Strictly speaking, the roots of these changes go back to the mid-seventeenth century and the beginnings of the reign of Louis XIV. France was the new dominant power in Europe and Louis, who came to the throne in 1643, loved power. Under him France became more and more centralized and his reign became a byword for absolutism. Painting was affected no less than anything else. The first change came in 1648 when the Royal Academy of Painting and Sculpture was established. This was designed to be much more than a craft guild—which already existed and to which it was opposed. The idea was that the Academy would help improve the standard and status of French art. At that point Italian art was still felt to be superior to French art, something which the newfound self-confidence of the French would not tolerate. This determined both the character and the functioning of the Academy over the next century and a half, for its important and lasting concern was its desire to improve the *status* of artists. To this end, the Academy encouraged discussions of aesthetics, discussions that featured not just artists but other intellectuals by whom the artists wanted to be accepted. This had obvious parallels with the Humanist controversies of Renaissance Italy. But in this case the consequences were rather different. The most important was that the critical circle grew wider and wider over time; it eventually involved the general public.

A second element which the new Academy fostered was the importance of history in providing a subject for painting. Despite their new-found power, the French still looked to Rome, where Nicolas Poussin, among others, was working. The painting of historical scenes came to be regarded as the highest form of art and it was felt that current moral issues could be tackled in the guise of scenes of Greek or Roman gods, which reinforced the strength of allegory as a form of art.

Finally, because the Academy was eager to overtake the guild in importance and to improve the status of artists, membership was only granted to artists who were judged worthy. Pictures on a given (historical) subject were prepared for an annual exhibition in the academy. Thus was born the "Salon."

These three elements—the greater role of the public and public criticism, history painting (allegory), and the Salon—would interreact one hundred years later to produce what is in some ways the most extraordinary artistic milieu the world has yet seen, culminating in the great works of David and his crucial role in the French Revolution.

The part played in all this by the Dukes of Orléans was not confined simply to their collections and patronage, important though that was. The regent and Pierre Crozat also headed the intellectual community surrounding the arts in the early years of the eighteenth century. As such, they maintained and developed the notion of the Salon at a time when it might have disappeared.

For various reasons, the Salon, which had begun in the second quarter of the seventeenth century, had closed down in later years and did not reopen until 1737. During that time, quite simply, Orléans and Crozat filled that gap. Crozat became the head of the intellectual community surrounding the arts after the death of Mansart in 1708. He provided support for a number of figures in the art world, including Roger de Piles (whom he provided with 1,500 livres per year [$23,000]). And his accumulation of drawings by the old masters, besides being such a fine collection, was an important technical resource that drew many artists to his house. Charles de Lafosse actually boarded at Crozat's for a while; and Antoine Coypel was a regular guest during the time he was first painter to Orléans.

Crozat held weekly "reunions" attended by, among others, Coypel's son Charles, Pierre-Jean Mariette, the celebrated connoisseur, Nicolas Vleughels, a future director of the Academy at Rome, the abbé Dubois, whose *Critical Reflections on Poetry and Painting* was an influential aesthetic, the Comte de Caylus, and Louis Petit de Bauchaumont. The reunions were a shadow academy, where the learned theorizing about aesthetics actually outstripped the academy proper. Italian artists and amateurs, mainly from Venice, were entertained there, and from 1721 Crozat's Salon produced published works and with the help of Mariette bound books were also produced containing prints of the great collections belonging to the crown and to the regent, and Crozat's own. This set a pattern of *recueils*—engraved reproductions—which were widely distributed later in the century.

The circle around Crozat and the regent played a number of other roles. It served as a mediator between the theoreticians of the academy and the needs of an expansive urban aristocracy, now liberated after Louis's death; it was international and had a keen sense of curatorial responsibility which helped give exposure to French artists who could not get to Rome to see the great old masters; and it provided an understanding forum where artists on the leading edge could take the risks they are prone to take.

If Crozat's reunions were vital in keeping alive the notion of the Salon, the Orléans collection, even after the regent's death, was important in the formation of taste *because of its accessibility*. In 1727, a guidebook to Paris by a German writer, Joachim Nemeitz, said of the Palais Royal: "The new gallery, with various rooms embellished by fine paintings, is the most remarkable part of the palace." Furthermore, it added that the royal collection in the Louvre was, by contrast, almost inaccessible and its pictures "in very poor condition." In the same year another close friend of Orléans and Crozat, Dubois de Saint-Gelais, helped to make the pictures in the regent's collection still more accessible by publishing a detailed catalog. What was notable about this, apart from the fact that it was done at all, was that it was organized along fairly modern lines. The organization of the entries was not arbitrary (as was the way the pictures were displayed on the walls) but rather alphabetical, by artist. Saint-Gelais also included a few words on the character of each painter.

Another example of the effect Orléans had on the public may be seen from a survey made in France of the possessions of 1,247 merchants and artisans who died in Paris between 1726 and 1759. This showed that there was a "considerable vogue" for prints after Poussin's *Seven Sacraments,* many in a complete edition and specified as belonging to "the cabinet of the Duc d'Orléans." This shows how famous, by the standards of the day, Philippe's pictures had become.

In their efforts to keep alive the idea of the Salon and maintain accessible collections, neither the regent nor Crozat could anticipate the course which events would take down the century. But the changes would be profound. The same is true of their patronage. The most famous artist patronized by Orléans and Crozat was Watteau. Philippe could not have imagined that Watteau would lead to David but in fact the story of the eighteenth-century art world and its vicissitudes in France may be told through four artists: Watteau, Boucher, Greuze, and David.

Besides having great ability as a painter, Watteau also marked a turning point in the history of art so far as patronage is concerned. Watteau had no important commissions from Church or crown and he was working before the great public debates surrounding the salons which came into vogue later in the century. That is why he became important in one crucial sense: he created, albeit unwittingly, the concept of the individual artist, loyal to himself, and himself alone.

A second achievement was to create a new kind of picture, the *fête galante,* which did not need an overt story as its subject matter but, harking back to Giorgione, treated human *psychology* as its central element. Watteau stood for the fact that there are truths to human nature as well as the more objective truths of nature in general, which was the concern of the Enlightenment. Not only was this new: it was probably essential to the emergence later in the century of a strong link between art and politics.

Watteau was received into the Academy in 1712, sponsored by Lafosse and Coypel, friends, respectively, of Crozat and Orléans. The minutes of the proceedings show that the subject of the work he had to paint was left to him. This was revolutionary and reveals that the highly structured organization of the arts, which had radiated from the monarch, was already beginning to change. Watteau was of course in the tradition of the Rubénistes, and looked back to the great Venetians. Although this helped to create the Rococo, Watteau was more than a decorative painter. While his pictures do not have a moral purpose, like a conventional allegory or a religious picture, they do have a psychological purpose—to create *mood.* This was his innovation and if Titian is the first modern painter in his techniques, Watteau is the first modern painter in his motivation. It could not have happened without the development of a salon and the greater interest in and access to art by a wider public.

There are those who regard the Rococo as hardly a style at all, and at most a puny one. But it is delicate art and a style, like a boxer, can be slight but still pack a punch. Rococo saw something pompous and absurd in Louis XIV's court at Versailles. Its attitude was summed up perfectly by Matthew Prior, who visited the palace and was struck by the ludicrousness of the King: "His house at Versailles is something the foolishest in the world; he is galloping in every ceiling, and if he turns to spit he must see himself in person, or his Vice Regent in the Sun." And of course there was the undisputed fact that, for all his splendor (and maybe because of it), Louis had left France nearly bankrupt. At the same time, in the realm of the intellect, advances in philosophy and science everywhere had taken the wind out of the sails of the Baroque. What appealed in this climate was an art that was not overly ambitious or grand, an art that did not take itself too seriously. The tradition of Rococo looked back past Rubens, to Correggio and Veronese. These two had never lost their fame but were appreciated in the regent's and Crozat's day as never before. Indeed, two of Veronese's paintings were at this time probably the most famous in all Europe. One was *The Family of Darius Before Alexander,* then still in Venice at the Palazzo Pisani, but now in the National Gallery in London. The other was *The Marriage Feast at Cana,* in the Louvre. Both paintings were copied and the subject of many a pastiche. President Charles de Brosses believed he owned the original sketch for *Darius.* But then, so did many others. Crozat himself had both a drawing and a copy of *The Marriage Feast at Cana.* And even Goethe offered an erudite analysis of what was going on in the picture. In fact, the universal popularity of Veronese at the beginning of the eighteenth century was one of the factors which stimulated a vogue for itinerant Venetian painters, who were welcomed as far afield as England, Spain, and Poland, but nowhere more so than in Paris.

Watteau is not always regarded as a pure Rococo artist. In a way he was too serious. Yes, his subjects are clowns, dancers, picnickers in a glade. But there was an added dimension: his pictures contained psychological insight. Indeed that insight is their raison d'être. High Rococo art, by contrast, has no such purpose. Like Mannerism, it is highly artificial and presupposes in the spectator a cultivated and prepared mind, an awareness of what the artist is trying to do. At the same time, it is an uncritical, art in that it willingly accepts the structure of society and, more, even flatters its dreams of glamour and pleasure. If this makes it sound rather like a cross between Mannerism and Veronese's art, it is no more than the truth.

The two leaders of High Rococo were Boucher and Tiepolo. The latter, a Venetian, owed a great deal to Veronese, as even a cursory examination of his paintings will show, but even Boucher had his love of

women who were incandescently, "impossibly" blond. And both painters, once more harking back to Veronese, barely attempted any psychology: instead what they offered was a flight from reality.

Boucher started out as an engraver of prints after Watteau. He finished
his distinguished career as the director of the Academy but the professional road was by no means always smooth. For example, he was at
loggerheads several times with the general public in its newfound role as
collective art critic. This had something to do with the fact that his career
also spanned the reopening of the Salon.

Having won the Prix de Rome in 1723, Boucher did not take up his
prize and travel to Italy until four years later but he stayed there until
1731 and was then elected to the Academy in 1734. Three years later the
Salon reopened in the Salon Carré of the Louvre and from then on was
mounted regularly every other year on odd-numbered years. It began on
August 25, the feast day of St. Louis (and therefore the King's name day)
and lasted from three to six weeks. While it was running, the Salon was
the greatest public spectacle in Paris. It was also public now in a way that
it had not been before. Louis XIV was long dead, the Rococo was in full
swing, and France's spirit had revived. It had grown a good deal more
irreverent than it had been in the bad old days of absolutism. Although
the seventeenth-century Salon had been in theory open to all ranks, according to contemporary accounts it resembled ritual and had become set
in its ways, rather like a political or religious ceremony. In 1737, by
contrast, all types did mix together. This in itself was a novelty adding to
the attraction. And as a result the public began to take on a self-conscious
awareness about itself and its role as arbiter of taste in a way that had not
happened before.

And so, just as Watteau was the first great artist to survive without any
important commissions from the Church or the crown, so Boucher was
the first painter of note who had to face the newly self-conscious public
who flocked to the salons. He did not relish it. The early relationship
between artist and the wider Salon public was stormy. In 1747, Boucher
designed a frontispiece for a booklet, defending the Academy against the
attacks from the public. It was headed "Painting mocked by Envy, Stupidity, and Drunkenness" and showed painting in despair, hooted at by
harpies and braying asses. Two years later, Boucher was among a group
of painters harshly criticized for its selection of "tired and irrelevant"
themes and its "implicit contempt" for the interests of the Salon public.

At this stage, the "contempt" charge may well have been justified.
Most of the paintings displayed at the newly reopened Salon were not
intended to be shown there. As with many of Boucher's own compositions, these pictures had started life as private commissions and thus re-

flected the tastes of the better off, tastes which did not necessarily agree with those of the wider public. Here again Boucher was typical: while the wider public complained about the irrelevance of his work and his contempt for them, he was growing rich. At one point he was earning 50,000 livres a year (about three quarters of a million dollars at modern values) so it is not surprising that he fell out with the public: their criticisms threatened those earnings.

Boucher numbered among his patrons both the Lenormand family (that of Mme. de Pompadour) and Orléans. This, despite the fact that he, like many other fashionable painters of the time, was regarded by them as "dull and hopelessly vulgar, much patronized and condescended to" and quite lacking in any wider learning or culture outside painting. So again the status of the painter had changed. It was not so long since Crozat and the regent had treated Watteau and other artists of their time as near equals.

Apart from the few satirical engravings he did, the wider public never had much influence on Boucher's style. But the third painter of note in eighteenth-century France *did* take that public far more seriously. This was Jean Baptiste Greuze. Greuze shared with Watteau and with David, who was to come after him, the status of brilliant outsider, an uncompromising genius who never belonged to the academic establishment but was simply the dominant talent of the day. This was important in a political sense because the King was the patron of the Academy and its officers were therefore official appointments. As a result, an outsider was almost by definition an *opponent* of the Academy's aesthetics. Boucher apart, the history of important French painting in the eighteenth century is the history of outsiders challenging the ancien régime. The parallel with the wider political scene was not lost on the participants and provided a link between these painters, on the one hand, and the house of Orléans, on the other. This link may have been no more than symbolic at times, but it was an age that was heavy with symbolism.

Greuze's main achievement was the invention of a new type of picture that was enormously popular with *both* the Academy *and* the general public. Until Greuze, the gap between educated taste and that of the wider public was obvious and as a result the relationship was uneasy, as Boucher's experience had shown. Until Greuze, the connoisseurs of French society could claim, with justification, that their taste was better than the general public's because only they, through their superior education, could properly understand the moral allusions in academic history painting.

Greuze, however, invented a picture which sought to narrow the gap. On the one hand, his pictures were set in the present day, in scenes which everyone could understand, such as the betrothal of a village girl (the episode caught at the moment when the dowry changes hands with the families crowded around on either side). On the other hand, it posed moral dilemmas which were just as noble, just as learned, just as *sensitive* as those raised by the grandest history painting. Greuze's pictures were capable, therefore of just as much analysis as the Academy's. According to one interpretation of the betrothal picture, for example, the painting showed what was happening to the bride's soul "at the moment of this so thoroughly desirable and so thoroughly dreaded revolution." Elsewhere it was noted that Greuze's work concentrated on the civic, as opposed to the religious, moment of the encounter. This was read as meaning that the two families joined by this union were Protestants, since they had been banned from performing the sacraments since 1685.

There were other sociopolitical aspects of the picture which attracted comment at the time, quite apart from Greuze's use of color, shadow, and compositional elements. The social class of the figures was also the subject of much "interpretation." And so although Greuze had painted what at first sight might appear to be a mere genre picture, an eighteenth-century version of the Roman *bambocciata,* in fact his works were also thoroughgoing pieces of social commentary and criticism. It was an aesthetic advance in itself but it was equally important as a form of picture which linked the two tastes—of the Academy and of the public—in pre-revolutionary Paris.

After Greuze's early successes, there was no going back so far as the general public was concerned. The fact that its taste had coincided with that of the better-informed nobility legitimized their view and from then on there were no longer two publics, merely one Salon audience.

Greuze himself helped the process still more, later on in his career. In an attempt to show that he could do it all, he switched to more traditional history painting, portraying Roman rulers facing moral dilemmas. These works were not received as rapturously as his early works but that was not the point. Despite the changed setting, the *themes,* the moral dilemmas, remained the same. This had the effect for many people of making the allegorical method even more obvious. This move of Greuze's prepared the way for David.

Like Greuze, David was an outsider of immense talent who took on the Academy. As with Greuze, this battle of outsider versus establishment was seen by the public as symbolic of the battle between the corrupt ancien régime and those agitating for change. However, the situation David found himself in was rather more pointed than that of Greuze. This was partly because he was a better artist, able to frame the dilemmas more incisively, but also because the artistic movement known as Neoclassicism had by then begun and because the political situation in France had itself sharpened. The Neoclassical movement is considered more fully in a later chapter, when it had an even greater impact on the fortunes of *Wisdom and Strength,* but the role of David's career is considered here.

The Academy's tradition of history painting naturally lent itself to Neoclassicism and so did the political situation. In the 1780s, in France especially, paintings became ever more austere and uplifting. Heroic themes and examples of virtue were used consciously by artists to stress the need for a program of national renewal in France and a return to the values of antiquity: purity, uncontaminated motives, and—something that became the revolutionaries' credo—simplicity. Until 1785, any one of a small number of artists could have emerged as the champion of this approach, but in that year David painted *The Oath of the Horatii* and his position as the most uncompromising Neoclassical painter and critic was never in doubt after that.

In *Horatii* and the pictures which came after, David's work employed static forms and a rigid masculinity. There was no padding. Backgrounds were often dramatically bare. The dominant values were asceticism, order, and economy. In addition, *Horatii* had a brutal and open message. The picture shows the sons of Horatius vowing to fight for Rome against neighboring Alba even though they were related to the people they had to kill. It does not glory in the call to arms, to revolution. But the light in the picture glints most on the swords and on the arms outstretched to grasp them. The picture is not sentimental: it is tough.

These are men putting the state before everything else, willing to make a sacrifice though they do not dress it up in romantic garb. It is awful as well as awesome and it is as well to remember that revolution, in this context, is a term borrowed from astronomy, meaning a return to a position already established by the cyclical nature of history. Thus the Roman setting of the picture is not an avoidance mechanism or a softening of the message by transferring it to another time and another place: the *re*birth of primitive, or antique, virtues and social and political innocence was one of the aims of the Revolution when it came. In addition to that, David's method of painting, its clarity, its abruptness, its stark monumentality, was a challenge to the Rococo generally.

By David's time, the role of the public in the Salon had swelled well beyond what it had been in the seventeenth century and in 1737 when it reopened on a regular basis. The artist was now regarded as a political figure, partly due to the central role which the Salon played in the spectacle of Paris. All this is significant for the biography of *Wisdom and Strength* because David himself was a frequent guest of Égalité at the duke's country seat, St. Leu, and at least one of his paintings was identified with the Orléans cause. This was his rendering of *Paris and Helen,* painted in 1789 and generally believed to represent the Comte d'Artois as the seducer and Marie Antoinette. This was a widely held rumor at the time and one which gave comfort to the Orléans camp, since she and Égalité were on very bad terms.

Right up until the Revolution, therefore, in one way or another, the house of Orléans was an integral part of the flammable mix of politics, salon intrigues, combative pictures, and pamphleteering which railed against the ancien régime and worked for change. When that change came, it was complete, turning the country upside down for a while. Even so, the consequences for the regent's picture collection might not have been so spectacular had it not been for the personality and character of his great-grandson Égalité.

15.
Égalité

Égalité, Louis Philippe Joseph, fifth Duke of Orléans, had all the bad
qualities of his great-grandfather the regent and none of the good ones.
Born on April 13, 1747, Louis Philippe entered a world which, in the
words of one historian, looked upon itself as perfect; and if you were on
the right side of the divide, it was. Except for that curse from his grandfather, Louis Philippe was as well placed as anyone could be. Great care
was taken with his education—though it was scarcely the kind of care we
should take nowadays. Even at night, his tutor, the first valet de chambre,
and the *valet de chambre de garde* slept in the same room with the young
duke and had to present a report the next day. In such company, it is
hardly surprising that Égalité learned only things "that would be interesting to tailors."

As a boy, Égalité ran the risk of developing a hunchback inherited
from his mother's side. To treat this the doctor hung him on a door to
stretch his limbs. The young duke was also one of the first children in
Paris, and perhaps *the* first, to be inoculated against smallpox. The Turks
had developed the technique at the beginning of the century and it gradually spread to Geneva and London. The young duke was treated by a
Swiss doctor who made his name in the process; perhaps because the
Orléans had taken the lead, inoculation became all the rage in Paris and
the Swiss medic became very rich.

Égalité's official life began when he was twelve, in 1759. He made his
first visit to Versailles, was received by the Dauphin, and exercised some
of the privileges of his rank. For instance, he handed the King his shirt at
his levee and gave the Queen her napkin at dinner. More strenuously,
three years later his father presented him with his first mistress. Old
Orléans traditions died hard and before long he was enjoying the company of rakes, pub-crawling, and brothel-creeping, to such an extent that
the policeman whose job it was to report on the royal pleasure — seeking
was overcome by the repetitious boredom of it all.

The next stage in this by now familiar Orléans development was marriage. This took place in 1769, to Louise Marie Adélaïde, the only
daughter of the Duke of Penthièvre, Grand Admiral of France. Louise
Marie Adélaïde's brother, Prince Lamballe, a roué of the first order, had

died of syphilis a few months before, leaving her the sole inheritor of her father's fortune. This was so immense that Louise Marie Adélaïde, though not a royal personage, was actually the richest woman in the land. The sequence of events which culminated in the marriage naturally fueled all the old anti-Orléans jealousies. It was rumored—of course—that Louis Philippe had encouraged Lamballe in his debauches so that he would find an early grave. Then Orléans could take up with Marie Adelaïde who had suddenly become so much more attractive.

The newlyweds set up home in the Palais Royal, vacated by the duke's father after his morganatic marriage. As the century wore on, the Palais Royal became the center of political opposition in France. But it all began innocently enough. It stemmed partly from the house of Orléans's intellectual traditions (the regent's legacy) but also from the family's uncomfortable legal position in being so near to the throne but not, for most of the time, part of the governing elite. It was a recurrence of the old problem that had kept the young regent idle. As princes of the blood, the Orléans were of the first rank in French society, but their very proximity to the throne always made them an ever-present threat to the royal household of the day. This is what made everyone else ready to see the house of Orléans as a rival court. They thus became the natural focus of anything, however trivial, that was antiestablishment.

On top of this was the tradition, established by the regent, of allowing the gardens of the Palais Royal to be open to everyone. As the Revolution approached, the gardens became a natural rallying spot for all radical groups, the forum for venting all radical ideas. During the eighteenth century there was no shortage of new or liberal ideas: Montesquieu, Diderot, Rousseau, Condillac, d'Alembert. Just as their ideas, and indeed their persons, were welcome inside the Palais Royal, so the popular representation of what they stood for was seen outside, in the gardens of the palace. It is true that Orléans was responsible for having Voltaire imprisoned during the regency, but the circumstances were exceptional and do not change the overall picture.

The house of Orléans's position as a rallying point was given added force by a specific event which took place when Louis Philippe was twenty-four. Chancellor Maupeou attempted to abolish the Parlement of Paris and replace it with the absolute power of Louis XV. Even Égalité's father was roused from his natural indolence to oppose this and he took his place as head of the council of princes and magistrates, which made up the parlement. Égalité enthusiastically played his part in the proceedings, signing all the letters of protest, defying all manner of restrictions, and refusing, with his father, to take his place in the new council with which Maupeou attempted to replace the parlement. As a result, both he and his father were exiled for a time. Later they were readmitted to the court but they stuck to their guns and, when Louis XV died the next year, they refused to attend his funeral because that involved the recognition of the new council, which would be present officially. All this made the Orléans very popular in the streets of Paris, at the expense of the court.

Nor did Égalité's Anglophilia help his popularity at Versailles. He had been attracted to English customs and habits even before he crossed the Channel himself. He was one of those who set the fashion in Paris for the English frock coat, one of the first to do away with powdered hair, and also one of the first to wear shoes instead of slippers—all English fashions. He helped to popularize horse racing in France and Englishmen were always welcome at the Palais Royal. At the royal court, however, English ways were deplored. More significant, later on, once the Revolution was under way, speculation was fueled about Égalité's actual aims: people wondered whether he was not in fact a secret agent acting on behalf of the English designs.

His motives over the English were also called into question after the Battle of Ushant. The year was now 1778 and Benjamin Franklin was already in France to plead the American cause against Britain. News of the capture of General Burgoyne had produced a sensation and Louis XVI had signed a formal treaty of recognition and friendship with the American rebels, making war between France and England certain. Égalité came from a family which had distinguished itself in battle, so he entered the navy and was given command of a ship. Unfortunately for Égalité, the Battle of Ushant took place in weather that was extremely difficult. It was difficult to maneuver the ships, lives were lost, and many men were injured. But no ship of either side was sunk or taken as a prize. It was a messy, unsatisfactory battle and in such circumstances both sides claimed victory. More important, because there were no undisputed facts, such as prizes taken or ships sunk, exaggerated descriptions of who had shone in this generally lackluster conflict began to circulate. As luck would have it, Égalité was among the first to go home to Paris and make his report. He was greeted as a conquering hero, received by the King, and feted at the Opera. The cheering crowds outside the Palais Royal refused to disperse until he had appeared on the balcony. It was a reception quite out of keeping with what had actually happened but Égalité, desperate for recognition and no doubt believing that he had, after all, played a part in a victory, enjoyed his reception. But then other versions reached Paris and tongues started wagging.

It was now said that Égalité had hidden himself while the fighting took place; it was said that his ship suffered fewer casualties than any other; it

was said that he responded slowly to orders that might have been decisive. And all this against a background in which he had been one of the
first to present *his* version in the capital. The changeabout was so total
that an official inquiry was ordered. This exonerated Égalité completely
but in a sense that only made things worse: that he was cleared smacked
of a cover-up. Égalité himself did not help matters by taking umbrage
and applying for a job in the hussars—as if to turn his back on the navy
the minute things did not go his way. In addition to everything else,
Égalité acquired a reputation as a devious schemer and a coward. It all
was taken into account when the Revolution came along: there were
even those who suspected that he had deliberately let the English off the
hook at Ushant.

Nor did it help when he began to speculate with the Palais Royal itself.
For this was a move which, in the words of one of his biographers (and a
not unsympathetic one at that), turned him into, not the Grand Admiral
of France that he sought to be, but the "Grand Pimp of the Kingdom."
Égalité's efforts with the Palais Royal, as with so much else in his life,
began well enough. Between 1770 and 1780 he decorated the left wing
of the palace and built an observatory. He turned the Galerie des
Hommes Illustres and the remainder of the Galerie Richelieu into a
ballroom and built new stables. He reorganized the picture gallery, the
Oppenordt room, and established a museum for arts and mechanical
trades. All of this was laudable but, by this time, Égalité, who had married the richest woman in France, was in financial trouble. Indeed his
gambling, which was prodigious, and his general extravagance were such
that his income of 800,000 livres a year (over $12 million at 1980s rates)
was entirely mortgaged from 1776 to 1780. Then, when the Opera
burned down yet again, in June 1781, he saw his chance. He persuaded
the King to let him rebuild it but also, at the same time, enclose the
Palais Royal gardens on three sides with buildings which he would rent
out as apartments and shops, thereby rectifying the imbalance in his fortunes.

The construction of the new buildings and arcades took two and a half
years to complete and, to do him justice, Égalité threw himself into the
work with a gusto that he had rarely shown for anything else. He was
made fun of at court. "We don't see our cousin any more since he has
become a shopkeeper," quipped the Comte d'Artois. And he was made
fun of by the people. Mysterious "street signs" appeared among the
buildings, reading "Rue d'Ouessant" (Ushant) or "Rue Saint Esprit" and
so on.

Still, by January 1, 1785, the new gardens and arcades were ready.
One feature of the garden was its mature trees, cleverly planted a year

before the reopening so that they would have time to take hold (they were already thirty years old when they were planted). These transformed the project, to everyone's delight, making it a wild success. As one visitor wrote: "This enchanting place is a small luxurious city in a big one. One could call it the capital of Paris. You find everything here."

But although the new Palais Royal was a success and once again a fashionable spot, it was with a different group of people. No longer was it only the aristocracy who strolled there now. "You could not hope to know what was going on in town unless you strolled through its arcades or under its trees at least once a day," wrote one frequenter. Cafés, marionette shows, aristocratic gamblers, wineshops, brothels, and all manner of clubs rented the theaters, booths, and apartments. The *Journal de l'Almanach du Palais Royal* kept people informed about every new pleasure available in the great bazaar. The gardens gave the police more to do than the rest of Paris put together. It was the home of the Club des Américains, frequented by the many young aristocrats who had fought with Washington and Lafayette in America. The new buildings had cost twelve million livres ($408 million) and the annual rents brought in 550,000 ($30 million). This, plus the agricultural holdings and the canal rights which Égalité held in several parts of the kingdom, made him again the richest man in the country. Yet this time marks the beginning of the financial difficulties that helped ruin the house of Orléans.

It is not easy to see where all the money went unless he had chronic and huge gambling debts. This is all too likely. Or, as some critics have alleged, perhaps Égalité hid the money away in England against the day when a revolution might make some outside source of funds indispensable. What is known is that the commercial and fashionable success of the revamped Palais Royal had a very mixed effect on Égalité's reputation and on the standing of the house of Orléans. This was partly because as usual the court and the rest of the aristocracy were willing to believe that a success on the part of the Orléans was bound to be a threat. But overriding that the actual nature of the commercial success was unwholesome: low-level trading, theater, gambling, and prostitution. This was hardly a distinguished business.

There was really no way out for him. Even though the public eventually began to forget the unkind limericks they had spoken about his cowardice at Ushant so that his popularity rose again, the nobles around the King were another matter. They whispered that Égalité had deliberately solicited this popularity because he was not fully welcome at court. It was said that one of the reasons for this was the intense hatred that had grown up between Égalité and the Queen, Marie Antoinette. This had developed after Ushant, when the Queen had made a quip about Orléans's cowardice and prevented him becoming, like his father-in-law, a high admiral of France. People saw, or thought they saw, rivalries everywhere.

Whatever truth there was to all this, the ultimate effect was that, as 1789 approached, the Palais Royal gardens, if not the palace itself, became a center for anything antiestablishment. Many of the radical pamphlets that were circulated prior to the Revolution and that contributed to the political atmosphere of 1789 were printed in the gardens of the Palais Royal. There is no doubt that their anti-Antoinette flavor reflected Égalité's feelings, whether he had a hand in them or not. And the Palais Royal was more than just a printing press: the fact that pamphlets were produced there gave them a certain stamp: they were not the "official" opposition exactly, but close. With such things happening under his nose and on his property, it is easy to see how Orléans acquired such a controversial image.

Égalité's's role in the French Revolution has been described by historians as "one of the most debated points in history." That is an understatement, but whatever he did or did not do, the fact remains that what he did put *Wisdom and Strength* on the move again.

A major reason for the ambiguity over Égalité's role is that, despite what had gone before, the house of Orléans was monarchist by tradition and its members, even he, took very little interest in revolutionary and republican politics. In 1777, for instance, while Lafayette and other Frenchmen were fighting and dying in the American War of Independence, the battle of the century, Égalité bet the Comte de Genlis that he could prick 500,000 holes in a piece of paper before the count could go from the Palais Royal to Versailles and back. He even went into "training" for this event—which he lost.

There were still four years to the Revolution when, in 1785, Orléans made three controversial trips to England. There is little doubt that at this time he went to London to make substantial deposits of money. What no one has ever been able to find out is whether the money was deposited to oil Égalité's ever-lively gambling urges or whether, as hostile historians claimed later, it was left in a safe place against the day when he might needs funds. During one of the English trips, in April, Orléans was painted by Sir Joshua Reynolds. Reynolds was then at the height of his popularity and indeed portrait painting itself was very much in vogue all over Europe. In Paris, for instance, the rage was for works by Mme. Vigée-Lebrun, wife of Jean Baptiste Pierre Lebrun, the man who was now in charge of the Orléans collection. Reynold's portrait of Égalité is one of his best works and shows the duke at thirty-eight. Dressed as a colonel general of the hussars, his figure is heavy but dignified. The small, but fleshy and sensuous Bourbon lips are prominent and Reynolds did not shrink from at least hinting at the debauchery in Orléans's life, which had begun to take its toll. He charged the duke 250 guineas for the picture, which friends considered expensive. But Égalité paid up, had several engravings made, and in the following year presented the original to his friend the Prince of Wales.

The visits to England were provocative enough, but more was to come. In 1787, with the French economy in poor shape, Charles Alexandre de Calonne, the Minister of Finance, proposed to rectify this through taxes, including one on land. This would have been unpopular at the best of times but it coincided with the first rumors of Marie Antoinette's extravagances. Accordingly, parlement refused to register the law. This set parlement against the King once again and a long tug-of-war ensued. Louis XVI exiled parlement, recalled it, tried other measures. The battle culminated in a seven-hour debate of parlement at which both the King and Égalité were present. At a crucial point, Orléans rose and faced the King with the all-important question on everyone's lips: Was the meeting they were now engaged in a royal meeting of parlement, in which case a vote should be taken on the King's proposal? . . . Or was it a *lit de justice?* The King answered that it was a royal session of parlement. Égalité, taking his courage in both hands, replied that therefore what the King was trying to do, to force the issue without a vote, was illegal.

This caused a sensation. For a prince of the blood to oppose the King so obviously and so publicly was unprecedented and treasonable. Moreover, at a time when the monarchy was beginning to become unpopular, it made Égalité a favorite with the wider public. For a while, therefore, the duke was at the head of the opposition to the King, something that was made all the more obvious when Marie Antoinette, letting her hatred of Orléans override her good sense, insisted he be exiled once again. It made no difference that Égalité acted as he did because, as a major landholder, he stood to lose most by the King's proposed taxes. In the charged atmosphere of the day, the duke must have known that his action would set him in opposition to the crown. And add to the Orléans mystique.

The next time Égalité stood up against the King came in 1789 itself but early on in the year, before the Revolution proper began in the summer. On April 28, a crowd of five or six thousand marched on the house of a rich factory owner, a M. Reveillon, on the pretext that he had treated his workers badly. This was not true. Moreover, many of those present had never worked for Reveillon. The important point is that they were later identified as habitués of the gardens of the Palais Royal. In addition, Égalité, allegedly on his way to the races at Vincennes, came across the mob in the Rue Monteuil. He got down from his coach, talked to the people, and wished them well. Later, as the mob attacked the troops guarding Reveillon's house, and many of the mob were killed, they were heard to cry out: *"Vive la maison d'Orléans."*

The affair did not end there. Parlement set up an inquiry into the march and the deaths which resulted. But no sooner was it begun than, mysteriously, it was dropped. Was this because Égalité, then the hero of parlement, was behind the whole thing? It was widely believed that the duke had financed the affair—at twelve francs a person since this was the sum found, wrapped in envelopes on the bodies of several dead rioters. But it was not a revolutionary riot, however much it may sound like one. Reveillon had defeated an Orléanist candidate in an election and it was, more than anything, an act of revenge. But it showed what men were prepared to do, how the social order was breaking down. And of course it showed the house of Orléans identified with the forces of opposition in French society.

The Reveillon riot marked the beginning of what the French writer Augustin Cochin called "the inconceivable tyranny of the Palais Royal." This was the period when Égalité was enormously popular, leading the opposition to Marie Antoinette which culminated in his election as president of the National Assembly. It was from the Palais Royal, at this time, that the vicious whispering campaign against the Queen began. Whatever more active role Orléans was to play in the events of later months, there is no doubt that on the eve of Revolution he was the figurehead behind which the forces of opposition were gathering. He may never have been anything but a figurehead. Historians still disagree over the matter. But figureheads are necessary, certainly in the early stages of a popular movement.

From then on, events accelerated and deteriorated. "There was a crescendo of fêtes, fireworks, speeches, harangues, disorders, and distractions amounting to madness" in the Palais Royal gardens and arcades. According to police reports decent people now never ventured into the palace gardens, where frenzied orators shouted that Versailles should be pulled down and that Orléans should be declared general-in-chief. At times, money was thrown from the windows of the palace to the crowds below.

No wonder that the duke's part in the events of July 14 and the Revolution proper should be hotly debated at the time and ever since. Orléans gold was believed to be at the bottom of every antimonarchy movement. The trips to London, the deposits of money, his wife's huge Penthièvre income—all this was conveniently remembered. Since Égalité had been a figurehead in recent months, the rumors are scarcely surprising. Nor is it strange that several histories of the French Revolution have been written with a marked anti-Orléanist slant. There is no doubt that the Orléanist party became a recognizable faction in the politics of the day.

And yet, read any modern history of the French Revolution and you will find that Égalité features in only a very minor way, if at all. The duke suffered the fate of many figureheads. He became an early *victim* of a revolutionary movement in a way that has become much more familiar since. Once the Revolution proper started, he himself, and any political ideas or ambitions he may have had, were overtaken by events which got quickly out of hand. It is quite possible that Égalité did want to become a constitutional monarch, as existed in England. For that reason it is probably true that he did finance certain crowd scenes, including, as has been claimed, the storming of the Bastille.

Yet, the likes of Danton, Talleyrand, and Robespierre were to prove more than a match for him: once the ball had started rolling, Égalité was relegated to a supporting role. But that was not how it was seen at the time. The royal family certainly saw him as enough of a threat to have him sent away, from October 1789 to July 1790, on a "mission" to England. This was yet another exile and this, more than anything, accounts for why Orléans was no more than a figurehead from then on, and an increasingly remote and dated one at that.

Whatever his actual role, so far as *Wisdom and Strength* was concerned, Égalité's involvement with the antimonarchy forces was to prove crucial. For it was the duke's shortage of cash, brought on by his financing of crowds and mobs, and his gambling, that led him to sell the Orléans collection. Égalité had never been interested in the arts. True, he was the patron of Choderlos de Laclos, author of *Les Liaisons Dangereuses*. Ironically enough, in that work Laclos recreated the dissolute and debauched world of the regent, as if to remind the Orléans dynasty that, despite its grand aims, there was a dark side to its nature. But Égalité did not appear to take much pride in the collection though it was looked after well enough. For example, when the Baroness d'Oberkirch visited the palace in 1782 she recorded that she had been shown around by an old valet de chambre. This man, she said, had served the regent, had never left the palace, and was then aged over eighty. "But he is still sprightly and knows a thousand stories, a thousand things one might otherwise ignore. It is his happiness to show you the Palais Royal; he walks with you and tells you the history of every piece, every corridor. When one tries to tip him he returns it fiercely."

By then, the Orléans collection was officially under the direction of Jean Baptiste Pierre Lebrun. Lebrun was born in 1748 and was "the last (and possibly the greatest) in a long and distinguished line of eighteenth-century French dealer-connoisseurs," exactly the type of individual Crozat had been. Lebrun started life as an artist and in 1776 had married Élisabeth Vigée, who was to become probably the most famous portrait painter of her day in France and the friend of almost everyone who mattered at that time. Mme. Vigée-Lebrun's *Memoirs* are the main source of information about Lebrun's character; but, as a disillusioned wife, she may not be wholly reliable. She says that she did not want to marry him at first but that her mother, thinking him rich, insisted upon it. But, she adds, although he had a sweet nature, he also had a passion for women of easy virtue and for gambling that caused the ruin of his fortune. Perhaps that is what appealed to Orléans.

Lebrun is an important figure in the history of art because he was one of the first dealer-connoisseurs to dream up the idea of the "rediscovery" of once-forgotten artists. In doing so he permanently changed the artistic taste of France, not to mention the very function of the art dealer.

Lebrun managed well throughout the Revolution, considering his position on the eve of it. Having bought paintings for the King and been curator for both Égalité and the Comte d'Artois, his already shaky position was not helped by his wife, who had painted almost everybody who was anybody in the ancien régime and was one of the first émigrés. In fact, Lebrun was forced to issue a pamphlet defending his wife and explaining that her motives were purely personal and had not the slightest thing to do with politics. Worse, the first volume of Lebrun's monumental book on Flemish, Dutch, and German painters appeared slap in the middle of the Revolution—1792—with an embarrassing pro-monarchy introduction. In the second volume, Lebrun changed his tune—successfully, because he remained in favor and helped the Bonapartes form the Musée de Louvre.

But Lebrun's book is more interesting than the circumstances of its publication. It is noteworthy for its novel grouping of painters. For the first time, painters were not grouped in alphabetical or chronological order, but according to masters and followers. Broadly speaking, this is still the way painters and painting are regarded today. Lebrun's main achievement, though, stemmed from his realization that taste could be led, a breakthrough that created the modern art dealer as he is known today. Until Lebrun, it was the fashion, for financial reasons, for dealers and everyone else to attribute as many paintings as possible to established artists. Naturally a Titian was worth more than something that was not a Titian. Lebrun was the first to realize the commercial significance of the fact that there were many artists who were *unknown but just as good* as the known painters, if only the public could be made to appreciate their work.

As a result of Lebrun's insight, therefore, the art dealer became more than simply an entrepreneur, a man who had access to paintings and a similar access to clients who could afford his wares. Instead, the dealer became something much more worthwhile—a real man of taste himself, someone whose eye was very important. He became an insider, who could obtain a really good painting cheaply by recognizing an artist who had merit but who at the time was simply not appreciated. After Lebrun, dealers became a sort of cross between evangelists and venture capitalists. It does not matter that Lebrun was feathering his own nest in making his breakthrough. It was a breakthrough nonetheless. Lebrun traveled in Spain and elsewhere and helped rehabilitate many names which we now take for granted as first-rate: Holbein, Ribera, and Louis Le Nain, among others.

Despite all this activity, and despite the fact that he bought for the King and the Comte d'Artois, Lebrun does not seem to have added appreciably to the Orléans collection (reinforcing the view that Égalité was not interested in art: what money he had he spent elsewhere). Lebrun's own collection contained a number of important old masters and was displayed in a specially built set of rooms in the garden adjoining his own house in the Rue de Cléry. In the days before the Revolution the Lebruns held weekly salons at which painters and musicians of the day would gather.

Three years before the Revolution, in 1786, while Lebrun was in charge of the collections, the galleries of the Palais Royal were refurbished. When John Trumbull, an attaché at the American legation, was in Paris in that year, he visited the Palais Royal and found workmen "employed in taking down the old gallery, in order to rebuild the whole in a modern style." The pictures, he reported, had been "placed in the middle of each room, on great easels and obliquely to the light, resting partly upon each other, and with such small intervals that it was impossible to view the large pictures with any advantage or satisfaction."

No sooner was this refurbishment complete, however, than Égalité surprised Lebrun. Contrary to his father's express wishes, he began to sell off parts of the art collection. The timing was ambiguous. The year was 1787, two years after the new gardens had opened in the Palais Royal; it was becoming clear that the enormous income they generated was still not enough to support Égalité's extravagant habits. It was also close enough to the Revolution for his enemies to say later that he had sold off his art to finance his political ambitions.

The first part of the collection to go was the engraved stones, sold to

Catherine the Great of Russia for a sum of about 450,000 livres (about $7 million). The money did not last long. In the following year, Égalité unsuccessfully attempted to borrow 500,000 francs at 20 percent. Or- léans reduced his requirements to 300,000 francs but it still did no good. It was probably this failure which determined him to sell the collection, including *Wisdom and Strength,* because an inventory of everything was now drawn up. It showed that there were 478 paintings: 295 Italian, 147 from the northern schools, and 36 French.

Given his background and his Anglophilia, Égalité's first thought was to sell to the English. He used as his agent Nathaniel Parker Forth, who in February 1773 had served as George III's special envoy to the court at Versailles. He had become a close friend of Égalité's while the latter was still Duke of Chartres. On Forth's advice, the inventory which was drawn up was presented in the first place not to any distinguished and wealthy collector or amateur and not to a dealer. Rather, Forth's advice reflected very much the fashion of the times, another new development in the art world. For the first person to be offered the Orléans's gallery was the auctioneer James Christie.

James Christie was probably the most interesting auctioneer the world has seen. "Tall, good-looking with agreeable manners," he was also a very witty man, on equal terms with many of the most brilliant figures of his day in England: Reynolds, Garrick, Sheridan, Gainsborough. It was Christie who helped to make the auction rooms of London fashionable meeting places.

Before Christie's time, auction houses had rather dubious reputations as they were associated with, and probably originated on, the field of battle, when the victors disposed of their spoils. A spear would be stuck into the ground to attract attention and the loot spread around it: *sub hasta,* "under the spear" sales had begun. After this had become an accepted way of selling, auctions were conducted in ancient Rome by a special magistrate, the *magister auctionis,* who was assisted by a *praeco,* or crier, whose job it was not only to call out the bids but also to amuse the crowd with jokes and witty remarks. According to Suetonius, Apponius was one of the first to suffer the auction nightmare when he accompanied Caligula to a sale. He fell asleep in the heat, started nodding his head, and awoke to find he had become a principal buyer. After the Reforma- tion, Catholics in England sent objects to France to be sold. The French auctions were famous but a good way from being perfect, with dealers' rings widespread. Indeed, the dealers pulled down the posters advertis- ing the sales so that the nobility would not attend. Tolerably accurate catalogs were introduced around 1760.

In this way auctions became rather racy affairs. In England, the first records of auction sales with any kind of modern flavor occurred in the seventeenth century. They usually took place on the death of the owner of the property to be sold. There was an Auction House in Ave Maria Lane in London, but Tom's Coffee House or the Outroper's Office in the Royal Exchange were popular venues too. There are references to art auctions in the writings of Samuel Pepys, who explains how he tried, but failed, to acquire a Holbein at auction. Book sales were very popular early on, although many people used agents to buy books in bulk, to fill up space, rather than because they were interested in particular works. Sotheby's began in 1744 as an auction house devoted solely to books.

At that time the sale of goods by "inch of candle" was also not uncommon. The practice originated at Lloyd's and was apparently used for part of the Commonwealth sale. The practice continues even today in Beaune, Burgundy, for the annual sale of wine. The bidding continues until the candle has burned down an inch. Whoever made the last bid when the mark is reached gets that lot. Hogarth used a special clock with much the same function when he sold his pictures from his home.

The first regular auction room, as we would recognize it today, opened in Covent Garden in 1690. It was run by a man called Edward Millington and was called "Le Vendue." In winter the sales took place at four o'clock in the afternoon, which suited the convenience of gentlemen who in those days dined in midafternoon. In spring, when society moved out to the fashionable spa of Tunbridge Wells, Millington moved out too, taking his pictures and his objets d'art with him.

Millington was followed about 1720 by Cock, who had his sale room on the great piazza, also at Covent Garden, where Hogarth was a frequent visitor. Cock was followed in turn by Langford and by this time— the mid-1700s—the collecting of old masters was becoming so fashionable in England that English painters found it hard to sell their works. A letter in the *St. James's Chronicle* of April 25, 1765, strikes a surprisingly modern note: "It is a well-known melancholy truth," wrote the author, "that the tribe of auctioneers, connoisseurs, picture-dealers, brokers, menders, etc., etc., have monopolised the trade of pictures, and by their authority, interest, and artifices with the great have made it a matter of ridicule to purchase any modern production, or encourage an English artist. By this craft the leaders of taste of these kingdoms acquire fortunes and credit, whilst many of our painters, men of genius, and industry, are absolutely starving."

It was an attempt to remedy this state of affairs that led, in 1765, to the formation of the Society of Artists of Great Britain, which became the Royal Academy three years later. First located in Pall Mall in the print warehouse of its treasurer, Richard Dalton, it later moved to Somerset

House, and the Pall Mall premises became the premier auction rooms in London. It was there that James Christie set up his firm in 1766.

There are a number of accounts of Christie's origins, including one that he started out beating feather beds for an upholsterer. However, the most reliable version holds that he was the son of an English father and a Scottish mother; she was a Macdonald and a relation of the indomitable Flora, the romantic Jacobite heroine who after the Battle of Culloden helped Bonnie Prince Charlie escape to Skye, dressed as a woman. Christie became an officer in the navy but resigned to become an auctioneer. After an apprenticeship, he opened for business on December 5, 1766. His pleasant, open face and his dignified presence gave him a persuasive aura on the rostrum that soon became legendary. In those days, Christie's main rival was Phillips's and not Sotheby's, which confined itself to books, manuscripts, and classical antiquities. Christie's was not concerned solely with art but dealt in all sorts of property. The following extract from *The Times* of London illustrates the scope of Christie's business and at the same time nicely illustrates Christie's proverbial abilities. The property being auctioned was the borough of Gatton in Surrey, ownership of which carried with it a seat in the House of Commons. It was probably the most valuable property ever to be sold by Christie in one lot and came under the hammer on April 17, 1800. *The Times* wrote:

> The Borough of Gatton was yesterday sold by Mr. Christie for the sum of £39,000. . . . An ocassion so admirably adapted to the eloquence of Mr. Christie did not present itself in vain, nor was this inimitable orator deficient in justness of idea and the *curiosa felicitas* of expression. The subject, necessarily great, involving in it a very desirable contingency, demanded extraordinary talents, and Mr. C. descanted with uncommon feeling on the virtue of a key belonging to the Borough which opened the gate of St. Stephen's Chapel and the gates of Paradise.

Christie was a man of his time. Thanks to individuals like Lord Burlington, the architect and connoisseur, the fine arts were becoming fashionable. The Grand Tour was now a necessary part of the education of every young aristocrat, which gave many of them a taste for art when they returned home. The manufacture of silver, porcelain, furniture, and glass as well as bookbinding, reached new heights in England, which have hardly ever been surpassed. The Adams brothers were designing beautiful interiors. In this world, Christie traded successfully in Pall Mall for thirty-six years; well before the end of the century the firm's premises had become the favorite rendezvous for art lovers of the fashionable world. Christie, with Reynolds, Gainsborough, and Horace Walpole, became a kind of court at which the tastes of the day were settled, where the decision was taken as to which artists were "in" and which were "out," not unlike Titian and Vittoria's group in Veronese's day. When Reynolds died in 1792, it was Christie who auctioned his collection at a sale which tells us which artists were then in favor: Rembrandt, Titian, Raphael, Tintoretto, Michelangelo, the seventeenth-century Bolognese and Roman painters, but no primitives. Christie's had become so fashionable by the 1790s that, at private viewings, an official from the opera was stationed at the door because he knew everyone who was anyone in society and could thus identify—and refuse entry to—any undesirables. The private viewings were so formal that Lord Chesterfield arrived in a coach-and-six, with his footmen in state liveries.

By the early 1790s, Christie was therefore the obvious person for Orléans to contact. However, an auction was not envisaged at that stage but rather a private sale. In those days there was not the distinction there is now between dealers and auctioneers and Christie sometimes speculated on his own behalf. For the Orléans collections, Christie appears to have tried two plans. At first he agreed with Orléans's idea to form a syndicate that would lodge 100,000 guineas ($9,200,000) in the Bank of England against the collection, which was to be taken by boat from Rouen to London. This plan ran into difficulty almost immediately. Christie's idea was to have the King, or someone else in the royal family, start the ball rolling. The Prince of Wales agreed to put up 7,000 guineas ($644,000) and his brothers, the Dukes of York and Clarence, each earmarked 5,000 guineas ($460,000). But it proved impossible to get anyone else to join in because, as one contemporary observer dryly noted, "at the division of the spoils the old fable of the lion and his partners in the chase would be realized."

After this plan foundered, Christie considered the idea of acquiring the collection on his own account, presumably with a view to auctioning it off separately in his Pall Mall rooms. He therefore dispatched a friend, Philippe John Tassaert (1732–1803) to Paris on his behalf. Tassaert, Flemish-born, had been an assistant to Thomas Hudson, Reynolds's master, and had been president of the Society of Artists since 1775. By the early 1790s he had become more of a connoisseur than an artist and therefore ideally placed from Christie's point of view. He traveled to Paris and from there wrote a series of letters to Christie, which the firm only recently reacquired and which have not yet been published. They provide a vivid account of the transactions and conditions in revolutionary Paris.

The first letter was written early in 1790. The duke had given Tassaert permission to study the collection. "The plot is Out. I have seen the pictures . . . 3 successive days." On first impressions, perhaps because of the "very bad light" or the pictures' "bad arrangement," they fell "in General very short" of his expectations. "Dont think I want to throw Cold water on the purchase of such a Collection," he wrote, "for in it are some of the finest pictures in the World . . . particularly the descent of the Cross by hanibal Carrache [now in the National Gallery], w^h [which] is the best picture in my opinion in the Whole Collection." He valued the pictures by schools and in his view the best of the Raphaels ("a damd fine picture, worth al the rest") was the *Madonna del Passeggio,* now regarded as a school piece (Sutherland Loan to the National Galleries of Scotland). Tassaert valued the collection at £20,500 (now about $2.5 million) and was disappointed by the condition of many compositions, adding that a lot of them "Comming in to a sale without a title in London would sell from 2 to 10 g^s [guineas] a piece." His next letter, dated June 7, was more enthusiastic and this was because, in the interim, Tassaert had found out that he had only seen part of the collection, and the smaller pieces at that. He had not realized this earlier because "the catalogue" (i.e., the inventory) was in alphabetical order rather than following "the Hang in the different apartments." He had therefore asked permission of a certain M. Lebrun—"an Officer in the Army and not Mons Le Brun our Acquaintance" [i.e., J. B. P. Lebrun, in charge of Orléans gallery] who was "Ordered by the duke to Superintend" him and "Supply all information requisite"—to prepare his own catalog. The scale of some of the pictures alarmed Tassaert, who counseled caution. "I tremble my dear friend at the idea of this great, for so I may very justly call it, undertaking of yours. . . . I presume if you can buy this Collection for 30 to 40 thousand pounds you may make a fortune out of it, but the whole depends on the cheapness of the purchass." The scale, indeed, gave Tassaert ideas about how it should be sold in England. He argued that rather than sell the collection "in parts to a Lord Shelburne or Lord Ashburnham" it should be exhibited in an elegant room "twice the Size of the Large Exhibition Room of the Royal Academy." And he added that half a guinea could be charged for admission which "might produce 8 or 10 thousand pounds." Set against that, however, "what with duty & new frames" and restoration, he calculated that £2,000 ($250,000) would have to be spent on the collection. With an exhibition of the kind he had in mind, Tassaert thought that with "a Raffle or a Lottery" £100,000 ($12 million) might "be made of the collection." Evidently, there was still a possibility at this stage that the King might buy. Tassaert was dismissive: "As to disposing of these pictures to the King of England you know thats quit out of the question he is to[o] nigardly to buy." He also thought that Benjamin West "or that mirror of wisdom and knowledge in the arts, Mr. Dalton would never advise him to such a purchase."

Tassaert was not unaware that his mission was a delicate one and that there were rivals everywhere. He counseled Christie "not to be to[o] Explicit in this business" with two rivals, Bertels and Vandergucht. "The former has a scent of my Arrand and is so very Jealous that Such a Collection should possibly be Come at, . . . he turned Quit pale and said the french would never suffer that Collection to depart the Kingdom." There was also the worry that any rivals might inflate Orléans's notions of what the collection was worth.

The longer he spent in Paris, the more enthusiastic Tassaert became about *Wisdom and Strength* and the other pictures. He particularly liked the Rubenses, the biggest of which were "not *too* Large to find room in the English collections." He admired Van Dyck's portrait of Lord Arundel and out of the Titians he thought "7 or 8 very capital." Interestingly, he regarded a picture by Sebastiano del Piombo as the single most valuable work. This was the *Raising of Lazarus,* which he thought was worth "1500 or more." His approximate valuation of the main pictures was £46,000 (now about $5.6 million).

Tassaert fell ill while he was in Paris. "I had nearly finished you Commission here with my life," he wrote in June. But Lebrun had helped him by having his own catalog redrawn up room by room rather than alphabetically, so that valuation would be easier. Tassaert had now arrived at a more stable view of the pictures: "Youll observe this Collection is not without Copies and some under the names of Great Masters, but with all that, its the finest Collection of Italian pict^rs I have ever seen by very great odds." The confidential nature of the whole exercise was again stressed. In his letters he only ever referred to a Mr. F——h, the manuscript being altered to "Forth" by a later hand. Tassaert was also worried by the attitude of the duke's staff. "A suspicion has arisen I see plainly Among the Officers and principal serv^ts seeing me daily at work with A Catalogue, the[y] look at me as if the devil him self had been sent from England." As well they might since they received considerable tips from the many travelers who went to see the collection.

The letters show that Tassaert was growing more aware of the difficulties of the projected sale. His time in Paris had alerted him to the possible objections that could be raised, even in the middle of revolutionary chaos. "I believe if you succeed in the purchase for y^r self it will make a great noise in paris whenever the pict^rs are Attempted to be removed, because they are public pict^rs and daily on view." He was not alone: Perrigaux, a French banker who acted for Christie, had learned why Christie was coming to Paris and was sure the scheme would fail. The story was also beginning to leak out. Where he ate near the Palais Royal, Tassaert overheard certain "notables" in "great dispute in there politiks": "the duke of orleans the[y] speak of with high Contempt and say if he could make money of Even his wife and children he would sell em." Tassaert had now arrived at a valuation. He recommended that Christie offer £33,000 for the pictures unless he planned to "sell them for the dukes account." As the arrival in Paris of Christie and his son to conclude the deal was now imminent, Tassaert added a postscript for the benefit of the youth, saying that he might "get a fine florid crimson in his face without any trouble or Expense" in Paris merely by brushing the cheeks of any of the "Old babies" who offered to kiss him: "they paint there faces up to there Eys."

After Christie arrived in Paris, Tassaert's letters stopped, so there are no details of how the transactions progressed, except that the Paris dealers got wind of the scheme, protested, and, either because of that or for some other reason, the whole thing fell through. All three negotiators— the two Christies and Tassaert—returned to London empty-handed.

But the idea did not die, not in Égalité's mind anyway. One thing that kept it alive was the existence of a rival scheme, that Louis XVI also sell some works of art in London. Twenty to thirty pictures were to be sold. These were selected by d'Angivillier, the intendant of fine arts, and valued by J. B. P. Lebrun at 960,000 livres ($15 million). But that scheme also fell through.

Throughout the late part of 1790, and into 1791, turmoil continued in Paris. It is now generally accepted that 1791 was the one year when Égalité might have become regent. Orléanism was never a political party as such, not in that first Revolution, but the movement did serve the purposes of those who believed that the French people would never accept the overthrow of the monarchy altogether but *would* accept the removal of Louis XVI and Marie Antoinette *provided* they were replaced by the cadet branch of the family, at least for a while, with Égalité as head of a regency council. Many of the people subscribing to this view were paid Orléans money. That money could not last forever: there may have been some left in London but as the Revolution gathered pace, as the King fled to Varennes, was captured and brought back, the need for funds became more acute than ever. A sale would probably have happened sooner but for the fact that Égalité was caught in a trap: the more he needed to sell, the lower the price he could ask.

He was also stubborn. But still, in 1791 the last act, so far as the Rudolf/Christina/Odescalchi/Orléans collection in France was concerned, began to be played out. It went through in two parts. When the inventory had originally been drawn up, the two largest sections were the Italian pictures and paintings from the northern schools. These were sold separately. First to go were the northern schools pictures. Sometime in the first half of 1791, Lord Kinnaird asked Thomas More Slade if he would help secure the collection. Kinnaird was married to Elisabeth Ransome, the daughter of a partner in the banking firm of Ransome, Hammersly, and Morland, later amalgamated with Barclays Bank. Kinnaird, who sat for Romney, was a keen lover of painting and he joined with Hammersly and Morland in trying to obtain the Orléans pictures. He and the others provided the capital and they left it to Slade to decide for himself what the pictures were worth. The introductions were again provided by Nathaniel Parker Forth and Slade was given a credit of 550,000 francs on Perrigaux's bank.

It was an exciting mission, for Slade arrived in Paris on the very day that Louis XVI fled the city and martial law was imposed. Now more than ever Égalité would have believed that the crown, or at least the kingdom, might be his. He desperately needed money. Despite the confusion, Slade presented himself at the Palais Royal; the guards were instructed to let him through so that he could examine the paintings. After two or three days, Égalité asked Slade to make a valuation and then to place an offer. This was unusual, to say the least, and reflected Orléans hurry and need for cash. As Slade wrote later: "This, I represented was contrary to all usage, as it was for His Royal Highness to fix the price and make a demand—all expostulation on this point was in vain." Orléans told Slade that unless he agreed to this procedure all negotiations were at an end. Slade had to agree and yet, when he did make his offer, the duke flew into a rage and charged that he had been "betrayed," that Slade was "in league" with M. Lebrun. His reason was simple enough. Slade's valuation of the collection differed from Lebrun's by only 20,000 livres ($300,000). It looked like connivance (and, no doubt, the atmosphere of Revolution made everyone a bit paranoid). Slade would not be bullied in this way and told the duke very firmly that he had never set eyes on Lebrun. However, in his letters Slade wrote that "this casualty . . . gave check to the affair."

Events were still in turmoil. Égalité continued to harbor the belief that he might become regent like his great-grandfather before him, and such a possibility could turn even the coolest head. He now went off the idea of a sale and instead borrowed money against the collection "for the purpose of influencing the public mind." A greatly dispirited Slade was forced to return to London empty-handed.

No sooner had he arrived in London than Slade learned from Lord Kinnaird that while he was traveling the French and Italian pictures in the Orléans collection had been disposed of, although the Dutch and Flemish paintings were still available. At this news the poor man turned around and left for Paris yet again. Back at the Palais Royal he was forced to make another valuation and another offer. This time his estimate was even closer to Lebrun's, being just 10,000 livres ($150,000) short. There were no charges of "connivance" this time, however. The duke's mind was elsewhere and the offer was accepted and an agreement signed.

Slade could not relax, however, not yet. Égalité refused to ratify the agreement since he had learned, or pretended to have learned, that Catherine the Great of Russia was interested in the collection and might pay more for it. He insisted that he would let the pictures go to the English only if "he was allowed the difference of exchange which was at that time exceedingly favorable to England." Not wanting to return to London empty-handed again, Slade consented to this and so paid 350,000 francs ($5.5 million) for the pictures.

Slade was still not out of the woods. Égalité's creditors had wind of the sale: and because he had pledged various parts of the Palais Royal to third parties, they now claimed the pictures as part of the furniture. Slade consulted a local lawyer who advised him to meet the creditors himself and plead his own case since he spoke fluent French. Slade reports: "I accordingly attended the first meeting of the creditors in the great hall of the Palais Royal—from thirty to forty claimants were present—I urged the justice of my claim, which they did not seem to allow; and I boldly declared that, if they would not suffer me to remove the pictures, I had the power, and would enforce it, of lodging a protest against their being sold to any other person; in which case, the duke could not satisfy their demands to any extent." This argument seems to have won the day and Slade was allowed to remove the paintings to a warehouse next to the Palais Royal for packing.

Even then danger loomed. While the packing was in progress a "parcel of people"—artists mostly and all rather hostile—surrounded him, saying it was shameful that such a part of the French heritage was leaving the country. Slade was also asked by what route the pictures were to leave Paris but he was prepared for this. He told the packers the paintings were to be sent via Calais but no sooner was the packing completed than the pictures were loaded onto a barge at night and sent down the Seine to Le Havre, from where they sailed to Slade's own home near Chatham. The pictures arrived and were hung at his house until the next London season, 1793. From April to June that year they were exhibited at the Old Academy Rooms, 125 Pall Mall (once used by Christie), and an entrance fee of a shilling a day or a guinea for a season ticket was charged. So successful was the exhibition that in the last week £100 a day was taken in entrance money, representing two thousand visitors. Among the pictures sold were Rembrandt's *The Mill* and Rubens's *Judgment of Paris* and *St. George and the Dragon.*

The Slade episode was confused enough: not for the first time was the Rudolf/Christina/Odescalchi/Orléans collection caught up in politics. But *Wisdom and Strength* and the rest of the French and Italian paintings had an even more confused and adventurous history during the Revolution. At precisely the time Slade was in Paris on his first visit, or immediately after and before he reached London, this portion of the collection was sold to the Viscount Édouard de Walckiers, a Brussels banker, for the sum of 750,000 livres ($11.7 million).

Walckiers was scarcely less "revolutionary" than Égalité. Extremely well connected, his grandparents being members of the famous banking family of Nettine, his interests combined banking, commerce, and politics. He was involved in the arming of the ships which traded with Africa and the East Indies, and various members of his family had political positions. He collected books and manuscripts and built an Italian-style villa at Laeken, using the architect Payen. It was ornamented by the statues of Godecharle and boasted pictures by Lens. For this Walckiers was known in Belgium as "Édouard the Magnificent." He was also very well connected in France, since all three of his Nettine aunts had made good marriages there. One was married to Jean Joseph, Marquis de Laborde, banker to the court; a second to Micault d'Harvelay, keeper of the royal treasury, who inherited the financial house of Montmartel; and the third to Ange-Laurent de Lalive de Jully, the great introducer of ambassadors and another great collector.

But Walckiers was not in the usual run of conservative bankers. He was a revolutionary. In the beginning he had been regarded as a brilliant addition to the family's tradition, but he had a fiery temper and this, aided by his contempt for the Belgian aristocracy (which, in fairness to Walckiers, was unsophisticated by Parisian standards), caused him to turn against his upbringing. In so doing he became the first of the Belgians to consider action against the Habsburg Austrians who still ruled in Flanders 140 years after Christina had passed through.

The events in France clearly had an influence on the young man (he was twenty-one when the Bastille was stormed) and it was generally believed that he financed the insurrection which took place in Brabant in December 1789. The parallel with Égalité is very close. Walckiers formed a group of volunteers who tried to use civil unrest to bring about their demands. They had some early successes but were eventually broken and Walckiers was forced to flee to France.

Later he was allowed back but he had not changed. The Archduchess Marie Christine and Maurice Metternich were in power and implacably imposed to any reforms. Walckiers, therefore, did not wait around to be arrested or worse, and he returned to Paris. There, in 1791 and 1792, he busied himself organizing the Committee of Belgians and Liègeois, a sort of revolutionary force in exile.

Extraordinary as it may seem, it was during this turbulent period that Walckiers found occasion to buy Égalité's collection of French and Italian masterpieces. He had always been drawn to the Italian taste and perhaps the broadly similar position in which both men found themselves made them sympathetic to each other. The sale may also have been oiled by political motivation: Égalité would have been pleased to accept an offer from someone who broadly agreed with his aims, and Walckiers, who had more ready money than Égalité, would have been pleased to help a comrade-in-arms.

The collection did not get very far, not just then anyway. Almost immediately, while the pictures were awaiting shipment to Brussels, Walckiers sold them to a relative, the Comte Laborde de Méréville, for 900,000 livres ($50 million–$65 million). Laborde's father was married to Walckier's aunt and he too would have known Égalité, since Laborde senior was a very brilliant man, also a banker who, at one stage in his career, had been royal treasurer. Laborde senior was so well regarded that when Louis XVI wanted to borrow £30 million ($1.5 billion) from the King of Spain, the Spaniard refused—but said he would lend Laborde £10 million ($500 million), because he knew he would be paid back.

Laborde senior had a passion for building and one of his houses was considered so beautiful that the Duke of Bourbon wanted to buy it. Laborde refused but the duke appealed to the King and to Marie Antoinette and they forced Laborde to part with it cheaply. He was not pleased, but he was not the type to harbor a grudge and, in the years before the Revolution, he built himself another very beautiful home and sank millions into it. With hindsight his only mistake was to engage in property development in Paris. He bought large tracts of land and had the foresight to build good roads on them. This increased the value of the real estate tremendously and he quickly amassed yet another fortune. That did not make him popular among the ordinary people of Paris. After the Revolution broke out, the mob eventually caught up with Laborde and he was guillotined in 1794. But that is running ahead of the story, for by that time his son had bought the Orléans pictures.

Given the family's wealth, it is no surprise to find that Méréville (as he was known to distinguish him from his father) was given the best education money could buy. As a young man he was well versed in the arts and letters. Following the fashion of the day, Méréville crossed the Atlantic and took part in the War of Independence. This gave him liberal ideas and when he returned to France he wanted to play a political role. He did this by taking a seat on the left side of the National Assembly, where he acquitted himself well on financial matters. But his political life did not last long. In 1791, with the Revolution getting out of hand and taking ugly and unforeseen turns, he left public life and devoted himself more to arts and letters. The next year Égalité decided to sell his pictures.

Here things get murky. There were four possible routes by which *Wisdom and Strength* and the other Italian and French pictures could have found their way from Orléans to Méréville. It could have been that all three men, Égalité, Édouard Walckiers, and Méréville, shared similar views and therefore liked dealing with each other. A second possibility is that Égalité lost a huge sum of money to Laborde senior at billiards and settled his debt with the pictures. This would imply that Walckiers and Laborde had formal banking connections. A third version is that Méréville had always wanted the pictures but, not having the ready cash, persuaded Walckiers to acquire them on his behalf. Once he had sold some land, however, he was able to pay off the Belgian. A final version, which fits the facts and the psychology of the situation best, is that when the pictures came onto the market, the situation in France was so uncertain that foreigners made the most likely customers. Sharing similar political aims, Walckiers was sympathetic to Égalité, on hand in exile in Paris, and able to indulge his interest in Italian art—all at the same time. However, given the turbulent nature of the times, Walckiers's own fortunes were always changing. After his various revolutionary adventures, he and a number of other bankers and financiers were denounced as speculators and spies. And it may have quickly become clear to him that he could not return to Brussels, at least for a while. So, when Méréville, who seems genuinely to have wanted to keep the pictures in France, made Walckiers a good offer, which gave him a tidy profit for pictures he could not display at home for the foreseeable future, he agreed.

Méréville built a special gallery for the collection at his private house in the Rue d'Artois: he was still hoping for a return to stability. But this was to misread the situation. Events now moved fast. On September 15, 1792, Orléans renounced his title and became Philippe-Égalité. A week later he took his seat as the last member of the newly constituted convention, which a day later voted for the abolition of the monarchy. On December 9, Égalité published his denial of kingly ambitions and the very next day the trial of Louis XVI began. Finally, as the new year started (though it was no longer the new year, the old calendar having been abolished), Égalité voted, on January 16, for the execution of his cousin, the king, and of the hated Marie Antoinette.

By then even Méréville could see what was coming. Before the end of 1792 he fled to England and it was from London that he watched, appalled, as first Louis XVI was guillotined and then Égalité. The renunciation and the public denials of political ambition had done no good at all. And in 1794, when the terror had taken hold, Méréville's own father, Laborde senior, met the same fate. Mereville kept hoping he could go back but, again, that was to misread the situation. He was at least more fortunate than most émigrés in that he had one asset that was worth a great deal of money and, unlike houses or land, he could take with him to London. The Orléans pictures.

16.
The Canal Duke

The first Englishman to possess *Wisdom and Strength* was Jeremiah Harman (ca. 1764–1844), a banker who enjoyed a high reputation in the City. He was a director of the Bank of England from 1794 to 1827 and governor from 1816 to 1818. The cost of the Napoleonic Wars made this an economically difficult time in England. And Harman was one of the experts consulted during the secret inquiry by Pitt and Lord Liverpool into the question of paper money. Harman was also a distinguished patron of the arts. He helped Charles Eastlake, later director of the National Gallery, to visit Italy and do the research for his book, *The Methods and Materials of the Old Masters.* When Harman died his collection was sold at Christie's.

Harman did not own the collection: it was "consigned to his house for safe-keeping" when Méréville eventually felt he could go back to France to see what was happening. According to another version, Méréville mortgaged the Orléans collection to Harman's banking house for £40,000 (roughly $5 million now).

Things did not work out in France for Méréville. Indeed, for a time reports circulated to the effect that he too had been guillotined. He had not been but he could not return to France permanently and the time had clearly come for him to dispose of the paintings and raise some funds for living in London. As soon as it got out that the paintings were for sale again, Harman was approached by an art dealer, Michael Bryan, acting on behalf of a consortium of three British lords: the Duke of Bridgewater (the Canal Duke), the Earl of Carlisle, and Earl Gower.

Bryan was chosen because he was one of the best-known dealers of the day and because he had an introduction. Born in 1757 in Newcastle upon Tyne, he moved to London in 1781 but then accompanied his brother to Flanders and worked in Bruges. While in Flanders he met and married the sister of the Earl of Shrewsbury. Bryan left Flanders in 1790 and lived in Throgmorton Street in the City, where he became an art dealer as well as an agent for his brother who had also returned to England and was by now a well-known clothier in Yorkshire. Bryan opened an art gallery in Savile Row and, later on, compiled the well-known *Biographical and Critical Dictionary of Painters and Engravers,* an excellent reference work still used in art libraries today.

After he returned to London, he continued to travel to the Continent in search of paintings. On one of these trips, in 1793 or 1794, he visited Holland. He was in Rotterdam when the order arrived from the French to intern all English people there. It was during his detention in Rotterdam that he met Méréville.

Nothing much happened until 1798. Méréville, still hoping for a return to stability in France, held on to the paintings. However, some five years after his father's death under the guillotine, he finally gave up all hope and the contact with Bryan was renewed.

The three grandees whom Bryan interested in the collection were led by Francis Egerton, third and last Duke of Bridgewater. Born in 1736, Bridgewater was therefore already an old man by the time the Orléans pictures came onto the market. He was a powerful and rich but decidedly eccentric figure who had been jilted as a young man by the famous Irish beauty Elizabeth Gunning, later the Duchess of Hamilton and Argyll. After that, Bridgewater remained unmarried, becoming steadily grosser, rarely washing, his Lancashire accent getting broader and broader as he spent his time away from London on his projects in the North.

Bridgewater was one of the first great industrialists. He devoted his time and energy to the development of his coal mines and, more significantly, to canals. He built a canal from Manchester to Liverpool and a second linking the Mersey to the Trent, earning him the title of Canal Duke. The Manchester and Liverpool Canal reduced the price of coal in Manchester from 7 pence to 3½ pence per hundredweight. And although it had cost £250,000 ($12.5 million) in all to cut the canal, toward the end of the century it was earning Bridgewater £80,000 a year ($14 million).

As a young man, Bridgewater had as his tutor Robert Wood, a member of the celebrated Society of Dilettanti. Wood was an explorer and somewhat wayward as a tutor: he believed that a man should "possess a dainty mistress, own racehorses, and sit up half the night dicing." But Bridgewater had also been sent on the Grand Tour as part of his education, and this exposed him to Italian art. While in Rome he had sat for Anton Raphael Mengs. Mengs, the son of the Dresden court painter, played an important role in the development of the Neoclassical style in art, a role which owed a lot to his association with Johann Winckelmann, then in Rome also. During his Grand Tour, Bridgewater visited the Canal du Midi. He spent time at Sète and followed the entire course of the canal for two weeks, studying its engineering features.

Bridgewater's own canal-building program was ambitious and costly and took up all his energies for many years. The first sign he showed of being interested in artistic matters was when he formed a friendship with Josiah Wedgwood and ordered from him "the most complete table service of cream china that the potter could make." It was not until the 1790s that the duke gave any thought to collecting but, between 1794 and the arrival of the Orléans collection, he made a number of judicious purchases. His late-flowering interest in art delighted his friends because, at the least, it provided him with exercise. By now, the port and the indolence had made the duke exceedingly fat and "it causes him to take exercise of walking much about his gallery and rooms." His hobby of collecting never turned into real knowledge and his involvement with the collection was as much that of a speculator as of an art lover.

The second man of the three was George Granville Leveson-Gower (1758–1833), Lord Gower and, in Charles Greville's description, that "leviathan of wealth." He was Bridgewater's nephew and had served as British ambassador in Paris in 1790–92 and thus knew all about the Orléans collection, having seen firsthand the circumstances that caused Égalité to divest himself of the paintings. Gower was a learned but somewhat dull man whose interest in art was fanned by his marriage to Elizabeth, Countess of Sutherland, who, in her own right was a beautiful and fascinating woman and an amateur artist.

The third man of the syndicate was Frederick, fifth Earl of Carlisle (1748–1825). Carlisle was a distinguished statesman who held various important offices including president of the board of trade and head of the commission which opened peace negotiations with the Americans in 1778. A most civilized man, he was very interested in the arts and in literary matters. He wrote poetry and his tragedy, The Father's Revenge, published in 1783, drew praise from both Samuel Johnson and Horace Walpole. Carlisle was a friend of Reynolds's, who painted his portrait. And he attended the very first dinner given by the Royal Academy.

That the Orléans collection should go to Britain may seem inevitable now but so far as the French, Italians, and Germans were concerned, England was a backward country artistically speaking. The Continentals took the view that the British as a whole had little experience of the old masters and were in fact constitutionally incapable of appreciating them. There may have been a grain of truth in this a generation or so before but, by the end of the eighteenth century, Britain was changing, and changing rapidly and permanently. There were several reasons for this of which the first and foremost was Sir Joshua Reynolds.

Reynolds, "historically, the most important figure in British painting," was born in Plympton St. Maurice in Devon in 1723, the son of the headmaster of the local grammar school and a man who had been a

Fellow of Balliol College, Oxford. Thus Reynolds was brought up in an educated household at a time when most English painters were little more than tradesmen. As an educated man, Reynolds traveled to Italy with Admiral Keppel, the same man who fought the Battle of Ushant against Égalité (see page 223). And his paintings make frequent allusion to old masters and antique sculpture, much as a writer or speaker might refer to earlier authors. This was new and interesting and the appeal to the educated eye, as well as Reynolds's own education, made him the equal and the friend of such contemporaries as Dr. Johnson, David Garrick, Oliver Goldsmith, and Edmund Burke. His fame was such that, in 1790, Empress Catherine of Russia sent him a small snuffbox, in gold and lavender enamel, in return for a copy of his *Discourses,* which he had sent her. Reynolds's *Discourses* was extremely influential, as it explored the "rules of art" and showed how later painters were influenced by earlier ones. In it, Reynolds does not admire Veronese.

Reynolds was equivocal about the Venetian school in general but of Veronese and Tintoretto in particular; however, he does absolve Titian. Indeed, Reynolds's bile was so marked that L. March Phillips, who introduced the Everyman edition of the fifteen *Discourses,* began by drawing readers' attention, in his very first sentence, to Reynolds's "frequent slighting and depreciatory allusions to the great Venetian colourists, and by the almost passionate note of warning sounded in them against the teaching and influence of these masters. The school of Venice is always referred to by Sir Joshua as the 'decorative' school; 'mere elegance' is defined as its principal object, and its 'ornamental' character is affirmed to be totally inconsistent with any achievement of the first order. Tintoret and Veronese are selected for especial condemnation."

Reynolds's *Discourses* were usually given to the students of the Royal Academy, from early December from 1769 on, on the occasion of the distribution of prizes. He frequently returned to what he considered the vexed subject of Venetian art (though he was very much influenced by it.) It was in his fourth *Discourse,* delivered in 1771, that his objections were most clearly delineated.

In this lecture he says plainly that the "glow and bustle" of Veronese and Tintoretto are completely contrary to the (more fitting) aims of Michelangelo and Raphael, that the two Venetians were "engrossed by the study of colour to the neglect of the ideal beauty of form," and that "their colouring is not only too brilliant, but, I will venture to say, too harmonious, to produce that solidity, steadiness, and simplicity of effect, which heroic subjects require, and which simple or grave colours only can give to a work." In his most antagonistic passage, he described Veronese and Tintoretto as ". . . the persons who may be said to have exhausted all the powers of florid eloquence, to debauch the young and inexperienced; and have, without doubt, been the cause of turning off the attention of the connoisseur and of the patron of art, as well as that of the painter. . . ."

Reynolds was aware that what he was saying was controversial. In the same *Discourse,* for example, he referred to a conference of the French Academy where Lebrun, Sébastien Bourdon, and others admiringly discussed Veronese's technique. But "debauch" was a strong term and reflected, or perhaps presaged, a time when the master no longer occupied the preeminent position he once did. Veronese was included among the artists represented in Paul Delaroche's semicircular mural at the École des Beaux-Arts in Paris in 1841, and on the podium of the Albert Memorial, completed in 1864. But Reynolds's comments stuck, and his anti-Veronese and anti-Tintoretto stance is remembered today.

All this intellectual activity by Reynolds did a great deal to raise the status of artists in England and when the Royal Academy was formed in 1768 he was the obvious choice as president. Knighted in 1769, he received a doctor of clerical letters degree at Oxford (unthinkable only a generation earlier) and he even became mayor of his native Plympton in 1772.

But it was not only Reynolds who accounted for the change. The English scene was changing in many other ways as well. There was an idea for an academy of painting at Oxford, suggested in 1786; English engraving was becoming very popular at this time too, even abroad, with Madrid and Paris healthy markets for prints by such artists as Sir Robert Strange. Another indication of the keen interest in art in Britain were the large numbers who crossed the Channel to look at the newly opened Louvre. People who made the journey included Benjamin West, then president of the Royal Academy, Fuseli (Füssli), Hoppner, Opie, Farington, Turner, Flaxman, Smirke, Charles James Fox, Kemble, Samuel Rogers, then Lord Chancellor, Mary Berry, Maria Edgeworth, and Fanny Burney. In England "art was more fashionable in 1787 than it had ever been before, and the practice of painting, modelling or design attracted innumerable amateurs, of all ranks from the King and his Consort downwards."

In addition to this, English painting was thriving as never before. Gainsborough had died only recently, in 1788, and Reynolds in 1792. J. M. W. Turner was twenty-three in 1798, the year the Orléans pictures went on display in Pall Mall, Benjamin West was sixty, Henry Raeburn was forty-two, Sawrey Gilpin, the animal painter, was sixty-five, and Hoppner, forty. Sir Thomas Lawrence was twenty-nine but already in the Royal Academy and painter to the King since Reynolds's death. George

Stubbs, the painter of horses, was seventy-four, William Blake, forty-one, and Zoffany, seventy-three. Paul Sandby, the great watercolorist, was the same age. Nollekens was sixty-one, Henry Fuseli was fifty-seven, and Westmacott, twenty-three. Joseph Farington, fifty-one, was a mediocre painter of topographical views, but he was in the middle of the diary that was to bring him more lasting fame than his pictures ever did. In other words, the last quarter of the eighteenth century saw more innovation and more good work produced in the fine arts than at any comparable period of time before or since: "Only in England, with no golden age on which to look back, could the eighteenth century be seen as a real advance in painting."

Attitudes to painting had changed too, in line with these other advances, with the result that collecting art grew more and more popular. Even so, Great Britain would almost certainly not have become anywhere near as rich as she did in old masters without the tumultuous years of the French Revolution and the Napoleonic Wars, which resulted in so many French collections crossing the English Channel.

When the Dutch and Flemish pictures from the Orléans collection came onto the market, they were exhibited for some months in Pall Mall. With *Wisdom and Strength* and the other Italian and French paintings a slightly different tactic was used. The trio of Lords had *two* valuations drawn up: one for public consumption and one for their own. The three men then selected the pictures which they liked and would keep. This amounted to close to ninety paintings which were valued at 39,000 guineas ($3.6 million). The remainder were offered for sale.

The exhibition opened on Boxing Day (the day after Christmas) 1798 and, since there were 295 paintings in all, two venues were needed: Bryan's own rooms, then at 88 Pall Mall, and the Lyceum in the Strand. The price of admission was two shillings and six pence and the exhibition ran for six months. It was a great success: "Nothing of even remotely comparable quality and quantity had been seen in England since the dispersal of Charles I's pictures a century and a half earlier." It may have been for this very reason "that the general public seems to have been almost too dazed to have reacted with the enthusiasm that might have been expected." Mary Berry wrote to a friend in March 1799, less than three months after the exhibition opened: "I am heartily sorry that you did not see these pictures for they are by far the finest—indeed the only real display of the excellency of the Italian schools of painting that I ever remember in this country. And then one sees them so comfortable, for there are fewer people go to the Lyceum than even to Pall Mall, for the pictures are all of a sort less understood and less tasted here: and besides, they are without frames; and besides, the Lyceum is out of the way; and besides, it is not near Dyde's and Scribe's, nor Butler's, nor any of the great haberdashers for the women, nor Bond St., nor St. James's St. for the men."

On some people, the impact of the exhibition was "unforgettable." No one recorded it more vividly than William Hazlitt, who was an aspiring painter at the time. He wrote: "My first initiation into the mysteries of the art was at the Orléans gallery; it was there that I formed my taste, such as it is: so that I am irreclaimably of the old school in painting. I was staggered when I saw the works there collected and looked at them with wondering and with longing eyes. A mist passed away from my sight: the scales fell off. A new sense came upon me, a new heaven and a new earth stood before me. . . . Old Time has unlocked his treasures, and Fame stood portress at the door. We had heard the names of Titian, Raphael, Guido, Domenichino, the Carracci—but to see them face to face, to be in the same room with their deathless productions, was like breaking some mighty spell—was almost an effect of necromancy."

During the exhibition, paintings to the value of 31,000 guineas were sold. All the ones not sold during the display were then consigned for auction at Bryan's Gallery by the auctioneers Peter Coxe, Burrel, and Forster in 1800. Peter Coxe was a poet as well as a businessman. He was the son of Dr. Coxe, George II's physician and brother of the Venerable William Coxe, archdeacon of Wiltshire. Coxe's most well-known piece of verse, published anonymously, explained itself in its fashionably long title: "Another word or two; or Architectural hints in lines to those Royal Academicians who are painters, addressed to them on their re-election of Benjamin West, Esq. to the President's chair."

The Italian and French pictures were thus broken up in three stages, those paintings chosen by Bridgewater, Gower, and Carlisle, those sold during the exhibition, and the remainder sold at auction. Those stages offer some guidance to the tastes of the day. The pictures selected by the three Lords included works by Bellini, Correggio, Lotto, Palma Vecchio, Poussin, Raphael, Titian, Velázquez, Veronese, da Vinci. But four other things stand out. One was the particular appeal of Tintoretto. They kept nine of his works, in comparison with only seven of the twenty-eight Titians and four of the sixteen Veroneses. The second was the enormous popularity of the Bolognese school. The three dukes selected thirteen Annibale Carraccis and six Lodovico Carraccis, plus several Domenichinos, Guido Renis, and Guercinos. And finally, they selected names we barely remember now: Luca Cambiaso, Peruzzi, Scarsellino da Ferrara, Spagnoletto, Turchi. Even allowing for the fact that the choice was limited in some cases (in Lottos and Bellinis, for instance), this is a somewhat strange mix by today's standards. The Lords showed, of course, a commendable enthusiasm in the range of their selection. But still it is worth recording that they preferred seven Guilio Romanos to either of the Michelangelos available or to the three Caravaggios and two del Sartos.

After Bridgewater, Gower, and Carlisle, the principle buyers during the exhibition came from a wide range of society: aristocrats, businessmen, and even the middle classes. One of these was John Bligh, fourth Earl of Darnley, who bought the four Veronese ceiling allegories now in the National Gallery in London, plus a number of Titians and Annibale Carracci's *The Toilet of Venus*. Darnley already owned a number of Venetian works which he had acquired through Thomas More Slade. Darnley was the patron of many artists of the day, including Gainsborough, Reynolds, and Hoppner, and among his jewels were several Van Dycks. Other aristocrats at the sale included the Duke of Bedford, the Earl of Suffolk, Earl Temple, the Earl of Wycombe, and Lord Berwick, who bought what many people consider to be the most beautiful painting of all, Titian's *Rape of Europa*, (now in the Isabella Stewart Gardner Museum in Boston). Other buyers included Sir Abraham Hume and his son-in-law Charles Long, later Lord Farnborough, who assisted both George III and George IV in the decoration of various royal households.

But the buyer whose purchases have had most effect on people was John Julius Angerstein. Of Russian extraction, Angerstein may have been the natural son of Empress Anne of Austria. He had made a fortune when very young by a series of spectacular underwritings which became known in the City as "Julians" (after his middle name). He had impressed the Prime Minister. And in his house in Pall Mall he built a sizable gallery to house his Claudes, extended fantastic hospitality, and entertained such artists as Sir Thomas Lawrence, who painted his portrait. Angerstein bought heavily at the Orléans sale and several years later, in 1824, his collection helped to found London's National Gallery.

Two things stand out about the Orléans sale itself. The first is that the effect of the exhibition was to increase taste in Britain for the old masters. Until that time in England, although there were a number of collections of old masters and antique sculpture, interest in painting was mainly directed to contemporary art, and contemporary English art at that. English collectors had not imagined that they, like their counterparts on the Continent, could own pictures on a large scale by the great Italian, Dutch, or French masters. But at the Orléans sale and after, the British aristocracy and leading businessmen found they could acquire old masters in appreciable numbers: this was to become an important element in creating the English country house as it exists today.

But perhaps the most startling thing to come out of the sale was that both the supposed Michelangelos were not sold until the end: neither

Bridgewater nor Gower nor Carlisle wanted them, they were not bought during the six months of the exhibition, and even when they eventually sold at auction, they went for ninety guineas and fifty-two guineas respectively. The regent's Watteau suffered an even worse fate, selling at auction for a pitiful eleven guineas. Other paintings not sold until the auction included Bellinis, Caravaggios, and one attributed to Giorgione. Compare that with the £4,000 ($250,000) at which certain Carraccis had been valued. Indeed, all thirty-three Carraccis were snapped up before the auction, all Domenichinos went, all four Spagnolettos, and both Schiavones.

Raphael, Poussin, Reni, and Velázquez seem to have occupied much the same position then as now in terms of general esteem. Among the Venetians, despite Bridgewater's enthusiasm, Tintoretto seems not have been as popular as Titian or Veronese. Of the twelve Tintorettos in the collection, all were sold but only four reached three figures. Titian's prices came second only to the Carracci and Raphael and were ahead of Poussin. Veronese held up fairly well, even though by now he had slipped in popularity well below Titian. Most of Veronese's pictures sold for between £200 and £300 ($18,000–27,000).

It was at this point, however, that the Veronese allegories, which had been together for two hundred years, since they had been brought under one roof in the Hradčany Palace in Prague by Rudolf II, were at last split up. *Mars and Venus United by Love* (now in the Metropolitan Museum, New York) was bought by Lord Winborne. *Mercury, Herse, and Aglauros* (now in the Fitzwilliam Museum, Cambridge) was bought by Earl Fitzwilliam. *Wisdom and Strength* was bought by one of two brothers who, together, spent a great deal of money at the auction: £5,046 between them, or half a million dollars at today's values. Among the other works acquired by these brothers were Veronese's *Vice and Virtue,* one of the Michelangelos, a Velázquez, and a (doubtful) Titian. *Wisdom and Strength* thus moved a short distance, from Pall Mall to Duchess Street, near Portland Place. And there it joined an extraordinary collection in an extraordinary house. For the man who had acquired the picture was a strange being: banker, traveler, writer, patron, designer of furniture and costumes, interior decorator, and aspiring architect. But above all he was a collector who wanted to be an arbiter of taste. He was the very opposite of Philippe-Égalité, Égalité, who had no interest in the arts and had given up his title. The new owner of *Wisdom and Strength,* in sharp contrast, was interested in the arts more than anything else and would stop at nothing to have himself elevated to the peerage. He even tried to bribe his way in. This extraordinary character was Thomas Hope.

Interlude Two:
Revolution in France,
the Napoleonic Wars,
and the Creation of
the Louvre

The movement of art around Europe in the last decade of the eighteenth century and the first decades of the nineteenth occurred on a scale unknown since the Thirty Years' War. It played a vital part in the distribution of art in the world's museums and great houses of today.

This movement occurred in four stages. First came the removal of collections *from* France by the members of the ancien régime, émigrés who fled the Revolution, usually to England, and who realized that the most readily convertible currency they could take with them was their art. As a consequence, the number of art dealers in London increased greatly. Second, there was the systematic plunder of art treasures carried out by Napoleon's armies, denuding the major collections in Holland, Belgium, Prussia, Austria, Italy, Spain, and even Egypt. This provoked great bitterness and resentment all over Europe. Third, the London dealers and other hangers-on, who saw the opportunity, scoured Europe, Italy especially, during the chaos, picking up pictures cheaply since potential victims of Napoleon were only too thankful to receive some reimbursement for art that, at any time, might be confiscated. These maneuvers—the transfer of ancien régime collections to London and the activities of English dealers in Europe—were among the chief reasons for the establishment of a thriving art market in London, where it has remained ever since. Finally, there was the restitution of the plundered works, forced on France after Napoleon's defeat by the allies. Unfortunately, not everything went back and what did, did not always go back to where it had come from.

The Orléans gallery was the biggest and the best to be dispersed. But the roll call of the other ancien régime collections was almost as impressive. Next in importance was that of the French minister, Charles Alexandre Calonne, which consisted of 359 pictures, containing masterpieces mainly of the Dutch, French, and Spanish schools. It, too, was sold in England, in 1795. In 1801, Citizen Robit's collection came under the hammer when Michael Bryan, in company with two other connoisseurs bought forty-seven of the best. Other collections that found their way to London included those of M. Paperrière, the receiver general, those of Érard and Lafitte, the Chevalier de Crochart, paymaster general of the French army, Lafontaine, the Prince de Conti, Sereville, Sabatier, Tolazon, Delahante, Randon de Boisset, the Duke de Praslin, the Prince Talleyrand (in 1817), and, last but by no means least, J. B. P. Lebrun himself, who was still alive and still managing to do the right thing at the right time.

To an extent, these losses were redressed when neighboring countries were invaded by France. Indeed, almost no collection in Europe was left intact. Rome was worst affected, especially the famous papal families, the Aldobrandini, Barberini, Borghese, Colonna, Corsini, Falconieri, Giustiniani, Chigi, Lanzelotti, Spada and Odescalchi, who lost many of their coins to Napoleon. In Genoa, the families of Balbi, Cambiasi, Cataneo, Doria, Durazzo, Gentile, Lecari, Marano, Mari, and Spinola sold the whole or part of their collections. The Palazzo Riccardi in Florence and the royal palace of Capo di Monte in Naples lost many admirable pictures. Lastly, a great number of churches throughout Italy parted with their altarpieces.

From 1798 the process was repeated in Belgium and Holland. Those collections that were not looted and removed to Paris were snapped up by English dealers, such as Michael Bryan or William Buchanan, and taken to London. The German art historian Gustav Waagen, visiting London during the first half of the nineteenth century, recorded that the following collections from the Netherlands had crossed the Channel: Van Zwieten, Van Hasselaer, Lubbeling, Van Leyden, Schlingelandt, Lormier, Braamcamp, and numerous others. "Two collections, moderate in size, but very choice, that of the Countess Holderness, formerly belonging to Greffier Fagel, and that of the banker Crawford, were sold by auction in London in 1802 and 1806."

Spain, the last to fall, was not as badly hit as elsewhere but even so several rich families and religious establishments were forced to surrender their Rubenses and Murillos.

Besides paintings, entire collections of drawings, manuscripts, engravings, woodcuts, miniatures, church silver, and sculptures of classical antiquity changed hands and crossed frontiers. Lord Elgin, for example, acquired his celebrated marbles in the first years of the nineteenth century.

It is ironic that the strength and depth of Britain's many collections should owe so much to the French. But they do, and in more ways than this. For events in France at the turn of the nineteenth century also determined the way we look at paintings today. For Napoleon, as well as sanctioning plunder on a widespread scale, also created the first public museum, an institution which changed the experience of art for all time. This was the Louvre.

Several factors led to the creation of the Musée du Louvre, the Emperor being only one. Another was the building of Versailles. As a result of that and the transfer of the court out of Paris, the palace of the Louvre was neglected and the royal collections became increasingly inaccessible. As early as the 1760s Denis Diderot, in the *Encyclopédie,* attacked this neglect and campaigned to have the Grande Galerie, that long walkway in the Louvre, opened to the public. Another element was that the French at this time led the world in the care of pictures. Robert Picault had invented the technique of transferring paintings from wood to canvas so that they could be moved around more easily. The French were therefore especially conscious of the lack of a proper collection in Paris: there was now no reason why paintings could not be moved.

From time to time, attempts were made to act on Diderot's suggestion but, in the end, it took an event as momentous as the Revolution of 1789 to bring about anything definite. For when the Revolution did arrive, a new element surfaced: the anticlericalism of the revolutionaries which resulted in the nationalization, on November 2, 1789, of ecclesiastical property and the seizure of works of art. What was to be done with all these paintings and other beautiful objects? Given the republican spirit of the times, when the monarchy fell, on August 10, 1792, the Girondist Minister of the Interior, Roland, immediately took steps to install a national museum in the home of the ex-King.

The early Louvre had its opponents, the citizens of Versailles among them. They were alarmed by the exodus of these great works to Paris and, for a while, they succeeded in stopping the government from adding to the Louvre. Leonardo da Vinci's *Mona Lisa,* for example, was one of the pictures held up for a time. The painter Jacques Louis David also opposed the Louvre for political reasons, aided and abetted by Lebrun, who was angry because he had not been appointed to the commission which ran the museum. David and Lebrun also objected to the widespread cleaning of pictures in the Louvre; there have always been those painters who have opposed any cleaning, which appears to make old masters especially vivid.

Despite the objections, however, the Louvre opened to the public on the scheduled date, August 10, 1793: the first anniversary of the fall of the King. The general public was admitted three days out of every ten, the rest of the time being reserved for artists and special entrants. Roland had forbidden the exhibition of works by living artists on the grounds that the intrigues to get their works accepted and displayed alongside the great old masters would have become problematic and unedifying. However, when the Grande Galerie opened, the works of living artists were exhibited next to it, in the Salon Carré. This room was known colloquially as the "Salon" and the word was used ever after for the exhibitions of the Academy, wherever they were held.

Besides the old royal collection and the works confiscated from churches, a final source of pictures for the gallery was paintings left behind by émigrés who had fled: these included important works by Mantegna and Perugino. The Louvre, finally opened, was *the* embodiment of revolutionary and republican spirit. Without it, what then happened might never have come to pass. For it became a trophy of conquest.

In the early 1790s France was at war as well as in the middle of a Revolution and it was this conjunction that had such important consequences for art. France had declared war on Austria in April 1792, the initial aim being to invade the Austrian Netherlands—Belgium. Things did not go according to plan, however, and in the next twenty years the fighting spread to Germany, Italy, Spain—even to Egypt. Early on in the hostilities the same thought occurred to several people: that artists and scholars should accompany the army secretly and carefully remove important works of art and scientific instruments and send them back to France.

They started in Antwerp, which fell to the French on July 24, 1794. Their first load comprised four Rubenses, including *Descent from the Cross* from Antwerp Cathedral, which was one of the two or three most famous pictures of the day. In all, about forty Rubenses were looted from Antwerp, Brussels, Ghent, Malines, and Alost, together with works by Van Dyck and Jordaens and also Michelangelo's marble *Madonna* from Bruges, by far the most important piece of sculpture in the whole of Belgium.

Belgium was an appetizer. In October 1794 a committee was formed to compile information concerning art works to be found in countries which the French armies were expected to invade. Detailed catalogs were drawn up for Holland, the Rhineland, and the pictures remaining in Belgium. All this paled, however, in comparison with the booty to be found in Italy. This campaign was also interesting because the general in the field now was Napoleon Bonaparte. Napoleon, therefore, did not initiate the plunder across Europe by the French. He merely inherited an attitude and approach that was already widespread. From now on his role was crucial but it was also, in a way, curious. As much as he was eager to obtain masterpieces and send them back to Paris, yet he was himself unmoved by pictures: his interest in paintings was not aesthetic. In the Louvre, Napoleon would walk right round the gallery without stopping anywhere. Perhaps Quatremère de Quichy was right when he said that Bonaparte was "devoured by anticipatory lust after the best things in each country, whether masterpieces and precious objects or men of talent and renown." It is also true that Napoleon shared with many Frenchmen the conscious desire to transfer the center of the civilized world from Rome to Paris.

Whatever Napoleon's motives, there can be no doubting his zeal. In Italy a special commission followed Bonaparte right across the country, only two days behind the front line, despoiling in succession Parma, Modena, Milan (the big Raphael cartoon *The School of Athens),* Bologna, and Cento. From the first two towns Bonaparte demanded twenty pictures as part of the armistice settlement; in Bologna, he concluded with the Pope's representative an agreement which enabled him to take a number of pictures, sculptures, and vases from Rome. In keeping with the Neoclassical tastes of the time, eighty-three pieces of sculpture were chosen and only seventeen pictures. The sculptures taken came mainly from the Vatican and the Capitoline: the Apollo Belvedere, the Laocoön, and the Belvedere torso. The pictures included Raphael's *Transfiguration,* Poussin's *St. Erasmus,* and Caravaggio's *Deposition.* The armies then moved on: to Verona (Mantegna's altarpiece in San Zeno), to Perugia (Raphael's *Madonna of Foligno,* nearby), then to Mantua and Venice, called upon to provide twenty pictures and six hundred manuscripts. The Veroneses taken included three of his huge feasts; and among the Titians taken were the *Death of St. Peter Martyr* (later known as *Martyrdom of St. Peter)* and the *Martyrdom of St. Lawrence.* Sebastiano del Piombo, Lotto, Palma Vecchio, and Giorgione all escaped.

The list of plunder shows that the premier attraction in Italy for the French was not Renaissance painting but antique sculpture. Apart from its own excellence, antique sculpture was regarded as very important for the education of the young. A lot that was the best in French painting— Claude and Poussin, for example—was inconceivable without it. After that, the most highly regarded painters were Raphael, Correggio, Veronese, and Titian, more or less in that order. The Bolognese painters of the silver age came next: Domenichino, Reni, Guercino, and the Carracci. And then one or two, but only one or two, early masters: Bellini and Mantegna. Tiepolo was out, as were da Vinci and Michelangelo, though in their cases this was partly due to the fact that their works were very rare. The idea that they were the dominating geniuses of the Renaissance was still some way off.

In the second campaign, Turin and Florence were taken. The Florence of the 1790s, however, was not the Florence of today. Giotto, Fra Angelico, Botticelli, Donatello, and Ghirlandaio were all "rediscovered" in the nineteenth century, well after the Napoleonic Wars. The main artists of the Uffizi at the time were Raphael, Correggio, Titian, the Carracci, Reni, plus Dou and Rembrandt. The French did not loot the Uffizi Palace, however, but turned to the Pitti since it was the palace of the ruling house. It contained no antique sculpture but a rich variety of paintings: Raphael's circular *Madonna della Seggiola,* Rubens's *Four Philosophers* and *The Horrors of War,* portraits by Van Dyck and Rembrandt, Titian's *Concert* and *The Three Ages of Man* (then ascribed to Giorgione). Several del Sartos were not taken. Turin was better represented in northern painters: Rembrandt, Van Dyck, Holbein, Teniers, "Velvet" Bruegel, Poussin, and Reni.

As a result of all this Italian plunder, Europe yet again saw convoys of wagons and mules similar to those it had seen a century and a half earlier, during the Thirty Years' War. The first French convoy went by land. "The wagons, drawn by oxen, were specially constructed. The cases containing the paintings and statues rested on rollers. The larger pictures were removed from their stretchers and placed one above the other with padding between; then rolled on cylinders which were supported from the ends. The cases were tarred on the outside and then covered with waxed cloth as further protection against wet. The first convoy, which contained the spoils of Lombardy, formed up at Tortona, near Alessandria, and continued by land to Paris over the Mont Cenis. The journey lasted from September 13 to the beginning of November 1796." Subsequent convoys, however, went by water for as much of the way as possible.

The third convoy, the greatest one, with the spoils of Rome and Venice, was given a huge reception. Its departure from Italy had been delayed because the Italians had tried hard to stop it. This made it even more of a prize and the bronze horses of St. Mark's were paraded through the streets of Paris together with live ostriches, camels, gazelles, vultures, and a military band. The celebrations lasted for two days and represented for the Republic a culmination of the Revolution, the celebrations were as close to an imitation of a Roman triumph as the revolutionaries ever achieved. With the arrival of this booty it really did seem as if the center of civilization had been dragged North, by oxen, over the Alps, from Rome to Paris.

After Italy came Munich in 1800. It did not have a great collection, certainly in comparison with the collections of Italy, but it did include

Altdorfer's *Alexander the Great at the Battle of Issus,* which became Napoleon's personal favorite and hung in his bathroom at St. Cloud.

By now the Louvre was becoming congested. The tally so far amounted to 1,390 paintings of the foreign schools, 270 French old masters, and more than a thousand of the modern French schools. There were 4,000 engraved plates, 30,000 engravings, 1,500 antique sculptures and other works of art in the form of Etruscan vases, porphyry tables, and so on. Besides that there were another thousand pictures at Versailles and six to seven hundred in storage in Paris. The Louvre, big as it was, and it was by far the biggest collection anywhere, could not accommodate more than half of what belonged to the French nation at that time. Thus was born the idea of spreading the lesser works, and even a few major ones, around the provinces.

The importance of the Louvre did not lie simply in the fact that it became a trophy of conquest. It also lay in the fact that its very existence sparked imitations. Under Napoleon as Emperor, the eighteenth-century academy of Brera, at Milan, was reconstituted and a similar one set up in Bologna. In 1808, Louis Bonaparte, as King of Holland, founded the Rijksmuseum in the town hall of Amsterdam. In 1809, Joseph Bonaparte, King of Spain, gave orders for the founding of a museum there. It took ten years but it led to the Prado.

The Louvre's effect on the British was almost as great. It helped pave the way for the regular exhibition of old masters in London at the British Institution and for the creation of the National Gallery. The Louvre also affected taste in Britain because it attracted so many British artists anxious to view its splendors. Turner was only one of many painters who made the journey across the Channel. Together with the Orléans sale, the Louvre helped to shift taste in Britain from sculpture to painting and from contemporary art to old masters.

In fact the Louvre quickly became famous outside its own country as countless people from all over Europe came to see what had been denied them before, either because the collections were private or because it needed a whole Grand Tour to take in what was now on show in one place—if the Louvre could be described as one place.

Yet, despite its vast dimensions, the Louvre had still not peaked. In July 1803, its name was changed to the Musée Napoleon and the next year Bonaparte assumed the title of Emperor. By then the museum had a new director general, a man who, in the world of art plunder, was almost an Emperor himself. This was Domenique Vivant Denon.

Denon, born in 1747, was no longer a young man when he got the job. But he had successfully outlasted every political crisis and change that had overtaken France. Like Égalité, he had even altered his name at one point, from Chevalier de Non to Citoyen Denon. And he had made friends with a succession of very different people ranging from Louis XV and Voltaire to Bonaparte and Pius VII. He was an artist and an author of erotica for which he composed both the drawings and the words. He was a far from obvious choice as director general of the Louvre, especially as Jacques Louis David badly wanted the job. But it was Denon who charmed Bonaparte and, once installed, he never looked back.

He traveled with the shock troops himself, knowing that a man on the spot can do anything while chaos reigns. In Germany he entered successive art centers with a free hand from the Emperor. Brunswick, Kassel, Schwerin, Warsaw—it almost reads like Gustavus Adolphus's rapid race through Europe in the 1630s. The Brunswick collection was possibly the best. It included Rembrandt's *Family Group* and Palma Vecchio's *Adam and Eve,* then attributed to Giorgione. From Kassel he took 299 pictures, including 16 Rembrandts (among them the great *Jacob's Blessing),* four Rubenses, and a Titian. Some two hundred pictures were taken from Schwerin; at Berlin and Potsdam the Prussian collection contained Frederick the Great's contemporary French art, Watteau especially, and Correggio's *Leda,* the painting which had left France a few years before, having been mutilated by the son of the regent. Denon made similar hauls in Danzig (Memling's *Last Judgment,* then attributed to Van Eyck) and took a few pictures by Bellotto and Palma Giovane from Warsaw.

Denon's first batch of booty was exhibited at the Louvre in October 1807 when it officially numbered 710 items: 368 paintings, 33 drawings, and the rest mainly sculpture. But in fact Denon had taken far more than this: he had also handed over substantial amounts to Napoleon's wife, Joesephine, who was collecting on her own behalf.

Next, Denon swooped down on Vienna where the imperial collections of Austria—Leopold William's pictures among them—were housed in the Upper Belvedere. Part of the collection had been packed up and evacuated before the arrival of the French troops so that although Denon got his hands on four hundred pictures, they did not include the best: Titian's *Ecce Homo,* Correggio's *Jupiter and Io,* Rubens's Ildefonso altar, Dürer's *Trinity,* Giorgione's *Three Philosophers,* and works by del Sarto, Tintoretto, and Velázquez. Some Bruegels fell to Denon, however, as well as Rubens's huge *Assumption of the Virgin,* which had to be sawed into three pieces before it could be moved.

Denon's activities, coming on top of everyone else's, made the Louvre without doubt one of the wonders of the age. The seal was truly set on that glory, moreover, when, on April 2, 1810, Napoleon and Marie Louise, his second wife, chose it as the setting for their marriage. A long strip drawing of this occasion, by Benjamin Zix, conveys the social and artistic glitter. Apart from the lines of distinguished people present, Zix's work shows that the ceremony was "overseen" by fourteen famous—and looted—old masters.

After this, Denon had just one further tour of plunder to undertake, but it was an important one. Until then, 1810, the museum had reflected the taste of the day. Raphael and Rubens came first, followed by Correggio, Veronese, and Titian, then the Bolognese school, the other northern masters, and finally the Neoclassical Poussins and Claudes. But this was the taste, essentially of the ancien régime and, as the nineteenth century grew older, tastes changed again. Denon sensed this, for in his final adventure, in Italy in 1811–12, he concentrated on primitive painters much more than had anyone before him. Now, for the first time since their death, attention was paid to the likes of Botticelli, Fra Angelico, Filippo Lippi, and Ghirlandaio.

Denon's achievements extended beyond his acquisitions. The catalogs which he produced showed that he was well ahead of his time. Rather than being just a list, they were set out as a series of brief biographies, compiled in such a way that Cimabue, Giotto, and Masaccio, for instance, were presented as successive steps in an artistic progression which culminated in Raphael. This is still essentially the understanding of today. Also, by looting the work of artists who were not esteemed in their own countries, Denon drew attention to them, made them valued, and—all of a sudden—valuable. This was especially true of the primitives. Denon opened people's eyes to what was under their noses.

In one sense, then, the Louvre under Denon and Napoleon was a magnificent achievement: it comprised the greatest collection of art ever brought together in one place. But it was equally fitting that the museum should not last long as it was. It had been filled by plunder and when the wars turned against France, the allies wanted everything returned.

The German and Spanish works were the first to go. Being less fashionable, fewer of their works were on show and the French had fewer objections anyway. But the Italian works were problematic. The Pope sent the sculptor Antonio Canova to negotiate the return of the Vatican's art objects but that was just the start of an enormous amount of toing and froing, plot and counterplot, which made the period so chaotic. The Pope had no armies to enforce his claims, the British at one point had *their* eye on some of the spoils, and all the while the French used every ounce of guile to prevent anything leaving Paris. In the end, however, the Duke of Wellington sided with Canova and the Pope and the states of Sardinia, Parma, Piacenza, and Tuscany had their claims met. Lombardy and Venice were by now part of the Holy Roman Empire, one of the allies, and so their treasures were returned not to Italy but to Austria, another complicating factor. For the French the final humiliation came when the horses of St. Mark's were taken down, prior to their return to Venice. No French turned up to watch, although some had tried by force to prevent the dismantling during the night when the work of detaching the horses was taking place. And they gloated unreservedly when the Lion of St. Mark's fell and broke into twenty pieces. (The creature now in Venice has modern legs and wings.) The French attitude was summed up by Baron Gros when he said at an oration for Denon's burial ten years later, in 1825: "Let them take them. But they have no eyes to see them with. France will always prove by her superiority in the arts that the masterpieces were better here than elsewhere."

Whatever the allies might have *wanted* to do with the plundered art in France, they were still faced with very difficult practical problems. Many works had been dispersed around the country, away from the Louvre. It was impossible to get many of these back, with the result that masterpieces may still be found in unlikely places in France. For example, Rubens's *Crucifixion,* plundered from the Capuchins church in Antwerp, is in Toulouse; the same painter's *Madonna and Saints,* which hung over his mother's grave, is still in Grenoble; and his *Last Supper,* from Malines, is still in the Brera in Milan. At least sixty-eight of the Stadouder's pictures in the Hague never returned; nor did forty-four from Munich, including yet another Rubens, the *Adoration of the Magi,* which is in Lyon.* And so, after a fashion, the Musée Napoleon was dismembered. Far more remained than is usually thought but it was not again to be the fantastic wonder it was for the brief period, when it was host to the Bonaparte wedding.

Still, the creation of the Louvre was a watershed in the history of art galleries and museums all around the world. Indeed, one can speak now in terms of "pre-Louvre" and "post-Louvre" epochs.

Museum was originally a Greek word, *mouseion.* This was applied to a sanctuary dedicated to the Muses of Greek mythology. Then it was used more widely and came to be applied to places of learning. For instance, it was used to describe part of the building that housed the library of Alexander the Great. Public art collections *did* exist in ancient Greece: according to Pausanias, writing in the second century A.D., there was a building in Athens near the Acropolis which contained a collection of paintings and was known as the Pinakotheke. But the idea then seems to have died

---

* A French art historian, Marie-Louise Blumer, tracked the fate of 506 paintings which had been removed from Italy: 9 disappeared and 249 were returned, but 248 remained in France!

out. No such thing was known in ancient Rome, although Roman generals did exhibit some of the statues they had plundered in Greece.

It could be said that in the Middle Ages the churches were the closest things to museums. Besides the carvings and the stained glass that were part of the fabric of the church, some, like St. Mark's in Venice or the cathedral at Halle in Germany, had displays of treasures and relics. But it was not until much later, the late fourteenth and early fifteenth century, that it added to the prestige of a prince or noble, such as Jean, Duke of Berry, to be surrounded by art and curiosities. Until that time, knights or nobles had moved around, from house to house or castle to castle, taking with them their silver, books, jewels, and tapestries. Once the idea caught on, however, it soon spread throughout Europe. Thus began the age of the *studiolo* or *scrittoio,* the *Kunst-* and *Wunderkammer,* of which Rudolf and, later, Christina were such passionate adherents. These collections were seen by the privileged few, courtiers and nobles making the Grand Tour, for example. But they were essentially private collections. The general public was not admitted and the collections bore the stamp of their owner's personal taste.

In addition to all this, the Italians, possibly led by the architect Sebastiano Serlio, came up with the idea of the *galleria* as a place to display the larger paintings. The *gallerie,* as is still true in some Italian cities today, were places to take exercise indoors when it was raining, and it came to be a part of all princely palaces across Europe.

These two things, the cabinet of curiosities and the *gallerie,* were joined by a third idea. This was put forward first in 1565 by Samuel van Quiccheberg, a Flemish doctor in the service of Albrecht V of Bavaria. Quiccheberg wrote a treatise advocating that the ideal museum should seek to represent the entire universe through the systematic classification of all subject matter. This notion proved very popular and was put into effect almost everywhere. The idea also grew that collections were worthy of study. In 1739, as a result of these developments, the Vatican collections were opened to the public. In the 1750s, parts of the French royal collections were made available to the public in the Palais du Luxembourg, and in 1759 an act of Parliament in Britain opened the house of Sir Hans Sloane, which he had given to the nation. Sloane collected all manner of things and the British Museum was born.

In all these instances, however, public access was very restricted and it took the French Revolution and the Musée Napoleon to change attitudes fundamentally. The unrestricted access brought about by the creation of the Louvre was enormously popular with the public, who clamored for more art, more exhibitions, more knowledge. Publications were produced which fostered the desire for education. Simultaneously but separately, the restitution of the art treasures to the various nations from which they had been taken by the French produced an awakening in the public of *heritage* as a concept associated with art. The practical result of this was that efforts were now made to found museums on a national basis.

The contents of these museums were very different from earlier collections. For instance, under Louis XV, any works the King disliked were placed in the Luxembourg, where he would not have to see them. At Potsdam, Frederick the Great collected pictures by Watteau because they were *out* of favor with the rest of the art world. Catherine II of Russia bought several private collections because she thought it her duty to do so. Princes could do that. The national collections, on the other hand, took Vienna as their model of organization, even if it was the *idea* of the Louvre which started everything. In Vienna, Christian von Mechel, director of the art collection, had arranged pictures in chronological order by schools, a pattern which was new then but is still the recognized form of display even today. He had also set up a print room, a feature which most other museums/galleries also sought to emulate.

Thus art galleries as they are known today derive more or less directly from Denon's Louvre, with acknowledgment to Von Mechel's Vienna. It shows in the dates when the national galleries of most countries were founded: Budapest (1802), Prague (1818), Madrid (1819), London (1824), Berlin (1830), and Munich (1836). Even then they were fairly static affairs. Little effort was made to add to them or round out the weak areas. Acquisition was usually by bequest and the administration was invariably in the hands of court officials, eminent artists, or connoisseurs, not scholars.

One final point. These national art galleries, consciously or otherwise, reflected the Renaissance attitudes: they dealt almost exclusively with the fine arts. Ever since painters freed themselves of the guilds, through that process which began with the Humanists and which turned painting into a liberal rather than a manual art, the fine arts and the decorative arts had been separate, more separate than they deserved to be. It was as a direct consequence of this that the great national galleries of paintings, as they are now known, were first formed.

The great collections of the decorative arts—those of the Rothschilds, Sir Richard Wallace, John Pierpont Morgan, Frederic Spitzer, Georg Hirth, the Musée de Cluny, or the Victoria and Albert Museum—came later and were thoroughly nineteenth century in conception. The industrial revolution played its part, too. This affected the understanding of, and attitudes toward, craftwork and at the same time created larger numbers of wealthy people who were neither royal nor noble in the old-fashioned sense at all. A new type of collector appeared and the whole art world changed again. This shaped the type of collection where *Wisdom and Strength* was to be housed for the next hundred years.

V

THE HOPES

17.
Thomas Hope,
the Ambitious Commoner

Wisdom and Strength was owned successively by an Emperor, a Queen, a prince of the empire, a regent of France, a royal duke who renounced his title, and three British Lords. In order to maintain this "social slide," it was time for the painting to be owned by a commoner. Thomas Hope, however, was no mere commoner. He would have hated to be described as a "mere" anything.

For Hope was extraordinary. He worked hard, very hard, at being out of the ordinary. For that reason, he is remembered now but, in his life, it was his undoing. Born around 1770 into a Dutch banking family, he made the Grand Tour on a grand scale, traveling extensively in Europe and the Middle East, acquiring knowledge and strong views about history and the arts. He then settled in London where he used those opinions to create for himself a position in Society. This he did more or less successfully although he is remembered now chiefly for his influence on British taste in clothes, gardens, and, above all, in furniture and interior decoration. He was caught up in that artistic movement which swept through Europe at the end of the eighteenth and beginning of the nineteenth century: Neoclassicism.

Hope was born in Amsterdam. The Dutch city was then flourishing, mainly as a result of the Far Eastern trade, in which the Hopes played a prominent part. The family had emigrated from Scotland in the seventeenth century to involve themselves in the commercial life of Holland.

The Hopes were remarkably successful in Holland and by the late seventeenth century had emerged as one of the most notable families in a city that was thriving with bankers. The memoirs of the times afford us several glimpses of the kind of life they led. Benjamin Franklin, for example, wrote: "At Amsterdam we were Recommended to thee Hopes, who are Rank'd amounge the greatest Merchants of Europe, one of them sent us his Coach to carry us to se evry thing curious in the City." Sir Joshua Reynolds also referred to the Hopes: "I have been more particular in the account of Mr Hope's Cabinet, not only because it is acknowledged to be the first in Amsterdam, but because I had an opportunity (by the particular attention and civility of its possessors) of seeing it oftner, and considering it more at my leisure, than any other collection." And finally, Baron de Frénilly, writing in 1786: "Amidst the forst of masts which covered the sea and made the port of Amsterdam into a second town . . . and amidst the painted trees and marble houses of Broek, there reappear before me the servants of the great banker Hope, dressed in their gold-gallooned livery and drawn up in a row along a white marble corridor, to receive, as we went out, the gold ducat which you paid for your dinner. . . . [These were] The millionaires of Amsterdam . . . [who] prided themselves on being frenchified, spoke only French, and lived entirely *à la Française."*

The banking family had been founded by Thomas Hope's grandfather, also called Thomas, who died in 1779. But it was under the management of Henry Hope, "our" Thomas's second cousin, that it enjoyed its period of greatest prosperity in the 1770s and 1780s. It was Henry who built a great Dutch country house on the estate of Welgelegen, near Haarlem, between 1785 and 1788. This house, called Het Paviljoen, was noteworthy for two reasons. One, its domed central hall was flanked by two galleries for the display of the Hope picture collection, important even in those early days. And two, it was the sole example of the Louis XIV style in eighteenth-century Holland: indeed it was so elegant and grand that after various changes of fortune, it was acquired in 1806 by Louis Bonaparte, then King of Holland.

The Hopes always regarded themselves as more than bankers. Thomas's mother always thought the English did not treat her with the proper respect. The Hopes liked to see themselves in much the same light as the Italian Renaissance bankers, who combined moneymaking with art patronage and lavish hospitality, mixing art, financial muscle, and political power in almost equal measure.

Thomas, born on August 30, 1769, was the eldest of three sons, the others being Adrian Elias and Henry Philip. As this was the era of the Grand Tour, the Hopes followed this fashion as extravagantly as they were to follow others. On and off, Thomas spent no fewer than eight years making the tour from the age of eighteen until he was twenty-six. He studied architecture in Turkey, where he stayed in the capital for nearly twelve months, and traveled in Egypt, Syria, Greece, Sicily, Spain, Portugal, France, Germany—and England.

While Thomas was away the political situation in Holland deteriorated and, with the approach of the French armies in 1794, the Hope family moved to England and Thomas settled in Hanover Square. It was from here that, at the age of twenty-five, he attempted to launch himself into English intellectual society. It was not to be straightforward, partly on account of Hope's singular personality: Hope was as difficult a character as Rudolf, Christina, Don Livio, the regent, or Égalité. The pictures show a small, dark-haired man, with a moustache and a straight nose, but he looks weak about the face and a little pasty. Lord Glenbervie wrote about Hope, in 1801, that he was "a little ill-looking man about thirty, with a sort of effeminate face and manner." He must also have been what we would call pushy. He quickly got about in London, becoming known almost immediately to the circle around Horace Walpole, and he made an impact on smart society in Brighton, entertaining, among others, Samuel Rogers. By 1801 he could also number John Julius Angerstein and the Princess of Wales as acquaintances, if not yet as friends.

Hanover Square did not satisfy Hope's ambition for long and in 1799, he purchased a grander town house from the former Countess of Warwick. Located on Duchess Street, it was not far from his cousin, Henry Hope, who lived in Cavendish Square. This was the first of Thomas Hope's two great houses. The other, his country retreat at Deepdene, near Dorking in Surrey, was bought much later. It is for the way Hope decorated these extraordinary mansions that he is remembered today.

At the same time as he began putting down these magnificent roots in London, he was still traveling. In France and Italy, he encountered first-hand the French soldiers' rapacious attitude to art: in Rome certain works which he had acquired were confiscated. But despite Napoleon, life was good and wherever he went Hope was accepted in the finest houses. Lady Hester Stanhope wrote from Naples, in 1802: "Here there are the most distinguished of our beaux: Lord Grantham, Algernon, Lord Montague, Sir Charles Douglas and Mr. Hope, Thomas Hope, I think needs no description. . . . Thursday, Mr. Hope, another ball." Hope was recognized as a civilized patron, and in 1800 he was admitted to the Society of Dilettanti, a club for fashionable people interested in the arts and had visited Italy. The next year he was invited for the first time to attend the annual dinner of the Royal Academy, a singular honor. With these advances, Hope could now anticipate that he was to have an even greater impact on London society. But the way he did it appears rather strange today: he was going to open his house to the public. *Wisdom and Strength* was to be part of an extraordinary exhibition of vanity, very fitting given the Latin inscription it bears.

For Hope was a man in the Crozat tradition, an "amateur," a self-conscious connoisseur. He felt strongly that a man of means, though he might not be an artist himself, could influence the thought of his day by his collecting and the display of his acquisitions. Hope felt that he had taste—the fruit of his travels, his studies, and his acquisitions—and he was determined to show it in such a way that he might influence his contemporaries. The contents of his two houses, not to mention the very bricks and mortar, represented a philosophy, a fully worked out intellectual system. Hope's approach may seem self-conscious, excessively precious, and condescending: a bit much in the late twentieth century. But it was very much in keeping with the attitudes of his day.

Hope acquired the Duchess Street mansion in 1799, the same year that he bought *Wisdom and Strength.* This was a fortunate coincidence, for the Orléans sale afforded him the ideal opportunity to realize his ideas about marrying the arts of the ancients with those of the contemporary world. The actual address of the house was 1 Mansfield Street and it was built as part of the Portland Place development by Robert Adam, the English Neoclassical architect and interior decorator who had studied in Rome. The dowager Lady Warwick, who sold the house to Hope, was the sister of Sir William Hamilton, the diplomat involved in restitution in Paris, and whose celebrated collection of vases Hope was to acquire later on.

The house was entered by two gates which led into a courtyard overlooked by two short, three-storied wings. Inside, the ground floor of the house was entirely given over to the servants with the exception of a circular entrance hall and a staircase hall. The staircase rose in one arm, returning in two and in later years a painting of Thomas Hope, in Turkish dress, by Sir William Beechey, greeted the visitor.

The principal reception rooms, including the dining room, were on the second floor. However, Hope and his family spent most of their time in the three private entertaining rooms and three bedrooms on the next floor. The second floor was designed entirely for Hope's large public entertainments and it was this part of the house that the most fashionable people in the London of his day were to come to know.

As soon as he acquired the house, Hope started to make alterations and improvements. In 1799 the property taxes rose from £350 per annum to £500, probably reflecting the large amount of building that was going on. The layout was important for it reflected Hope's view that his pictures, and his picture gallery, were only one part of the artistic spectrum, and not necessarily the most important part. The stairs to the second floor led to a large drawing room beyond which was the dining room. These two rooms occupied the center of the second floor and it was around them that nine other rooms were laid out and filled with Hope's collections.

The picture gallery, which came after an anteroom containing modern copies of antique sculpture, was a grand affair. It was two stories high with a large skylight at the top, a device Hope copied from the Louvre. Hope had designed this gallery himself—it was added to enclose the courtyard on its fourth side. Built and decorated in the Greek style, it was rather austere. Four columns supported the skylight, imitations of those in the Tower of Winds in Athens. There was a trabeated, or beamed, roof based on the Theseion and four Doric columns from the Propylaea, the entrance to the Acropolis. The gallery was not only decorated with Greek-style objects or features, it also took the overall form of a Greek temple. There was even an organ at the end which gave it, in Hope's own words, "the appearance of a sanctuary." Put simply, the room was an attempt to create something even purer than a museum, a sanctuary devoted to the Muses, and the effect was, as David Watkin says in his monograph on Hope, to make a religion of the arts. Not a museum as we would understand it today but a *museion* as originally conceived, a place where contemplation of *all* the Muses was encouraged. A replica, of sorts, of Christina's room of the Muses in the Palazzo Riario.

Wisdom and Strength and *Vice and Virtue* hung in this large gallery. They were sheltered from the light by huge curtains which would be drawn back on grand occasions. It seems from Hope's own drawings that the picture gallery is where he held his banquets and balls. When Hope first built the gallery, it was the pictures of the sixteenth- and seventeenth-century Italian schools that held pride of place. A drawing of the room made at this time shows *Vice and Virtue* in the briefest of outlines. *Wisdom and Strength,* very likely, was directly opposite.

Later on, after about 1805, Hope added the great canvases of Greek mythology which he was commissioning from contemporary artists like Benjamin West, George Dawe, and Richard Westall. "This room," writes Watkin, "must have been the first as well as one of the most uncompromising attempts to impose the forms of a Greek temple upon an English interior." Such an idea may seem strange now and it was new when Hope did it, as Watkin's comment shows. But this was Hope's life's work; trying to marry the arts of the ancients to the arts of his own time. His writings stress this in some detail. Hope thought that contemporary man could learn from the ancients, as the Humanists of the Renaissance had done. Like them he believed that there were secrets to be learned from this early art, secrets that were aesthetic rather than philosophical, secrets which, when applied to contemporary matters, would result in a new and "correct" art. He deliberately sought to improve taste, believing that he had the right to do so through his own travels and study. Nor was he alone in this.

After the picture gallery came three smaller vase rooms. Hope lived during a time when classical vases were the center of a new wave of scholarship. The interest in classical archaeology stimulated by Winckelmann and others in the middle of the eighteenth century showed people that these vases, so similar in shape to the untutored eye, were in fact valuable social documents: the equivalent of books and paintings combined. The costumes of the Greeks, the manners, the sporting habits, the manufacturing processes, even the migratory patterns, could all be deduced from a study of ancient vases.

Hope took care to ensure that his vases were displayed in the proper way, much as they would have been originally. In the first of the three rooms, therefore, they were shown in columbaria, or niches. The cupboards in the second room, which was narrower and had a barreled ceiling, were decorated with the Dionysiac staff entwined with the ivy leaves of Bacchus. The third vase room was the largest; around the walls it had banquettes that terminated in bronze chimaera, or monsters, and there was a round table supported by similar moldings. These were inspired by what had been uncovered at Pompeii. Hope's aim in these rooms, he said, was to achieve a "sepulchral" tone and, to our modern eye, to judge from his own drawings he seems to have succeeded all too well.

The rooms on the other side of the house, across the dining room, were entirely different in tone. One drawing room was variously known as the Indian Room or the Blue Room and it was decorated in, as Hope put it, the "Saracenic or Moorish" taste. There was a vaulted ceiling, copied from those common in Turkish palaces. It was painted in exotic colors and there were even aromas of the East in this room. There were banquettes with winged lions at the ends, large pictures of Eastern landscapes on the walls. Hope gave much thought to the gradation of coloring in this space: "As the colours of this room, in compliance with the oriental taste, are everywhere very vivid, and very strongly contrasted, due attention has been paid to their gradual lightening, as the eye rose from the skirting to the cornice. The tint of the sofa is deep crimson; that of the walls sky blue; and that of the ceiling pale yellow, intermixed with azure and with sea-green. Ornaments of gold, in various shades, relieve and harmonize these colours. Round the room are incense urns, cassolettes, flower baskets and other vehicles of natural and artificial perfumes." The large pictures in this room included three Indian views specially commissioned from Thomas Daniell.

Adjacent to the Indian Room was the Flaxman Room, also known as the Star Room, the centerpiece of which was a sculpture, *Aurora Visiting Cephalus on Mount Ida,* which Hope had commissioned from John Flaxman, an English Neoclassical sculptor. Flaxman was friendly with George Romney and William Blake and he worked for Josiah Wedgwood. At the end of the eighteenth century, Wedgwood was popularizing Neoclassical designs for his new "Etruscan" ware and with his help, Flaxman traveled to Italy where Hope commissioned the work he was to feature so prominently in his house. The Flaxman Room was heavily draped in curtains which were tinted, said Hope, to suggest "the fiery hue which fringes the clouds just before sunrise . . . [while] in a ceiling of cooler sky blue are sown, amidst a few unextinguished luminaries of the night, the rose which the harbinger of the day . . . spread on every side around her." The prose was as colorful as the room.

Between the Indian Room and the antechamber was the Egyptian, or Black, Room. The prevailing colors here were pale yellow and bluish green, relieved by the occasional introduction of masses of black and gold. The walls were topped with a large frieze of figures to suggest an Egyptian papyrus roll. The furniture was all decorated with Egyptian gods, the pictures picked up on related themes (*The Rest on the Flight to Egypt, The Finding of Moses,* etc.). But the prize exhibit was a genuine Egyptian mummy, which lay in a glass case near the center of the room. Not exactly what we would expect nowadays in a room which was frequently used for entertainment: but the Regency man of taste was expected to take these things in his stride.

The dining room was altogether less elaborate but even so Hope insisted on appropriate decoration wherever possible. The centerpiece of the chimney mantel was an elaborate Greek-style bust of Hope's brother Henry Philip, carved by Flaxman. On either side of the bust were the heads of horses: Henry Philip was known by his second name and in Greek Philip means horse — lover.

The final room on this, the public floor, was in some senses the most extraordinary. It was called a "Lararium" and had a curved, bamboo ceiling from which hung hundreds of tassels and swags of drapery. There was an early-seventeenth-century bronze copy of the famous Marcus Aurelius statue in Rome, wooden reliefs of Bacchus and Ariadne, busts of Dante and Napoleon, and a large ivory crucifix. Despite its fancy name, it is hard to escape the impression that this room contained the valuables which did not fit anywhere else.

Hope's house was finished some time in 1803 and no major changes were made until the autumn of 1819, when Hope added a large gallery to house about a hundred Dutch and Flemish pictures which his brother Henry Philip had inherited.

What is one to make of this collection, this self-conscious array of eccentric rooms? There are two answers. One lies within Hope himself and the second lies within the whole Neoclassical movement that swept Europe in the second half of the eighteenth century. Because Hope had traveled extensively, because he could afford to collect widely, and had been able to patronize the artists of his day, he defined for himself a unique role. For him, art—whether it was pictures, antique vases, furniture, or interior decoration in general—had to meet three requirements: character, beauty, and meaning. It was his insistence on that third requirement, meaning, which distinguished Hope from many others and which so imbued his decorative schemes with symbolism. This requirement gave an inner coherence to everything he collected and in the sense that everything displayed in one room had a single style his house resembled a modern museum. Hope's attitude was as different as can be from Rudolf's day, when all manner of different objects were put together (in a similar search for meaning, it should be noted). But it was also Humanist in its way, in that it valued the arts and crafts of the ancients; it recognized the value of earlier civilizations and carried implicitly the message that the modern mind has a lot to learn from ancient Greece, Rome, and Egypt.

By twentieth-century standards Hope seems rather didactic. Duchess Street would be overdone for modern tastes. But his behavior was not quite as extraordinary then as it appears now. For Thomas Hope was but one figure among many who were swept up in a new movement that was being followed across Europe. It was a movement which changed attitudes to the great colorists, including Veronese. This was the development of Neoclassicism.

The Age of Neoclassicism

Hope was in the thick of this latest artistic development, a development which reopened yet again the debate which had set Dolce against Vasari and the Rubénistes against the Poussinistes. It was a movement which divided attitudes toward Veronese, who, at this time, was more popular in France than in England. Hope's two houses, at Duchess Street in London and at Deepdene, fully embodied the Neoclassical idea. The architecture, the interior decoration, the furniture, the objects collected there were all of a piece according to Hope. Indeed, there were those who felt that he went too far in his search for artistic integrity. Hope saw *Wisdom and Strength* and *Vice and Virtue* as part of his vision even at a time when Sir Joshua Reynolds had relegated Veronese firmly to the bottom rung of the ladder of great artists. That Reynolds was influential did not bother Hope, for he saw himself in the Italophile Neoclassical tradition which had really started half a century earlier.

Just as Paris under the regency of the Duke of Orléans had rejected and reacted against the heavy, dark, religious art that had been in official favor during the last years of Louis XIV, a reaction that led directly to the Rococo stylishness of Watteau and the unserious mythologies of Boucher, so there was eventually *another* reaction: this time, against the lightheart-

edness. It happened around the middle of the eighteenth century and
Diderot, in his *Encyclopédie,* was but one of several voices raised against
the meaninglessness of the Rococo.

When it came, the move away from colorful but mindless frivolity was
led not by a Frenchman but by a German, Johann Joachim Winckelmann.
Winckelmann, who came from Dresden, was in many ways the first modern art historian. After he arrived in Rome he quickly established himself
as a knowledgeable antiquarian, serving as a guide to visitors and as a
mentor to artists. More important, his presence in Italy coincided with
the discoveries taking place at Herculaneum and at Pompeii. Until the
middle of the eighteenth century, excavations in Italy had been largely
fortuitous, made as a by-product of building works or because a particular individual—such as Queen Christina of Sweden—was interested in
enriching his or her private collection. But the collections built up in this
way by the great papal families such as the Farnese, the Barberini, the
Colonna, the Chigi, and the Borghese began to be dispersed in the 1720s
and 1730s. The Odescalchi, who had acquired Christina's sculptures
along with her paintings, sold the statues to Spain in 1724.

Partly as a result of this the Italians began to take a more lively interest
in their heritage and this led to more systematic excavations. Herculaneum came first in 1709; Pompeii followed in 1748. Rome also featured
in these excavations and developed a market in antiquities. English gentlemen on the Grand Tour, Russian princes, and German nobles all competed. Among the famous collections formed or begun at this time were
those of Charles Townley, the Earl of Leicester, the Earl of Egremont, the
Duke of Bedford, and Hope himself. Rome was a Mecca for artists, who
flocked there: Flaxman, Thorvaldsen, Stubbs, Wright of Derby, Vien,
Adam, Mengs, Goethe. The statues which were unearthed in the digs
(and it was statues rather than paintings or anything else which survived
in any numbers) were astonishing in themselves. But Winckelmann
added something extra.

He had become part of the household of Cardinal Albani who himself
had a wonderful collection of antiquities. By his patronage of Winckelmann, Albani allowed the German to write his magnum opus, the *History of Ancient Art,* which appeared in 1764. With this book Winckelmann
changed the course of art history. Besides containing some poetic descriptions of wonderful pieces of sculpture, Winckelmann, in that one
book, reestablished the primacy of ancient Greece in art. He outlined
three phases in Greek art, from the severe to the graceful, and in so
doing he quite simply redefined beauty for many people. By his persuasive theories and his prose, he reestablished the importance of form over
color, the superiority of line. He stressed again and again the importance

of intellect for the artist and gave artists something to strive for, a definition of beauty which he summed up as "noble simplicity and calm grandeur." In this he echoed older arguments of decorum.

Winckelmann saw in the purity of line and the austere simplicity of ancient statues a deep purpose: it represented the purity that was possible in society. For him, art took the place of religion. And of course it gave the artist—as the one who pointed the way—an important role in the creation of that purer society.

The impact of Winckelmann's ideas was felt immediately all over Europe. People as diverse as Mme. de Stael, Diderot, and Herder reacted enthusiastically. Moreover, just as Winckelmann had been fortunate in that the excavations in Italy had coincided with his arrival in Rome, reinforcing the researches he had made on already existing collections of coins and gems, so did certain other elements in eighteenth-century civilization fall into place, ensuring that his ideas seemed absolutely right for the times. The purity and cleanliness which he said all art should strive for contrasted sharply with the corruption and decadence evident in many places in what were to be the last years of the ancien régime. The implication that human nature was perfectible and *reasonable* accorded exactly with the notions of the Enlightenment and the gains being made in science in the last half of the eighteenth century. This all fostered the view that there are underlying truths in nature which, very often, can be used for mankind's benefit. With the growth of science and a reading public, art also became an *educator,* serving nature and science as it had once served the Church. The idea that there were eternal verities, simple and noble, in art therefore fitted well with the political beliefs of many people who would see in the French Revolution a return, or at least an attempt to return, to these ancient ideals.

Winckelmann's impact was therefore aesthetic, social, *and* political. This is why, later on in France, Neoclassicism became a political art form, bound up in the Revolution and, afterwards, with Napoleon's empire.

What Winckelmann had started reached its maturity between 1780 and 1795, years which were almost as turbulent artistically as they were politically. This is when most of the great Neoclassical masterpieces were created, in painting, sculpture, and architecture. As art historian Hugh Honour has said: "Among the painters there are David's great masterpieces, *The Oath of the Horatii, The Death of Socrates, Brutus* and *The Dead Marat.* Flaxman published his illustrations to Homer and A. J. Carstens executed his first monumentally severe drawings. For those attuned to them . . . these works have . . . an intellectual integrity which commands respect, a deeply moving emotional candour . . . which makes the period in which they were created one of the greatest in European history."

But Winckelmann's legacy was not a simple thing. Far from it. Many artists had responded to the call for a purified style by going well beyond the wishes of the originators of the Neoclassical idea. Not only did these artists abandon the frivolity of Rococo, but they removed all grace until they had achieved a bold, indeed a severe, art in which form and strength of outline dominate all else. Even though the works of these artists featured the ancient gods, they could not have been more different from Veronese's mythologies. Given the temper of the times, the morality—or moral—in this art was invariably revealed as grave and stoic, the figures as spare, robust, austere. There are no banquets, no fine clothes or jugs of wine. There is no joy. No one illustrates this better than Jacques Louis David.

Elsewhere, architecture and sculpture might flourish but it was in France and in French painting that the morality of Neoclassical art flexed its muscles most notably—and clashed with politics. David, more than anyone, was responsible for that collision.

Just as the Revolution was supposed to bring with it moral regeneration in life, so Neoclassicism was supposed to do the same thing in art. Neoclassicism, furthermore, showed that a wonderful world could exist without Christianity, a convenient parallel with the anticlericalism of the revolutionaries. The message is so strong that Michael Levey could well write that "so much eighteenth century painting lacked a cutting edge. David responded with the guillotine."

Note, at this point, the parallels with situations encountered before. The pictures of David and the other Neoclassical artists are not actually called allegories but they are clearly that. But note too how we have shifted from the Greek world to the Roman world. To a purist, as the Neoclassicists were supposed to be, this is an important distinction. After all, most classical sculptures were known only as Roman copies of Greek originals, and Winckelmann abjured copies. Greece was superior to Rome.

But to the revolutionaries, and to Napoleon afterward, it did not matter. To them, and him, Rome was no less ancient and no less pure, no less innocent, no less *glorious* than Greece. In fact, the French saw far more parallels with ancient Rome than with Greece. Rome was as purifying and as republican as Greece, but it offered additional military parallels. The activities of the conquering Roman generals had much more in common with the armies of the Revolution. This is why whole villages in France at this time adopted Roman names. It is why Napoleon himself adopted the style as the official one of the empire. Thus Neoclassicism, in its final flowering, became the Empire style.

The most important consequence was that art became standardized. After all, the empire stretched, in one form or another, from Amsterdam to Aranjuez, from Fontainebleau to Florence. A number of books appeared, including Hope's own *Household Furniture* (1807), which argued for consistency (carpets and architecture must match) and symmetry (furniture must look the same even if its functions vary). Standardization did not last—it never does in art. But that is not the point. What all this shows is how fully Hope embraced Neoclassical ideas and attitudes, how in touch he was with that whole world.

Clearly the Neoclassicists had a lot in common with the Humanists who influenced both Veronese and Rudolf. Like them they adored antiquity for the lessons it had to teach and the sheer beauty it had achieved. Like the Humanists, the educated people of the Grand Tour especially regarded themselves as an "in" group, privileged to have studied the ancients and ennobled by their associations with the pure and clean ancient sculptures. But allegory was now different in an important way. By now it had become—paradoxically—much more *direct.* There is no escaping the message. It does not require a thorough knowledge of the ancients to read a David picture. It does not flatter the viewer to be able to decipher it for it was meant to be understood *by all.* Part of its point is its accessibility. This, of course, was associated with its naked political impact.

It followed that more allusive allegories, such as those by Veronese or Correggio, were less to the taste of the times and fell out of favor, at least as allegories, although they were still admired as works of art in France. But the complicated iconography that had so attracted the Emperor Rudolf was not admired by the Emperor Napoleon. When David painted a hovering Victory in the sky of the *Distribution of the Eagles,* Napoleon asked him to remove it.

Neoclassicism was never as political in England as it was in France. Nevertheless, a political element was reflected in the fact that many of its adherents were proselytizing or didactic in their feelings about it. And, as we have seen, this description fits Hope. Hope was doubly crucial, however. He was not only a collector, a student, and a traveler, he was also rich enough and ambitious enough to move in Society, which, throughout his life, he tried to influence in the direction of Neoclassicism. This was a noble enough aim but it also illustrates another all-important element in his character. The fact is that Hope was Dutch and in some ways he never truly understood the British, on more than one occasion he fell afoul of British ways. Sometimes this antagonized people; it always made him look foolish. This foolishness was revealing, not only of the man but also of his times.

Hope's awkwardness first showed itself over the matter of his house and its opening to the public. Having prepared the rooms, Hope decided, early in 1804, that all was ready. Accordingly, on February 1, he sent out to sixty members of the Royal Academy tickets which were to admit "the bearer" and three friends to the Duchess Street mansion between February 18 and March 31. Reasonable as this may have seemed to a Dutchman, in London it was a social gaffe of the first order. He had invited people he wished to be accepted by as a social equal as if they were dealers or members of the press. It was an approach which was bound not to receive much sympathy. At a meeting of the Royal Academy Council on February 7 there was criticism of Hope and dismay was expressed at his lack of respect. The academicians felt they had been invited not as friends or fellow connoisseurs but that Hope had asked them so they would "talk up" his achievement.

What made the episode even worse, however, was the fact that at more or less the same time Hope published a pamphlet, the first of several he was to issue in his lifetime, which was little short of an attack on James Wyatt, the architect who was then president of the Royal Academy. Wyatt was to design Downing College in Cambridge but Hope's pamphlet argued in favor of the Greek revival and against Wyatt's plans. It would have been controversial enough for Hope to have pursued either one of these maneuvers. That he carried through both virtually simultaneously was extraordinary and it is no surprise to learn that the academicians retaliated and he was not invited that year to the Academy's annual dinner. The dinner was a prestigious affair and an opportunity for artists to show their appreciation to and respect for connoisseurs and patrons. This slight hurt Hope very much and, it should be said, divided the Academy. West and Farington were on his side but many others were against him. The decision was not reversed, however. And to make matters worse about two hundred copies of a satirical poem called "Hope's Garland" were delivered to the Academy on the day of the dinner. It was doggerel but it stuck.

A second episode was, if anything, more embarrassing still for it involved his wife, Louisa. Hope had met Louisa in Bath. She was the youngest child of William Beresford, archbishop of Tuam in (southern) Ireland, who later became the first Baron Decies. Louisa was not Hope's first choice as wife and Louisa had not accepted him at first either, being already in love with her cousin, also called William Beresford. But Louisa's friends persuaded her at the time that Hope was a splendid catch and they were married on April 16, 1806. The marriage does not, therefore, appear to have been a love match but no matter. Hope was always devoted to his wife and children and the relationship was a great success.

Louisa, who came from good Tory stock, was as British as can be and well connected. Her background helped Thomas just as his money helped his wife become a great Society hostess. Their parties were attended by many of the most fashionable nobles, royalty, even Lord Byron himself. The Neoclassical artistic setting which Hope created in Duchess Street made his evenings more than mere entertainments. But that only meant that the Dubost incident was even more painful.

Antoine Dubost was a French artist living in London who, in 1807, had sold a painting of *Damocles* to Hope for 800 guineas. After that Hope asked Dubost to paint his wife's picture. This was shown at the Academy in 1808 but severely criticized. According to Dubost, Hope had liked the picture until he listened to the comments of others, some of them Dubost's rivals. One of these was Benjamin West, who had praised *Damocles*. Dubost put it about that West had been angered, however, when Hope hung *Damocles* next to a picture by West, which was then seen to be inferior. In turn this annoyed West and, given that the portrait of Louisa Hope was so inferior to *Damocles,* the story began to circulate that this latter painting, which Dubost had brought with him from Paris, was not his at all, since no one had actually seen him execute it. Hope himself came round to this view, and erased Dubost's signature from the picture.

The sap was rising. But no one could foresee the way Dubost would take his revenge. It came on May 28, 1810, when this advertisement appeared in the *Morning Chronicle:*

> Exhibition at No 65 Pall Mall of an extensive view of Hyde Park on a Sunday, executed upon a scale of 22 feet by Mr Dubost, author of the picture of Damocles, in which are introduced a correct likeness of the distinguished frequenters of this fashionable resort . . . ; also a collection of some other pictures. Admission 2s 6d., catalogue 6d.

In fact, what soon began to attract attention was not the view of Hyde Park but number three among the "other pictures," entitled *Beauty and the Beast.* The *Morning Chronicle* correspondent described it as "a vile caricature on a most amiable lady whose family too liberally encouraged the ungrateful caricaturist, and for which he deserves nothing so much as a kicking."

The fact is that Thomas Hope was one of the plainest men in London and his wife one of the most lovely. It was these two whom Dubost had represented as *Beauty and the Beast.* The Beast was shown next to a chest of jewels and money, some of which he was showing to Beauty, who was distraught at the sacrifice implied in the gift. Beauty, moreover, was a good likeness of Louisa Hope, copied from the one Dubost had shown at the Academy and which everyone thought inferior to *Damocles*. The Beast likeness was not so close to Hope himself but he did nonetheless wear around his neck an eyeglass on a string, just as Thomas did.

Naturally, word soon flashed around London of this unusual and outrageous libel. Hope had the public's sympathy but that did not stop them going to look. Even the Prince of Wales and his brother the Duke of York went. The receipts of the exhibition, modest at first, multiplied tenfold and might have increased still more had not Mrs. Hope's brother, the Reverend J. Beresford, attacked the picture with a knife and cut it to pieces.

The matter did not end there, however, for six months later Dubost brought an action against Beresford for destroying the picture and claimed a thousand pounds in damages. The case was heard before the Lord Chief Justice and the court was crowded with notables. The case brought out two facts of interest which no doubt influenced the verdict, namely, that Dubost was present when Beresford attacked the picture and yet did nothing to stop him and that Dubost had told the doorkeeper that he did indeed mean *Beauty and the Beast* to represent the Hopes. The Lord Chief Justice took the view that the picture was a libel and should have been destroyed. It was, he said, worth no more than the canvas, wood, and paint used in its construction. The jury took the hint and awarded Dubost £5 in damages and 40s in costs. Dubost was finished in London and would never exhibit there again. But he retained his taste for fireworks since he was later killed in a duel in France. As for Hope he held on to *Damocles,* despite the unpleasant end to his relationship with Dubost.

It is easier to sympathize with Hope over this episode than with the Royal Academy ticket business or his attack on Wyatt. At the same time, one can also imagine him becoming rather a figure of fun in society. On the one hand he took himself seriously as a leader of taste; on the other he was looked upon as—well, as Dubost saw him. That he had his clumsy, insensitive side there can be no doubt as the affair of his attempted ennoblement proves.

This first occurred in 1823, well after his marriage when he tried to buy himself a peerage. This was difficult at the best of times, but Hope compounded the error by approaching, or had approached on his behalf, the Prime Minister of the day, the Duke of Wellington. A certain Mr. Bromley had an interview with Wellington and offered £10,000 on Hope's behalf. As Mrs. Arbuthnot explains: "The Duke was civil to the

man, but told him he had made an egregious mistake in coming upon
such an errand to him and sent him out of the house. . . . The man,
whose name is Bromley . . . had been on a similar errand to the Duke
of York who had kicked him out of his house. . . . The Duke had a
letter from Bromley repeating the offer . . . and describing the person
who wants it [the peerage] so accurately that the Duke found out who it
was at once. It was Mr. Hope and what is most incredible, it seems Mr.
Hope must have known of it for he took no steps to deny it when the
Duke of York told him of it. The law officers very much wished the Duke
of Wellington to prosecute Bromley, but he will not do it as he does not
wish to expose Mr. Hope."

This episode also shows how un-English Hope still was a quarter of a
century after he had arrived. No one could really think that Wellington
was the kind of man Lloyd George was to become. Hope was not ennobled.

In each of these incidents Hope showed himself to be, not just socially
gauche but somewhat accident-prone. In no case did he do anything
illegal, but one can imagine society's frowning disapproval. And indeed,
in another matter which should have shown him in better light we see
that the compliments he received were decidedly backhanded. This occurred on the publication of his novel, *Anastasius.*

Anastasius was published in 1819 and was an immediate success. This,
despite the fact that it is very long, "cumulative rather than coherent,"
according to one critic, and extravagantly picturesque. Its success may
have had something to do with the fact that it was published anonymously and there was wild speculation as to its author, Lord Byron himself being the most popular choice. In fact the poet went so far as to say
to Lady Blessington, "that he wept bitterly over many pages of it, and for
two reasons—that first, that *he* had not written it, and secondly that Hope
had. . . . He added, that he would have given his two most approved
poems to have been the author of *Anastasius.*"

Flattering—or is it? Byron's remark was hardly his most gracious and
there is more than a suspicion that Hope was not exactly welcomed as an
author. The plot of the book, a rambling tale set in Constantinople and
Cairo, was not exactly autobiographical but there was undoubtedly much
of Hope's own experience in it. Apart from its didactic nature, the most
important thing about *Anastasius* was that most people, like Byron, found
it hard to believe that Hope was capable of producing so fine a work. But
write it he did and it confirms that, despite his gaucheness, Hope had
talents for more than simply spending his inherited money.

It is doubtful that he was ever fully accepted in London society as a
true Englishman. But, as the years passed, he did make a contribution to

the artistic life of his day. Hope may not have been fantastically popular but his influence *was* acknowledged. After opening Duchess Street to the public, the rest of his life's achievements would fall into three areas. There were his books about art, the most important and influential of which were *Household Furniture* and *Costume of the Ancients.* Second, there was his patronage of the artists of the day, the most important being the sculptors Flaxman, Thorvaldsen, and Canova. And third, there was his acquisition of Deepdene, his country house near Dorking in Surrey, and his creation there of a "picturesque" setting that fitted in with his theories and influenced many of his contemporaries. *Wisdom and Strength* and the other Veroneses remained in Duchess Street throughout Thomas's life but later on, after the family had been through several changes in fortune, they were moved to Deepdene, where they remained for many years.

Household Furniture (1807), perhaps Hope's best-known book, is best understood through its illustrations, which show how Hope adapted furniture designs from the decorations on such things as Greek vases. He actually had them made up, keeping very close to the ancient patterns, for the Duchess Street house.

The reaction to *Household Furniture* was mixed. *The Satirist* made fun of him, and Sydney Smith in the *Edinburgh Review* wrote a long, hostile article in which he attacked the very existence of the book, not just the way Hope treated the subject. Smith considered that Hope was a jumped-up nouveau riche, writing pretentiously about "lamps, sideboards and cradles" as though they were works of art on a par with more traditional things.

Hope's two books on dress, *Costume of the Ancients* (1809) and *Designs of Modern Costume* (1812), also had their pretentious aspects although neither seems to have been reviewed quite so virulently as *Household Furniture.* In the 1812 book Hope did with women's dress what he had done with furniture. From a study of clothes on classical vases he had adapted contemporary dress to the ancient designs. As a result he had some influence on Regency taste in this area but not as much as he had hoped and hardly any at all on men's dress. Perhaps people could not accept that a foreign banker could be an expert on architecture, furniture, gardening, *and* clothes.

He was much more successful, and perhaps in the long run more important, as a patron. John Flaxman was already in Italy with Wedgwood's help when he met Hope and it is worth pointing out that, at the time, Hope was only twenty-two. It is indicative of his sensibility that he should have singled out Flaxman from the large number of artists then in Rome. Hope gave Flaxman a commission to restore the Torso Belvedere to a group as *The Marriage of Hercules and Hebe* at a fee of 700 guineas. Hope also commissioned a copy of the *Apollo Belvedere* in black-veined marble and a group of *Aurora and Cephalus,* which was to become the focal point of the Flaxman Room in Duchess Street. The next commission was different again: for 109 illustrations of the works of Dante at one guinea each. In some ways this was the most fruitful collaboration between the two men for it was these illustrations that were to bring Flaxman his greatest fame (he did Homer, Aeschylus, and Hesiod as well as Dante).

Bertel Thorvaldsen (ca. 1770–1844) is generally regarded nowadays as the only Danish artist ever to achieve an international reputation. Thorvaldsen won a scholarship to Italy in 1796 and lived in Rome until his triumphant return to Denmark in 1819. His rise to fame was not however straightforward or easy. When Hope came across him in Rome in 1803 the sculptor was despairing and about to return, unsuccessful, to Denmark. To Thorvaldsen's astonishment, when Hope entered his studio he was immediately delighted by a rather severe *Jason,* which was unfinished. He was so taken with it that he even offered more money for it than the young sculptor was asking.

The sculpture was important in Thorvaldsen's career for it was his first fully Neoclassical work, showing the influence of Canova and one would have expected him to hasten to complete it, the more so as Hope's commission was backed up by a legal contract. In fact, it took the artist another three years to finish it and another *eleven* before Thorvaldsen wrote to Hope saying that the sculpture was a work of his youth and asking to be allowed to try another subject. Hope was unmoved and placed the affair in the hands of a bank, which started to pressure Thorvaldsen. He then got irritated with Hope and the completed sculpture did not in fact reach Hope's possession until the spring of 1828, a quarter of a century after it had been commissioned. With it came a number of peace offerings: two bas-reliefs and a bust of Hope's son, Henry. Hope emerges from the affair much better than Thorvaldsen. He wrote an elegant letter of thanks when he finally received the *Jason* and, in all, was to commission eleven works from the Dane. He appreciated the sculptor's talent and would not let the dispute between them blind him to that.

Thorvaldsen was an example of the new, Blake-inspired "liberated" artist of the nineteenth century. His elevated opinion of his art and of his own position in the order of things led him to think that his works could not be produced to order.

Quite different, in temperament anyway, was Antonio Canova (1757–1822). Canova was the most famous Neoclassical sculptor of all. He was brought up in Venice, spent time in Rome in 1779/80, and moved there

permanently in 1781. In 1797 the French invasion caused him to flee but
later he accepted Napoleon's invitation to go to Paris. There he became
an admirer of the Emperor and made several busts of him and also one of
Nelson (unfinished). He disapproved of the looting of art treasures practiced by Napoleon's troops, however. Around 1800 Canova offered
Hope a cast of his *Perseus,* which Pope Pius VII refused to allow out of
Rome. Perhaps worried about the quality of the cast, Hope refused. But
a few years later he had more fruitful contact and acquired a *Venus.* Hope
admired it very much and placed it very prominently in Duchess Street.
Wanting to be greeted by it at each of his houses, he commissioned a
copy of it for Deepdene.

Hope's patronage of painters was not as decisive, in art historical
terms, as his friendships with sculptors. Besides the awful Dubost the
other artists he had links with were Benjamin West, Richard Westall,
George Dawe, and Benjamin Haydon. Not names that would rank with
Veronese perhaps but, for all his faults, Hope was, with the exception of
Turner, a patron of some of the finest artists of his day.

Another way in which Hope was in the thick of fashion was the part
he, and *Wisdom and Strength,* played in the establishment of the British
Institution. This was how the picture was first seen by the general public
since it had been on show in Rome during Christina's day.

Agitation for a national collection of treasures in England had been
repeatedly forestalled. Both the Royal Academy and the British Government had refused bequests which might have been used as the basis for a
National Gallery. There *were* paintings and sculptures to be seen in London, but they were in private collections that were open to the public at
various times. For instance, John Feltham, in an 1804 guide to the capital,
listed twenty-one such collections (and which shows that Hope's plan to
open his house to the public was not so strange as it may now appear).
But it was not at all satisfactory.

At the same time there was also a disquiet felt in many quarters about
the Royal Academy. This institution had a dual aim: to aid modern artists
and to supervise a national collection. But the Academy was going
through a difficult period when there was widespread dissension from
within about the direction it should take: the position of president was
bitterly fought over and at one point in 1803 five council members were
suspended. It was perhaps only natural for outsiders to begin to think of
an alternative to the Royal Academy.

One or two early plans, involving Henry Addington, William Beck-
ford, and even the Prince of Wales, came to nothing. The divisions,
however, did spawn both the Society of Engravers and the Society of
Painters in Watercolors, and these proved that alternatives to the Acad-

emy could succeed. And so, when a plan for the British Institution was published in May 1805, it received widespread attention and support.

The idea of the Institution, which had royal patronage almost from the start, was twofold. In the first place it aimed to provide a venue where contemporary British art could be shown and sold. Second, there were to be loan exhibitions of the old masters which had been pouring into British private collections since the French Revolution. The Institution was therefore to be a hybrid: both a national gallery and a commercial gallery. It was felt that the public, which had acquired a taste for old masters since the Orléans sale, would flock to see the great Italian and Dutch schools. At the same time it would be drawn to the British paintings and seek to purchase them.

The initial management of the Institution was invested in a committee of subscribers, chaired by George Legge, third Earl of Dartmouth and including Richard Payne Knight, the connoisseur and writer on art, and Thomas Hope. In contrast to the exclusiveness of the Academy, involvement in the Institution was freely available. Anyone who paid more than fifty guineas per year was called a governor. Subscriptions were sufficient for the Institution to acquire three rooms at 52 Pall Mall, and its first exhibition opened in February 1806. It was a great success with more than ten thousand admission tickets being sold. What seems to have caught the public's imagination was indeed the mix of the old and the new. Sixteen grandees loaned twenty-three old masters and, at the same time, £11,000 was taken in the sales of new works, on which the Institution charged artists a 20 percent commission. With the monopoly of the Academy broken, the British Institution proved very popular for many years, always maintaining its mix of the old and the new. Hope lent *Wisdom and Strength* and *Vice and Virtue* twice to the institution. First in 1816 by Thomas and again in 1835 by his son Henry.

The aim of the old master exhibitions was not only to enable the public to see some wonderful pictures but also to allow artists to copy them, or at least parts of them—there were special rules forbidding the copying of an old master in its entirety. Hope was a great supporter of the Institution for, in its exhibitions, its declared aim was to bring "civil refinement" to the public "calculated to raise the standard of morality and patriotism; to attract the homage and respect of foreign nations, and to produce those intellectual and virtuous feelings, which are perpetually alive to the welfare and glory of the country."

The success of the Institution, its mixing of old masters with contemporary works, its lay membership, as opposed to the professional artists of the Academy, all had a marked effect on taste and helped shape the climate that enabled the National Gallery in London to be formed in

1824. When the British Institution was closed in 1867, it had become a victim of its own success. It no longer stood out since what it had pioneered had become commonplace. Hope's part in all this was typical of his belief that art was ennobling and that it was his duty as a civilized and wealthy man to help widen the appeal of great painting. It was charitable in the best sense.

Though he was never ennobled, toward the end of his life Hope did make peace with those around him. His wife, Louisa, was chiefly responsible for this: where he was plain and gauche, she was beautiful and graceful; where he was a foreigner and therefore long an outsider, she was brilliantly connected and at ease with everyone. The Hopes became close friends of the Princess of Wales and it is probable that Hope lent her money. Later they even became friendly with the Duke of Wellington and the Duke and Duchess of Clarence, who became, in time, King William IV and Queen Adelaide. Louisa was eventually appointed woman of the bedchamber.

With Louisa's help and contacts, the couple became known for their magnificence and splendor. In the memoirs of the period there is no shortage of references to the Duchess Street balls and dinners. Elzabeth Spencer Stanhope, for example, describes one: "At half past eleven [in the evening] we set out for Mr. Hope's rout, but after waiting in the street *till near one,* we found to get in was impossible!" According to the novelist Maria Edgeworth it was so crowded on one occasion that many guests did not reach the door. Relating yet another occasion, Miss Edgeworth wrote: "We have been to a grand night at Mrs. Hope's. The rooms really deserve the French epithet 'superbes.' All of beauty, rank and fashion that London can assemble, I may say in the newspaper style, were there. The Prince Regent stood one third of the night holding converse with Lady Elizabeth Monk, she leaning gracefully on a bronze ornament in the centre of the room in the midst of the sacred but very small circle etiquette could keep around them. About nine hundred people were at this assembly, the crowd of carriages was so great that after sitting waiting in ours for an hour the coachman told us there was no chance of our reaching the door unless we got out and walked. . . . I asked Mr. Hope who someone was—I really don't know half the people here, nor do they know me and Mrs. Hope even by sight. Just now I was behind a lady who was making her 'speech' as she thought to Mrs. Hope, but she was addressing a stranger."

Even Byron was impressed. In 1821 he wrote in his diary, referring to a night of revelry at Mrs. Hope's: "I was in love and just nicked a minute when neither mothers nor husbands, nor rivals nor gossips, were near my then idol, who was beautiful as the statues of the gallery where we stood at the time."

Deepdene also became a social center at the time of the Derby, the great classic horse race at nearby Epsom. The famous or titled people who stayed with the Hopes included Lord Tankerville, Lady Westmeath, Prince Schwarzenberg, and Prince Karl of Württemberg. Louisa was always sparkling and in this she was much aided by Thomas's nature: he could afford to spoil her and did. At Christmas 1823 she was dressed, according to Lady Grenville, "in solid gold, with rare birds flying in different directions out of her head."

The elevation of Louisa, to woman of the bedchamber, came in 1830. By then, too, Thomas's eldest son Henry had also been honored and appointed groom of the bedchamber to George IV in the last months of his reign. This recognition did not command universal support. Lady Holland, for example, noted that "persons are surprised at Mrs. Hope being a *Woman* of the Bedchamber. The services are not dignified; & at court she cannot be admitted into the Circle, or be spoken to as her own station entitles her to otherwise. She gains the fan and gloves."

If Hope was bothered by this he did not show it. He was, at that time, much immersed in the preparation of a curious work, his last, entitled *Essay on the Origin and Prospects of Man.* This left him in a weak condition and, in January 1831, when he went out in an open carriage in a fog, he caught a cold. An inflammation of the chest developed and he became seriously ill. Even to the last he was devoted to Louisa, telling Maria Edgeworth, when she went to see him, "that he was ill only of a plethora of happiness, that he had everything this world could give," adding, "I am happy, blessed with such a wife and such a son!"

He died on February 2, 1831. Ten days later the "strange, half-foreign and ever enigmatic connoisseur" was buried in a mausoleum at Deepdene. The funeral was simple and unpublicized and one cannot help feeling that Thomas Hope was not really missed.

18.
Downhill at Deepdene

Thomas Hope's will provided for his wife, children, and servants. But he also made specific arrangements for the preservation of his two houses and their contents. Louisa was to have use of Deepdene for life and it was then to pass to his eldest son, Henry Thomas. He gave all his "pictures, prints, drawings, statues, fictile vases, engraved stones, marbles and other curiosities of that nature, and all my books, manuscripts, maps and charts . . . and my house in Duchess Street with the appurtenances and furniture—to my executors in trust for my son Henry." In the event of the death without heirs of his wife and children, Duchess Street and its contents were to be made over to the British Museum.

Henry Thomas was a good enough son. Educated at Eton and Trinity College, Cambridge, he attended the university, however, for only a year, becoming a bachelor under the long-obsolete system by which degrees were conferred without examination on undergraduates claiming to have royal blood in their veins. Henry's claims were based simply on the fact that the female line of his family descended from the Plantagenets.

He held a minor appointment at the courts of George IV and William IV and became a Member of Parliament, representing the rotten borough of East Looe from 1829 to its disenfranchisement in 1832 (the borough, and the House of Commons seat that went with it, had been bought by the family). After the Reform Bill of 1832, Henry Thomas made no attempt to reenter Parliament although he retained an interest in politics and in the early 1840s helped to form the Young England Party, a Conservative group led by Benjamin Disraeli. Henry was close to Disraeli and during this period Deepdene became the country headquarters for the party and the retreat where Disraeli was able to devote himself to literary work. In fact, in the general preface to his novels, Disraeli says that it was Henry Thomas Hope who first urged him to put his political ideas into literary form. And his very first political novel, *Coningsby,* is dedicated to Henry with the explanation, in an accompanying note, that it was "conceived and partly executed amid the glades and galleries of Deepdene."

This was a reference to the fact that Henry set about transforming the country house after his father died. Thomas had acquired Deepdene in 1807. Until 1791 the house had been the home of the Dukes of Norfolk. Hope's aim in buying Deepdene was to create a classical, Italianate landscape of the sort found in, say, a Claude picture. This approach, the creation of "picturesque" landscapes, was part of the Neoclassical movement. As in Claude's pictures, picturesque gardens and houses sought a kind of classical peacefulness and austerity. Such landscapes were thus characterized above all by irregularity: the roof of the house would be glimpsed unexpectedly above the trees, vistas would open up in surprising ways: all in strong contrast to the more artificial gardens, or parklands and carefully regimented trees that were favored in England throughout most of the eighteenth century.

One of the early descriptions of Deepdene, which had been in existence since the middle of the seventeenth century, refers to a "long hope," meaning a long valley. Thomas must have known of this coincidence, and it was bound to have pleased him. As early as 1655 there was an amphitheater garden, caves, and an "elaboratory." Later, vineyards were added and a subterranean passageway was dug through a hill so that the sea could be glimpsed (at least, in theory). The house was surrounded by one hundred acres.

Hope seems to have been content with Deepdene for several years and made no additions until 1818, when he added two side wings, one capped by a tall tower. The main building phase came in 1823 when he added the features that probably determined the character of the house more than anything else. This was an orangery, conservatory, sculpture gallery, and indoor amphitheater—all tacked on together at an angle of forty-five degrees to the main building. Just as at Duchess Street, Hope sought at Deepdene to marry the art of the ancients with modern taste. In Surrey he wanted the pure "picturesque" environment of an Italianate landscape with antique sculpture.

Deepdene was not the classic grand British country house, at least not in appearance. There was no rolling parkland as many of his contemporaries had but instead the house became a kind of palazzo, surrounded by Italianate grounds. The house, more surprising in its features than most grand houses, was sculpted into the land around it rather than being the focal point either at the top or the bottom of a vista. Inside, there were all sorts of alcoves, niches, and other surprises.

It also meant that some of the Duchess Street atmosphere was reproduced, with sculptures by Flaxman and Thorvaldsen, paintings by West, Westall, and Reynolds. There was an Egyptian room and a sculpture gallery. The amphitheater, for instance, had busts and other figures displayed around the seats. Doors, walls, and ceilings were decorated with designs taken from vase paintings, the whole very busy and consciously thought out.

During Thomas's time the house was visited by many distinguished politicians and literary people. It was the fashion then for the lady of the house to keep a book in which friends wrote elegant extracts, original or otherwise, an elaborate version of today's visitors' book. Among the entries were contributions from Sir Henry Englefield, a well-known anti-quary, the historian Sismondi, the poets Sir Walter Scott, Thomas Moore, and George Crabbe. There were contributions from Samuel Rogers, the chemist Sir Humphry Davy, and the Comte de Lieven. Other visitors included the Russian ambassador in London, the eminent numismatist Richard Payne Knight, also a key picturesque theorist, the first Lord Ellesmere, the German poet Schlegel, and, last but not least, the Duchess of Clarence, later Queen Adelaide.

Thomas's achievements with Deepdene were considerable. But Henry, for his part, made the house even more Italianate than his father had. He changed the whole atmosphere from a calm Poussinesque world to a thoroughgoing Renaissance palazzo. He did this by the addition of loggias, balustrades, belvederes, and more chimney pieces. Deepdene, in fact, became one of the earliest examples of the fashion for early Victo-rian Italian architecture on a massive scale (the Travelers' Club and the Reform Club next to it in Pall Mall in London perhaps being the most familiar). In the hall the balustrades are straight out of Veronese's *Feast in the House of Levi.*

Several descriptions of the Hope residences are contained in Disraeli's novels. Henry, who was still unmarried, and Disraeli belonged to the Young England Party, which was run by aristocrats who believed in gov-ernment that was likewise "aristocratic and agrarian, half-feudal and half-*ancien régime.*" It was therefore only natural that Disraeli's books should be set in a Hope-like environment. In his 1837 novel, *Henrietta Temple,* Ducie Bower, the main country house of the novel, is described in this way:

A facade of four ionic columns fronted an octagonal hall, adorned with statues. . . . The lofty walls were covered with an Indian pa-per of vivid fancy. . . . A large lamp of Dresden china was sus-pended from the painted and gilded ceiling. . . . [In the dining room] . . . the ceiling was painted in grey tinted frescoes of a clas-sical and festive character, and the side table, which stood in a recess supported by four magnificent columns, was adorned with choice Etruscan vases. . . . The air of repose and stillness which distin-guished this apartment was heightened by the vast conservatory into which it led, blazing with light and beauty, groups of exotic trees, plants of radiant tint, the sound of a fountain, and gorgeous forms of tropical birds.

Lady Bellair's town mansion is likewise decorated:

Bellair House was the prettiest mansion in Mayfair. It was a long building, in the Italian style. . . . All the reception rooms were on the ground floor and were all connected. [In the centre was] . . . an octagon library, lined with well-laden dwarf cases of brilliant volumes, crowned with no lack of marble busts, bronzes and Etruscan vases. On each side opened a magnificent saloon, furnished in that classic style which the late accomplished and ingenious Mr. Hope first rendered popular in this country.

In the 1830s and 1840s, therefore, Deepdene was as much at the center of things with Henry in residence as it had been while Thomas was alive.

The English country house, as personified by Deepdene, has played a unique role in the history of art, no less than in other aspects of social history. Deepdene was typical of its time and of the way in which these houses developed through the centuries.

The great period of the English country house (and the Scottish manse) stretches forward from late medieval times until the late nineteenth century, when cheap American corn made the rich landowners of England much, much poorer. Death duties were introduced in England in 1894 and began to eat away at the formidable stability which, for four or five hundred years, had produced the "powerhouses" of Britain, mingling great architecture, great art, politics, and a glamorous way of life that is enviable even today.

The changes that overtook the great houses reflected not just architectural tastes but the very development of European civilization. Medieval houses, for example, were simply divided into a hall, kitchen, and chapel. Bedrooms, chimneys, closets, and towers were introduced one by one, each a new concept or, as with chimneys, a new piece of technology that helped to establish new styles of living. The development of chimneys, for example, enabled the great houses to be split into smaller rooms, thus increasing privacy, which had hitherto scarcely existed.

The order of houses reflected the order of society. On the one hand there was the segregation of the classes—servants were increasingly kept out of sight; and on the other hand there was the segregation of the sexes —dressing rooms became common as, in time, did smoking rooms and billiard rooms. Technology, such as the remote bell, enabled the servants to be segregated even further and servants' wings were introduced.

The organization of the country house was thus, at any one time, a microcosm of the wider world around it and Deepdene was no exception. Indeed, Deepdene stood at the center of two important developments in the history of the country house. One was the interaction between learning and the life of the country house and the other, strange as it may seem, was the development of the ball.

In the early country houses the walls were decorated with tapestries—for warmth as much as for decoration. The success of the chimney, however, meant that as houses grew warmer tapestries were needed less and less and the owners of these great buildings developed a taste for different sorts of decoration. This led, in the sixteenth century, to the rise in popularity of portrait painting. Portraits occupied the galleries. An Italian innovation, galleries had been introduced to provide for indoor exercise.

Throughout the seventeenth and eighteenth centuries, especially the latter, the taste for learning and for collecting grew apace: libraries were introduced into the great houses and to the portraits were added numerous other paintings and antiquities collected on the grand tour. The high regard in which learning was held at this time was reflected in the fact that libraries were not simply places of study, but they were also *living rooms* much as they are today.

Deepdene, no less than Duchess Street, was part of all this—and in more ways than one, for together with the fashion for learning and collecting went an interest in foreign (often Italian) ideas and architecture. In imitation of Italian villas, English houses became for a while *less* regular, less symmetrical. They became, in some ways, more informal, making use of conservatories, French windows, and informal gardens. This was the picturesque movement of which Deepdene was one of the best examples in early nineteenth century Britain.

The development of the ball reflected a different set of beliefs. Throughout the eighteenth century entertainments got larger. Society was itself larger and more mobile: Bath, Tunbridge Wells and Scarborough were all as social as London. This was the period which saw the growth of assemblies (and assembly rooms), but hostesses emulated these in private. Reception rooms got larger, but for a really large ball this was often not enough: the whole of the second floor of the house would be opened up for entertainment. Reaching the top of the stairs, guests would circulate through a series of rooms—dancing in one, cards in another, conversation or gossip in a third. We have already made a tour of Thomas Hope's second floor in Duchess Street, laid out in just such a circle. It was hardly different at the Deepdene, with Henry Thomas and his wife equally as lavish in their hospitality as Thomas was in his.

The development of the ball was also responsible, in part, for another innovation, one which helped to produce the golden age of the country house. This was the house party. The ball may have provided the focal point for a house party (which often lasted for much longer than the weekend of modern times), but there were at least two other contributing factors. One was the much improved state of English roads, which made many more places accessible. The other was the state of the countryside: improvements in agriculture in the second half of the eighteenth century meant that planting, draining, and enclosing now became the rule rather than the exception. This not only made the countryside more fun; it meant that landowners became richer—and could entertain more.

Just as the ball helped to spawn the house party, so the house party helped to spawn the luncheon! With the men out shooting and often not returning until dark, dinner, which in the early nineteenth century was often eaten at 4:30 or 5:00 P.M., was put back to 6:30 or 7:00. Luncheon —informal and mainly for women—was served to fill the gap.

In most people's minds, however, the country-house party of nineteenth-century Britain has become closely associated with one thing above all else—what might be called the "power weekend." In the power weekend, successful individuals—wealthy aristocrats, leading politicians, industrial or financial wizards, actors and writers—all gather for a period that is part relaxation, part mutual admiration, part social climbing, and part work. One reason why politics loomed so large in these gatherings was because, in the nineteenth century, land was one of the main objects of political attention. Both Thomas and Henry Thomas lavishly entertained all types of people, but it was Henry Thomas who typified the trend most. In its move to Deepdene, *Wisdom and Strength* was once again following the mainstream social and intellectual trends of its day.

Yet one thing has been overlooked so far Deepdene, although it was to have been left to Henry eventually, had originally been intended for Thomas's widow, Louisa, in her lifetime. Where was she all this time?

After Thomas died, Louisa mourned for two years. However, in November 1832, she married her cousin and childhood sweetheart, William Carr, now Viscount Beresford and the man who had caused her to hesitate when Thomas had first proposed all those years ago. Viscount Beresford was a soldier of fortune, at least to begin with, a man who saw action all over the world. He fought in Egypt, South Africa, Toulon, and Corsica. He captured Buenos Aires *and* Madeira; he was taken prisoner in South America but escaped; he lived in Portugal where he ran the army and visited Rio several times. In the 1820s he had been asked to become commander in chief in India but declined. Eventually he came home and involved himself in domestic politics. He was offered a place in the cabinet under Wellington but turned it down. He fell out with Wellington over Irish politics. It was a hectic life but after he married Louisa the couple lived relatively quietly at the Beresford family seat at Bedgebury Park in Derbyshire. They still mixed with the leading Conservatives of the time, and Louisa still saw Queen Adelaide. But it was not on the same scale as when Thomas was alive.

On his deathbed, Thomas had said he was happy, blessed with "such a wife and such a son." When his brother Henry Philip died in 1839, that happy family feeling was destroyed, as a bitter family quarrel developed. Henry Philip had been a more straightforward person than Thomas while he was alive but his death created severe complications. Both brothers had been avid collectors but their tastes were rather different. For instance, whereas Thomas preferred Italian paintings, Henry Philip liked Dutch and Flemish. In fact it was he who actually owned the northern school pictures which hung in Duchess Street.

Although many of these paintings were first-rate, Henry Philip was chiefly known across Europe for his fine collections of jewels. Chief among them was the Blue diamond, which had—and still has—one of the most notorious histories of any gemstone. It was believed to have originally been part of a larger stone, weighing 112.5 carats in the rough; it was bought in India by the traveler Tavernier, who sold it to Louis XIV in 1668. It was recut for the King, who wore it as a pendant on a light blue ribbon. After his death, however, its history is uncertain. At the time of the Revolution the regalia included a triangular diamond of the same color as the Blue diamond, which weighed 67.5 carats, which is about right for the Tavernier recut. This stone was stolen but, in 1830, a similar blue diamond, weighing 44.5 carats, came to light in the hands of a certain Daniel Elias and was believed by experts to be the Tavernier. It was bought by Henry Philip for a price not recorded; but an 1839 catalog of his stones describes it as worth at least £30,000 ($3.3 million now). The stone was of a deep sapphire blue and when it belonged to Henry Philip it was mounted as a medallion with a border of small rose diamonds surrounded by twenty brilliants of equal size.

Henry Philip had many other jewels, including 110 other diamonds, 148 pearls, 19 Oriental rubies, 33 sapphires, and 12 emeralds. But it was the Blue diamond, now known more notoriously as the Hope diamond, which has attracted attention because of the alleged bad luck that has always been associated with it. To begin with, Tavernier was torn to pieces by dogs; Marie Antoinette was guillotined; a French minister who got possession of it after that died before long in prison. Other unlucky owners included a Persian merchant drowned at sea, a Sultan who lost his throne, and a Russian prince who was assassinated. Today the Hope diamond is in the Smithsonian Institution in Washington, D.C.

Although the Hopes do not appear to have shared in the bad luck linked to the diamond, the stone did feature in the unseemly series of events which followed Henry Philip's death. The problem appears to have developed because he did not divide up his collections in his will. Rather, to avoid death duties, he disposed of them by deeds executed in his lifetime. However, his memory in his later years was far from good and these deeds became a source of bitter disagreement. No fewer than three deeds were found after his death. These purported to give the jewels to different nephews and in one of them he did not even name the beneficiary. The lawsuits dragged on for years. Eventually, in 1849, it was settled. Alexander took most of the smaller stones and Henry Thomas took eight of the principal ones, including the Blue diamond. Thus the notorious gem joined the same collection as *Wisdom and Strength.*

The family quarrel must have spilled over into the public domain, and perhaps provided as much amusement for spectators as the Dubost libel of earlier years. But Henry Thomas's life was unaffected: his social whirl was as grand as his father's, perhaps more so. Throughout the memoirs of the 1830s and 1840s, the Hope hospitality is continually referred to, on the whole, approvingly. Disraeli himself is a source. In one of his letters to his sister, he refers to a ball at Duchess Street in 1834 when they "supped off gold and danced in the sculpture gallery." In 1837 there was a dinner there that was "sumptuous but dull." In 1840, at another dinner, Disraeli sat next to Samuel Rogers who consumed "an immense dinner" and with whom he had formed a close acquaintance before the end of the evening on account of "each despairing of his other neighbour"; that occasion was dull, too. In the same year Disraeli stayed at Deepdene with his wife and described the place as "a perfect Italian palace full of balconies adorned with busts." The Disraelis were back at Christmas, which was very festive with Henry Thomas giving everyone rather lavish presents. Mrs. Disraeli, for example, received "two beautiful specimens of Dresden china."

The gift underlines the fact that Henry Thomas shared his father's love of fine art objects and increased the collections at Deepdene. In fact he seemed to prefer that house to Duchess Street, for he sold the latter in 1849 and built another in Piccadilly. It was lavish, with much decorative detailing, all carried out by French craftsmen at a cost of £18,000. This was when *Wisdom and Strength* moved from Duchess Street to Deepdene, where it was to spend the rest of the century.

Other changes were in the offing, like marriage. Henry Thomas did not marry until after his mother died. He may have been holding off to spare his mother's feelings because his bride was Adele Bichat, a French woman with whom he had long been acquainted, who was not the kind of high society figure whom his parents would have wanted their son to marry. Adele's background did not matter to Thomas, though: by then he had the kind of social acceptability that his father never quite achieved. Like Thomas he became a vice president of the Society of Arts, but in addition he was a founder, in 1836, of the Art Union of London and also of the Royal Botanical Society. He also helped organize the Great Exhibition of 1851 and he became chairman of the Eastern Steam Navigation Company, founded to launch Brunel's great ship *Leviathan.*

Henry Thomas also became a father. Thomas would have been mortified that his granddaughter Henrietta was born illegitimate. But she grew up to be a great beauty, which evidently outweighed her bastard status: in 1861, a year before Henry Thomas died, she made a sparkling marriage to Lord Lincoln, eldest son and heir to the fifth Duke of Newcastle. For Thomas that would surely have obliterated any shame brought on the family by Henry Thomas's wrongdoing. With his granddaughter a duchess, it followed that his great-grandson became the seventh Duke of Newcastle. The Hopes were finally admitted to the nobility.

The Newcastles, though grand, were a divided family of strong-willed individualists. Prior to the union between Lincoln and Henrietta, the family had been through the second most sensational divorce case (after Henry VIII's) which England had seen. It was notorious because Lincoln's mother, the duchess, had appeared as the *defendant,* something unprecedented at that level of society. That court case was only one of the great indignities faced by Lincoln's father. Earlier, he had fallen out with *his* father to such an extent that when he stood for Parliament his father had put up a candidate—who was successful—against him.

Lincoln reacted to all this unpleasantness by cultivating his own eccentricity, gambling. In fact, it was Lincoln's gambling which led indirectly to his meeting Henrietta. In 1860, when Lincoln was twenty-seven, he had been forced to flee England on account of his racing debts which amounted to a staggering £230,000, (at least $100 million now). His father had refused to see him for more than a year so Lincoln went to France, to Nice. It was there that he met and fell in love with Henrietta. Newcastle was outraged when he was told that Lincoln planned to marry. The Hopes, however, were very much in favor of the marriage and it is not hard to see why. The Newcastles, however much they might noisily object, were on the way down. Successive dukes had played their part in politics, or tried to, but their estate at Clumber in Nottinghamshire, for all that it had been designed by the great Barry, was losing money heavily, the Newcastle fortune slipping away even without Lincoln's help at the racetrack. It was a perfect marriage of convenience.

The convenience was not lost on Society. Lady Londonderry, for example, observed to her son Lord Adolphus that the marriage was much "talked of in England, & not pleasantly, as it is known that illegitimacy & gambling debts made the *fond* for the barter of Wealth and Rank, & it is thought the young Lady has been sold for a ducal coronet." Though unpleasantly phrased, this was no more than the truth, for the understanding between the parties was that Henry Hope would pay all Lincoln's debts and settle £10,000–£12,000 ($440,000–$525,000) a year on his daughter, with an additional £50,000 ($2,200,000) a year for the couple after his death. As Lord Stanley observed in his diary: "The match is not brilliant as to rank, certainly, but it saves the dukedom from ruin, otherwise inevitable."

Henrietta and Lincoln were married on February 11, 1861, in Paris. Gradually, Newcastle came to accept the marriage. He met Henrietta about a month after the wedding though he still refused to see his son for the rest of that year. Then, however, the couple were invited to Clumber during the visit of the Prince of Wales. Thus through Henrietta the Hopes were finally admitted to the highest society in England. Thomas would have been very proud.

Or he would have been proud had Lord Lincoln reformed his ways. But he did not. The next year, 1862, he again ran up huge racing debts and this time it was Henry Hope who got very angry, since he had to meet those debts. One important effect of this was that, at his death later that same year, Henry Hope left his money and Deepdene not to the couple but to Henrietta, knowing that if he placed too much in the hands of Lincoln it would soon all be gone.

Henrietta gave birth to a son and heir, Henry Pelham Archibald Douglas, in 1864, less than a month before the fifth Duke died. Lord Lincoln succeeded as sixth Duke and so Henrietta, as Duchess of Newcastle, became the first Hope to bear the sort of title Thomas always coveted. Clumber, the ducal home, was not the largest of country homes, but it was still magnificent and contained many treasures. Paintings by Rembrandt and Rubens adorned the dining room, and the drawing room was decorated with objects obtained from the Doges' Palace in Venice. Perhaps the finest room of all was the library, which contained many fine books, including volumes of rare engravings by Van Dyck, Hogarth, and Holbein.

Because her eldest child would inherit all this, and because Lincoln, the sixth Duke, died young in 1879 — at the age of forty-five—Henrietta left Deepdene and everything in it, including *Wisdom and Strength,* to her second son, Henry Francis Pelham Clinton Hope. He was not to acquire the house, however, for some years, since the duchess had remarried. In 1892, when the duchess's second husband died, she decided to rent out Deepdene. And here some earlier names return to the story. For it was let to Colonel Lord William Beresford, namesake and descendant of the Lord William Beresford whom Henrietta's grandmother had married after Thomas died. *This* William Beresford was no less colorful than the earlier one.

Colonel Lord William Leslie de la Poer Beresford, recipient of the Victoria Cross and a Knight Commander of the Indian Empire (1846–1900), was famous in his time as a sportsman, a soldier, and a wit. Educated at Eton, he at first joined the 9th Lancers, stationed in Dublin, but he spent much of his life in India, where he joined the viceroy's staff. He won the Victoria Cross, Britain's highest award for bravery, in South Africa when he rescued an injured soldier in the face of an attack put at three thousand Zulus from only two hundred yards away. "Fighting Bill," as he became known after this incident, was also a keen racing man. He kept many horses wherever he was stationed, often winning and almost as often falling off, for he loved to ride himself. After a particularly nasty accident, he was given a one in a hundred chance of survival by the doctors. He recovered.

He came back to England in 1894, bringing with him some servants and several of his beloved horses. In June of that year he paid a first visit to Deepdene as a guest of Lily, Duchess of Marlborough. She had rented the house since 1892 when her husband, the eighth Duke of Marlborough, died. Lilian, so called, it was said, because her name rhymed with "million," was the daughter of Cicero Price, commodore of the United States Navy, and she had been married first of all to Mr. Louis Hammersely, an immensely wealthy New Yorker who, when he died, had left his large fortune to his wife. This fortune, once she had married Marlborough, helped restore Blenheim, the ancestral home of Winston Churchill.

Lord William had gone to Deepdene in the first place to attend the Ascot races. Later in the year, in September, his engagement to Lily was announced. The news surprised a lot of people. It was not a long engagement and the couple were married on April 30, 1895, after which they both moved into Deepdene.

An account of the house at the time, written by a friend of Lord William's, reads as follows: "The Deepdene . . . that lovely place . . . stands on the eastern side of the old coaching road near Dorking. On the north the London, Brighton and South Coast railway winds. The grounds around the house are amongst the most beautiful in England, when the rhododendrons are in flower the gardens and grounds are a blaze of colour and a delight. It is charmingly secluded and yet near enough to the world to easily see as much of it as might be desired."

The house had been leased to Lily in 1892 for twenty-one years and so it was here that the couple spent their last years. Since Clumber had so many treasures of its own, Henrietta had not moved anything out of Deepdene, which was as stuffed with art now as it had been in Thomas's and in Henry's time. Into all this, Lord William imported his own tastes: his Indian and South African sporting and military trophies. "The dining room, the billiard-room, the front hall and indeed every nook and corner were filled with them . . . guns, spears, assegais [Zulu spears], antlers, racing cups and beautiful inlaid vases are arranged in profusion. Also regimental trophies of which he was fond and proud."

By then it seems that most of the paintings had been moved into the billiard room. Although we cannot be certain, it is likely that this is where *Wisdom and Strength* was located: it would have been natural for the Victorians to place a scene of partial nudity in what was a uniquely male room.

Lord William and Lilian entertained a great deal at Deepdene. Both were well connected and of the highest rank and their guests included King Edward VII, then Prince of Wales, the Sassoons, Mr. Charles Moore, and Winston Churchill.

Though he was by now fifty Lord William set about becoming a "character" in Surrey. Every year, on his birthday he entertained eighteen hundred local schoolchildren in the park at Deepdene. And with one of his horses, Harry, he took to racing the train between Burford and Dorking, for bets, of course.

He also set about winning the Derby. To this end he bought many horses, and when he died he had forty. He also attracted from America the famous jockey Tod Sloan. Sloan had been riding, very successfully, for William Collins Whitney in America, but Whitney let him go to Britain because he was planning to be in England himself at that time. Sloan, riding Democrat, gave Lord William his greatest year in 1899, when he won eleven races including the Coventry Stakes at Ascot, the Champagne Stakes at Doncaster, the Imperial Stakes at Kempton Park, and the Dewhurst Plate at Newmarket. He also won the Thousand Guineas that year with another horse, Sibola.

But his greatest chance of winning the Derby came in the next year when he leased from Lady Meaux a two-year-old called Volodyovski. With the help of Democrat and "Voly," Lord William came second in the list of winners in 1899 (after the Duke of Westminster) and again in

1900 (after the Prince of Wales). His health, however, was failing. He had caught dysentery in India some years before and never fully recovered. In December of 1900 he ate some game that was too high, which led to peritonitis. Given his already weakened state, he did not pull through and died before the year was out. His death caused a great sadness throughout the racing world—there were poems in his honor printed in the *Sporting Times*—but the final sadness did not come until the following June, when Volodyovski, now back with Lady Meaux, did indeed win the Derby.

Lily survived Lord William by a few years and stayed on at Deepdene. Around her, however, the world was changing. Agricultural and social changes made the large country estates of Great Britain harder and harder to keep up. Deepdene was not especially large but Clumber and the Newcastles were beginning to feel the squeeze more and more. In 1898, Lord Francis Pelham Clinton Hope had succeeded in breaking the entail on the Dutch pictures which Henry Philip had collected and which had been bequeathed to him by Henrietta. The pictures by then were in the South Kensington Museum (forerunner of the Victoria and Albert) and he sold the collection en bloc to a syndicate consisting of Otto Gutkunst, representing Colnaghi, and Asher Wertheimer, the Rothschilds' favorite dealer.

Gutkunst, at that point, was quite close to Bernard Berenson, who persuaded the former to sell him some of the Hope collection, including two Rembrandts, for Mrs. Isabella Stewart Gardner of Boston. These were thus the first Hope pictures to cross the Atlantic.

Some years later, after Lillian had died, Lord Francis decided to sell more paintings and this time among those he chose to go was *Wisdom and Strength*. Veronese's allegory thus joined the next great wholesale movement of art: across the Atlantic to America.

19.
Enter the Dealers:
Agnew, Colnaghi, Knoedler

Lord Francis, once he had decided to sell off *Wisdom and Strength,* had the choice of three great dealers in London: Agnew, Colnaghi, and Duveen. Or, of course, he could have put the picture up for auction. A few years later, when circumstances forced him to sell the *entire* contents of the house, at what became known as the Hope Heirlooms Sale, he preferred Christie's. But for the paintings, Lord Francis chose a dealer, Agnew.

The Newcastle archives, or at least part of them, took a direct hit by a bomb during the Second World War, so it may never be known for certain why Lord Francis chose a dealer on this occasion. Two reasons, however, are likely. One is that a dealer offered discretion, certainly in comparison with the public auction rooms. And families like the Newcastles, very proud of their distinguished past but feeling the pinch, may not have wanted the fact of their slide broadcast widely. A second reason, and possibly a more powerful one, was that dealers offered more money. This may seem difficult to understand viewed from this end of the twentieth century, when the highest prices for art are almost all fetched in the auction rooms. But circumstances were very different then. The most obvious difference was that collecting in America was beginning to be a factor in the art market. At that time, however, it was the dealers and not the auctioneers who benefited most from this development. There was no air travel, no transatlantic telephone, no telex. The number of serious collectors was much smaller than now and few of them would have dreamed of crossing the Atlantic to attend art auctions as people do all the time now. The main dealers, on the other hand, all had offices, or at least representatives or associates on both continents and made a healthy living shipping paintings regularly on the great liners which were, at the time, the sole way to cross the ocean.

The firm of Agnew and Son goes back to 1817. In that year, Thomas Agnew was taken into partnership by Vittore Zanetti, an Italian émigré who had premises in Market Street in Manchester. At that point the firm was not only, or even mainly, art dealers. A newspaper advertisement described it this way:

Carvers and gilders, Looking-glass and picture-frame manufacturers, Opticians, Ancient and modern English and Foreign printsellers, Publishers, and dealers in Old Coins, medals and all kinds of Curiosities. . . . they always have on hand a very extensive assortment of Chimney and Pier glasses, Mirrors, Girandoles, Bronze Figures, Lamps, Lustres, Telescopes, Microscopes, Opera and Reading Glasses, Mathematical instruments, Spectacles of every description, suitable for all ages; Primed Canvas &c. with every requisite for Artists. Boarding schools supplied with designs for Embroidery Work on Silk and needlework Neatly and permanently framed. Barometer, thermometer, Hydrometer, and Saccharometer Maker, on the most improved construction, warranted correct. Paintings restored, New lined and cleaned with the greatest care, on very moderate terms. Ancient and modern paintings bought, sold and exchanged.

Apart from listing their dealing in pictures as the last specialty of all, as Geoffrey Agnew says, in his history of the firm, "The list reads like that of a 17th century German collector's Kunstkammer." Or even a modern junkshop.

The young Agnew who was taken into partnership had served as an apprentice since 1810. The Agnews were originally from Wigtonshire in Scotland, although John Agnew, Thomas's father, had crossed the border and settled and married in Liverpool. The partnership between Zanetti and Agnew was a success from the start although in the early days it was the manufacture of frames which was the most profitable side of the business. This was gradually replaced by print publishing (as was also true of Colnaghi's) and by the time Thomas retired in 1861 his firm had published over a thousand prints and was one of the leading printsellers in the country. During this period before photography, magazines like the *Illustrated London News* were enormously popular for their engravings of views of historic events: everything from great fires to state occasions.

Zanetti retired in 1828. It was around this time that the picture dealing side of the business began to look up, and the first purchases were made at Christie's in London. The taste of the firm, at that time, was not for old masters but for contemporary English works by Constable, Turner, and Etty. The large fortunes accumulated in the mid-nineteenth century by Manchester merchants gave a tremendous impetus to art collecting.

Thomas's eldest son, William, followed him into the business and was to develop his ideas on a far greater scale. He and his younger brother, Thomas Jr., became partners in 1851 and the timing may have had something to do with the fact that Thomas Sr. by then had numerous commitments elsewhere. Art dealers, or whatever it was that the Agnews were at that time, had become much more substantial people than their counter-parts in, say, Christina's Rome. Thomas Sr. was now a well-known figure in Lancashire and numbered among his friends the lakeland poet Charles Swain. As mayor of Salford in 1851, Agnew received Queen Victoria.

During the 1850s William started traveling to London and buying more heavily at Christie's. In 1860, the firm opened its first London office, in Waterloo Place. In the next thirty-five years, William was the preeminent dealer in England and it was that prominence which caused *Wisdom and Strength* and *Vice and Virtue* to be offered to his firm rather than to Colnaghi or Duveen.

William was as friendly with Gladstone as Henry Thomas Hope had been with Disraeli. This is an added reason why Lord Francis approached Agnew. The Newcastles had always been close to Gladstone as well, so they all moved in the same "set." William entertained at his home the Prime Minister, Lord Rosebery, painters such as Millais, Burne-Jones, and Leighton and musicians like Hallé and Mme. Neruda. In 1872, he joined the board of *Punch* magazine, becoming chairman in 1890. By then he had also been elected Liberal Member of Parliament for South East Lancashire, which seat he held for six years. He was a great advocate of the Manchester Ship Canal, a founder of the National Liberal Club, and vice president of Great Ormond Street children's hospital.

He was a busy man but he did not neglect art. For William was just as sharp in that world as his father had been. It was William, for example, who first noticed that tastes were changing again in the 1870s, when people once again began to veer away from contemporary works toward the eighteenth century and even further back to older masters. It was William who fashioned links between the firm and the great aristocratic collections in England: Lord Lansdowne, the Rothschilds, Lord Rosebery, Lord Westmorland, Lord Albermarle, and so on. And it was William who first formed a link with the New York firm of Knoedler, a link which has continued until today.

By the late nineteenth century, Agnew was becoming a force to be reckoned with in the art world. Indeed, the firm itself claims that, over the years, it has been Christie's biggest customer. Whether or not that is true, the remark points up the fact that, during the nineteenth century and, indeed, up until the Second World War, Christie's was a much more successful auction house in the realm of paintings than was Sotheby's. Sotheby's still specialized mainly in books and there was at this time no real competition between the two.

As the 1890s approached, William had no shortage of help in the business. There were his sons, George and Morland, and his nephew Lockett (Thomas's son). But William was still fully involved and the last decade of the century saw what were his greatest achievements—the formation of two of his greatest collections: those of Sir Edward Cecil Guinness and of Sir Charles Tennant. In all, Sir E. C. Guinness (later Lord Iveagh) bought 240 pictures and drawings from Agnew, including 34 Reynoldses, 16 Romneys, and 15 Gainsboroughs. According to Geoffrey Agnew, it was because of William and Guinness that the great Joseph Duveen became an art dealer in the first place. At the time Iveagh was collecting, the Duveen family dealt mainly in porcelain, furniture, and objets d'art. One day, Guinness bought a number of Spanish screens from the firm. Although the elder Duveen was pleased with the sale, the younger Joe was not: "While we were selling screens to Guiness for a few hundred pounds, Agnew's were selling him pictures for many thousands. There and then I decided I would be a picture dealer."

William Agnew retired in 1895 and Morland and Lockett took over in London (with George running the Manchester office until 1902). The old master field remained strong, but so did eighteenth-century, nineteenth-century, and Victorian paintings. It was about this time that the firm, already international, acquired a number of new American clients, among them George Gould, "Judge" Elbert H. Gary, J. G. Johnson, E. T. Stotesbury, P. A. B. and J. E. Widener, and, above all, J. Pierpont Morgan. The great Morgan, founder of the Metropolitan Museum of Art in New York, at that time had a house in London where he kept his paintings. From Agnew he bought no fewer than two hundred pictures and drawings.

The years up to the First World War were very strong in the picture market: the boom in both contemporary works and in old masters continued. Agnew by now had strong international links, with Sedelmeyr and Wertheimer in Paris, and with Knoedler and Duveen in New York. They also often took "shares" in pictures with Colnaghi in London. Among the paintings they handled were two magnificent Turners, *Cologne* and *Dieppe*, which went for £57,000 ($7,752,000). (These now hang in the Frick, in the same room as *Wisdom and Strength*.) The strength of the market was reflected in the prices. In 1912 a Rembrandt was sold through Agnew for £63,000 ($8,568,000); in the next year two works by Reynolds went for £110,000 ($14,960,000) and a second Rembrandt, for £59,000 ($8,024,000). It was thus a good time to sell important old masters and, for a family who perhaps prided itself on its discretion, Agnew was the obvious choice.

Records show that *Wisdom and Strength* was sold as part of a pair, with *Vice and Virtue*, for £11,000, or $1.5 million. Veronese was thus not then regarded as being in the same class as Turner or Rembrandt, or Reynolds for that matter. Although Agnew was in charge of the transaction, the records also show that the company acted in cooperation with two other firms, each of which had a third share in the paintings. These two firms were Colnaghi and Knoedler.

Later in their histories, Colnaghi and Agnew were to show some remarkable similarities in their development, but their beginnings were very different. Colnaghi was older than Agnew, having been founded in the mid-eighteenth century by an Italian pyrotechnist, Giovanni Battista Torre. Torre came to London in the 1750s and worked with the Brock firework family. With them he helped to put on a magnificent display at Marylebone Gardens. He then moved to Paris where he opened a shop which was known as the Cabinet de Physique Experimentale, selling scientific equipment and books. In 1767 Torre moved back across the Channel and in Pall Mall in London opened a small branch of his firm, which was managed by his son Antony. The Torres continued in fireworks, however, and in 1771, at the invitation of David Garrick, Giovanni Battista returned to Marylebone Gardens to give a "firework drama" called the Forge of Vulcan: it created a sensation.

Though he was a brilliant pyrotechnist, fireworks were then frequently banned by the police and both the Torres could see that selling prints was safer. Their first major success in this area occurred in 1775 when they published *Caricatures of the English* which was very popular on both sides of the Channel (although French buyers of these prints at the sales in England outstripped the English by three to one). As a result of the success of this series of prints the firm lost its scientific flavor.

Giovanni Battista died in 1780 and now Paul Colnaghi entered the scene. A charming and intelligent man, he came from a distinguished Milanese family though he was obliged to leave the city and go abroad when his father died in debt. He traveled first to Paris and there joined the great "rendezvous" which gathered at the optician's shop, Ciceri (during the Enlightenment, opticians were at the forefront of the passion for science). Ciceri had at one stage been a partner with Antony Torre but no longer was. The intellectuals of the day gathered at Ciceri's shop in the Rue St. Honoré and included among their number Benjamin Franklin. Colnaghi became a great favorite at Ciceri's and was pressed to go to America. But he declined, having received an offer from Antony Torre to be the latter's agent as a printseller in Paris with a shop in the Palais Royal. This opened in 1784 (Égalité had just refurbished the palace) and began by selling Reynolds portraits in mezzotint; these were known in France as the *manière anglaise.* The next year Colnaghi moved to London, by which time the shop there had transferred from Market Lane to 132 Pall Mall. The two men clearly hit it off, for Colnaghi married

Torre's sister-in-law and, toward the end of the eighteenth century, Torre made over the business entirely to Colnaghi.

Trade foundered during the French Revolution but Colnaghi weathered the storm by publishing the firm's second series of famous prints. This was the *Cries of London,* probably the most famous of all colored stipple prints, showing the charm of eighteenth-century life but revealing its more somber aspects too. Two other types of print also served the firm well. One was the topical portrait. For example, Colnaghi published a likeness of Nelson after Hoppner's portrait. It was released on the very day that the news of Trafalgar reached London, a brilliant move. Second, as war dragged on, Colnaghi began to supply the government with views of beleaguered towns. These were very useful for the army and it was through these that Colnaghi came to know a number of important and influential people. In 1799 the firm moved again, this time to 23 Cockspur Street, and Colnaghi now became a rendezvous itself "for the 'upper ten thousand' who collected prints."

This was a fashionable time for the print and the print publisher. Colnaghi held a three o'clock levee, "crowded with beauty and fashion." He was appointed printseller to the regent and he was also asked to arrange the royal collections before they moved to Windsor. The Duke of Orléans, Égalité's son and the future King Louis Philippe, who was then in exile in Twickenham, also consoled himself by collecting from Colnaghi prints showing French glory.

The good fortune did not last. Paul Colnaghi's two sons, Dominic and Martin, now entered the business—with disastrous results. Dominic was not so bad. He went to Italy to buy armor, which was then a new collecting specialty, and he sold it to Dr. Meyrick where it helped to form the Wallace Collection. Dominic was also one of those who encouraged John Constable and helped him to gain acceptance. But, as is recorded in Constable's own diaries, Dominic's younger brother, Martin, was quite different.

Paul was by now planning to retire but Martin's extravagances nearly ruined the entire family. It got so bad that the rest of them bought him out and he started up on his own. There then followed an extraordinary period when Dominic and Martin met only at the sales where they would bid ruthlessly against each other. Though one brother was now out of the firm, his loss was more than made up for by the gain, unusual at the time, of a sister. Paul Colnaghi's daughter Caroline had married John Scott, the editor of the *Champion.* But Scott was killed in a duel with a journalist whose scurrilous articles on Keats in *Blackwood's* had aroused his anger. As a tragic widow, Caroline was given a full partnership and helped to carry on the Colnaghis' successful publication of print series. The military connection continued too and the firm sent Simpson as the first war artist to the Crimea.

The latter part of the nineteenth century was marked by a waning of the print and the firm's slow transition to paintings proper, which had something to do with the arrival of new blood in the form of E. F. Deprez, O. C. H. Gutkunst, and Gustav Meyer. These three developed the firm greatly. And it was Otto Gutkunst who, in 1898, in partnership with Asher Wertheimer, bought from Lord Francis Pelham Clinton Hope the great collection of Dutch and Flemish pictures that had been assembled by Thomas Hope's brother, Henry Philip, and which included pictures by Massys and Vermeer. The son of an auctioneer in Stuttgart, Gutkunst was as fine a collector as he was dealer and his own collection eventually went to the Ashmolean Museum in Oxford. This marked a great period for the Colnaghis: among their deals at the time was the Darnley Titian, *Europa and the Bull,* for Isabella Stewart Gardner and the seven Van Dycks from the Marquis Cattaneo of Genoa. Paintings which they acquired for Frick included Bellini's *St. Francis in Ecstasy,* Titian's *Pietro Aretino,* and Goya's *The Forge.* Later on, they combined with Knoedler in the great Hermitage deal. (See below p. 329.)

Knoedler, which now has offices in New York only a few doors away from the Frick Collection, dates back to 1846, when Michael Knoedler, the founder, arrived in Manhattan from France. He was then acting for the firm of Goupil, a well-known company of French engravers. He set up an office at 289 Broadway, on the corner of Duane Street. The engraving business brought him into touch with American painters and the wider art world. Knoedler was very impressed by the fact that, in the early 1850s, a picture sold in New York for three hundred dollars. This was such a lot for a painting in Manhattan at the time that Knoedler immediately wrote to France expressing doubt that a picture "could ever again be sold in New York for as large a sum."

In 1854 he returned to France, married, and brought his wife back to New York. There, he took larger premises, still on Broadway but further north. After a few more years he bought out the Goupil interest in the firm and from then on traded under his own name. In 1859 he moved again, even further up Broadway. His period there covered the Civil War when there was a marked drop in sales. This brought about a broadening of the art works Knoedler dealt in and he now showed both European paintings and contemporary American artists.

Because of the unstable political conditions, paintings in those days were usually paid for not in money but in gold. But the appetite of Americans for fine art was growing despite this and already Knoedler was acquiring a number of distinguished clients. Among them were John

Taylor Johnston, who was to become first president of the Metropolitan Museum, and Aaron Healy, first president of the Brooklyn Museum. Another client was Charles Crocker of Sacramento, who bought eight paintings in the month after the Union Pacific made its first transcontinental run, proving that the art business was truly nationwide.

In 1869 Knoedler moved again, to 170 Fifth Avenue, on the corner of Twenty-second Street. This was considered a daring and even dangerous move, "for it was doubted that the business section would expand so far up-town." But prices went on creeping up. In 1875 the Corcoran Gallery in Washington bought from Knoedler one of the first purchases from an American dealer by an American museum. Collis P. Huntington of the Union Pacific and John Jacob Astor started collecting about now, also using Knoedler.

In 1877, Knoedler's eldest son, Roland, reached his twenty-first birthday and became a partner in the firm, thus making it M. Knoedler and Company, the title it has been known by ever since. It was not a moment too soon since the elder Knoedler died the very next year. The firm could have gone under at that point but Roland prospered as his father had done, and later on he brought in his younger brothers, Edmond and Charles. The expansion continued and another move was made, still farther uptown, to 355 Fifth Avenue, on the corner of Thirty-fourth Street, opposite the Waldorf Hotel. Roland and the other sons were proving as astute as their father, for this intersection quickly became the city's busiest thoroughfare. B. Altman and Company now occupies that site and Benjamin Altman himself became one of Knoedler's most valued clients.

Now, the names in the Knoedler old record books become very familiar. For the immense industrial expansion which followed the Civil War in America and the new era of railroads had its impact on the world of art. William H. Vanderbilt bought a Meissonnier from Knoedler for the then record price of $16,000; other names that recur include Cornelius Vanderbilt, John Jacob Astor, Henry M. Flagler of Standard Oil, Charles Stewart Smith, one of the founders of the Fifth Avenue Bank, Henry O. Havemeyer, Stephen V. Harkness, William Rockefeller, California governor Leland Stanford, publisher John A. Harper, and W. A. Roebling, the builder of Brooklyn Bridge. Jay Gould bought twenty-two pictures in two days, as Charles Henschel, in his history of Knoedler's says, "an indication that collectors then had a very different attitude from those of today." He also adds: "It was then the fashion to hang pictures from floor to ceiling, and I even remember a Philadelphia collector who hung pictures on the back of his front door because there was no room left anywhere else. Also, the sales books show that waves of buying would suddenly occur in a given locality and, presumably, one collector would start others buying."

In 1895 the firm opened a branch in Paris and, shortly after, another branch in London. The first non-Knoedler was also brought into the firm. This was an astute move, for Charles Carstairs was a talented and courageous dealer. During his thirty-year association with the firm, Knoedler began dealing in earlier and earlier pictures, which, in time, appealed to a number of truly great collectors, such as Andrew Mellon and Henry Clay Frick.

The official history of Knoedler continues the story: "At the turn of the century there began that great importation of paintings which now fill our institutions of art, and many of the greatest masterpieces of Europe passed through our hands in this period when millions of dollars worth of painting came into the country each year. Intense competition developed between the principal collectors, such as Henry Clay Frick, P. A. B. Widener, Charles Taft and Andrew Mellon, and prices were paid which would have seemed fabulous to [Michele Knoedler]. In 1901 we sold our first important old master when the Boston Museum bought Velázquez's *Don Balthazar and His Dwarf*."

Knoedler remained a family firm. Michele's grandson, Charles Henschel joined in 1904 and continued as a director until after the Second World War. As the twentieth century stretched forward, more and more old masters arrived from Europe—a wholesale movement which is considered in the next interlude. In 1907 the firm acquired the seven great Cattaneo Van Dycks from Colnaghi: these pictures are generally considered to have comprised the first exhibition of important old masters ever held in America.

In 1911, Knoedler's bought the old Lotos Club at 556 Fifth Avenue, in what was yet another move north, the sixth, as the firm dutifully followed the growth of Manhattan in its inexorable move up the island. And it was in this year, 1911, that *Wisdom and Strength* made the journey across the Atlantic, to Knoedler's vaults.

20.
Pentimento:
Wisdom and Strength Ages

Wisdom and Strength remained at Knoedler's for about fifteen months. Since it had hung, together with *Vice and Virtue,* at Deepdene for more than sixty years, where it had been comparatively neglected, the picture was now cleaned. This highlighted a change that had come over *Wisdom and Strength,* a change that set it apart from its close companion of more than three hundred years. Thus this book is about one painting and not two. The picture had aged.

What happened specifically was that an earlier idea of Veronese's, a billowing of cloth about which he had had second thoughts and had painted over, now showed through and disfigured the picture. The new, or rather old, section showed itself above the left shoulder of Wisdom and it fitted so awkwardly into the composition that it suggested Veronese had changed his mind fairly dramatically while working on the painting.

When such a change happens it is known as a *pentimento* and it is merely the most vivid aspect of aging in old masters. In developing a pentimento, *Wisdom and Strength* is by no means atypical since most museums and galleries have examples of pentimento.

Knoedler did not have the detailed records of *Wisdom and Strength,* as the Frick Collection now does, so the dealers may have thought that the pentimento was a recent change. In fact, that is not so. Several copies of the painting—Boucher's, for example—depict the painting *already* showing the pentimento. So does an engraving of the picture, in J. Couché's book, *La Galerie du Palais Royal,* published in 1808.

There appears to be no set timetable for when pentimenti will appear. With *Wisdom and Strength* this change appears to have taken place in the first hundred and fifty years of its life and, since then, it has been fairly stable. In general, pentimenti are left as they are when they occur in museum-owned works but in any case with *Wisdom and Strength* the pentimento is not large and does not seriously distort the painting. It merely adds interest for us to wonder how differently Veronese at one stage imagined his composition was going to be.

Old master paintings can in fact age markedly. Understanding this process is important to restorers so that its worst effects can be checked. For the rest of us it is of interest because it helps us understand how old masters may look different now, as compared with their appearance when they left the artist's studio. Probably the single most striking example of aging in an old master is the yellowing, or browning, that takes place with time. This "golden glow," as it has been called, is what attracts many people to old masters. But did the artists themselves anticipate the yellowing? Did they like it? Did any of them try to avoid it? This is important because, from time to time, when restorations are undertaken, they invariably remove the "golden glow"—to the consternation of many art lovers. Is this a good thing? Should paintings be seen as their makers intended them to be? Or as we would rather see them now, very often with the mellowing effect of the intervening centuries added? There is no easy answer since modern artists are likely to want one thing —to see what the artists originally intended—and certain collectors may want another.

Although the development of the great galleries of the world has helped enormously to improve the access of the public to wonderful pictures, for many restorers the idea that a museum is a "safe haven" is far from obvious. The very act of putting a painting in a museum usually means that a picture will be restored, to "look its best." *Wisdom and Strength* has been cleaned twice since it has been in the Frick, in 1930 and 1961–62. The same is often true when a painting changes hands, as has happened more frequently since the growth in importance of the auction houses. Many pictures are "restored" before they are sold.

There is so much controversy over what is and what is not good conservation that the "centralization" of pictures in museums is not always a good thing. When paintings were scattered across an entire country, across Britain or France for example, then the paintings could all grow old separately, restored piecemeal so that not too much collective damage could be done. Once in a museum, restoration can occur on an unprecedented scale. Ironically, this means that over the years it is the major masterpieces that have been tampered with, whereas, by comparison, minor works have been left alone. It also means that in subtle ways many masterpieces that were once quite different from one another are now "unified" by the hidden hand of the restorer.

Restoration has advanced considerably since the seventeenth century when a Frenchman suggested that the best way to clean a dirty picture was simply "to pee on it." Nevertheless, despite these advances, the problems have not disappeared. The prevailing aesthetic is apt always to influence what goes on. For example, in the eighteenth century restorers invariably lightened pictures, whereas in Victorian times they invariably darkened them. It may be that with the impact of advertising, with its need for raw, easily assimilable images, we in our own time are actually *less* ready to respond to the sensibilities of other times and therefore allow greater crimes to take place in the name of restoration than was allowed in the past.

There are three kinds of aging in an old picture. First, there are those changes that occur naturally due to time. Paintings are made up of layers of chemicals and other substances which change at different rates over the centuries. Second, there are those changes brought about by man in his attempt to counter the natural effects. And third, there are the "unnatural" things that tend to occur with objects that have a long life. In other words, accidents of one sort or another can occur: flooding perhaps, or theft, which often involves violent movement or the picture being kept for a while in an unsuitable environment.

Such changes occur in three areas: in the medium, in the pigments, and in the canvas or wood on which the painting is produced. Of all painting media, egg tempera is the most stable. Early authorities even argued that eggs from town hens were better than eggs from country hens because they were paler. This is why those very complicated and detailed northern European paintings—of Van Eyck or Campin or Van der Weyden, say—are still so fresh today. That and the fact that they are painted on panel (poplar in the north, oak in the south), not canvas. Oil, on the other hand, is nowhere near as stable. Linseed oil is the worst: it yellows, grows darker, and becomes more brittle with age. Poppy oil and walnut oil, Veronese's favorites, are somewhat better, though far from perfect. Artists were well aware of these differences from quite early on. For example, in his picture of a *Family Group,* Lorenzo Lotto, according to researches carried out at the National Gallery in London, used walnut oil in the woman's white cuffs and linseed oil in the man's black cap.

Besides darkening, different pigments react differently with oil. White and blue are most affected, white for the obvious reason that it is altered most by darkening, and blue because, in order to make a vivid color, the original pigment, lapis lazuli, has to be left in fairly large particles. Thus it needs a lot of oil to surround these particles and bind them together, and this has the visual effect of making it darker.

Veronese developed his own glue to bind his blues. This was made from leather clippings, a technique known as *a guazzo.* De Mayerne, a friend to Rubens and Van Dyck, reports that both men were concerned with the yellowing effect of oil and that the latter's remedy at least was to mix his pigments with fish glue. Rubens observed, for instance, that oil darkens more if it dries in the dark but that in sunshine there is a bleaching effect. He was therefore able to avoid the worst of the yellowing effects.

Not everyone tried to avoid it. Nicolas Poussin observed to his pupil Canini that the Titians then in Rome, which were already about a hundred years old, were yellowed in the fleshy sections; he added, however, that he thought the Venetians had intended the effect because it did not apply anywhere near so much in other parts of their paintings. Van Dyck evidently agreed with Poussin since he admired the golden glow of Venetian works and inserted yellow into his own flesh tones in imitation of them. The flesh in old masters has always been one of the most vulnerable areas to cleaning and restoration.

As oil ages it becomes more transparent. This is the process which results in pentimenti. With darker grounds you tend to get fewer pentimenti but there is instead a loss of subtlety. There are also much sharper changes in tone than the artist ever intended. The paintings of Poussin are victims in this regard: the faces of his characters stand out far more than they are meant to.

A different kind of problem occurs if too much oil is used: then the oil separates out and forms a layer on top of the paint. This dries and hardens into a brittle wrinkled effect which interferes optically with the progress of natural light. Leonardo da Vinci's *Virgin and Child* in the Alte Pinakothek, Munich, is a striking example of this.

Apart from the changes in the oil in which the pigments are mixed, the pigments themselves may change over the centuries. Many old masters had their own idiosyncratic or even secretive ways of preparing their pigments, not to mention the fact that the various schools, like the Venetian and the Florentine, habitually differed in their painting practices. But some generalizations are possible. For example, copper green and several dark browns usually darken with time, many red pigments fade, and ultramarine bleaches when it comes in contact with an acidic atmosphere. But it is important to say that other changes which have taken place are not as systematic as they would have been had there been a standard way of painting all over Europe. For instance, the flesh in Italian primitives, particularly where a shadow was depicted, often had green painted under the pink; nowadays the pink has become transparent, the green underpainting shows through and the figures sometimes look quite ill.

Early yellows were also vulnerable, India yellow perhaps most of all, being made from cow's urine. Among the blues, it was discovered that azurite may blacken if cleaned with alkalis. Copper resinate, a common green, was discovered to turn reddish brown over time, especially unfortunate in that it gave spring vegetation an autumnal tinge.

Venetian paintings are also vulnerable to aging on at least three other

grounds. One stems from the use of glazing. This glazing, or the application of many layers of subtly translucent layers of pigment, is the most
personal, the most idiosyncratic, and the most delicate of techniques,
responsible for the great beauty of Venetian art. In many cases, the master himself took a direct part only when laying in the shapes and in the
glazing: that may have been the only visible part by the master's own
hand. It would be asking too much for any restorer to recapture the
glazing. Second, the Venetians made wide use of impasto, heavy layers of
paint which stand out in lumps. This is very vulnerable to relining, often
being subtly flattened in the process. Third and finally, some painters,
like Tintoretto, treated the huge canvases for public commissions with a
rapid technique that made great use of halftones. But these were so thin
that in no time the brown ground which he used showed through and
made the paintings very dark.

In general, Veronese's paintings have aged better than the more dramatic compositions of Tintoretto, Rembrandt, or the Caravaggists. The
fact that his paintings retained their daylight effects was of special interest
to the artists of the early eighteenth century, who began to imitate or
adapt the gray-green grounds which he and others, like Correggio favored. Canaletto, Boucher, and Gainsborough all benefited and it is no
coincidence that their works, like Veronese's, are relatively well preserved today.

Much of what is known about the aging of paintings comes from the
various cleanings carried out by restorers. Yet ironically it is these cleanings themselves that have created the most controversy. This stems from
the fact that it is the changes that occur over time in varnish which
divides people more than anything else.

The cleaning of pictures has gone on everywhere and at all times. Yet
on four occasions the divisions over varnish have erupted into bitter
controversies: in 1796, over the Italian paintings which the conservators
in the newly created Louvre had cleaned; in 1846 at the National Gallery
in London; in 1919, when the Frans Hals paintings were cleaned in
Haarlem; and in 1947, again at the National Gallery in London, where
Sir Kenneth (later Lord) Clark had ordered many pictures to be cleaned
during their evacuation out of London during the Second World War. In
all four cases, the issues were much the same. On each occasion, when
the varnish was removed so too was the "golden glow" which for many
people was the main attraction of old masters. Indeed there were even
reports during the 1846 incident that "gallery varnish" or "licorice" had
been washed over the cleaned pictures to reduce the "shocking crude-
ness" revealed by the removal of the varnish. Right up until our own
day, when the cleaning of Michelangelo's Sistine Chapel has caused many

people to object to what they see as the crudity revealed by overrestoration, the issue has remained the same: we have got so used to seeing old masters literally through the mists of time that we cannot accept them being vivid. For varnish not only yellows old paintings, it mellows them. Some collectors like this, but professional restorers and many artists do not. They dismiss it as part of the "cult of the old" and argue that it interferes with our understanding of great art. And they point to the damage that such an attitude has already had on paintings in the past.

The aging of varnish is composed of several elements. There is its yellowing, its darkening. Not only does this give an overall glow to a picture but it reacts differentially with different colors. Rubens, for example, is generally regarded as the most accomplished painter of flesh, an effect he achieved by mixing blue in with the other pigments. Yellow varnish makes blue more green and this utterly changes Rubens's skin tones after a while (though other parts of his pictures are less affected). Rubens was aware of this and was therefore very careful with the varnish he used. Even so, after three hundred years even the best varnish yellows somewhat and the flesh on a clean Rubens is quite different from that on an uncleaned one. The lilac-colored flesh in many of Guido Reni's paintings is the result of a similar process.

A second element is the development of a disfiguring craquelure. These are fine cracks which form because the ground, the pigment, and the varnish contract at different rates. Different kinds of pigment, different ways of painting, and different centuries may produce characteristic forms of craquelure. Some, for instance, are round, like a spider's web, others are rectangular nets, like a soccer goal. They are in general irreversible effects of aging, although skilled restorers can sometimes alleviate the worst craquelure.

A third effect of varnishing occurs particularly with painters who lay their pigment on in thick layers of impasto, Rembrandt, for example. Here, over the years varnish may settle into the little furrows formed by the hairs of the brush and these darken to form lines which the master never painted. Rembrandt's *The Adoration of the Shepherds,* in London's National Gallery, is such a case: Joseph's right eye has a squint which the master never intended. *Wisdom and Strength* suffers a similar blemish, according to a note in the Frick archive.

These are not all the ways that the aging of varnish and oil can disfigure a painting but they are enough to show why there has always been so much controversy when old masters have been cleaned: people had simply got used to the golden glow or "gallery tone" and many thought that it was what the old masters *intended* their paintings to look like. In recent years the restorers have had the better of the argument. As a cursory look around Madison Avenue or Bond Street galleries will show, the taste now is for pristine, clean, and *bright* old masters, very often restored to the point where they look as though they were painted yesterday.†

The last category of factors which affect the aging of paintings are the changes brought about by man himself, which have been a factor ever since Renaissance priests used to bless paintings by sprinkling them with holy water. The introduction of tinted varnishes is only one of many ways restorers may subtly change the appearance of old masters. Another is the transfer of paintings from one surface to another. The most common type of transfer is from wood to canvas. Most early paintings were done on oak or poplar panels although later mahogany was also used. Wood is not quite as stable a support as it might appear; it becomes more susceptible to temperature differences as it ages and cracks; and it is also susceptible to rot and woodworm. And it is heavy, meaning that big compositions on panel are difficult to move around. This is one reason why, in eighteenth-century Paris, Citoyen Hacquin, under Napoleon, developed his technique for the transfer of certain old masters from panel to canvas. It is not as dangerous as it might appear for in fact oil paint forms quite a tough, if very thin, layer.

When a panel suffers woodworm or blistering due to flooding, for instance, then a transfer is obviously prudent. Otherwise, the method is not used as often now as it once was, for there is a general feeling among connoisseurs and art historians that, during transfer, something subtle is lost. Robert Frost said of writing that "the poetry is the bit that gets lost in translation" and similarly, in transferring paintings, some of the life and warmth which the wood can give to a composition is lost: it becomes colder, flatter. Given all this, it is surely extraordinary that Titian's great *Ariadne and Bacchus* was finally fixed to composition board, making it unnaturally rigid, because it was taken off the wall so much in order to be photographed.

Other aspects of earlier restorations which may affect the appearance of paintings include lining, retouching, and overpainting. Lining or relining a canvas involves gluing and ironing a canvas which may mean that the impasto is slightly flattened and some texture and details of brushwork may also be lost. This most affects painters like Titian whose brushwork was precisely the point—part of the artist's signature. Rey-

† In one sense the golden glow may have made a major contribution to the development of modern art. As one scholar says: "Had the masterpieces been the shining examples they are now again becoming, would the revolt of Turner, Constable and the Impressionists and all the exciting subsequent developments have happened . . . ?" An unanswerable—but thoroughly intriguing—question.

nolds, for example, was renowned during his day for his "cheesy" texture, and this, too, is very vulnerable to lining.

Dealers, insofar as they reflect fashions, also change paintings. Duveen always had the pictures he sold very highly varnished, so that his wealthy clients could see their reflections in the masterpieces they owned. At one time there was a fashion for Salomes to have the head of John the Baptist overpainted with a vase of flowers; at other times landscapes were made more "interesting" through the addition of hunting scenes, or royalist collars on portraits were converted to puritan ones.

The travels of *Wisdom and Strength* have been at the heart of this book: The picture has seen a great deal of movement. But movement involves risk and whereas *Wisdom and Strength* has been lucky, other masterpieces have been much less so.

For instance, in 1627, when the Gonzaga paintings were taken from Mantua to the coast and shipped from there to England by sea, the ship they were loaded onto was also carrying two other types of cargo—currants, which had begun to ferment, and mercury sublimate in casks. The fermenting currants caused evaporation of the mercury sublimate and, by the time the paintings were unloaded in England, they were totally black. Most of the pictures were successfully cleaned by the restorer, who first tried pure saliva, then warm milk, and finally, pure alcohol. This removed all the stains on the oil paintings but perhaps the rarest painting of all, Mantegna's *Triumph of Caesar,* which was regarded as a national trophy in Mantua, was very badly affected as it was executed in watercolors. This is what accounts for its very bad state of preservation now.†

Apart from the pentimento, and despite its many travels and the fact that it has had many different owners, *Wisdom and Strength* is in a basically sound condition. In general, it has aged a good deal better than many other old masters. It is a predominantly red picture so some fading will have occurred, but there has been no appreciable darkening, at least in comparison with other old masters of similar age. There is nothing much in the way of disfiguring craquelure and there appear, from the condition reports at the Frick, to be no major areas of retouching. According to the file, a small hole was repaired in 1945 and repainting is visible along the upper, right-hand and bottom edges of the picture. In the wings of Cupid "the ultramarine has been partially changed to green."

† The looting of masterpieces by the Nazis during the Second World War naturally resulted in widespread damage to many works, quite apart from the vast number that were completely destroyed, by both sides, either by bombing or by shelling. The records of the Allied Monuments, Fine Arts and Archives Commission show that "almost every item" had suffered some sort of damage.

These are only minor imperfections, however, and overall the painting seems stable, so that its appearance should hold up well in the future. More than anything this is due to Veronese's own techniques. If you look at his paintings in the museums of the world, especially those which were also painted for Rudolf, you will see that the pictures retain that "morning freshness," that "lunar coolness" mentioned in the opening chapter. It was that freshness which the dealers—Agnew, Colnaghi, and Knoedler —thought would appeal to the Americans.

Interlude Three:
Into America

The movement of European painting and other treasures across the Atlantic at the end of the nineteenth and at the beginning of the twentieth centuries was the third great shift in art since the Renaissance. Once again *Wisdom and Strength* played a part in the transfer.

A number of factors made art collecting in the United States rather different from Europe in general and from Great Britain in particular. For example, the country house, as it exists in Europe and especially in Britain, is comparatively rare in America and was even more so in the nineteenth century. In most places, because commerce and industry were supreme in America, the manufacturers, shopowners, and merchants made their homes in the towns. The country was somewhere to go to *from* the towns rather than vice versa. The significance of this for collecting was that it meant there was no continuity. The town houses changed so much, just as the towns around them were changing, that there was little thought, and less time, for collecting. And because the country houses, when they existed, became very much second homes, their collections, when they existed, were second-rate too. Until the early part of the nineteenth century at least, the collections in America were invariably composed of either inferior works or copies.

A second factor was financial. Until 1909, works of art imported into the United States were subjected to an ad valorem duty. This was so heavy that, in 1906, a collector had to pay $150,000 in tax on works valued at $80,000. Not only did this mean that the art that was available in America was of poor quality, it also meant that the early dealers and auctioneers had a poor reputation as they were always trying to pass things off as more valuable than they really were. Furthermore since few museums existed, scholarship was rare. This combination of factors led to an overall atmosphere in which art collecting and dealing were shrouded in mystery and hardly popular.

Moreover, collectors had to look to Europe and even go there themselves to find works, since there was no native art that was particularly esteemed. This was another hindrance to collecting. In such circumstances it was not surprising that many collectors and dealers were ignorant and that this led to a proliferating trade in "certificates of authentication," most of which were not worth the paper they were written on.

What indigenous art there was often went unrecognized until the artists had proved themselves in Europe. This was true, for example, of John Singleton Copley and Gilbert Stuart, both of whom traveled to Britain. The former remained there and the latter returned to make a name for himself as a portrait painter. That was typical too: portraits and landscapes comprised early American taste in indigenous art. So far as European old masters were concerned, fake or original, Americans by and large preferred Italian and French works to Dutch.

The first of the great American collectors was JJJ—James Jackson Jarves—though his name means less these days than some of the others. Born in Boston to a well-to-do glassmaker, he traveled widely, including an early trip to Hawaii. But then he moved to Europe, discovered the Louvre, and settled in Florence. In Italy he met the Brownings, Mrs. Trollope, and John Ruskin. Through them, Jarves acquired a passion for what he called "gold background pictures." And this is still what makes him significant today: he was the first American to collect the Italian primitives systematically. In doing this he was going very much against the spirit of the times. Not only did many people regard what he collected as fakes or copies; even when it was undoubtedly genuine they did not like it. Nathaniel Hawthorne once said that Cimabue and Giotto "might certainly be dismissed henceforth and forever, without any detriment to the cause of good art."

Jarves's collection was eventually acquired by Yale University. Now, when we list the painters whom he collected, we see that his eye has been well and truly vindicated, for at Yale you may now find works by Taddeo and Agnolo Gaddi, Bernardo Daddi, Gentile da Fabriano, Sassetta, Giovanni di Paolo, Antonio Pollaiuolo, Domenico Ghirlandaio. Jarves continued to collect throughout his life and remained ever open to new ideas. In 1876 he published *A Glimpse of the Art of Japan,* one of the first books of its kind by a Westerner. His interest in Far Eastern art was another important strand that affected American collecting.

The other great collectors, whose names are now so well known, began their acquisitions well after Jarves, mainly because they acquired their fortunes later, during the American industrial revolution — that is after the Civil War.

Isabella Stewart Gardner's collection, now housed in the building in Boston which she built especially for her pictures, is unique in the Western world. Fenway Court is decorated in the Venetian style and, like the Frick, always has fresh flowers, shrubs, and plants. This is true even today, as a clause in her will stipulates that the flowers in the house must always be fresh. Isabella Stewart Gardner was a friend of many famous people, many of whom advised her on her collecting. She was close to Henry and William James, to John Singer Sargent, and to Henry Adams. But the man who had the greatest influence on her collecting was Bernard Berenson whom she had known as a brilliant student at Harvard. Berenson helped Mrs. Gardner acquire four Rembrandts, portraits by Dürer, Holbein, Rubens, Van Dyck, and Velázquez, all via Colnaghi. Other works she acquired through BB, as he was affectionately known, were painted by Giotto, Simone Martini, Fra Angelico, Masaccio, Giovanni di Paolo, Giovanni Bellini, Botticelli, Pollaiuolo, Giorgione, Titian, Raphael, and Francesco Guardi.

Although his interests were much the same as Mrs. Gardner's, J. G. Johnson was a very different soul. The son of a blacksmith, he was a self-made man who became the greatest corporate lawyer of his time, an adviser to J. Pierpont Morgan, Henry Frick, Widener, and Havemeyer. Johnson regarded with horror the prices *they* paid for pictures and aimed to buy well, and more cheaply, himself. He developed the idea of forming a collection which would show the main phases of painting in the Western world; he was more selective than Mrs. Gardner and worked hard at developing his taste, befriending or corresponding with the great scholars of the time: Bernard Berenson, Roger Fry, Max J. Friedländer, and Wilhelm von Bode.

Johnson's collection is especially noteworthy because it included fine examples of early *northern* painting, which until that time had not been particularly popular in America. His northern European paintings included some fine works: Van Eyck's *St. Francis Receiving the Stigmata* (the first Van Eyck to reach the United States), and paintings by Robert Campin, Rogier van der Weyden, Dirk Bouts, Hans Memling, Bosch, Mabuse, Bruegel the Elder, and Dürer. Johnson, working hard at the development of his taste, was one of the first Americans to realize the appeal of Hals, van Ruysdael, the van de Veldes, Pieter de Hooch, and, above all, Rubens, then not highly regarded in North America.

A quite different group of collectors was interested in the more recent past. If the older collections were dominated by Italian and, to some extent, German and Flemish art, the collectors wrapped up in more recent works were far more concerned with French art. Three phases in French painting were especially popular in America: Salon art, the Barbizon school, and Impressionism. Collectors, who included people like John Jacob Astor and William H. Vanderbilt, all had pretty much the same sorts of pictures in their collections: Bouguereau, Meissonnier, Lefebvre, Corot, Delacroix, and Courbet.

One reason for the popularity of French painting had to do with the fact that Americans actually played a part in some of the events. For example, Americans were at the center of the revolt over the Salon which resulted in the triumph of the Barbizon school. While in Europe, the New England painter William Morris Hunt got to know Jean-François Millet, one of the leaders of the Barbizon school. Seen as socialists, the Barbizon painters were vilified in many quarters, and several of them lived in desperate poverty. Nonetheless Hunt popularized their work in America and, in particular, helped Quincy Adams Shaw of Boston compile a collection of Barbizon school paintings. For this reason Boston now has one of the best collections of Barbizon painting in the world.

One of the aims of the Barbizon school was an exact, unprettified depiction of peasant life and scenery, painted on the spot. In this they are generally regarded as the precursors of the Impressionists. This being the case, it is not in the least surprising that the Americans should have taken so readily to Impressionism proper, with the result that today some of the world's greatest Impressionist collections are in the United States.

In this the role of Mary Cassatt, an American Impressionist painter herself, was crucial. She was a Philadelphia woman of independent means who went to Europe to study painting. She settled in Paris and became friendly with the Impressionist circle, especially Degas. She was also acquainted with Paul Durand-Ruel, a Parisian dealer who had started out handling Barbizon school painters but came increasingly to deal in the Impressionists. To begin with he was by no means successful, and Mary Cassatt helped him out financially. But in 1885 the American Art Association invited him to organize a large Impressionist exhibition and this *was* a success.

As a result, two major collectors began to acquire Impressionist works through Durand-Ruel and Cassatt. One was Henry O. Havemeyer, whose wife was a friend of Mary Cassatt's. He concentrated on Degas, Manet, Monet, Pissarro, Courbet, and Cézanne. The other collector was Mrs. Potter Palmer, who in the 1880s and 1890s was the much-admired social arbiter of Chicago. Her collection was not especially large—it included four Renoirs, three Pissarros, and a Manet. But that was not the point. Because of who she was, collecting Impressionists became *the* thing in the Midwest and her example and enthusiasm meant that midwestern America became one of the centers of Impressionist collecting. In turn this enabled the Art Institute of Chicago to become one of the greatest repositories of modern French art in the United States, if not the world.

Parallel with the developing interest in European, and especially French, art went a fascination with Far Eastern works. At times it seems that the further from America a work originated, the better it was re-

garded. Americans did not really collect their own artists until after the
Civil War.

The war had two effects on the art world. The first was to stimulate
that interest in American art: because so much had been destroyed, people naturally turned to art which recorded what had been lost. People
also paid more attention to what they had been fighting over. Collectors
like William Corcoran, George Hearn, and Andrew Mellon now turned
to American art. The passion grew as the nineteenth century came to a
close, so much so that colonial portraits were heavily forged, or else
English portraits were doctored. American art has remained strong ever
since.

Henry Clay Frick, and the Frick Collection, however, belonged to a
quite different tradition of American art collecting. Frick was part of a
group of men, the "great all round collectors," who acquired first-class
examples of paintings from every age. They could do so because of the
fantastic wealth they amassed following the Civil War, during the American industrial revolution. This was the second, and most important, effect
of that war on art.

In this super league there are seven names to conjure with: the magnificent seven. They were Pierpont Morgan, Benjamin Altman, Collis Huntington, the Wideners, Andrew Mellon, Samuel Kress—and Frick. Three
others, Jules Bache, Charles Taft, and John Ringling, were not quite in
the super league, but later on they too had significant collections.

The emergence of the collections of great masters in the United States
took place in the 1890s and the first two decades of the twentieth century. As a result of the great social and economic changes brought on by
the Civil War, there came into existence a class of incredibly wealthy men
operating on scale unrivaled by their contemporaries anywhere else in
the world. The dominating motive behind a number of collections was
simply the acquisition of the best, the very best across the whole range of
art. In many cases, Frick for instance, the men became very knowledgeable and truly passionate collectors. At the same time this was often allied
with the feeling of power that exclusive possession gave them. Already in
America a magnificent collection was also a pathway to social acceptability: "The merchant princes and industrialists of the time formed a class in
society analogous to the commercial aristocracy in Venice; and they
wanted to show that American wealth could show cultural achievements
that could rival those of Europe." They also refused to buy contemporary
works and most if not all looked forward to immortality through their
collections: from an early date most of these wealthy men anticipated
that, at their deaths, if not before, their collections would be given to the
nation.

If anyone among the magnificent seven was the senior figure it was probably Pierpont Morgan. Born in 1837 he did not start collecting seriously until the 1890s, when he was already into middle age and by which time Frick was under way, too. Morgan came from a Connecticut family of merchants, farmers, and theologians and he was very well educated. This may explain why he began by collecting manuscripts and books. On the other hand, Morgan never seemed to show any scholarly ambition to form a historical collection. Rather, he simply wanted the greatest collection of masterpieces, of one kind or another, in America. He was advised to an extent by Joseph Duveen's uncle, Henry. But he also relied on Hercules Read, keeper in the department of British and medieval antiquities at the British Museum, on Agnew, and on Bernard Quaritch for books. More than the others, Morgan specialized in buying *entire* collections: the Gréau collection of ancient glass, the Gaston Labreton collection of faience, the Marfels collection of watches. Among the masterpieces he acquired were the Mazarin tapestry (later in the Widener collection), Fragonard's decorative panels made for Mme. du Barry (now in the Frick Collection), paintings by Ghirlandaio, Raphael, Hals, Rembrandt, Van Dyck, and also a series of English works by Reynolds, Romney, Hoppner, Constable, Turner, and Gainsborough. These latter included the celebrated *Duchess of Devonshire,* stolen from Agnew and recovered in Chicago before Morgan acquired it. He also owned a marvelous collection of miniatures: Holbein, Hilliard, Samuel Cooper, Richard Cosway, and Andrew Plimer.

Morgan became president of the Metropolitan Museum in 1904 and resolved to make it the home of one of the greatest collections of all time, on a par with the Vatican and other great European collections. However, the city of New York would not provide the buildings in which to house his collection. Therefore, although he brought his paintings over from London, where they had been kept until the American customs law was changed in 1909, when he died in 1913 most things passed to his son.

Benjamin Altman, although Morgan's almost exact contemporary, was very different. A recluse who hardly ever went to Europe, he bought mostly through Duveen, Knoedler, and Jacques Seligmann, a dealer in Paris. Like Frick, he collected Barbizon school pictures at first but then disposed of these and began collecting old masters. He was strongest on the northern schools, his Italian works were less good, and, like Morgan, he had little taste for primitives.

The Huntington family, Collis P., his wife, and his son Henry, also bought through Duveen, creating a first-rank collection, especially strong in Flemish and Italian works. P. A. B. Widener had a wider range. His

son Joseph inherited the collection in 1915 and was responsible for win-
nowing it down from about five hundred paintings to the hundred or so
which were eventually given to the National Gallery in Washington. The
Wideners also began with the Barbizon school, turning to old masters
only later. According to one servant, the Duveen vans would arrive
weekly at the Widener house, laden with all manner of objects. The
family home, Lynnewood Hall, was superbly decorated, its chief feature
being a passage gallery occupied solely by Bellini's *Feast of the Gods.*

Samuel Kress created not one, but two, collections, in each case with a
different idea in mind. The pictures which hung in his New York apartment were almost entirely Italian. He was "helped" initially by rather
unscrupulous dealers and what he bought was not very good. Then he
took advice and acquired steadily better works for which he often liked
to have certificates of authenticity. Finally, but only after Morgan died,
did he consent to buy through Duveen. Kress's collection, which consisted of 375 paintings and 16 sculptures, was entirely Italian and contained works by Duccio, Giotto, Fra Angelico, Botticelli, Piero della
Francesca, Bellini, Giorgione *(Adoration of the Shepherds),* Titian, Raphael,
and Tintoretto. Much of this collection came from Britain.

The other Kress collection was put together much later, after 1939
when the Kress Foundation was established. The aim here was to buy
works and place them in eighteen museums around the country, usually
in cities where the Kress five-and-ten-cent stores had branches. Italian
pictures still dominated the Kress collections but French and Flemish
works were now admitted. Kress's collection was possibly the largest
ever formed by one man and surely few people can ever have seen it in
its entirety.

Frick apart, the last of the megamillionaire collectors was Andrew Mellon. Mellon and Frick had similar origins and their collections, to begin
with at least, seem to have had similar aims. In the end, however, they
developed very differently. Both were from Pittsburgh. They were
friends and business partners as young men and both derived their
wealth from the steel industry that made Pittsburgh what it was. At the
age of twenty-one, Frick, in partnership with his two cousins, founded
Frick and Company for the manufacture of coke, a product distilled from
coal used in the manufacture of steel. The Frick company became a major
supplier to the Pittsburgh steel industry and in order to expand his company Frick borrowed money from a relatively new bank, Thomas Mellon
and Sons. Frick's second request for a loan prompted Judge Mellon to
investigate the firm and its prospects. The report submitted is revealing
about Frick. Part of it read: "Lands good, ovens well built; manager on
job all day, keeps books evenings, may be a little too enthusiastic about

pictures but not enough to hurt; knows his business down to the ground; advise making the loan."

The Mellons were not the types to be put off by this first indication of Frick's interest in art. At the age of thirty and having made his first million, Frick set off on a tour of Europe with his friend Andrew Mellon, the son of the judge. For each man it was to be an important event, leading indirectly to the creation of both the Frick Collection and the National Gallery of Art in Washington. On that trip, as on later ones, they were both very impressed by the Wallace Collection in London and Frick himself set out to emulate the same kind of atmosphere in his own collection (some would say he surpassed it). Mellon did not go that far but it seems that Wallace's taste in Dutch seventeenth-century and English eighteenth-century art accorded with Mellon's preferences, too.

Mellon was like several other American collectors in that he discarded much of what he had bought early on. Of Scottish descent, he was very canny and used only a small number of dealers, Duveen and Knoedler included. He would have a picture hang in his Washington apartment for weeks to be sure that he liked it. Early on, for example, he refused to buy a Raphael because it did not give him pleasure.

All this made his collection a highly personal one, but then he was clearly a most singular man. His plans for the creation of the National Gallery in Washington date from 1927 but were probably gestating for some time before that. By then he was well aware of Frick's plans for *his* collection and he had seen what others among the "magnificent seven" had done. Once he had made up his mind about the gallery, Mellon's collecting increased as he tried to form a collection representative of painting from the thirteenth century to the early nineteenth. Among his greatest acquisitions was a marvelous *Nativity with Saints* by Duccio, part of the predella (the bottom strip of an altarpiece) of the great *Maestà* in Siena, which he secured by exchange with the Kaiser Friedrich Museum for a German panel which Hitler wanted back.

But Mellon's greatest and most controversial coup was his acquisition of no fewer than twenty-one masterpieces from the Hermitage in Leningrad in 1930. By the spring of 1930 the strains of the first Five-Year Plan and collectivization in Soviet Russia were beginning to show. In desperate secrecy, and after a decade of denying that they would ever sell off any of their masterpieces for ready cash, the Russians finally decided that some art had to go in order to finance the state. Russia was especially rich in painting, mainly as a result of the acquisitions of Catherine the Great. The Russians had already been selling off antiques and jewelry (hundreds of tons per month) to alleviate their enormous troubles but the paintings were different. They would attract far more attention and highlight the fact that collectivization was not working. Hence the secrecy on the Russian side.

The need for secrecy on Mellon's behalf was equally urgent. In 1930 Mellon was seventy-five and one of the most powerful men in America. He had been Secretary of the Treasury since 1921 and, according to one wit, "had three presidents serve under him." That was part of the problem. By that time Mellon had controlling stock interests not only in his banks but in an enormous number of other large and important companies: Aluminum Company of America, Gulf Oil, the Union Steel Company, the Standard Steel Car Company, and the New York Shipbuilding Company. This brought widespread and continual criticism of the man and his policies for the perceived conflict of interest. This was made much worse when Mellon's policies were seen to be at least partly responsible for the stock market crash in 1929 and the Great Depression which followed. For Mellon to press ahead and spend millions of dollars on art when so many of America's poor were starving, and for a government official to deal with Communist Russia, a government that was not even recognized officially, would obviously look very bad if it had got out. More, the Russians were in effect "dumping" art on the market in much the same way that they were dumping other things at low prices, a practice which was putting Americans out of work. What Mellon planned to do was not so much illegal as deeply, deeply distasteful.

The deal was handled with great secrecy at the New York end by Charles Henschel, the grandson of the founder of Knoedler. In April 1930 twenty-five paintings left Russia, twenty-one of them for Mellon. They included five Rembrandts, four Van Dycks, two Raphaels, a Botticelli, a Rubens, a Titian, a Velázquez, and Veronese's *The Finding of Moses.*

This fabulous deal, worth more than $6 million at the time, and nearer $150 million now, was consummated by June 1930 but it was not announced for five years. Mellon denied it every time the rumor surfaced. The reason was still the same: he continued to be very unpopular in some circles. Worse, in 1931 impeachment proceedings for conflict of interest were begun against him in Congress. Mellon's response was to resign. The impeachment proceedings were dropped but now the tax authorities turned on him, charging that he had failed to pay more than $3 million in taxes due for 1931. Part of Mellon's defense, in a sensational court case which took place in March 1935, was that he had set up a charitable trust and donated his paintings to the trust, thus making him eligible for certain tax breaks which the Internal Revenue Service had not taken into account. Among the witnesses at the trial, which centered partly on the value of art, was Henschel of Knoedler and Duveen.

The result of the trial was a draw: the tax liability was settled out of court but it was accepted that Mellon *had* intended to create a National Gallery in which the Hermitage paintings would feature as one of the main attractions. But before that Mellon had died. It is curious that one of America's most distinguished galleries should have had such a controversial beginning.

Since that time works of art have continued to pour into America, from Europe and all over the world. But with Mellon's death the golden age of the magnificent seven came to an end.

VI

NEW
YORK

21.
Roger Fry and
the Art Historians

From the sixteenth to the nineteenth century, art history as a discipline had been an informal activity, virtually indistinguishable from connoisseurship or even from the practice of art itself. Vasari was an art historian as well as a painter. In his sparring with Lodovico Dolce he both recorded the history of art and discussed its theory. Giovanni Pietro Bellori, Christina's librarian, wrote art history through the lives of the great painters of his day. Crozat helped finance and publish the first important art history book, Dubois de St. Gelais's catalog of the Orléans collection —the cataloging method was itself an advance. Winckelmann was probably the first *systematic* scholar on a grand scale. But Jean Baptiste Pierre Lebrun, besides being curator of the Orléans gallery, was a "rediscoverer" of forgotten painters and therefore an art historian of almost equal importance since by his discoveries he, like Winckelmann, changed our attitudes to the past.

After the French Revolution, because so much great art was changing hands, a number of Englishmen—scholars and dealers—began to record this movement. Thus the works of Buchanan, Bryan, Westmacott, and Waagen, a German who traveled widely in Britain looking at the collections, mark the first time that art history became popular. In turn, this meant that general books about it were worth printing.

In the nineteenth century, John Ruskin straddled both art history and art criticism, adopting a role as close to Vasari as any of his other predecessors. Ruskin could afford to travel widely and in 1840 he met Turner, who so impressed him that he made him the star of his most influential book, *Modern Painters*. (The echo with Vasari is repeated here, to the extent that Ruskin's close links with Turner paralleled Vasari's with Michelangelo.) Ruskin's career had its ups and downs. But his importance lay in his influence. In the English-speaking world at least, art history and art criticism were accepted after him as they had never been before—this was true even though he died insane.

Art history as we know it today, however, really began in the nineteenth century. The great dispersals of art throughout Europe and America and the high prices that were at stake meant that the *authentication* and *provenance* of a work of art took on an added importance. It was as a result of this that Giovanni Morelli became the first of two brilliant personalities to revolutionize art history and give it its modern flavor.

Born in 1816 in Verona, Morelli trained as a doctor and also became a politician. He was quite old, over seventy, when his art books began to appear in the 1890s, but when they did they changed the face of art history. Morelli maintained and set out to prove that the smallest details in a painting—the hands, the ears, the joints—are what matter in deciding whether a painting is genuine or not. He maintained that these tiny details, because they *are* details, show a consistency within each artist's oeuvre. And because the details are so tiny the painter could not help but reveal himself unconsciously in them: they constitute in other words a kind of signature which is very difficult to forge. (This was the era when Freud was making his discoveries about the unconscious.) As a result of Morelli's work, many famous masterpieces in museums had to be relabeled, including no fewer than forty-six in Dresden.

Other founding figures of art history, who concentrated on *historical* research, included Aby Warburg, Heinrich Wölfflin, and Jakob Burkhardt, but the other man who, with Morelli, really introduced a new approach, was Bernard Berenson.

Strictly speaking, Berenson was a connoisseur, connoisseurship being but one branch of art history. In 1895, during an exhibition of Venetian art in London, Berenson published a pamphlet which asserted confidently that the exhibition positively teemed with attributions that were either blatantly wrong or greatly overexalted. A bitter controversy ensued but the young art historian who had dared to publish the pamphlet was in general vindicated and he was set on the road to fame and fortune as the most celebrated art historian of modern times.

Berenson, "BB", was born in eastern Europe but his parents had emigrated to Boston and he was educated at Harvard. There he made some important friendships, among them Isabella Stewart Gardner, who helped him financially so that he was able to travel to Europe and look at paintings. The impact of his Venetian pamphlet was such that within five years he was able to establish himself at I Tatti, his villa outside Florence, where he remained until he died and which he left to Harvard. For years Berenson roamed over Italy. Using his own version of Morelli's method, he was able to bring a new confidence to the attribution of many important pictures. It was through Berenson that the practice of naming painters "Master of this . . ." or "Master of that . . ." became widespread. Hitherto it had been the practice to group as many pictures as possible under the rubric of known masters but Berenson and others like him at the turn of the century were no longer content with this. If they could discern a fresh and individualistic hand they said so and if there was no name to attach the hand to they called him "Master of . . ." and added on some trait, or place, or other detail that *was* known. Thus through Berenson we now have the Master of the Bambino Vispo *(Lively Christ Child)* after a painting with a wriggling baby in it, or the Master of the Castello Nativity, a painter who executed a Nativity that was once in the town of Castello. And so on.

Berenson married Mary Pearsall Smith, sister of the writer Logan. She was as much of a personality as he, and through her BB became a member of an elite social/intellectual group that included such figures as Henry James, Oscar Wilde, and Bertrand Russell, in its wide-ranging ambit. If Berenson was the most conspicuous art historian of that first generation, he was by no means the only one or, in the long run, necessarily the best. As Denys Sutton, the then editor of *Apollo,* put it, this was a time which saw "the rise of the connoisseurship of early Italian painting and a gifted generation now began to sort out the different personalities of this School. . . . It was the start of the age when the great international art dealers—the Sedelmeyers, Duveens, Agnews, Seligmans and Wildensteins—engaged in sharp competition for the acquisition of important pieces, and, correspondingly, it proved a favourable moment for the expert, who could make, or break, an attribution."

The importance of the expert was not only his aesthetic sensibility but his detailed knowledge of collections and collectors around the world, so that if an American had a gap that he felt like filling, the expert would know exactly where to look. Berenson apart, one of the most formidable other art historians was Wilhelm von Bode, director of the Kaiser Friedrich Museum in Berlin and a man who, in his way, was equally impressive. Bode had an incredibly wide learning and an unrivaled knowledge of private, especially English, collections. His memory was excellent and this enabled him to enrich his museum magnificently: whenever anything came on the market, Bode knew about it and was ready with an offer. Bode's long-term importance lay in his belief that artists from north of the Alps equaled, if not outweighed, those from Italy. This was, if not new, an unusual view of art at the time, and it was very influential. He also researched Italian sculpture and Rembrandt. Bode taught many men who went on to run museums themselves so his tastes lasted and may be seen in many European galleries today, especially in Germany.

Besides some remarkable acquisitions, including several pictures from Lord Francis Pelham Clinton Hope, Bode expanded the Berlin museums, developing a new style of presentation, in which more attention was paid to the framing and presentation of pictures. Under him all pictures were

not treated as equal: the more important ones were given greater prominence.

Apart from a rise in the number of first-rate scholars, another sign that
art history as a discipline was developing, was the publication of a number of new journals. It was now that the *Jahrbuche* of the Vienna and
Berlin Museums appeared, publishing scholarly analyses and descriptions
of recent acquisitions and other, more general, articles. In France in 1859
the *Gazette des Beaux-Arts* appeared and in Italy *L'Arte* was published. In
London in 1903 there appeared what was to become the most influential
journal of all. Though it had a far from easy birth, the *Burlington Maga-*
zine was to become the house journal for art historians, the bulletin board
where all serious art books aspired to be reviewed and, more important,
where every scholar of note who "rediscovered" a "lost" painting would
make the announcement.

Berenson was on the editorial board of the *Burlington* from its incep-
tion. So was Roger Fry, another art critic and historian, an Englishman
who wrote better than Berenson. Fry could have become as great an
authority on Italian art as BB but he preferred to be more a leader of
taste. Later on, he was the chief champion of Impressionist art in Britain.
And Fry was the man who advised Henry Frick to buy *Wisdom and*
Strength.

The Frys are a distinguished Quaker family in Britain, related to the
famous Bristol chocolate-making Frys. Fry was born in 1866, the son of
Sir Edward Fry, a lawyer and later a judge. Roger was brought up with
five sisters in an authoritarian household and was rather relieved to be
sent away to school. After attending Clifton College in Bristol, he won an
exhibition at King's College, Cambridge, to read biology. Early on, however, he determined to change his studies and to follow art.

At Cambridge he made a number of influential friends, including Ferdinand Schiller, Lowes Dickinson, and Edward Carpenter, and he was
elected to the Apostles, the Cambridge secret society that numbered so
many brilliant men among its members. By the time he graduated, Fry
was set on becoming a painter and he traveled in Italy and France. He
encountered Impressionism early on in his travels but it was the old
masters who first attracted him, Italian old masters particularly and, chief
among them, the Venetians.

Back in England, Fry made two moves decisive in his life. First, he fell
in love and married Helen Coombs, a fellow artist. They were very
happy but, before long, Helen would show signs of the mental illness
that was to hamper both their lives severely. And second, Fry began to
write. All his life, he followed two careers, one as a painter and the other
as a writer and theoretician about art. His paintings, though charming,

never have quite the immediacy or appeal of a true master; they are not derivative but show clearly the influence of the various innovations Fry was to approve, Impressionism mainly and Cézanne in particular. His writing, however—the range of subjects he wrote about and the enthusiasm he stimulated in himself and in others—has had an enduring appeal. It was in this capacity that he influenced Frick to buy *Wisdom and Strength.*

Early on Fry wrote a book about Giovanni Bellini, a work so successful that it gained him a regular slot writing about art for the *Pilot* magazine, a London-based periodical. At that time far less was known about painters than is the case now and so Fry's book was actually more original than might appear. The next book he planned was one on Veronese: the publishers even announced it. At this time, Veronese seems to have been Fry's favorite artist. In a letter to his mother from Venice, written in May 1891, he writes: "The paintings are all I expected and more; of course I knew Titian and Paolo Veronese to some extent before, much more than I knew Tintoretto, and knew that they were both very great painters. If one must compare, then I think I should say that Paolo Veronese was the greatest painter so far as technique and purely pictorial things go. Titian is the greatest man." But the book on Veronese never appeared.

Already Fry was drawn to more modern painters. In 1895, for instance, he journeyed to Giverny in France, where Monet lived. But it was Fry's writing on Italian art that was his main concern at this stage. It was on this basis that he was invited to join the *Athenaeum,* a journal with a much greater following and more prestige than the *Pilot.* He was also invited to participate in the consultative committee for the *Burlington Magazine,* which was founded in March 1903. He joined a distinguished group of men which included Lord Dillon, the Earl of Crawford and Balcarres, Sir Sydney Colvin, Sir Herbert Cook, Charles Eliot Norton of Harvard, and Bernard Berenson.

Fry and Berenson came to know each other very well though they fell out later (Berenson fell out with almost everybody sooner or later). Given his interests, Impressionism and modern art, Fry was perhaps bound to fall behind on Italian painting at some stage; but in the early years of their friendship Fry was just as sharp as Berenson was, his connoisseurship aided by his activities as a restorer. Fry helped to restore the Mantegnas in the Royal Collection at Hampton Court and Van Eyck's *St. Francis Receiving the Stigmata,* now in the J. G. Johnson Collection in Philadelphia. Several attributions of well-known pictures, such as Sassetta's *Journey of the Magi* in the Metropolitan Museum, are also Fry's.

In 1904 Fry's life changed again when he met William Laffan, an American journalist and collector who was also a friend of J. P. Morgan. It was at Laffan's instigation that Fry was asked to cross to New York to try to secure funds to help ensure the *Burlington*'s continued survival. During that trip Fry met Morgan and a new plan was floated: for Fry to become assistant curator of the Met. This nearly foundered for by then Fry's reputation was such that he was also offered the directorship of London's National Gallery by the Liberal Prime Minister Campbell-Bannerman—at the time, a much more prestigious job. But Fry would not go back on his word to Morgan.

Fry was never entirely happy in New York. Helen had remained behind in England, the threat of her illness, which recurred from time to time with increasing severity, hanging over them. Nevertheless, even though he was only there for two years, Fry's achievements in America were considerable. He extended the Met's collection and rearranged the galleries. Among the acquisitions he made were Goya's *Don Sebastian Martinez,* Giovanni di Paolo's *Paradise,* and Holbein's *Portrait of Benedikt von Hertenstein.* In general Fry's acquisitions were welcomed though he was criticized for what was seen as his neglect of native American painters. Although he resigned from the Met after two years, Fry stayed on at the museum as an adviser until 1910, during which time he helped the museum acquire still more works, including Renoir's *La Famille Charpentier* and Whistler's *Arrangement in Flesh Color and Black: Portrait of Théodore Duret.* Already, therefore, before *Wisdom and Strength* ever came on to the market, Fry had had a definite influence on the old masters to be seen in New York.

While he had been assistant director, Fry's contract had enabled him to spend six months a year in Europe looking for paintings. So he never lost touch completely with what was going on in England: indeed, he was in the thick of it. He became a member of that group of writers, artists, and intellectuals that has come to be known as the Bloomsbury group. He first became friendly with Clive and Vanessa Bell, the latter being Virginia Woolf's sister. So friendly were these three that Vanessa Bell and Fry had an affair with Clive Bell's full knowledge. Hardly Quaker behavior. Through them Fry got to know his fellow painter, Duncan Grant. He portrayed Lytton Strachey and, briefly, enjoyed yet another affair, this one with Lady Ottoline Morrell. And of course he met all the other members of the group: E. M. Forster, John Maynard Keynes, Desmond MacCarthy.

Fry's membership of the Bloomsbury group, and in particular his friendship with the Bells, helped to nurture his interest in modern painting. The years 1910–12 were a turning point for him, and for modern painting in Britain, for by that time there was considerable curiosity being entertained about modern French art.

It was now that Fry conceived of and organized the show that was to make him truly famous. This was the "imposing and impressive" exhibition "Manet and the Post-Impressionists," which he mounted at the Grafton Galleries between November 8, 1910, and January 15, 1911. Among the 154 items on show were 8 Manets, 21 Cézannes, 20 Van Goghs, 37 Gauguins, 9 Vlamincks, 3 Derains, 6 Roualts, and 2 Picassos. The show sparked great hostility among the old guard and many of Fry's followers were astonished to find that the cultivated commentator on the old masters had "gone over to the other side."

Despite this initial hostility, however, the show, and a second like it in 1912, had a profound influence on taste in England. From then on Fry championed modern art, and not just French modern art. He arranged shows for Augustus John, Wyndham Lewis, William Rothenstein, among others. Like Rudolf, the regent, and Thomas Hope, Fry saw no dichotomy between the arts of the different ages and indeed wrote more than once of Cézanne's debt to the old masters, Veronese among them.

From then on, Fry echoed Thomas Hope especially and tried to marry the arts of the ancients with the arts of the moderns. To begin with this was simply getting the strange new art accepted but later, in his Omega workshops, he tried hard to have artists adapt their "pure" art to the design of everyday objects, utensils, and furniture. Omega never really caught on but Fry's battle for modern art was a resounding success.

However, at the very time he was organizing his post-Impressionist exhibition in London, Fry was also busy acquiring old masters for another American collector. In the first instance, in April 1910, Fry traveled to Poland to acquire a very distinguished Rembrandt, the *Polish Rider,* for Henry Frick.† Fry had known Frick since 1906 when he raised money from him to help the *Burlington.* He had also dealt with Knoedler, Frick's dealers, who had approached Fry the same year in his capacity as a curator at the Met with Frans Hals's *Portrait of a Painter,* which eventually found its way to Frick. Fry therefore had a reputation and in London he was half way from America to Poland. Not that Fry seemed overly familiar with Frick as he left for Poland, as he wrote to his mother:

> Just now I have to go to Poland to buy for Mr. Frick a very important picture. Please don't say anything about this yet. The picture is so important that when it becomes known it will create great excitement. The whole business came upon me very suddenly and I have, I hope, transacted the affair satisfactorily. The owner is a rather stupid country gentleman [Count Tarnowski] who insists on selling the picture in his chateau; that's why I have to go and get it, as I

† The authenticity of this picture has recently been doubted by the Rembrandt Research Project in Amsterdam.

must see it before buying. The picture costs £60,000, so it is an important affair. It's tiresome and rather hateful work but I couldn't refuse to do it. I hope Mr. Frick will be more decent to me than his fellow millionaires.

When Fry said that he "couldn't refuse to do it," he was not speaking here of any special obligation to Frick but of the fact that his financial resources were very low at that point, since his regular income from the Metropolitan Museum had ceased. And whatever he was paid by Frick for his journey to Poland, the man certainly seems to have been "more decent" than other millionaires. Less than a year later, Fry was working for Frick again.

Knoedler had dealt with Frick for many years since Frick was one of the Americans who did not immediately fall for Duveen. So they may have offered him the Veroneses which Agnew had bought from Lord Francis Pelham Clinton Hope without Fry's intervention. But as it happened, it was Fry who first drew Frick's attention to them. Later on, Fry's enthusiasm for Veronese waned. In 1929, for instance, on one of his trips to Venice, he wrote in a letter:

> We went this morning to St. Sebastiano, a little church right on the outside of the town to the west where hardly anyone goes. I hadn't been except once in extreme youth and I was astonished to find anything to complete and perfect. Built by J. Sansovino so that the building has a certain Florentine *tenue,* very refreshing after the rather sloppy magnificence and exhuberance of the Venetians. The inside is painted almost all over like a casket by Veronese—ceilings, walls, organ shutters, organ case, sacristy ceiling, in fact wherever he could put either an oil painting or a fresco. And it was evidently a kind of pious devotion. For all is *soigné* and exquisitely delicate and sensitive, some of his very finest things and such adorable decorative settings, great swags of ivory white-grey with deep bronze medallions, then golden brown monochrome and leading up at central points to the full Venetian chord of blues and reds. . . .
>
> I forgot, at Sebastiano there was one very late Titian which somehow knocked all Veronese's loveliness a little silly. It was so tremendously *important.*

But, in 1911, Fry had no hesitation in recommending to Frick that he snap up the two Veroneses that had become available from the Newcastle family. Having been acquired in 1911 for £11,000 (approximately $1.5 million) with Agnew, Colnaghi, and Knoedler each taking a one-third share, Frick bought them in 1912 for $220,000. This is a quite normal markup for art dealers, and is in any case not quite so large as it seems since, at the time, there were roughly five dollars to the pound. Even so it was a tidy profit, though presumably Fry was paid something for his advice, either by Knoedler or by Frick.

And so, in 1912, *Wisdom and Strength,* accompanied as it had always been by *Vice and Virtue,* made its last but one physical move. Knoedler's had then just bought a new set of premises at 556 Fifth Avenue. This was the old Lotos Club at Sixty-sixth Street. The Veroneses therefore moved just a few doors up Fifth Avenue to where Frick lived temporarily at 640 Fifth. A year later, the paintings moved to their final home on Seventieth Street and Fifth Avenue. It was probably the shortest and most uneventful journey they had ever made.

Henry Frick's "Paradise"

Henry Clay Frick's interest in art is not easily explained. Born in 1849, he came from a rural part of southwestern Pennsylvania, the son of John W. Frick, a farmer. Frick senior was a fourth generation American, whose ancestors had emigrated from Switzerland and followed William Penn in search of religious freedom. Before that the Frick family was of Celtic-Burgundian origins and could be traced back for generations.

Frick, who was always called Clay, even as a boy, received little formal education. He started work very young, as a clerk for his two uncles and as a bookkeeper for his mother's father, Abraham Overholt, who was a flour merchant and a whiskey distiller. The earliest clue we have to Frick as an art collector is the fact that, even as a young man, he was a fastidious dresser, a boy who borrowed money for new suits and dressed himself from the age of fifteen. All of which suggests an interest in aesthetics.

But Frick was not a fop, far from it. He was always determined to make a million by the time he was thirty and one way to do this was suggested by his cousin Abraham Tintsman, who was much older than he and the manager of the family distillery. Tintsman believed that the coal on the family land could be made into more profitable coke. Tintsman never acted on his dream, but Frick did. When he was just twenty-one, he bought 123 acres, borrowing most of the money from within the family. That got him the land but no working capital. His next move was the start of the Frick legend for he took a train to Pittsburgh and went to see Judge Thomas Mellon. Frick asked Mellon for a loan of $50,000, a sizable sum in those days, the more so for a young man. He got what he asked for, though, partly because he promised to pay back at what was then the very high rate of 10 percent but mainly because he said that with the money he planned to build fifty coke ovens. Mellon shared Frick's belief in the future of steel. Before the year was out Frick was back in Pittsburgh to see Mellon again: he wanted yet more money to build another fifty ovens. Mellon was inclined to give it to him but felt it would be prudent to send someone up to Bradford, where the Frick land was, to scout out the conditions. This led to the famous report, already mentioned, which noted his enthusiasm for paintings but even so advised making the loan.

From then on Frick never looked back. Both borrowings were paid off within two years and he was on his way to earning his first million well before he was thirty. From the start Frick showed the resourcefulness and the stubbornness that were to make him famous. In 1873–74, for instance, when he was still in his middle twenties, the economy took a serious turn for the worse. Wall Street panicked; Frick did not. With proper money hard to come by, he printed his own. That is to say he printed certificates that could be redeemed at his company store. It tied people to him but in times of hardship it guaranteed that people could eat and it made him popular.

Frick made much more than a million by the time he was thirty. On his thirtieth birthday, he had one thousand employees, shipped nearly a hundred carloads of coke every day, and possessed the capacity to produce 80 percent of the coke needs of the entire steel industry in the region. His genius for management was so widely recognized that, in 1889, when he was forty, the Carnegies brought him into their firm as the man who could reorganize the steel business. Frick became company chairman and acquired a 2 percent interest to begin with. Over the next few years his interest would rise to 11 percent, a notable achievement. By 1891, Frick was in control of the greatest steel company and the largest coke company in the world.

Then the Homestead strike took place.

This single episode, more than anything else, gives a vivid picture of the sort of man Frick was. The Homestead strike, in Homestead, Pennsylvania, took place in 1892, an election year, but the seeds lay in a wage settlement made between the Carnegie management and the Amalgamated Association of Iron and Steel Workers in 1889. Before that time there was no relationship between pay and skill or between pay and output, with the result that unskilled men were sometimes earning from five to ten times the amount received by trained mechanics. The union accepted that some financial restructuring was necessary and fair but refused to go along with other changes which the management wanted to introduce at the same time.

So obdurate was the union that the Carnegie management requested protection from the civil authorities. The sheriff agreed and steamed up the river with a posse of a hundred men. Met by an even larger crowd of workers, the posse was unable to land. The sheriff retreated and the Carnegie management was forced to surrender.

The effect was disastrous. With the new wages they had to pay the men, but without the other changes they wished to introduce, the firm would be at great financial risk if the price of steel were to fall. This is exactly what happened between 1890 and 1892: dropping by more than a third. The firm started losing money heavily.

The next wage settlement fell due in 1892 and by then there had been two more significant changes: Frick had arrived as head of management and the work force had become even more politicized. One reason for this was that, of the thirty-eight hundred men in the factories, many were not native-born and did not speak English. They followed whatever leadership their union happened to have.

In May, Frick announced his new proposals to the union negotiators. They were not radically different from what anyone was used to but they included a reduction in earnings for the highest paid workers and, equally important, tied the pay of everyone to the prevailing price of steel. The union made counterproposals which were different, but not very different. Frick, however, took the view that the union's arithmetic did not work and in any case he was convinced that the company belonged to the management and not to the workers. Now was the time to be firm. He announced that, unless agreement was reached, he would be closing the mills on July 1 and reopening them five days later, unless prevented by force. His idea was that, in reopening, men would be taken on piecemeal on new contracts favorable to the company, breaking the force of the union. Since the area had a history of union power and violence, Frick must have known what to expect. He had simply taken a decision to force the issue.

The union's response was prompt and equally firm. It turned itself into a quasi-military outfit. Four thousand union men were organized into three watches, each of eight hours so that the company's premises were "guarded" all around the clock. The men were even given ranks, such as "commander" and "captain" and each captain had a certain part of the factories to guard. No management personnel, or sheriff's deputy, was allowed past the picket.

Frick had anticipated much of this. In advance, he had made inquiries of the Pinkerton security agency as to whether there would be enough men available to retake the factories by force. He was assured that there were. After dark, on the evening of July 5, three hundred Pinkerton guards were towed in barges up the river to Pittsburgh. Boxes with arms in them had already been placed on the barges. However, the military organization of the strikers was better than anyone thought: the barges were spotted, the steam whistles shrieked the alarm, and the men came scrambling from their beds. The Pinkerton men were met by a force of about a thousand. Firing broke out on both sides and the Pinkerton men were driven back. Oil was pumped onto the water and set alight. Eventually, the Pinkerton guards had no choice but to surrender. To begin with, the white flag with which the guards surrendered was riddled with bullets. But then they were allowed off the barges, which were set on fire. Although they had been promised safe passage away from Homestead, they were in fact made to run the gauntlet. The strikers and their families lined the streets and punched and kicked and robbed the men. Two men died and thirty were injured, one so badly that he committed suicide later.

Next day a state of siege was declared by the union leaders. The men had confiscated the weapons belonging to the Pinkerton guards, along with many rounds of ammunition. By now all the union wanted was official recognition, not more money. But this, Frick would not give, arguing that the forcible appropriation of the firm's property precluded any discussion whatever. At this point the Pennsylvania national guard was invoked and the state governor appeared at Homestead to say that he would spend whatever it took to get back the firm's property. Eight thousand men were sent to a military base nearby. Eight thousand trained national guardsmen could have massacred the four thousand untrained workers at the Homestead if it had come to a fight. But in fact the national guard repossessed the factories on July 12 without encountering any resistance. It was probably the first sensible move anyone took in the whole sorry epic.

The publicity which surrounded these events may be imagined. That the strikers took the law into their own hands cannot have made them many friends but neither was Frick's curt firmness calculated to make him popular. Two important consequences arose from the episode. The first occurred on July 23, more than a week after the troubles had subsided. On that day, a Saturday, a twenty-five-year-old Russian, Alexander Berkman, marched into Frick's office and shot him. The bullet pierced the lobe of Frick's ear, then entered his neck near the base of his skull and passed down between his shoulders. As Frick fell, Berkman fired a second bullet into the right side of his neck. A colleague of Frick's, who had been in the room with him, now tackled Berkman and prevented him from firing a third shot. But Berkman wrenched his left hand loose, slipped a dagger from his pocket and stabbed Frick three times, once in his hip, once in his right side, and the third time tearing open his left leg below the knee. By now Frick was bleeding profusely but still he managed to throw himself on Berkman and pin his assailant's arms to the floor. Then others arrived and the Russian was fully overpowered. Still, the drama was not over. As the sheriff arrived, Frick noticed that Berkman's jaws were working—he was chewing something. His mouth was forced open to reveal a capsule containing enough mercury fulminate to blow all those present to' eternity.

Frick was of course attended by doctors. But despite what had happened to him, he arranged for his sick wife to be informed of the events and dictated this telegram to his aged mother: "Was shot twice but not dangerously. H. C. Frick." The same wording was sent to Carnegie, who was abroad, with this addition: "There is no necessity for you to come home. I am still in shape to fight the battle out." Indeed he was. Patched up, Frick did not go to the hospital but finished the day's work, settling the details of a loan and signing several letters and documents. He was not allowed to go into work for some days after, but nonetheless had a telephone installed by his bed at home and his secretaries came to his house every day after the doctors had gone. He made it clear immediately that, despite his injuries, his attitudes had changed not one bit.

Finally, should there have been any doubts about Frick's strong constitution, they must have been dispelled eleven days later, on August 3. On that day his son, born less than four weeks before, died tragically and was buried twenty-four hours later. Frick spent the evening of that Thursday by the bed of his stricken wife and next morning rose early, took the open streetcar to the office, and started work at eight o'clock, as usual. Two weeks had still not elapsed since the assassination attempt. "Those who hate him most," wrote the New York *World,* "admire the nerve and stamina of this man of steel whom nothing seems able to move." Nor would he accept a bodyguard. "If an honest American cannot live in his own home without being surrounded by a bodyguard, it is time to quit." Clearly Frick did not intend to quit.

The second consequence of importance arising from the Homestead strike was not personal but political since 1892 was a national election year. Each of the two leading candidates, Harrison for the Republicans and Cleveland for the Democrats, was standing for a second term, with Harrison the incumbent. (Cleveland had been elected in 1884, had lost in 1888, and now was running again.) To make a long story short, aides of Harrison became involved in the Homestead saga, in a vain attempt to have the union recognized. It was unsuccessful and, in many people's eyes, was an attempt to treat with men who were rioters and assassins. It was hardly a wise move by the Harrison camp and Cleveland was elected by a landslide.

Frick never said anything and certainly apologized to no one. But Carnegie reflected the general view in a letter to Frick from Venice in which he confessed "that Homestead did much to elect Cleveland—very sorry —but no use getting scared."

Few people can be summed up so trenchantly and so well in one episode. But the Homestead strike shows that, compared with Rudolf, Christina, the regent, Égalité, the Hopes, and the Newcastles, Frick was straightforward and incredibly strong. Like them, though, his virtues were also his vices: he was firm but stubborn, single-minded but also obsessive.

That single-mindedness, however, does help explain why Frick was able to amass such a collection of great art at a time when there was so much competition from the other rich men of the day. Though his interest in art is not easily explained, Frick's love of painting was nevertheless genuine—it was within him from an early age. In his teens the walls of his rooms were covered with prints and sketches and some of his contemporaries recalled that once or twice he tried his hand with the brush. His interest in painting grew steadily and as his wealth increased his knowledge and judgment developed. Like many of his contemporaries, he was attracted at first to the French school. He seems to have begun collecting seriously in 1895, when he was forty-six and still living in Pittsburgh. He bought a number of pictures abroad, many of which he disposed of as his tastes changed. He learned quickly. Within three years, he had parted company with all but a few of his early Barbizon school acquisitions and bought seventy-one paintings which, according to his official biographer, were "fairly representative" of Rembrandt, Nattier, Hoppner, Reynolds, Watts, Corot, Daubigny, Rousseau, Alma-Tadema, Greuze, Monet, Bouguereau, and others.

Frick's collecting was, to an extent, bound up with his relationship with his other rich friends, especially Mellon and Carnegie. It was with Mellon that Frick had first traveled to Europe. Frick was not yet thirty and they were relaxing, learning French, getting to know Europe, and looking at art. For both of them the high spot on that and later trips was the Wallace Collection in London. Its combination of paintings, furniture, and carpets all laid out in a natural way in the house for which they had been intended appealed very much to both men and affected their aims for their own collections. The Frick Collection is very much in the spirit of the Wallace Collection.

Frick and Mellon met every Sunday morning to discuss art but they had much in common besides that. For example, they were both extremely taciturn. When they traveled abroad on their first trip to Europe, they advertised for and actually employed another young man, whom they took along "to do the talking."

The Frick Collection as it is now also owes something to Frick's relationship with the Carnegies. After Homestead, Frick had branched out. He took a dominating interest in the Oliver Mining Company, so they

could obtain high-grade Bessemer ore more cheaply; he built the Pittsburgh, Bessemer and Lake Erie Railroad so he could obtain transportation for the ore more cheaply. He bought a fleet of six steamships to
transport the ore more cheaply across the Great Lakes. Eventually, he
had created a company where, from the moment the crude ore was dug
from the earth until the finished steel was produced, not a single dollar's
profit or royalty was paid to anyone other than the Carnegie Steel Company. In doing so he transformed the profitability of the company. When
he took hold in 1889, its earning power was less than $2 million a year;
by 1899 it had reached $40 million.

In the process, however, Frick had become too big for Carnegie. Carnegie liked to spot brilliant young men and he got on better with them
than with his equals, which Frick now was. Moreover, whereas Carnegie
was dictatorial, Frick was stubborn and a clash was inevitable. It arrived
in 1899 in a classic manner, with a fight over the price the Carnegie
Company should pay for Frick coke. As a result, Carnegie attempted to
drum Frick out of the firm on terms which were so unfavorable and so
unfair to Frick that he was forced to take Carnegie to court. Once more,
the publicity was sensational. And, as usual in such cases, no one
emerged unscathed. Frick won far more than Carnegie wanted to give.
And he was still preeminent in his field. When, in 1901, negotiations
were opened for the formation of the United States Steel Corporation,
Frick was called in to negotiate with the Rockefeller interests for the
purchase of their large ore deposits and their Great Lakes steamers. But,
in a way, the sour Carnegie episode was the beginning of the end of one
phase in Frick's life. Within a few years he had given up the chairmanship
of his own company and had moved to New York, preferring to be close
to the financial activities of Wall Street and away from the industrial
heartland.

It suited his collecting too. Frick had wanted to house his paintings in
Pittsburgh but had been advised that the heavy smoke associated with
steel manufacture could damage them. This is the main reason why the
Frick Collection, formed by an industrial baron from Pittsburgh with
Pennsylvania steel money, is where it is now, on Seventieth Street and
Fifth Avenue in New York City. In New York, Frick at first leased a
former Vanderbilt house at 640 Fifth Avenue. The house at Seventieth
Street was built in 1913–14 on the site of what had been the Lenox
Library (now incorporated into the New York Public Library at Forty-
second Street and Fifth Avenue). Frick spent about $5 million on the
house (it would cost almost twenty times that now). By coincidence the
architect was Thomas Hastings of Carrère and Hastings, who were also

building the new public library. The sculpted decorations for the house were by the Piccirilli Brothers and most of the rest of the interior was the work of an English designer Sir Charles Allom, of the firm White Allom. The private rooms were done by Elsie de Wolfe.

After his early interest in Barbizon school painting, Frick next began to turn to English portraits and Dutch works of the seventeenth century. In 1901 he bought the first of several Turners, his first Vermeer, and a Monet landscape. During the next years he added a Hobbema, a Cuyp, a Ter Borch, and pictures by Lawrence, Reynolds, Romney, and Gainsborough. He bought El Greco's *St. Jerome* in 1905, the same year that he acquired Van Dyck's *Ottaviano Canevari* and Titian's *Pietro Aretino,* which was his first Italian Renaissance picture. The Vermeer and the El Greco show that Frick was not as conservative in his collecting habits as in other areas of his life: at that time only one other picture by these artists was in an American museum.

From then on, Frick's collecting took the following course:

1906	Rembrandt	*Self-portrait*
1907	Anonymous French	
	fifteenth century	*Pietà*
1908	Constable	*Salisbury Cathedral*
1909	El Greco	*Purification of the Temple*
	Van Dyck	*Frans and Margareta Snyders*
1910	Rembrandt	*The Polish Rider*
1911	Velázquez	*Philip IV of Spain*
	Vermeer	*Officer and Laughing Girl*
1912	Holbein the Younger	*Sir Thomas More*
	Veronese	*Wisdom and Strength*
		Vice and Virtue
1913	Van Dyck	*The Earl of Derby, His Wife and Child*
	El Greco	*Vincenzo Anastagi*

Each of these works was exceptional and the acquisitions established Frick as a major collector. The French *Pietà* was the first work which he bought on Fry's recommendation and shows that both men were alive to this type of painting at a time when its charms were only just being rediscovered. Apart from the Veroneses and *The Polish Rider,* Fry also advised Frick to buy the Holbein.

Frick was offered advice on all sides about which paintings to buy but always seems to have made up his own mind. He would hang works in his home for many months and he was nobody's fool when it came to price. There is in the Frick archive a celebrated letter which Frick wrote to Duveen:

New York
May 24, 1916

Dear Mr Duveen,

I wish you would make a complete list of everything
you have in my house "on approval." This to include all
articles (some of which, of course, you do not expect me to
purchase) and affix thereto the price of each, as I desire to
take up the matter with you very soon.

Let me caution you to be very careful in making up
your mind what you want to charge me for each article; I
will not pay extravagant prices. You are entitled to a good
profit—that I am willing to pay.

Frick's collection was formed much more with Knoedler's help than
with Duveen's but even with them he was no easy touch. On one occasion Charles Carstairs of Knoedler was in London and cabled excitedly to
Frick that he had just bought Constable's *Salisbury Cathedral* and Turner's
Mortlake. But Frick replied curtly, "Thanks, neither." He followed this
with a letter:

While I have the greatest confidence in your judgement, yet, having
two Turners, I would not care to purchase a third until after I have
seen it. The Constable I probably should have, but it seems to me
the price is very high.

The Fricks moved into the new house at Seventieth Street in 1914.
The house was specifically planned for Frick's pictures—the memory of
the Wallace Collection was still strong and this planning is why the house
has such superb proportions. That year, the year the First World War
broke out, Frick acquired a lot of new paintings, including three Goyas,
three Whistlers, two large Turners, Degas's *Rehearsal,* Manet's *Bullfight,*
and Renoir's *Mother and Children.* At this time his favorites, the pictures
he hung in his private rooms, were the Degas, the Monet, the El Greco's,
Purification of the Temple, and the Turners.

Toward the end of his life Frick added the "accoutrements" to his
collection: porcelain, Limoges enamel, and Renaissance bronzes. It
would appear that his tastes were still changing, still widening since there
exist a number of architectural drawings by Carrère and Hastings for
additional galleries to the east of the building, including a large two-
storied room designed specifically for sculpture. But in these years he
also acquired the series of Fragonard canvases called *The Progress of Love*
and the Boucher panels of *The Arts and Sciences.* His liking for Italian
Renaissance pictures was now firm, and he acquired Bellini's *St. Francis in
Ecstasy* and Titian's *Man in a Red Cap.* His last picture was his third

Vermeer, *Mistress and Maid,* which joined his list of favorites immediately.

Throughout his life Frick had suffered from inflammatory rheumatism and, on November 7, 1919, he became ill with ptomaine poisoning and a cold. He was allowed up by the nurse to "sit with my pictures" and the success of this appears to have given him the impression that he was better than he was. The next day he insisted on visiting his grandson. Exhaustion followed and the doctor was called. This man informed the family that he would no longer treat someone who disobeyed his instructions (both Frick and the doctor appear to have been stubborn on this occasion) and removed himself from the case. A replacement was found but he never gained Frick's confidence. Eleven days later he died.

Ever since Frick and Andrew Mellon had visited the Wallace Collection in London all those years previously, Henry Clay Frick had had it in mind to form a collection to leave to the nation. By the time he built the house on Seventieth Street the idea had coalesced. In a letter written during the First World War, Frick queried whether it was right for anyone to spend so much on art at such a time. But he answered his own question, justifying his actions because he was contemplating making a gift to the public.

This is exactly what he did. On his death he bequeathed in trust his residence and the paintings in it to establish a public gallery of art, "for the use and benefit of all persons whomsoever." It was Frick's wish that the collection should always be displayed in the way he had assembled it. For this reason, when one visits the house now, besides the works of art, one also finds fresh flowers in the rooms, ticking clocks, no display cases, and a minimum of restraining ropes. It is as near an ordinary house as it can safely be.

Unusually, Frick also left an endowment for the acquisition of further works. In his lifetime he had been unsuccessful a number of times in obtaining what he wanted, notably Holbein's portrait of *The Duchess of Milan,* Velázquez's *Portrait of Innocent X,* and the Donne Altarpiece by Hans Memling. The Trustees have therefore continued, where possible, to acquire works of a standard in keeping with Frick's own and the intervening years have seen added to the collection works by Duccio, Van Eyck, Piero della Francesca, Ingres, and others.

The house stayed more or less as Frick left it until Mrs. Frick died twelve years later, in 1931. Then a number of additions were made as he himself had intended (he had left money for this, too). The carriage court was built around and covered over to form an interior garden court. As designed by John Russell Pope, this brilliant idea gives the building today its unique feel. Two extra galleries, the Oval Room and the East Gallery, were added and a small assembly room where lectures, seminars, and concerts of chamber music are occasionally held. The building and rearrangement took four years and the Frick Collection opened to the public just before Christmas in 1935. Later Miss Helen Frick, Frick's daughter, established the Frick Art Reference Library, a collection of books, journals, and photographs in honor of her father. This is part of the same complex of buildings but has its own entrance at the other side of the block, on Seventy-first Street. Miss Frick died in 1984.

In 1949 the first catalog of the collection was published, with an introduction by Sir Osbert Sitwell. It was the author of the catalog who at first came to the conclusion that Albrecht, Duke of Bavaria, had owned *Wisdom and Strength* before Rudolf (see page 35ff. earlier). In joining the Frick collection, *Wisdom and Strength* renewed acquaintance with several names that have already featured in the narrative: Van Eyck, Titian *(Pietro Aretino)*, Van Dyck *(Portraits of Frans and Margareta Snyders)*, Boucher and Fragonard (a whole room to each, the former painted for Madame de Pompadour), Reynolds, Lawrence and Turner.

Of all the rooms in the house, the West Gallery, where *Wisdom and Strength* currently hangs, is the most impressive. According to the official account: "The West Gallery was planned from the start as an imposing setting for a major portion of the Collection, recalling the gallery of Hertford House (home of the Wallace Collection), those of English country houses, and ultimately the royal salons of the Renaissance and Baroque periods. . . . The grand scale of the West Gallery (96 × 33 feet) has permitted a fascinating juxtaposition of works of art in the manner Mr. Frick preferred: Corot alongside Hobbema, Rembrandt confronting Velázquez, Vermeer opposite Veronese. Renaissance bronzes and furniture, as well as the subtle, abstract designs of three Isfahan carpets, further enrich the gallery."

This is where, four hundred years on, after adventures unequaled in the world of art, *Wisdom and Strength* came to rest. For at least three reasons this was fitting. First, throughout its life Veronese's canvas has been typical of its time, its movement always reflecting the artistic fashions of the day. Who can doubt that North America, New York especially, is, in the twentieth century, the focus of artistic production and of much of the art trade just as Venice, Prague, Antwerp, Rome, Paris, and London were in their day? Second, it is only fitting that such a masterpiece should keep company with so many other great works. Third and last, where better to end your days than the place we all want to be? John

Canaday, a correspondent of the New York *Times,* fastened on to this when he was writing about the Frick Collection in 1981. For art lovers he was saying no more than the truth when he described the building and its contents at Seventieth Street and Fifth Avenue as "Paradise."

Epilogue

That is not the end of the story. Not quite. True, *Wisdom and Strength* has remained in the Frick Collection on Seventieth Street and Fifth Avenue where, to judge by photographs taken in the 1920s, it has occupied the same piece of wall for over half a century. However, since the painting was acquired by Frick in 1912 a number of echoes from the past have been heard again. Elements in the narrative—the great families, the splendid locations, the fabulous collections—have suffered dramatic changes of fortune. Some of these changes have been sad, others have involved pleasant surprises. They all keep alive the interest in *Wisdom and Strength,* each new development adding a fresh twist to the story, a new epilogue.

The sad sequels all involve the decline of the great dynasties encountered in these pages, the grand families who at one time were rich and powerful. The Odescalchi family, although they inhabit the Palazzo Odescalchi in Rome to this day, have gradually sold Don Livio's marvelous collections. The first to go were the statues, sold in 1724 to Philip V of Spain. Most of the drawings went in 1789, sold to the Teyler Foundation in Haarlem, where they have remained. Five years later the gem collection went to the Vatican. The decline has continued into modern times: latest to go were the remaining eight books of drawings for which Don Livio was particularly famous; they were sold for varying sums between 1950 and 1970.

The fate of the Hope collections was rather different. They were sold in one fell swoop at a mammoth eight-day event at Christie's in July 1917. Canova's masterpiece, *Venus,* was one of the stars and sold for £1,155. The portraits included Lawrence's painting of Mrs. Hope and Raphael's depiction of the engraver, Marc Antonio Raimundi, which fetched £4,515 (that would be a mere $361,000 now). The Egyptian sculptures and the famous Hamilton vases ran to twenty-three pages of illustrations in the catalogue. In all the sale realized £135,301 ($10,800,000 now).

Deepdene itself was sold in 1920, when it was bought by Surrey County Council and turned into offices. After the Second World War it changed hands again, passing to British Rail, who also used it as offices. When David Watkin was writing his book on Hope, from 1963 to 1965, to get permission to visit the house he had to telephone a BR official at Waterloo Station in London, who shared an office with the platform announcer. British Rail sold the house in 1969 to a property developer who demolished Deepdene and built more offices on the site.

The Newcastles soon followed the Hopes. The pictures and furniture from Clumber were sold at Christie's in July 1921. The treasures included some of the best Limoges, majolica and china to the value of £35,244, and several of Thomas Hope's pictures that had passed to Clumber. The ninth Duke of Newcastle, who sadly died in November 1988 after helping me research part of this book, wrote that the Newcastle archives had been deposited by his father, Francis, with the family's legal advisers. During the London Blitz of 1940, these premises took a direct hit and everything was destroyed, including portraits of Henrietta and Adele. Such records as remained passed to Nottingham University.

More happily, Queen Christina, who in her day was never entirely satisfied with her rank as a Queen without a realm, was accorded a singular and, some may think, rather grisly honor in 1965. Chosen as the subject for a Council of Europe exhibition, as a "personality of European culture," her sarcophagus in the Vatican was opened and a cast of her silver death mask was taken for exhibition. The Queen would probably have been much happier with her standing in posterity's eyes than in those of her own day.

So too with the Orléans family. Despite the futility of Égalité's career and his execution, Louis-Philippe, his son and the regent's great-great grandson, became the Citizen King of France in 1830. Égalité's extraordinary personality extended its influence even after his execution. In 1823 an Italian woman named Maria Stella arrived in Paris with the strangest of stories. She claimed to have received a letter from her father, one Lorenzo Chiappini, after his death, which said that she was in fact the daughter of Égalité and his duchess, Marie Adélaïde de Penthièvre. The story was that Égalité had so desired a male heir that he had taken his wife to Italy, to the small town of Modigliani, and there befriended a local jailer. The jailer's wife was at the same stage of pregnancy as the duchess and it was agreed between the two men that if Égalité's wife gave birth to a daughter and the jailer's wife to a son a swap would be made. Maria Stella, who made a brilliant marriage for a peasant girl and who was supposed by some to bear a striking resemblance to the Orléans family, spent several years trying to prove her claim that such an exchange had been made. In France she was regarded by many as mad but the British Peerage refers to her as the "presumed daughter of the Duke of Orléans." She died in 1843, five years before Louis-Philippe's reign came to an end.

Under Louis-Philippe another account of the collections of the Palais Royal was drawn up, in 1823, also by Vatout. This ran to four volumes and described 278 portraits. But although most of the Orléans family was portrayed, along with the French Kings, Queens, and mistresses, including Christina and Rosalba, the quality of these pictures is disappointing.

There have been a number of pleasant surprises involving the discoveries of works of art associated with *Wisdom and Strength*. The Boucher copies turned up in 1929, the Marquis of Bute's in 1971, and the Russian drawing of the cherub at the foot of the painting was discovered at the Moldavian museum Kishinev in April 1973. Sotheby's, now more of a rival to Christie's than Phillips, sold a copy of *Wisdom and Strength* in October 1965 and a second copy turned up in the same saleroom in June 1984.

But by far the happiest and most extraordinary sequel to the biography of *Wisdom and Strength* took place in 1962. In that year the Czechoslovakia Academy of Sciences was allowed access for the first time to make a comprehensive study of Prague Castle, "with a view to full restoration and adaptation to present-day requirements." The director of this project was Dr. Jaromír Neumann, who, with his colleagues, "came face-to-face" with material that had been locked away for centuries. To his astonishment, Neumann found that "the celebrated collections amassed in the sixteenth and seventeenth centuries by Emperor Rudolf II, King of Bohemia, and later rulers had not entirely disappeared in spite of repeated ransacking, sales, removals and auctions." Masterpieces, sometimes heavily overpainted, by such artists as Titian, Tintoretto, Rubens, Hans von Aachen, Pordenone, and Palma Giovane were all discovered, including three Veroneses.

Subsequent research showed that one of the pictures was a *Portrait of the Goldsmith Jakop Kinig*. Kinig's son, König von Königsfeld, was chamberlain to Rudolf II, so the picture must have found its way to Prague Castle at that time where it had formed part of the Emperor's collection with *Wisdom and Strength* and the other Veroneses. Some of the other pictures found at Prague, it turned out, had been acquired by the Archduke Leopold William, who had bought the collection of the Duke of Buckingham at Antwerp in 1648. In other words, these were some of the paintings which Queen Christina had seen in the course of her journey South. Late in 1975 Rudolf's coffin was opened, as Christina's had been before, and the brown-gold silk and velvet clothes in which he had been buried were removed and restored.

Following these discoveries and developments, Prague Castle was renovated and six rooms used to recreate, as far as possible, the "feel" of Rudolf's great collections. There, in Rudolf's stables, one floor below what used to be the New Hall, the center of the Emperor's Art Cabinet, the great Venetian works of Titian, Tintoretto, and Veronese are now displayed. From that time, too, Rudolf II has merited more attention from historians. This culminated in 1988 with the publication by Dr. Thomas DaCosta Kaufmann of *The School of Prague,* a complete catalog *raisonné* of the paintings at Rudolf's court. In the same year an exhibit, "Prague Around 1600: Art and Culture at the Court of Rudolf II" opened in Essen and continued in Vienna until 1989. Thus the crisscrossing of the different elements in the story, which have been such a feature of it in the past four hundred years, thus continues through today. The beginning of the narrative almost becomes the ending.

Almost, but not quite. Finally, in 1988, at a conference in Venice to mark the four-hundredth anniversary of Veronese's death, Klara Garas, formerly Director of the National Gallery of Hungary, again addressed the thorny question of whether *Wisdom and Strength* was commissioned by Albrecht or Rudolf. A resolution of this would have made the perfect ending to this story, like a denouement at the end of a whodunnit. Unfortunately, although a seductive oil sketch had just been discovered by a dealer in New York, which may have been produced around the time of the Frick picture, it was no real help for dating purposes. Dr. Garas, in fact, had no new research to report and although she personally leaned toward Albrecht, rather than Rudolf, her account was inconclusive. The final mystery remains.

Appendix:
A Note on Money

As anyone who has ever tried to relate prices in one period of history to other periods will know, it is a deceptively complex task. Different ages attach different values to different objects. When one is comparing different currencies at different times, the problem becomes even more difficult. We know from our experience in recent years how quickly and how much exchange rates can vary. In researching this book, I was advised by the economics departments of two universities that currency conversions couldn't be done. Nonetheless, it seemed to me that, since prices *are* a feature of this story, and since regular works of art history rarely explore the topic, some attempt, however crude, should be made to convert values. For a general reader it is a help to know what value, say, 25,000 scudi, a currency which no longer exists, represented in a particular year. Was it closer to $25,000, at 1988 rates, 25,000 Italian lire (roughly $200), or 25,000 Japanese yen ($20)?

I have, therefore, used two methods to convert prices to present-day values.

For sterling and dollars. The Bank of England produces a table of the Retail Price Index, adjusted for present-day values, and stretching all the way back to the year 1270. This table offers a simple guide to conversion. Thus for 1270, you need to multiply prices then by 291.08 to arrive at 1988 values. So, for 1799, when Thomas Hope bought *Wisdom and Strength* for £300, that figure was 17.69. In 1988 terms, therefore, Hope paid the equivalent of $26,500. For sterling/dollar conversions I have therefore made this calculation and then multiplied again by whatever the prevailing exchange rate was at the time (for instance, in the early twentieth century, when *Wisdom and Strength* crossed the Atlantic, there were five dollars to the pound, rather different from now). Many economists believe the Bank of England table, despite its unimpeachable source, to be very inadequate and to underestimate the differences between the past and now.

For other currencies. In medieval times the nearest to a standard coin was the Florentine florin and the Venetian ducat (see Barbara Tuchman's *A Distant Mirror*). Theoretically at least, these coins were supposed to contain between 3.5 and 4.5 grams of gold. Equally theoretically, the florin, ducat, franc, livre, ecu, mark, and pound were all supposed to be equivalent. Coinages varied, of course; different economies strengthened and weakened, as now, altering exchange rates. Moreover, before the age of the telex and the videoscreen, shifts in the value of gold could not be accommodated from one country to another with the ease and speed that occurs now. An added complication was that, from time to time, the price of gold has been pegged officially for political reasons. One can see why academic economic historians are so wary of comparing relative values over time and why the calculation is so fraught with difficulty. Still, gold is now unpegged, and so, in this book, values expressed in the above currencies have simply been recalculated at the current gold price for 1988 ($445 per ounce at the time of this writing). In other words, a figure of 50,000 ducats equals 50,000 × 3.5–4.5 grams of gold, or 172,000–225,000 grams. This equals 6,067–7,800 ounces. The 1988 value of this weight of gold is approximately $2,700,000–$3,470,000.

This will be much too simple for many academics, but it does give plausible results. For example, according to Brian Pullan in *Crisis and Change in the Venetian Economy in the Sixteenth and Seventeenth Centuries,* master builders earned up to 52,000 soldi (or 420 ducats) per year. Applying the calculation as set out above, this gives a 1988 figure for their earnings in the range $23,300–$29,900.

Though it has many shortcomings, it does at least have the merit of being a fairly simple and easy method to understand. It must be emphasized a final time, however, that this is a crude guide to value and is intended only as a general aid for readers.

Notes and References

INTRODUCTION: THE SEARCH FOR *Wisdom and Strength*

Page xiii: "Each painting is unique and contains the secrets of its own history." The phrase is Sarah Walden's in *The Ravished Image,* St. Martin's Press, New York, 1985.

Page xviii: Henry Frick's "Paradise": John Canaday, "Business As Usual [Quiet] in Paradise, The Frick Collection." *New York Times,* December 22, 1968.

PART ONE–VENICE

CHAPTER 1: THE FIGURES: FASHION AND BEAUTY IN RENAISSANCE VENICE

I have relied chiefly on: Pompeo Molmenti, *Venice: Its Individual Growth from the Earliest Beginnings to the Fall of the Republic,* translated by Horatio F. Brown, John Murray, London, 1907 and 1908, especially part II, volume I, "The Golden Age," and part III, volume I, "The Decadence"; *Rich and Poor in Renaissance Venice,* by Brian Pullen, Blackwell, Oxford, 1971; *Studies in the History of Venice,* by Horatio F. Brown, John Murray, London, 1907, especially volume II, chapters 2, 3, and 4; *Venice and History: Collected Papers of Frederick C. Lane,* Johns Hopkins Press, Baltimore, 1966.

Pages 3ff.: For the plague is Venice and Italy, see also: Fernand Braudel, *The Mediterranean and the Mediterranean World in the Age of Philip II,* Collins, London, 1972; Molmenti, "The Golden Age," pp. 54ff.; and Carlo M. Cipolla, *Faith, Reason and the Plague in Seventeenth Century Tuscany,* W. W. Norton, New York, 1979.

Pages 6ff.: On Veronese, my chief sources have been: *Veronese: L'Opera Completa,* by Terisio Pignatti, Alfieri, Venice, 1976; *Veronese's Drawings: A Catalogue Raisonné,* by Richard Cooke, Sotheby's Publications, London, 1984; *Veronese: I Geni della Pittura,* by Maria Luisa Rizzatti, Mondadori, Milan, 1976; *Painting in Cinquecento Venice: Titian, Veronese, Tintoretto,* by David Rosand, Yale University Press, New Haven and London, 1982; *L'Opera Completa del Veronese* (part of the Rizzoli Classici dell'Arte series), Rizzoli, Milan, 1968. Other sources: David Rosand, "Veronese and Company: Artistic Production in a Venetian Workshop," Introduction to "Veronese and His Studio, in North American Collections," Birmingham Museum of Art, October 1–15, 1972. This catalogue shows the Robert Draper and Rhode Island copies of *Wisdom and Strength;* Sylvie Beguin and Remigio Marini, *Tout l'Oeuvre Peint de Veronese,* especially: "Le Gout pour Veronese en France." Detlev Baron von Hadeln, "Pictures Left by Veronese in

His Studio," *Burlington Magazine,* volume 53, 1928, pp. 3–4; G. Gattinoni, "Inventario dei mobili di Casa pro Indivisi tra il Reverendissimo Sigr. Abbate D., Francesco Calliari, et la Commissario del quondam Eccte Sigr. Gabriel Calliari fu Suo Fratello nella casa per essi habitata a S. Geremia in Venetia," Venice, 1682, pp. 1 and ix–xiv; Deborah Howard, *Architecture and Patronage in Renaissance Venice,* Yale University Press, which contains a section on the sorts of people Veronese used as models; Carlo Ridolfi, *Le Maraviglie dell'Arte (della Pittura),* two volumes, 1648, reprinted by Grote, Berlin, 1914–24.

Page 7ff: "The Venice Veronese painted"—see: Molmenti, *op. cit.,* "The Golden Age," *passim.* For lace, for example, see pp. 138ff.; for dancing and banquets, see chapter 4.

Page 7: For the people in Veronese's Venice, see: Oliver Logan, *Culture and Society in Venice, 1470–1790: The Renaissance and Its Heritage,* Batsford, London, 1972, pp. 20–37, 68–92, and especially 220–55; Hale (ed.), *op. cit.,* chapters 3 and 8.

Page 10: For the Doges and Dogaressas of Venice, see: *The Dogaressas of Venice,* by Edgcumbe Staley, T. Werner Laurie, London, n. d. 1911(?).

Page 15: For male fashions, see: Molmenti, *op. cit.,* "The Golden Age," chapter 13.

Page 16: For the use of models and their payment, see: *ibid.,* p. 201.

Page 16ff.: "The Venice Veronese did not paint"—see: Pullen, *op. cit.,* part II, chapters 1, 3, 4, 5, and 6; for prostitution, bigamy, and music, see: Molmenti, *op. cit.,* "The Golden Age," chapters 7, 8, and 9 respectively; for education, see: Molmenti, *op. cit.,* "The Golden Age," pp. 248ff.; and for coteries and academies, see: Molmenti, *op. cit.,* "The Golden Age," pp. 282ff.; for a quite different kind of art from Veronese's, see: Samuel Edgerton, Jr., *Pictures and Punishment: Art and Criminal Prosecution During the Florentine Renaissance,* Cornell University Press, Ithaca, New York, 1985.

Page 20: For details on the daily life of Titian, Tintoretto, Sansovino, etc., see: Molmenti, *op. cit.* "The Golden Age," chapter 7.

Page 22: For Palladio, see: *Palladio,* by James S. Ackerman, Penguin Books, Harmondsworth, 1981, *passim.*

Page 22: For prostitution, games, etc., in sixteenth-century Venice, see: Molmenti, *op. cit.* "The Golden Age," chapter 12.

Pages 24ff.: On the general position of Venice, see: Pullen, *op. cit.,* part I, chapters 5 and 6, and part II, chapter 5; also J. R. Hale [ed.] *Renaissance Venice* London, Faber & Faber, 1973. Brown, and Braudel, *op. cit., passim.*

Page 26: On Aretino, see M. W. Roskill, *Dolce's "Aretino" and Venetian Art Theory of the Cinquecento* (text of his *Dialogo della Pittura,* translated, introduced, and with a commentary by M. W. Roskill), Monographs on Archaeology and the Fine Arts, New York, 1968; also Molmenti, *op. cit.,* "The Golden Age," p. 225.

Page 26: For Veronese's life in Venice, see: Cocke, *op. cit.,* pp. 5–20; Pignatti, *op. cit.,* pp. 7–99; and Rosand, *op. cit.,* 163–81.

Page 27: On Dolce's theories and influence, see: Roskill, *Dolce's "Aretino" and Venetian Art Theory of the Cinquecento, op. cit.*

Page 28: On the Council of Trent, see: *The Survival of the Pagan Gods: The Mythological Tradition and Its Place in Renaissance Humanism and Art,* by Jean Seznec, Pantheon Books, New York, 1953 (though I have used the edition published by Princeton University Press in 1972), pp. 264ff.

Page 29: For details of the Battle of Lepanto, see: Braudel, *op. cit.,* volume II, pp. 1088–1142; and *Venice: The Greatness and the Fall,* by John Julius Norwich, Allen Lane, London, 1981, especially chapter 18.

Page 30: For Veronese before the Inquisition, see: *A Documentary History of Art,* selected and edited by Elizabeth Gilmore Holt, Anchor Books, Garden City, New York, 1958, volume II, pp. 65–70.

Page 31: For the visit of Henry III to Venice, I have used Molmenti, *op. cit.,* "The Golden Age," pp. 88ff., but there are several accounts.

CHAPTER 2. THE COMMISSION: WHY THE EMPEROR CHOSE VERONESE

Page 33: For the Albrecht version, see: "Veronese's Omnia Vanitas and Honor et Virtus post Mortem Floret," by Richard Cocke, in *Pantheon,* volume 35, 1977, pp. 120–25; the first Frick Collection catalogue, 1949; "Albrecht V. und Seine Zeit," in *Münchner Jahrbuch der Bildenden Kunset,* volume 10, pp. 147–225; J. Stockbauer, *Quellenschriften für Kunstgeschichte,* VIII (1874), 29, pp. 32–36 and 43; S. Killermann, *Die Miniaturen im Gebetbuche Albrecht,* 1911.

Page 36: For the Rudolf version, see the Frick Collection catalogue, both the 1949 version, volume 1, pp. 262–70, *and* the 1968 version, pp. 272–83.

Page 37: For the rough-drawn coronet, see: E. Tietze-Conrat, *Arte Veneta,* volume 7, 1953, pp. 93ff.; and Richard Cocke, *Pantheon, op. cit.,* p. 121; for details of Rudolf, see: *Rudolf II and His World: A Study in Intellectual History, 1576–1612,* by R. J. W. Evans, Oxford University Press, 1973, pp. 84–115 and 162–95.

Page 39: For Rudolf's commission to Veronese, see: Pignatti, *op. cit.,* volume 1, page 147; for Veronese's Commissions in general, see Pignatti: *op. cit.,* volume 1, pp. 251–60; for Renaissance contracts in general, see: *The Renaissance Artist at Work: From Pisano to Titian,* by Bruce Cole, Harper & Row, New York, 1983, pp. 49–56; for Rudolf's commissioning habits, see: Evans, *op. cit.,* pp. 164ff.; *Renaissance Art in Bohemia,* by Jiřina Hořejší *et al.,* Hamlyn, London, 1979, pp. 174–84; and *Princes and Patrons: Patronage and Ideology and Four Habsburg Courts, 1517–1633,* by Hugh Trevor-Roper, Thames and Hudson, London, 1976, pp. 85–126.

CHAPTER 3. THE THEME: THE SECRET MEANINGS OF ALLEGORY

For this chapter I have relied on: *Dictionary of Subjects and Symbols in Art,* by James Hall, John Murray, London, 1974; *A History of Ideas and Images in Italian Art,* by James Hall, Harper & Row, New York, 1983; *Pagan Mysteries in the Renaissance,* by Edgar Wind, Oxford University Press (revised edition), 1980; and Seznec, *op. cit.* In the Frick Collection catalogue of 1949, the picture is described as *Allegory of Virtue and Strength,* where it is pointed out that the picture was known in 1621, in the inventory prepared in Prague, as *Glorious Virtue and Strength.* Wisdom's usual attributes are a helmet, spear, or owls—therefore Virtue is more suitable (p. 265).

Page 45: Humanism—see: Seznec, *op. cit.,* pp. 96ff.

Page 45: Cassone—see: Cole, *op. cit.,* pp. 48ff.

Page 46: On Ficino, see: Seznec, *op. cit.,* pp. 58–72 and 96ff.

Page 49: On Christianity, the Counter-Reformation, and allegory, see: Seznec, *op. cit.,* pp. 264ff.; and Hall, *A History of Ideas, op. cit.,* chapter 8, pp. 297ff.

Page 51: For the situation of Venice, see: Hale, *op. cit.,* chapter 6, pp. 318ff., and chapter 14, pp. 409ff.; and *The Genius of Venice,* catalogue of an exhibition held at the Royal Academy of Arts in London in 1983, edited by Jane Martineau and Charles Hope, pp. 16–20; see also Rosand, *op. cit.,* chapters 1–4, pp. 1–46.

Page 51: For Dolce, see Roskill, *op. cit., passim.*

Page 52: For the social standing of the artist, see: Cole, *op. cit.,* pp. 28ff.; and in Venice, see: Rosand, *op. cit.,* chapter 2, pp. 7–14.

Page 54: For the Venetian painters' guild, see: Cole, *op. cit.,* pp. 21ff.; and Rosand, *op. cit.,* pp. 15 and 28.

Page 57: For accounts of the individual gods, see any of a large number of iconographical works; among them: Gilbert F. Cope (ed.), *Christianity and the Visual Arts,* London, 1964: George Ferguson, *Signs and Symbols in Christian Art,* New York, 1954; A. Katzenellenbogen, "Allegories of the Virtues and Vices in Mediaeval Art," in *Studies of the Warburg Institute,* volume 10, London, 1939; *Renaissance and Renascences in Western Art,* by Erwin Panofsky (Institute of Art History, Uppsala), Stockholm, 1960.

Page 63: For the "decay" of allegory, see: Hall, *op. cit.,* pp. 335ff.

CHAPTER 4. THE OVERALL APPEARANCE: COLORS, CANVAS, PAINTING TECHNIQUE

Page 64: For female beauty in Venice, see: Molmenti, *op. cit.,* "The Golden Age," chapter 13; Rosand, *op. cit.,* section 1, chapter 3, pp. 15–25, and section 4, chapter 5, pp. 163–66.

Page 64: For canvas, miniver hair for brushes, etc., see: Cole, *op. cit.,* chapter II, pp. 57–136; see also the National Gallery (London) *Technical Bulletin* for reports in paintings by Veronese in its collection. For the history of pigments, see: Arthur Pillans Laurie, *New Light on Old Masters,* London, 1905; Arthur Pillans Laurie, *The Painter's Methods and Materials,* Dover, New York, 1967; Arthur Pillans Laurie, *The Pigments and Mediums of the Old Masters,* Macmillan, London, 1914; M. P. Merrifield, *Original Treatises . . . on the Arts of Painting,* London, 1849, reprinted 1967; James Maroger, *The Secret Formulas and Techniques of the Masters,* London, 1948; Max Doerner, *The Materials of the Artist,* Hart Davis, London, 1949.

Page 68: For details of Veronese's drawings, see: Cocke, *op. cit.,* pp. 72, 85, 128, 129, 309, and 362; for a more general discussion of drawing, its history, and its relationship to painting, see: *Drawing: History and Technique,* by Heribert Hutter, Thames and Hudson, London, 1968, especially pp. 7–77; Jean-Luc Bordeaux, "A Sheet of Studies for Veronese's Four Allegories of Love." *Burlington Magazine,* volume 117, number 2, 1975, pp. 600–3.

Page 71: For the Venetian manner of painting, see: the references given for pp. 30ff.; John Steer, *Venetian Painting,* Praeger, New York, 1970; Giovanni Morelli, *Italian Painting,* Murray, London, pp. 234–45 and 259–324.

Page 72: For Veronese's technique, see: Hans Tietze and E. Tietze-Conrat, *The Drawings of the Venetian Painters,* J. J. Augustin, New York, 1944, especially pp. 1–28: "The Role of Drawing in Venetian Art"; F. J. Mather, *Venetian Painters,* Allen and Unwin, London, 1937, with a section on Veronese "as an influence *against* Mannerism" (my italics).

PART TWO–PRAGUE

CHAPTER 5. RUDOLF'S MAGIC COURT

I agree with Lord Dacre (Hugh Trevor-Roper) that without the work of Dr. R. J. W. Evans, of Brasenose College, Oxford, it would hardly be possible to tread on this difficult ground. I have made heavy use of his book *Rudolf II and His World*, mentioned above. My debt is almost as great to *Renaissance Art in Bohemia*, by Jiřina Hořejší *et al.*, also referred to above, and to Hugh Trevor-Roper's own book, *Princes and Artists: Patronage and Ideology at Four Habsburg Courts, 1517–1633*. Other sources on mannerism include: "Observations on the Painting of the Maniera," by S. J. Freedberg, *Art Bulletin*, xlvii, 1965, pp. 187ff.; *Mannerism and Anti-Mannerism in Italian Painting*, by W. Friedlander, 1957; "The Counter-Reformation and Mannerism," by Nicholas Pevsner, in his *Studies in Art, Architecture, and Design* (originally published in 1925, English translation published 1968); and *The School of Prague: Painting at the Court of Rudolf II*, by Thomas DaCosta Kaufmann, University of Chicago Press, 1978, especially pp. 103–23; Karl Vocelka, *Rudolf II und Seine Zeit*, Hermann Böhlaus Nachf, Wien, 1985; H. Zimmerman, "Das Inventar der Prager Schatz- und Kunstkammer vom. 6 Dezember, 1621," in *Jahrbuch der Kunsthistorischen Sammlungen des allerhöchsten Kaiserhauses*, volume 25, 1905, pp. xiiiff.; K. Chytil, "Umění a Umělci na Dvoře Rudolfa II," Prague, 1920; K. B. Mádl, "Obrazárna a Umělci Rudolfa II v Praze," in *Pamatky Archeologicke*, volume 22, Prague, 1906–8.

Page 77: For mannerism in Prague, see: Evans, *op. cit.*, pp. 163ff. and chapter 7, pp. 243–74; and *Mannerism*, by John Shearman, Penguin Books, Harmondsworth, 1967.

Page 78: *Difficoltà*—see: Shearman, *op. cit.*, pp. 21 and 41.

Page 80: For Spranger, Savery, etc., see: Evans, *op. cit.*, pp. 165–74 and 243 and 268; Shearman, *op. cit.*, pp. 30–33; but for Arcimboldo, see also Simonetta Rasponi and Carla Tanzi (eds.), *The Arcimboldo Effect: Transformations of the Face from the Sixteenth to the Twentieth Century*, published by Bompiani, Milan, 1987, to accompany an exhibition with the same title at the Palazzo Grassi, Venice. See especially pp. 35–142.

Page 82: *Concetti*—see: Shearman, *op. cit.*, pp. 21 and 41.

Page 83: "The occult arts"—see: Evans, *op. cit.*, chapter 6, pp. 196–242.

Page 85: Brahe and Kepler—see: *ibid.*, pp. 136–38.

Page 86: *"Wunderkammer"*—see: *ibid.*, pp. 176ff., but also *The Origins of Museums: The Cabinet of Curiosities in Sixteenth- and Seventeenth-Century Europe*, Oliver Impey and Arthur MacGregor (eds.), Clarendon Press, Oxford, 1985.

Page 86: On the inventory, see: "Das Inventar der Rudolfinischen Kunstkammer von 1607/11," by Erwin Neumann, in *Queen Christina of Sweden: Documents and Studies*, Magnus von Platen (ed.), Analecta Reginensia 1, Kungl. Boktryckeriet P. A. Norstedt & Söner, Stockholm, 1966, pp. 262–65; *The Arcimboldo Effect*, *op. cit.*, "The Treasures and Art Chamber of Prague," a translation of the inventory ordered by the Prince of Liechtenstein in 1621, pp. 133–42.

Page 88: On Matthias, see: Evans, *op. cit.*, passim.

Page 89: On the Letter of Majesty, see: *ibid.*, pp. 60–70.

CHAPTER 6. FORGOTTEN FOR THIRTY YEARS

For the Thirty Years' War in general there are innumerable accounts. I have used, C. V. Wedgwood, *The Thirty Years War,* Methuen, London, 1938 and 1981, especially chapters 2, 7, and 11; R. J. W. Evans, *The Making of the Habsburg Monarchy, 1550–1750,* Oxford University Press, 1979; Michael Roberts, *Gustavus Adolphus: A History of Sweden, 1611–32,* London, 1953 and 1958; J. V. Polisensky, *The Thirty Years War,* Batsford, London, 1971 (trans. R. J. W. Evans), especially chapter 5, on Bohemia; J. V. Polisensky, *War and Society in Europe, 1618–1648,* Cambridge University Press, 1978; C. E. Morris, *Bohemia,* T. Fisher Unwin, London, 1922 (second edition).

Page 91: For the role of the Jesuits, see: Wedgwood, *op. cit.,* pp. 176–77.

Page 93: For Swedish military practices, see: Wedgwood, *op. cit.,* chapter 7, pp. 269–334; Roberts, *op. cit., passim.*

CHAPTER 7. DOWN THE ELBE

For the Sack of Prague I have used: Olof Granberg, *Kejsar Rudolf II:s Konstkammare och Dess Svenska Öden och om Uppkomsten af Drottning Kristinas Tafvelgalleri i Rom, och Dess Skingrade,* Gustaf Lindströms Boktryckeri, Stockholm, 1902; Olof Granberg, *La Galerie de Tableaux de la Reine Christine de Suède,* Ivar Haeggström, Stockholm, 1897.

Page 96: For descriptions of the castle interior, see: Granberg, *Kejsar Rudolf, op. cit.,* pp. 22ff.

Page 97: For the journey down the Elbe, see: *The Plunder of the Arts in the Seventeenth Century,* by Hugh Trevor-Roper, Thames and Hudson, London, 1970, pp. 44–45.

INTERLUDE ONE: THE DISPERSAL OF ART IN THE SEVENTEENTH CENTURY

Hugh Trevor-Roper's *The Plunder of the Arts in the Seventeenth Century,* referred to above, served as my initial guide to this field. See also: Alfons Lhotsky, *Die Geschichte der Sammlungen,* Vienna, 1941–45; Josef Svátek, *Die Rudolphinische Kunstkammer in Prag,* Vienna, 1897; for the Mantuan treasures, see also: D. Chambers and J. Martineau (eds.), *Splendours of the Gonzaga,* exhibition held at the Victoria and Albert Museum, London, 1981.

Page 100: For the Bohemian nobility proposes sale of Rudolf's collection, see: Trevor-Roper, *op. cit.,* pp. 17–18.

Page 100: For the Vatican's acquisition of the Heidelberg library, see: Trevor-Roper, *Plunder of the Arts,* etc.

Page 101: For the disposal of the Gonzaga collections from Mantua and their subsequent fate in England, see: *Splendours of the Gonzaga, op. cit.;* on the Commonwealth sale, see: Sir Claude Phillips, *The Picture Gallery of Charles I,* London, 1895; Oliver Millar (ed.), "Abraham van der Doort's Catalogue of the Collection of Charles I," *Walpole Society,* volume XXXVII, 1958–60; W. C. F. Nuttall, "King Charles I's Pictures and the Commonwealth Sale," *Apollo,* October 1965.

Page 102: For the dispersal of the Munich collections and the Swedish campaigns, see: Trevor-Roper, *The Plunder of the Arts,* pp. 38–47.

PART THREE–QUEEN CHRISTINA

CHAPTER 8. CHRISTINA'S STOCKHOLM

In 1966 the Council of Europe held an exhibition in Stockholm entitled "Christina: A Personality in European Culture." This exhibition covered every aspect of the Queen's life, including her collecting. The Vienna copy of *Wisdom and Strength* traveled to Stockholm as one of the exhibits (so did *Vice and Virtue*). The catalogue for this exhibition, which contains a number of essays on the Queen as well as very detailed entries for the items displayed, has been my main source for this and the following two chapters. Its full publishing details are: *Christina of Sweden: A Personality in European Civilisation,* Eleventh Exhibition of the Council of Europe, Nationalmuseum, Stockholm, National Musei, Utställningskatalog 305, Egnellska Boktryckeriet AB, Stockholm, 1966. But throughout these notes the catalogue is referred to as *Christina (Europe).* Other sources were: *Queen Christina of Sweden: Documents and Studies,* Magnus von Platen (ed.), *op. cit.,* 1966; *Queen Christina,* by Georgina Masson, Farrar, Straus & Giroux, New York, 1969.

Page 107: For Stockholm as a "green town," see: *Christina (Europe),* pp. 106ff.

Page 107: For the division of Stockholm, see: *ibid.,* pp. 108ff.

Page 108: For Christina "that dreadful woman . . . etc.", see: Trevor-Roper, *Princes and Artists,* p. 125.

Page 109: For Christina's belief that her mother found her ugly, see: Masson, *op. cit.,* p. 21.

Page 109: On Tessin's abortive plans for the gallery, see: *Christina (Europe),* p. 424.

Page 112: For Christina's correspondence with Orsini, see: *ibid.,* p. 432 and elsewhere.

Page 112: For Holm entrusted with the collections, see: *ibid.,* p. 428.

Page 113: On the Bregys in Sweden, see: Masson, *op. cit.,* pp. 125–30.

Page 113: For Descartes's arrival, see: *Christina (Europe),* p. 206; Masson, *op. cit.,* pp. 127–32.

Page 115: For Christina's coronation, see: Masson, *op. cit.,* pp. 136–38; *Christina (Europe),* pp. 179–84.

Page 117: For Chanut's description of the Queen, see: *Christina (Europe),* p. 396; Masson, *op. cit.,* pp. 113–14; for details on other men at court, see: *Christina (Europe),* pp. 44–53 and pp. 184ff.

Page 119: On Bourdelot, see: *Christina (Europe),* p. 207.

Page 120: "Christina and Art." This was a special section of the Council of Europe Christina exhibition and was reflected in the catalogue. See: *ibid.,* pp. 416–581.

Page 124: Abdication. This too was a section in the Christina exhibition. See: *ibid.,* pp. 232–35; Masson, *op. cit.,* pp. 175–217.

Page 126: For the Queen's extraordinary behavior, see: Masson *op. cit.,* pp. 130–41.

Page 127: The "Fortuna"—see: *Christina (Europe),* p. 430.

CHAPTER 9. SOUTH, TO ROME

The primary source for Christina's journey south is Galeazzo Gualdo Priorato, *Historia della Sacra Real Maestà di Christina Allessandra Regina di Svetia,* Rome, 1656, translated into English by John Burbery, London, 1938. This chapter has also made use of the same works as the previous one. The Council of Europe exhibition devoted an entire section to the Queen's journey south and I have relied most heavily on this account *Christina (Europe),* pp. 226–97, though Georgina Masson's book has a chapter on the journey also.

Page 130: For Hamburg and Texeira, see: *Christina (Europe),* p. 240.

Page 131: For Antwerp's golden age—Rubens, Jordaens, etc.—see: Leon Voet, *Antwerp: The Golden Age,* Mercatorfonds, Antwerp, pp. 351–62.

Page 133: For Leopold William, see: *Christina (Europe),* pp. 242–49; but also Wolfgang Prohaska, *Das Kunsthistorische Museum,* Vienna, Scala, Florence, pp. 3 and 8–10; R. J. W. Evans, *The Making of the Habsburg Monarchy, op. cit, passim.*

Page 135: For the Bollandists, see: *Christina (Europe),* p. 247.

Page 136: For Christina's public conversion at Innsbruck, see: *ibid.,* pp. 250–57.

Page 137: The Queen enters papal territory—see: *ibid.,* p. 258.

Page 137: Meets Orsini—see: *ibid.,* pp. 267–68.

Page 138: Enters Vatican by the back staircase—see: *ibid.,* pp. 269ff.

Page 138: Bernini designs stool to overcome problems of protocol—see: Masson, *op. cit.,* pp. 249–50.

Page 139: The Queen's official entry into Rome—see: *ibid.,* pp. 269–79.

CHAPTER 10. CHRISTINA IN BAROQUE ROME

In addition to the references given for the previous two chapters, for this one I have also relied on Francis Haskell, *Patrons and Painters: A Study in the Relations Between Italian Art and Society in the Age of the Baroque,* Chatto and Windus, London, 1963; P. Hollingworth, *History of the Intrigues and Gallantries of Christina, Queen of Sweden,* London, 1927; C. D. N. Bildt, *Christina di Svezia e Paolo Giordano Orsini,* Archivio della Reale Società Romana di Storia Patria, Roma, 1906; C. D. N. Bildt, *Queen Christina's Pictures in the XX Century,* London, 1904; Olof Granberg, *La Galerie de Tableaux de Christine de Suède,* Stockholm, 1897.

Page 142: For Bernini, Barberini, etc., see: Haskell, *op. cit.,* pp. 24–62.

Page 143: "The artistic temperament,"—see: *ibid.,* pp. 21–23.

Page 143: On Cortona, see: *ibid,* pp. 38–84 and *passim.*

Page 144: For Christina's political ambitions, see: *Christina (Europe),* section on "Political Activities in Rome," pp. 344–63; Masson, *op. cit.,* pp. 255–300 and 338–42.

Page 146: For Azzolino's "flying squadron," see: *Christina (Europe),* pp. 281–82; Masson, *op. cit.,* pp. 258–59; *Dizionario Biografico degli Italiani,* volume 4, p. 767.

Page 147: For Christina's change to French allegiance, see: *Christina (Europe),* p. 346; Masson, *op. cit.,* pp. 265ff.

Page 148: For the Duc de Guise's description of the Queen, see: Masson, *op. cit.,* p. 274.

Page 150: For the Palazzo Riario, see: *Christina (Europe)*, pp. 318–28; also Giovanni Battista Falda (attrib.) "Perspective View of the Palazzo Riario with Its Garden and Casino," engraving, Rome, Gabinetto Nationale delle Stampe, Inv. No. F.C. 131179; S. Vänje, "Palazzo della Regina Studier i Drottning Christinas Romerska Miljö," Stockholm, 1965; Granberg, 1896, *op. cit.;* O. Sirén, *Nicodemus Tessin D.Y. Studioresor*, Stockholm, 1914, pp. 182–265.

Page 151: "Christina's True Realm"—the phrase is Georgina Masson's, in Masson, *op. cit.*, chapter 10, pp. 345–390.

Page 151: For Bamboccianti, see: Haskell, *op. cit.*, pp. 132–43. For Salvator Rose, see: *ibid.*, pp. 126–53.

Page 153: For Mola, see: *Christina (Europe)*, pp. 470 and 474. For Bellori, see: *ibid.*, pp. 530ff.; Haskell, *op. cit.*, pp. 158–61.

Page 153: For patronage in Rome, see: *ibid.*, part I, pp. 3–166.

Page 155: For dealers in Rome, see: *ibid.*, pp. 120–25.

Page 157: *Bentveughels*—see: Haskell, *op. cit.*, pp. 20 and 130.

Page 157: Christina's collections in Rome. A section of the Stockholm exhibition was devoted to this. See: *Christina (Europe)*, pp. 422–581.

Page 159: For Christina's statues and drawings, see: *Christina (Europe)*, pp. 438, 440, and 444–69.

Page 160: For the layout of the Riario, see: *ibid.*, pp. 318–72 and references to p. 150 above.

Page 161: For scholars and academies in Rome, see: "A Note on Christina and Her Academies," by Ruth Stephan, in *Queen Christina of Sweden: Documents and Studies*, Magnus von Platen (ed.), *op. cit.*, pp. 365–71.

Page 163: For opera, theater, and music in Rome, see: *Christina (Europe)*, pp. 402–14; "Alessandro Scarlatti et Son Opéra L'Honestà negli Amori, Dédié à la Reine Christine," by Gustaf Hilleström, and "Amour et Mars Vaincus. Allégorie Politique des Ballets de cour de l'Époque de la Reine Christine," by Lars Gustafsson, both in *Queen Christina of Sweden: Documents and Studies, op. cit.*, Magnus von Platen (ed.), pp. 159 and 87, respectively.

Page 164: For the Queen's final illness, see: Masson, *op. cit.*, pp. 385–89.

Page 166: For social changes overtaking Italy, see: Haskell, *op. cit.*, part II, pp. 169–241.

Page 166: On Richelieu, Mazarin, and Louis XIV, see: Haskell, *op. cit.*, pp. 175–76 and 180–87.

CHAPTER 11. THE PAPAL NEPHEW

Marcel Roethlisberger, "The Drawings Collection of Prince Livio Odescalchi," *Master Drawings*, volume 23–24, number 1, 1985–86, pp. 5–30, is one of the most accessible accounts of the Odescalchi family. Also: Edward de Syrmia, *At the Head of the Nations: The Rise of the Papal and Princely House of Odescalchi*, Pleasant Valley, New York, 1978. For the Odescalchi firearms collection and a note on the background of the family, see: Nolfo di Carpegna, *Armi da Fuoco della Collezione Odescalchi*, Edizioni Marte, Rome, 1968. I am grateful to Burton Frederickson, at the Getty Museum in Malibu, California, for allowing me to inspect the Odescalchi inventory and other material in the Provenance Index. For Pope Innocent XI, see also Ludwig von Pastor, *Geschichte der Päpste*, volume XIV, number 2, Freiburg, 1930, pp. 685ff. and 776ff.

Page 170: For the layout of the Odescalchi palace, see: Roethlisberger, *op. cit.*, pp. 11–14; Thomas Ashby, "The Palazzo Odescalchi in Rome," in *Papers of the British School in Rome*, volume VIII, 1916, pp. 68ff., and volume IX, 1917, pp. 79–89.

Page 171: For Odescalchi's acquisition of drawings, see: Roethlisberger, *op. cit.*, pp. 10 and 13; see also the contract of the sale of Christina's art to the Odescalchi in *Christina (Europe)*, p. 434.

Page 172: For the history of drawings collections, see: Roethlisberger, *op. cit.*, pp. 15ff.; Heribert Hutter, *Drawing: History and Technique*, Thames and Hudson, London, 1968, pp. 7–77.

PART FOUR–THE HOUSE OF ORLÉANS

CHAPTER 12. PIERRE CROZAT'S HARD BARGAIN

The best single account of the sale of the Christina/Odescalchi collection to the Duke of Orléans is to be found in: Casimir Stryienski, *La Galerie du Régent, Philippe Duc d'Orléans*, Goupil & Co., Paris, 1913; but see also: Olof Granberg, *La Galerie de Tableaux de la Reine Christine de Suède*, Ivar Haeggström, Stockholm, 1897; Margret Stuffman, "Les Tableaux de la Collection de Pierre Crozat," *Gazette des Beaux Arts*, volume LXXII, July–September, 1968, pp. 5–144. Other accounts include: J. Couché, *Galerie du Palais Royal, Gravée d'après les Tableaux des Différentes Écoles Qui la Composent, avec un Abrégé de la Vie des Peintres et Une Description Historique de Chaque Tableau*, Perronneau, Paris, 1808, in which *Wisdom and Strength* is shown engraved in volume II, p. 45. The contract for the sale of the collection to Orléans is given in the references for p. 171 above.

Page 178: For Crozat's family and background, see: Stuffman, *op. cit.*, pp. 13ff.; see also *Bioghraphie Universelle*, 1852, volume 9, pp. 534–35. On Crozat and "amateurs," see also: M. J. Dumesnil, *Histoire des plus Célèbres Amateurs Français*, Paris, 1856; P-J. Mariette, *Descriptions Sommaires des Desesins des Grands Maistres d'Italie, des Pay-Bas et de France du Cabinet de feu M. Crozat, avec des Réflexions sur la Manière de Dessiner des Principaux Peintres*, Paris, 1741; J-B. Lacurne de Sainte-Palaye, *Catalogue des Tableaux du Cabinet de M. Crozat, Baron de Thiers*, Paris, 1755 (reprinted 1909).

Page 181: For Crozat's sojourn in Rome, see: Stryienski, *op. cit.*, pp. 15ff.

Page 182: For Ricci and Rosalba, see: Stuffman, *op. cit.*, pp. 22ff.

CHAPTER 13: THE SCANDALOUS REGENT

There are many diverse accounts of the life of Philippe, Duke of Orléans. I have taken my title from: W. H. Lewis, *The Scandalous Regent*, Deutsch, London, 1961; I have also used: J. H. Shennan, *Philippe Duke of Orléans, Regent of France, 1715–1723*, Thames & Hudson, London, 1979; C-E. Engel, "Le Régent Collectionneur," in *Le Régent*, Paris, 1969, pp. 58–65; G. Atkinson and A. C. Keller, *Prelude to the Enlightenment*, London, 1971; Dom H. Leclerc, *Histoire de la Régence*, three volumes, Paris, 1921; Louis de Rouvroy, Duke of Saint-Simon, *Historical Memoirs*, now edited and translated into English by Lucy Norton in three volumes, London, 1967–72. See too Lucienne Ercole, *Gay Court Life, France in the Eighteenth Century*, Harper, New York, 1932, and finally Olivier Bernier, *Louis the Beloved*, Doubleday, Garden City, New York, 1984, pp. 28–43. On the regent's pictures, see: P. Crozat, *Recueil d'Estampes d'après les plus Beaux Tableaux* . . . *Duc d'Orléans,* Paris, 1729–42.

Page 183: For Philippe's character, see: Shennan, *op. cit.,* pp. 126–33; Lucy Norton, *Saint-Simon at Versailles,* Hamish Hamilton, London, 1958, pp. 3–10, 116–21, and especially 216–24.

Page 183: For Monsieur's tastes, see: Shennan, *op. cit.,* pp. 11–12.

Page 184: For Orléans as the idol of Paris, see: *ibid.,* p. 13.

Page 185: For Orléans's intellectual interests, see: *ibid.,* pp. 126–33.

Page 185: Starts collecting—see: Stryienski, *op. cit.,* pp. 10ff.

Page 186: Acquires pictures as favors—see: *ibid.,* pp. 11ff.

Page 188: For "incest" with his daughter, see: Shennan, *op. cit.,* pp. 128–29.

Page 188: For the poisoning scandal, see: *ibid.,* p. 131.

Page 190: For orgies, see: Ercole, *op. cit.,* pp. 13–48.

Page 192: For Philippe and Watteau, Coypel, Oppenordt, etc., see: Shennan, *op. cit.,* pp. 14, 132, 133; see also Thomas Crow, *Painters and Public Life,* Yale University Press, 1985, pp. 39–42.

Page 193: For the Palais Royal, see: J. Vatout, *Le Palais Royal: Son Histoire et Sa Description,* Didier, Paris, 1852. This has chapters on the Palais Royal under Monsieur, the regent, and each of his successors down to Louis-Philippe, King of France; for the layout, see: pp. 103–40.

Page 195: For negotiations with Odescalchi, see: Stryienski, *op. cit.,* pp. 11–30.

Page 201: For the Canal du Midi, see: L. T. C. Rolt, *From Sea to Sea: The Canal du Midi,* London, 1973.

Page 202: Quote from the Mercury newspaper—see: Styrienski, *op. cit.,* p. 32; see the same source, pp. 43ff., for a note on the Veroneses in Orléans's collection.

Page 203: For details of the Palais Royal, see: Vatout, *op. cit.,* pp. 323ff.

CHAPTER 14. THE PALAIS ROYAL: THE MOST BEAUTIFUL HOUSE IN EUROPE

For France, Paris, and the House of Orléans in this period, see: Bernier, *op. cit., passim;* Crow, *op. cit.;* Michael Levey, *Rococo to Revolution,* Thames & Hudson, London, 1966. Other sources: Vatout, *op. cit.;* N. E. Restif de la Bretonne, *Le Palais Royal,* Paris, 1790; E. Dupezard, *Le Palais Royal de Paris: Architecture and Décoration de Louis XV à Nos Jours,* Paris, 1911, a history of the building with a good introduction, many architectural plans, a number of fine engravings, and excellent photographs.

Page 205: For the regent's son, see: Bernier, *op. cit.,* pp. 43–52.

Page 206: For distorted histories of Orléans, see: Evarts Seelye Scudder, *Prince of the Blood,* Collins, London, 1937, pp. 313–16.

Page 207: For Philip the Fat, see: Bernier, *op. cit.,* p. 235, and the Scudder book on Égalité referred to above.

Page 208: For copying, see: the catalogue for the exhibition Creative Genius, at the Drawings Center, Soho, New York, July 1988. This exhibition juxtaposed copies next to originals, or good-quality photographs of originals, drawing attention to the unique qualities in selected artists (e.g., a Parmigianino copy of a Raphael showed *both* how important the facial expressions are in Raphael *and* how mannerist ideas developed from the High Renaissance).

Page 209: Boucher copies—I am grateful to Bernice Davidson, of the Frick Collection, for allowing me access to the collection's files on *Wisdom and Strength*.

Page 211: For the public and art, see: Crow, *op. cit.*, especially chapters 1, 3, and 4.

Page 215: For the popularity of Veronese, see: Walden, *op. cit.*, pp. 56ff. See also Reynolds's Fourth Discourse, delivered 10 December 1771; Michael Levey, *Rococo to Revolution*, Thames & Hudson, London, 1966, pp. 20ff.; Gerard Reitlinger, *The Economics of Taste*, Barrie and Rockliff, London, 1961, pp. 484–86; Sylvie Béguin and Remigio Marini, *op. cit.*

Page 215: On Boucher, see: Crow, *op. cit.*, p. 7 and plate 3.

Page 217: On Greuze, see: *ibid.*, pp. 138–47.

Page 218: On David, see: *ibid.*, pp. 202–55.

CHAPTER 15. ÉGALITÉ

As with the regent, there are several accounts of Égalité's life, many of them hostile. I have relied on Scudder, *op. cit.*, and to a lesser extent on Amélée Britsch, *La Maison d'Orléans à la Fin de l'Ancien Régime, La Jeunesse de Philippe Égalité*, Payot, Paris, 1926; but I have also made use of W. H. Helm, *Vigée-Lebrun: Her Life, Works and Friendships*, Hutchinson, London, 1916; Maurice Rheims, *Art on the Market: Collecting and Collectors from Midas to Paul Getty*, London, 1961 (better known by its original French title, *La Vie Étrange des Objets*).

Page 221: For Égalité's upbringing, see: Scudder, *op. cit.*, pp. 9ff.

Page 222: For the Palais Royal as the center of opposition, see: *ibid.*, pp. 51ff.

Page 223: For Égalité's Anglophilia, see: *ibid.*, p. 106.

Page 224: For speculation with the Palais Royal, see: *ibid.*, pp. 93–96.

Page 229: For Lebrun, see: Helm, *op. cit.*, pp. 16–23; and Francis Haskell, *Rediscoveries in Art*, Cornell University Press, New York, 1976, pp. 26–38. See also *Biographie Universelle*, pp. 498–505.

Page 231: For the sale of the collections, see: Denys Sutton, "The Orléans Sale," *Apollo*, 1983, pp. 357–72; for the history of auctions, see: Rheims, *op. cit.*, Percy Colson, *A Story of Christie's*, London, 1950, pp. 1–18.

Page 235: Fable of the Lion and the Lamb—quoted in *Apollo*, November 1966, p. 371. I am grateful for Messrs. Christie's for granting me access to some of Philip Tassaert's unpublished letters.

Page 241: On Walckiers, see: *Biographie Nationale de Belgique*, volume XXVII, columns 38–42; on Laborde, see: *Biographie Universelle*, pp. 286–302.

CHAPTER 16. THE CANAL DUKE

This period in British art history is richly documented. I have used: William Buchanan, *Memoirs of Painting*, London, 1824; C. M. Westmacott, *British Galleries of Painting*, London, 1824; G. F. Waagen, *Works of Art and Artists in England*, three volumes, Murray, London, 1838, especially pp. 314–43; William Whitley's three indispensable books: *Artists and Their Friends in England, 1700–1799*, two volumes, the Medici Society, London, 1928; *Art in England 1800–1820*, Cambridge University Press, 1928; *Art in England 1821–1837*, 1930. See also: Gerald Reitlinger, *The Economics of Taste*, *op. cit.* Other sources: Francis Egerton, Eighth

Earl of Bridgewater, *Family Anecdotes,* Paris; Denys Sutton, "The Orléans Sale," *Apollo, op. cit.*

Page 245: For Harman's collection, see: Christie and Manson, "Catalogue of the Very Celebrated Collection . . . of Jeremiah Harman, 17 May 1844."

Page 245: On Bryan, see: *Dictionary of National Biography,* volume III, p. 155; see also *Bryan's Dictionary of Painters and Engravers,* in five volumes, Bell, London, 1903; for Coxe, see: *Dictionary of National Biography,* volume III, p. 420.

Page 246: For Bridgewater, Gower, and Carlisle, see Denys Sutton, "The Orléans Sale," *Apollo, op. cit.,* pp. 362–63; Egerton, *op. cit.;* B. Falke, *The Bridgewater Millions: A Candid Family History,* London, 1942.

Page 248: For Reynolds on Veronese, see: Sir Joshua Reynolds, *Discourses,* Dent, London, 1945, Fourth Discourse, delivered December 10, 1771, especially p. 52.

Page 251: Hazlitt, on the Orléans sale, is quoted in Haskell, *Rediscoveries in Art, op. cit.,* p. 43.

INTERLUDE TWO: REVOLUTION IN FRANCE, THE NAPOLEONIC WARS, AND THE CREATION OF THE LOUVRE

The standard work in this area, in English, is Cecil Gould, *Trophy of Conquest: The Musée Napoléon and the Creation of the Louvre,* Faber, London, 1965, but for other matters covered in this chapter, see also Oliver Impey and Arthur MacGregor (eds.), *The Origins of Museums,* Clarendon Press, Oxford, 1985. Much other material may also be found in Gustav Friedrich Waagen *Works of Art and Artists in England,* three vols., London, 1838: *Treasures of Art in Great Britain: Being an Account of the Chief Collectors of Paintings, Drawings, Sculptures, Illuminated Manuscripts, etc., etc.,* three vols.; supplement: *Galleries and Cabinets of Art in Great Britain: Being an Account of More than Forty Collections . . . Visited in 1854 and 1856, and Now for the First Time Described,* 1857, and Whitley's three volumes.

Page 260: On Denon, see: Gould, *op. cit.,* pp. 87–111.

Page 263: On the dispersal of booty around France and the nonreturn of many items see: M-L. Blumer, "La Commission pour la Recherche des Objets de Science et des Arts en Italie (1796–1797)," in *La Révolution Française,* January–July 1934; M-L. Blumer, "Catalogue des Peintures Transportées d'Italie en France de 1796 à 1814," in *Bulletin de la Société de l'Histoire de l'Art Française,* 1936.

PART FIVE–THE HOPES

CHAPTER 17. THOMAS HOPE, THE AMBITIOUS COMMONER

The standard work on Hope is: David Watkin, *Thomas Hope, 1769–1831, and the Neo-Classical Idea,* John Murray, London, 1968. But see also: David Watkin and Peter Thornton, "New Light on the Hope Mansion in Duchess Street," *Apollo,* September 1987, pp. 162–77. On Hope's pictures, see: Waagen, *Treasures of Art,* volume II, John Murray, London, 1854, pp. 112–25; A. Wertheimer, *The Hope Collection of Pictures of the Dutch and Flemish Schools,* London, 1898. On Hope's other works, see: Geoffrey Waywell, *The Lever and Hope Sculptures. Ancient Sculptures in the Lady Lever Gallery, Port Sunlight, and A Catalogue of the Ancient Sculptures Formerly in the Hope Collection, London and Deepdene,* Gebr. Mann Verlag,

Berlin, 1986. For Hope's vases, see: E. M. W. Tillyard, *The Hope Vases,* London, 1923. Also: Sandor Baumgarten, *Le Crépuscule Néo-Classique Thomas Hope,* Didier, Paris, 1958. For the early nineteenth century in Britain, the picturesque movement, the public display of pictures, and dealers, see: Bernard Denvir, *The Early Nineteenth Century: Art, Design and Society, 1789–1852,* Longman, London, 1984, chapters 2.2, 2.6, 2.8, 2.15, 3.9, 4.6, 4.18, 5.1, 5.2, 5.3, 5.6, and 6.14.

Page 271: For Lady Stanhope's quote, see: Watkin, *op. cit.,* p. 9.

Page 272: For Duchess Street, see: Watkin, *op. cit.,* pp. 93–124, and Watkin and Thornton, *op. cit.,* p. 163, for a slightly different account.

Page 273: For the Westmacott reference, see: Westmacott, *British Galleries of Painting and Sculpture,* London, 1824. pp. 21ff.

Page 276: On Neoclassicism in general, see: Hugh Honour, *Neo-Classicism,* London, 1967.

Page 277: For Winckelmann, see: Honour, *op. cit.,* pp. 50–62 and 116–17.

Page 279: ". . . David responded with the guillotine": see Michael Levey, *Rococo to Revolution, op. cit.,* p. 166.

Page 281: For Hope's house being open to the public, see: Watkin, *op. cit.,* pp. 10, 14, 100.

Page 282: For the Dubost incident, see: *ibid.,* pp. 40–41.

Page 283: For Hope's attempts to buy peerage, see: *ibid.,* pp. 25–26.

Page 284: On *Anastasius,* see: *ibid.,* pp. 5–7, 65–66.

Page 285: On Hope's patronage, see: *ibid.,* pp. 30–60.

Page 288: On the British Institution, see: Peter Fullerton, "Patronage and Pedagogy: The British Institution in the Early Nineteenth Century," *Art History,* volume 5, number 1, March 1982, pp. 59–73.

Page 289: For Byron being impressed by Hope, see: Watkin, *op. cit.,* pp. 5–6.

CHAPTER 18. DOWNHILL AT DEEPDENE

Page 291: On Disraeli, *Coningsby,* and Henry Thomas Hope's role in its genesis, see: J. A. Froude, *Lord Beaconsfield,* Sampson, Low, Marston, London, pp. 108ff.

Page 292: For Henry Hope's achievements with Deepdene, see: Watkin, *op. cit.,* pp. 182–85; for the later life of the Hopes, see H. W. Law and I. Law, *The Book of the Beresford Hopes,* Heath Cranston, London, 1925; Mrs. Stuart Menzies, *Lord William Beresford,* Herbert Jenkins, London, 1917.

Page 297: At least twenty people are supposed to have died after wearing, or possessing, the Hope diamond. Apart from a mountain of newspaper clippings, for a good, not overly sensational, and accessible account of the Hope diamond, see: Balfour, *Famous Diamonds,* Collins, London, 1987.

Page 299: On the Newcastle family, see: F. Darrell Munsell, *The Unfortunate Duke: Henry Pelham, Fifth Duke of Newcastle, 1811–1864,* University of Missouri Press, Columbia, 1985; Kathleen, Duchess of Newcastle, "Clumber," *Pall Mall Magazine,* volume XXIII, number 1, 1901.

Page 300: For Lincoln's wedding, see: Munsell, *op. cit.,* pp. 273–74.

Page 302: For Churchill at Deepdene, see: Winston Churchill, *My Early Life,* Butterworth, 1930, p. 105; for other pictures and art works at Deepdene, see: Christie's sales catalogues, volume VI, 1917, July–August, "One hundred important pictures by old masters . . . from the Deepdene" and "The Hope heirlooms sale," 20 July, 1917; for the appearance of Deepdene, see: J. Britten, *History . . . of the Deepdene, 1821–26,* Drawings Collection, Royal Institute of British Architects.

CHAPTER 19. ENTER THE DEALERS: AGNEW, COLNAGHI, KNOEDLER

Page 304: For Agnew, see: Sir Geoffrey Agnew, *Agnews, 1817–1967,* London, 1967.

Page 308: For Colnaghi, see: D. Colnaghi and Co. *Colnagi's 1790–1960,* London, 1960, with an introduction by Elfrida Manning.

Page 310: For Knoedler, see: *A Catalogue of an Exhibition of Paintings and Prints of Every Description on the Occasion of Knoedler, One Hundred Years, 1846–1946,* New York, April 1 to 27, 1946, pp. 5–9. I am also grateful to Nancy Little, former librarian and archivist of Knoedler, for her cooperation.

CHAPTER 20. PENTIMENTO: Wisdom and Strength AGES

I am grateful to Helen Glanville, restorer of Dulwich Picture gallery, London, for help with this chapter. She is in no way responsible for any mistakes that remain. I have also relied on Sarah Walden's outspoken book *The Ravished Image,* St. Martin's Press, New York, 1985, and on H. Ruhemann, *The Cleaning of Paintings,* Faber, London, 1968. On pigments through the ages, see most recently: R. D. Harley, *Artists' Pigments c. 1600–1835,* Butterworth's, London, 1972; see also the references for chapter 4 of this book and Helen Glanville's three articles in *The Artist,* for October, November, and December 1966, respectively: "Deterioration of Media," "Deterioration of Pigments," and "The Effect of Restoration on the Surface Appearance of a Painting."

Page 314: On yellowing, see: Glanville, "The Deterioration of Media," *op. cit.;* on pictures "done up for sale," see: Walden, *op. cit.,* p. 14.

Page 315: For how advertising may change our taste in art, see: Walden, *op. cit.,* p. 19.

Page 317: On the extent to which masters actually had a hand in paintings ascribed to them, see: *ibid.,* pp. 136–37.

Page 319: Footnote—see: Ruhemann, *op. cit.,* pp. 50–51.

Page 320: On the journey of the Mantuan pictures to England, see: Walden, *op. cit.,* pp. 78–81.

Pages 320–21: On the appearance of a pentimento on *Wisdom and Strength* in the eighteenth century, see: J. Couché, *op. cit.,* p. 45 of volume II; I am grateful to Bernice Sanderson, of the Frick Collection, for allowing me access to the Frick file on *Wisdom and Strength,* in which a photograph of the copy attributed to Boucher also confirms the date of the pentimento.

INTERLUDE THREE: INTO AMERICA

For the history of collecting in America, see: W. G. Constable, *Art Collecting in the United States of America,* Nelson, London, 1964; Robert C. Williams, *Russian Art and American Money: 1900–1940,* Harvard University Press, Cambridge, Massachusetts, 1980; for Duveen and Berenson: Colin Simpson, *The Partnership: The*

Secret Associations Between Bernard Berenson and Joseph Duveen, Bodley Head, London, 1987; Nancy Hale, *Mary Cassatt,* Doubleday, Garden City, New York, 1975.

Page 324: On Morgan, see: Constable, *op. cit.,* pp. 108–12 and *passim.*

Page 327: On Altman, Huntington, etc., see: *ibid.,* pp. 112–15.

Page 328: On Kress, see: *ibid.,* pp. 133–37.

Page 328: On Mellon, see: *ibid.,* pp. 122–26; Williams, *op. cit.,* pp. 147–90.

PART SIX–NEW YORK

CHAPTER 21: ROGER FRY AND THE ART HISTORIANS

I have made use of Frances Spalding, *Roger Fry,* London, 1900; Deny Sutton, *Letters of Roger Fry,* two volumes, Chatto and Windus, London, 1972; Virginia Woold, *Roger Fry,* Hogarth Press, London, 1940; Roger Fry, *Vision and Design,* London, 1920; Mark Roskill, *What Is Art History?,* Thames and Hudson, London, 1976; Barbara Strachey and Jayne Samuels (eds.), *Mary Berenson: A Self-Portrait from Her Letters and Diaries,* Gollancz, 1983.

Page 336: For Morelli and art history, see: Roskill, *op. cit.,* pp. 20–24.

Page 336: For the Berenson letters, see: Maria Berenson, *op. cit.,* pp. 100–1 and 113–16.

Page 338: For the *Burlington Magazine,* see: Sutton (ed.), *Letters of Roger Fry, op. cit.,* pp. 212–14.

Page 339: For Fry in New York, see: *ibid.,* pp. 227–29. See also: "Roger Fry and the Metropolitan Museum," by James Pope-Hennessy, in *Oxford, China, and Italy Essays in Honor of Harold Acton,* edited by Ed Chaney and Neil Ritchie, Thames & Hudson, 1984, pp. 229ff.

Page 340: For the Bloomsbury Group and Fry, see: *ibid.,* pp. 44 and 69; for Monet and the Post-Impressionist painters, see: *ibid.,* pp. 298–301.

Page 342: For Fry in Venice on Veronese, see: *ibid.,* p. 147.

Page 342: For Fry's comparison of Titian and Veronese, see: *ibid.,* p. 641.

CHAPTER 22. HENRY FRICK'S "PARADISE"

For this chapter I have made full use of the material in the Frick art reference library, which contains a variety of press clippings, plus the official biography of Frick: George Harvey, *Henry Clay Frick: The Man,* privately printed, 1936. See also: Keith Roberts, "Frick, Gulbenkian and Co." See *Burlington Magazine,* 1972, pp. 405–11, for a quite different, and unusual, view of the Frick. Other sources: "The Frick at 50," *Art News,* April 1986, where the then director, Everett Fahy, discusses Fry's recommendation to Frick that he buy *Wisdom and Strength* and *Vice and Virtue.* See finally a series of five interviews which Helen Clay Frick gave in August 1959.

Page 344: On Tintsman's suggestion that Frick go into coke and steel, see: Harvey, *op. cit.,* pp. 29–37.

Page 345: On the Homestead strike, see: *ibid.,* pp. 106–86.

Page 347: For the Berkman assassination attempt, see: *ibid.,* pp. 135–39.

Page 351: Frick's taste turns away from the Barbizon school—see: *ibid.,* pp. 137ff.; Edgard Munhall, *Masterpieces of the Frick Collection,* The Frick Collection (distributed by Thames and Hudson), 1970, pp. 4–5. See also the entire issue of *Apollo* for May 1971, which is given over to the Frick.

Page 355: John Canaday "Business As Usual [Quiet] In Paradise, the Frick Collection." *New York Times,* December 22, 1968.

EPILOGUE

Page 357: For the fate of Odescalchi collections, see: Roethlisberger, *op. cit., passim;* for an account of the Hope heirlooms sale, see Reitlinger, *op. cit.,* volume 1, pp. 175ff.

Page 358: For the fate of the Newcastle collections at Clumber, see: Reitlinger, *op. cit.,* pp. 182ff; for the re-opening of Christina's tome, see: Allan Braham, "The Tomb of Christina," in *Queen Christina of Sweden: Documents and Studies*, Magnus von Platen, editor, *op. cit.,* pp. 48–58; for Louis Philipe, citizen king of France, see: *Louis Philippe Memoirs,* translated and with an introduction by John Hardman, New York and London, Harcourt, Brace & Jovanovich, *passim.*

Page 359: For recent copies of *Wisdom and Strength*, see the file on the painting in the Frick Collection. I am grateful to Bernice Davidson, Research Curator, at the Frick Collection, for allowing me to see this.

For the rediscoveries at Prague, see: T. Gottheiner, "Rediscovery of Old Masters at Prague Castle," *Burlington Magazine*, No. 753, Volume 107, December 1965, pp. 601–6; Jaromir Neumann, "The Picture Gallery of Prague Castle," 1967. For the reopening of Rudolf's coffin, see the catalogue for the exhibition, "Prague around 1600: Art and Culture at the Court of Rudolf II," held in Essen and at the Kunsthistorisches Museum, Vienna, 1988–89.

Page 360: For the new Veronese oil sketch, see: Terisio Pignatti, "Paolo Veronese: His Life and Art," *The Art of Paolo Veronese*, catalogue for an exhibition held at the National Gallery of Art, Washington, D.C., November 13, 1988, to February 20, 1989, p. 15.

Index

PETER WATSON, author of the award-winning *The Caravaggio Conspiracy,* has been a journalist for the London *Sunday Times,* New York correspondent of the London *Times,* and now writes for the London *Observer,* where his column on art is syndicated around the world. He has also written for *Connoisseur, Art and Antiques,* and the London *Spectator.* This is his sixth book.

NEW YORK
1911 –present ●

☆

ABB-5265